MODERNISM AND THE REINVENTION OF DECADENCE

In *Modernism and the Reinvention of Decadence*, Vincent Sherry reveals a new continuity in literary history. He takes the idea of decadence back to key events from the failures of the French Revolution and reads it forward into the cataclysm of the Great War. Following this powerful trajectory, Sherry's work of literary criticism and history begins with an exposition of the English romantic poets and ends with a reevaluation of modernists as varied as W. B. Yeats, Henry James, Joseph Conrad, Rebecca West, Djuna Barnes, Samuel Beckett, and, centrally, Ezra Pound and T. S. Eliot. This major new book will be essential reading for anyone working in modernist studies and twentieth-century literature more generally.

VINCENT SHERRY is Howard Nemerov Professor in the Humanities and Professor of English at Washington University in St. Louis. He is the editor of the forthcoming *The Cambridge History of Modernism* and the author of several major books on modernist literature and art. He is currently working on *A Literary History of the European War of 1914–1918*.

MODERNISM AND THE REINVENTION OF DECADENCE

VINCENT SHERRY

Washington University in St. Louis

CAMBRIDGE
UNIVERSITY PRESS

CAMBRIDGE
UNIVERSITY PRESS

32 Avenue of the Americas, New York, NY 10013-2473, USA

Cambridge University Press is part of the University of Cambridge.

It furthers the University's mission by disseminating knowledge in the pursuit of education, learning, and research at the highest international levels of excellence.

www.cambridge.org
Information on this title: www.cambridge.org/9781107079328

© Vincent Sherry 2015

First published 2015

Printed in the United States of America

A catalog record for this publication is available from the British Library.

Library of Congress Cataloging in Publication Data
Sherry, Vincent B.
Modernism and the reinvention of decadence / Vincent Sherry, Washington University, St Louis.
pages cm
Includes bibliographical references.
ISBN 978-1-107-07932-8 (hardback)
1. Modernism (Literature) 2. Decadence in literature. I. Title.
PN56.M54M6128 2014
809′.9112–dc23 2014027972

ISBN 978-1-107-07932-8 Hardback

in memory of
my father
old artificer

Contents

Acknowledgments

This book represents an attempt to reclaim the idea of "decadence" in the formation of modernist literature and, so, to adjust our understanding of the literary history of the long turn of the twentieth century. In the decade and more in which I have been working on it, one inevitable development has been the increasing appropriateness of a joke: the longer it took, the better its theme might be illustrated on the cover by a photo of its author. Old and new friends, former students and unexpected mentors, all in all, the several communities of scholars working in late-nineteenth- and early-twentieth-century studies, have restored me with their extraordinary resources of good feeling and shared purpose. Colleagues have helped me in ways little and large, sometimes conspicuously and materially and at other times subtly and unnoticed until later. For all these reasons, it is beyond the scope of one paragraph to represent the exact character of particular debts, which I list in the admittedly inadequate form of the alphabetized roster: Charles Altieri, Natalie Amleshi, Stephen Arata, Dan Blanton, Ronald Bush, Jean Cannon, James Chandler, Michael Clune, Ellen Crowell, Colleen Davis, Mara de Gennaro, Joshua Gang, Martin Lockerd, Marina MacKay, Tilar Mazzeo, Elizabeth Micakovic, Melanie Micir, John Morgenstern, Adam Parkes, Marjorie Perloff, Paul Saint-Amour, Heather Treseler, John Whittier-Ferguson, and Steven Zwicker. Jennifer Rust has been my closest reader and companion; beyond the critical and theoretical interests she has opened for me, her emotional support has meant everything. At the late stage of a manuscript evaluation for Cambridge University Press, Jed Esty and James Longenbach provided incisive readings and especially useful advice. The editorial and production teams at the Press have been equally helpful, and I want to thank Jeanie Lee, Christine Kanownik, Caitlin Gallagher, Sue Costello, and, especially, Ray Ryan, who, as Senior Acquisitions Editor, has helped in the editing of this acquisition in the most expeditious of ways. In the years of my work on this book, I have moved from Villanova University to Tulane University, where my debts to friends and colleagues are still felt, and, now, to Washington University in St. Louis, where the richness of literary and intellectual culture has been transformative for me, and where the assistance given by graduate students and English department staff has also been exceptional: I want to thank Meredith Lane, Courtney Andree, Kelly Camerer, and, in particular, Aileen Waters. Here I want to acknowledge also the special opportunities afforded by the Mellon Summer Dissertation Seminars and Vertical Seminars, in particular the graduate students in "Modernism and Decadence," "The Time of Modernism," and "Modernism at the Turn of the Century: The Question of Periodization."

Grateful acknowledgment is given to New Directions Publishing Corporation and Faber & Faber Ltd. for permission to quote from the following copyright works by Ezra Pound: *Collected Early Poems of Ezra Pound* (Copyright © 1976 by the Trustees of the Ezra Pound Literary Property Trust), *Personae* (Copyright © 1926 by Ezra Pound), *Pound/ Lewis* (Copyright © 1985 by the Trustees of the Ezra Pound Literary Property Trust), *The Selected Letters of Ezra Pound to John Quinn, 1915– 1924* (Copyright © 1991 by Duke University Press and the Trustees of the Ezra Pound Literary Property Trust), *Selected Letters 1907–1941* (Copyright © 1950 by Ezra Pound), and for the material of various literary essays and reviews gathered subsequently in *Ezra Pound's Poetry and Prose: Contributions to Periodicals* (Copyright © 1991 by the Trustees of the Ezra Pound Literary Property Trust). Grateful acknowledgment is also given for permission to quote from previously unpublished work of Ezra Pound, Copyright © 2014 by Mary de Rachewiltz and the estate of Omar S. Pound, used by permission of New Directions Publishing Corporation, agents. Every effort has been made to secure permission for quotation from copyright works.

Earlier versions of portions of the Introduction; Chapters 1, 3, and 4; and the second Inter-Chapter of this book have appeared as "Edmund Wilson's *Axel's Castle*: Modernism under Review," in *Modernist Cultures* (October 2012); "T. S. Eliot, Late Empire, and Decadence," *Modernism and Colonialism*, ed. Michael Valdez Moses and Richard Begam (Durham: Duke University Press, 2007); "Modernist Poetry and the Century's Wars," in *A Concise Companion to Post-War British and Irish Poetry*, ed. Nigel Alderman and C. D. Blanton (Oxford: Blackwell, 2009); "Prose Criticism," in *Ezra Pound in Context*, ed. Ira Nadel (Cambridge: Cambridge University Press, 2010); "'Where Are the Eagles and the Trumpets?': Imperial Decline and Eliot's Development," in *Blackwell Companion to T. S. Eliot*, ed. David Chinitz (Oxford: Blackwell, 2010); "Imagism," in *The Cambridge History of English Poetry*, ed. Michael O'Neill (Cambridge: Cambridge University Press, 2010); and "War and Empire, Modernism and Decadence," in *The Blackwell Companion to Modernist Poetry*, ed. David Chinitz and Gail McDonald (Oxford: Blackwell, 2014). Grateful acknowledgment is given to the publishers for permission to use this material in the present work.

For the beginnings of my interest in the subject of this book, I express gratitude to my daughter, Sophia, who, beyond developing her own ideas about it, continues to improve me. The debt I reflect in the dedication is appropriate – with or without the rather grandiose analogy of the Joycean allusion, which my father would have enjoyed. It says what I want to say about the literary history, here in a personal story: about influences at once contested and confirmed, and confirmed as they were contested, and recognized, in the end, as what one is made of.

The Codes of Decadence:
Modernism and Its Discontents

On the first of January 1914, for the first number of *The Egoist*, which is arguably the first journal of a nascent literary modernism in England, Ezra Pound takes up the theme of first*ness* in introducing his group to London literary society. He is presenting these modernists of the 1910s, however, to a readership that still holds the memory of a preceding generation, the so-called decade of decadence, the 1890s. The rhetorical energy of the piece goes to differences. The oppositions are forcefully drawn:

> "A generation came down to London resolved to speak as they wrote." For all that disastrous decade men spoke with the balanced sentence. There was great awe in the world.
>
> And then there came to London a generation that tries to write as it speaks – and these young men are termed petulant – a praise by faint condemnation?[1]

The difference Pound is claiming is a truism of literary history now. He is emphasizing the poetics of vital voice in his own decade against the artifice of written literature among Nineties poets. Those were writers, following the conceit that Max Beerbohm used to describe the style of Walter Pater, who are supposed to have wrapped their every sentence in a shroud; they interred their words in the stylized ritual of their written English. That was a manner characterized by Latinate syntax and vocabulary, not by idiomatic directness. Pound's assertion of his poets' difference from the writerly Nineties, however, comes through a fragment of syntactical parallelism – "a generation came down to London," "there came to London a generation" – that adapts the grammar of the generation who "spoke with the balanced sentence." Is this a heckling echo? Or involuntary homage? Or both?

This ambiguity shows again in the next sentence, where he asserts the convention-dismaying freshness of his generation: "And in the face of this [the writerly Nineties] are we in the heat of our declining youth expected to stretch the one word *merde* over eighteen elaborate paragraphs?"[2] Once again, Pound sets his fellow revelers cavorting in a poetics of live speech, kicking their heels up against the artifice of the paragraphs written in the English fin de siècle. His protest carries an exemplary version of the literary temperament to which he is objecting, however: this sentence rises perfectly to its own rhetorical question and period. His complicity with the sensibility of the writerly Nineties appears to be as unshakeable as his challenge to it is voluble.

Another harmonic chord is struck in that last sentence: "the heat of our declining youth." This figure recalls a signature conceit of the English Nineties. That was the generation Yeats would frame in his famous phrase as the "Tragic Generation," whose tragic figure, imaged in the persons of Aubrey Beardsley and Ernest Dowson and Lionel Johnson, featured an artistic youth consumed in its first flush. This figure of genius dying young was of course not invented by Yeats. It is the signal image of memory, which catches this figure of ruined youth as the emblem of the time. There was indeed something about that decade, the last decade of the last century before the last century of the millennium, that framed a feeling of late or last days or, even, aftermath. This sense of an ending is registered most intensely where it touched the young: they are growing into their maturity as the century is winding down and, in that temporal imaginary, are being force-ripened into this early consummation. The strongest measure of the ongoing power of this figure shows as its poetry endures, even – or especially – as Pound ostensibly rejects the legacy of the decade that generated it.

For it is his legacy. And he demonstrates this prepossession as he reiterates that signature figure. He repeats and expands its theme in an adjacent phrase, where he turns the Nineties conceit of autumnal spring into one of energetic decline: "We have attained to a weariness more highly energised than the weariness of the glorious nineties, or at least more obviously volcanic."[3] Anticipating the explosive spirit of *Blast*, the journal of vorticist modernism whose first issue would come several months later, Pound may be trying to outrun the riddle of the Nineties generation, ramping up the vitalist side of the decadent poetics of enervating strengths. In doing so, however, he puts his formulation into a piece of periodic prose – "we have attained to a weariness more highly energised than the weariness of the glorious nineties, or at least ..." – that is at least as elegantly and even languorously sustained as any period featured in the writerly art of the Nineties. Beyond a jejune vaunt, something more than the boast of a young modernism sowing its vocal oats in poetry, the polemic reads as a ritual of succession in which the identity of the predecessor, in being so heavily contested, is more intensely confirmed.

No less intensely, however, than obliquely. While Pound is obviously suppressing the legacy of the Nineties as a constitutive element in the art of his decade, the underlying connection emerges in his critical prose as a subtler music. This includes the semantics of syntax and a set of images as enigmatic as their now distant vintage, which is the two-decade-old crypt he is working in. These are the signals of a code. The "decadence" of the Nineties joins the modernism of the Teens, that is, but in cipher. This decadence is not just a contested predecessor, however. On the evidence of Pound's exceptional efforts at deflection, it is obviously proscribed. Just so, it is re-inscribed into a set of alternative counters, where, if it is recognizable under certain signs, it has also been removed from the admitted view of direct sight.

This suppression extends into the scholarship of modernism in much of the subsequent century. The attitude and practice may be taken back to an even earlier moment in the history of literary modernism, which reads as one of the original instances of the encryption that is occurring so fluently in 1914. It is a story that reveals a motive action, in the understanding of modernist aesthetics in subsequent critical formulations, for writing decadence so forcibly out of the critical account. This is a history of critical misprision that I will be following in this introductory chapter. Although much of this chapter engages with questions of nomenclature, and builds an understanding of the otherwise elusive counter of "decadence" through its range of associations and attributed significances, this review is necessary for the work of an alternate literary history. In addition to providing a good deal more than nominal content to the word, it makes evident the threat which "decadence" presents to established understandings of modernity as well as developing conceptions of modernism. This is a threat that comprises but also exceeds the queerness which, in the conspicuous instance of Oscar Wilde, was attached to decadence as its most infamous condition and which, in our consideration, may be recovered in the greater complexity of its presence in the sensibility that decadence and modernism will be seen to share.

The process of evolving an identity and a set of institutional values for modernism in the history of twentieth-century literary criticism reveals a great deal at stake aesthetically and politically. The innovations with which modernism is customarily identified bring it into line equally and severally with revolutionary and progressive political temperaments. At various key points in the story, which I will be pinpointing, the partisan motives of particular critics exert extraordinary influence in developing its ideological affiliations. These forces join to produce a construction of modernism against which the sensibility of "decadence" sets an equally elementary opposition, right – or wrong – from the start. Those understandings may have been modified over the last several decades, but the absence that decadence occupies in the formative story has never been filled in with the import it originally owns. This is sufficiently significant to have warranted all the proscription it undergoes in this longer story, beginning already at the turn of the twentieth century.

1.   Displacements

This event is the publication, in 1899, of Arthur Symons's *The Symbolist Movement in Literature*, which presents the first compendium in English literary criticism of the major writing of the European fin de siècle. Under this title, Symons's book will be hailed for more than a century as the hallmark volume for the inception as well as the understanding of modernist poetics. Some later readers may be unaware, and others may have forgotten, that this book represents an expansion and re-titling of Symons's 1893 essay, "The Decadent Movement in Literature." This precedent text reveals an internal history to Symons's conception and representation of "the symbolist movement," one that is fraught with second thoughts and the superscriptions they entail. It exposes a set of tensions in the developing conceptions of the origins of modernist poetry, and it points to a legacy of avoidance and deflection in the critical tradition stemming from it. The import of these developments may be framed through an understanding of the character and significance of this change in nomenclature.

"The Decadent Movement in Literature" takes decadence as the comprehensive identity for the most important work in the fin-de-siècle period. It acknowledges the reality of Impressionism and Symbolism as configurations of interest, but it makes these "isms" subsequent to decadence in development and subsidiary in significance. In this array, "decadence" serves equally as a term for an historical period and an imaginative attitude, which emerge jointly from a sense of the lateness of contemporary time. Thus decadence demonstrates "all the qualities that mark the end of great periods, the qualities that we find in the Greek, the Latin, decadence: an intense self-consciousness, a restless curiosity in research, an over-subtilizing refinement upon refinement, a spiritual and moral perversity." In literary expression, this "*maladie fin de siècle*" eventuates in a style which Symons represents in critical metaphors of decay that are strongly turned: here a verbal texture "high-flavoured and spotted with corruption," there a "dis-ease of form," everywhere the signs of "a civilization grown over-luxurious, over-inquiring, too languid, for relief of action, too uncertain for any emphasis in opinion or in conduct." He traces these characteristics through a range of famous and not so famous authors, culminating in verse in Paul Verlaine's poetry and in fiction in J. K. Huysmans' novel *À Rebours* (*Against Nature*, 1884), which, as Symons is intent to demonstrate, is the "one exceptional achievement" of both its author and the sensibility of decadence that it exemplifies.[4]

Without specific reference to this essay in *The Symbolist Movement in Literature*, Symons presents the epochal phenomena of his earlier construction as "something which is vaguely called Decadence." He now faults this term as being "rarely used with any precise meaning"; accordingly, he is now replacing it with "Symbolism." He adds several figures to the census of writers he has included in "The Decadent Movement," most notably Arthur Rimbaud and Jules Laforgue, but the crucial point to mark is the new and indeed antithetical emphases that the change in nomenclature is bringing to the same figures. Among these, Verlaine and Huysmans have been most remarkably transformed. Where Verlaine once evidenced the "exquisite depravity" that provides the establishing category of interest in decadent writing, he has now been put on a course of purgatorial suffering and spiritual improvement, where all his work is seen as a constant "struggling towards at least an ideal of spiritual consolation"; the fact that the French poet died little more than two years after "The Decadent Movement" was published seems to prescribe a very steep learning curve for this major reorientation. The same change shows in the chapter "The Later Huysmans" in *The Symbolist Movement*, which removes *À Rebours* from significant account. Huysmans' later conversion to Roman Catholicism is now posited by Symons as the defining endpoint of his career, subjoining all the earlier fiction into a developmental narrative to that event and focusing attention on novels which, in no uncertain terms in the earlier essay, he has relegated to insignificance (where they mostly remain). This critical emphasis on spirituality picks up one aspect in the sensibility of decadence, where, in Symons's earlier account, the feeling of reprobation works in consort and contrast with some notion of the potential – usually just a potential – for redemption. In 1899, however, this spirituality becomes the whole story: in his "Conclusion," Symons rigidifies it into a "doctrine of Mysticism" and presents it as nothing less than an imperative of absolute value for his chosen authors. And where the term "Symbolism" involves an invocatory concept of some "unseen world" that "is no longer a dream," which will replace "a visible world that is no longer a reality," this term configures a good deal less "precise meaning" than the now disapproved "decadence," which once owned the assurance at least of his own emphatic tropes.[5] With this change of names, however, Symons's critical account has taken the character of major value in his chosen authors and changed it, utterly.

W. B. Yeats, it may be readily discerned, provided the impetus for this renaming. The dedication of the book to Symons's new poetic mentor suggests an allegiance as intense and comprehensive as the homage is (still uncomfortably) sycophantic.[6] The local motives and profounder consequences of this change in nomenclature have yet to be explored. The motivating circumstances will be engaged at length in my first chapter, where Yeats's growing interest in Irish poetic nationalism and his concomitant involvement with the creative doctrines of the symbolic will be seen to be displacing the clichéd elements of an older decadence, its stylized deliquescence most obviously. The influence of this development on Symons's critical book will show most strikingly in the parallel narrative of his own poetic development, which includes some fairly bad imitations of the Irish poet. Ruefully humorous as it may be, this secondhand verse proves to be worth reading for assurance of where the power actually lay in this relationship. The important part of this story is not Symons's bringing *Symbolisme* to Yeats, as the Irish poet occasionally claimed.[7] It was the Irish poet who brought his emergent concern with national activism in literature to Symons's original interest in the French material – and so occasioned the renaming of the literary movement that, under the revised title of the book, would provide the main reference in subsequent literary histories for an original identity of modernist poetics.[8]

In order to put this construction of subsequent literary history into perspective, it needs to be recognized that Symons was polarizing *symbolisme* and *décadence* for reasons that are identifiably and polemically his (and Yeats's) own. Each of these terms corresponds with distinct literary values, and it will be the work of this Introduction to spell out what is at stake critically with their difference, but the poetic coteries originally associated with *décadence* and *symbolisme* in fin-de-siècle Paris actually overlapped. As Patrick McGuinness has documented, the two terms were conferred, in turn and even simultaneously, on the same authors. These appellations were brandished equally as weapons and blazons in the heady contests for dominance among individual talents seeking the greater strength of a group, even as their members routinely changed sides. In the longer run, and largely because of greater aptitudes in self-promotion, the writers identified as symbolists claimed that greater strength, and took on the mantle of advanced guard philosophers of artistic novelty.

This process is recalled by one of the primary players in the scene of the Parisian fin de siècle, Remy de Gourmont, in a journalistic series of 1910–1911, *Souvenirs du Symbolisme*. In one of these pieces, he characterizes the philosophical warrant of the *symbolistes* as self-conferred and somewhat pretentious and dubious. He opposes it to the stronger sentiment of *décadence* in the earlier days of this period, when, if this feeling was both compelled and limited by the youthful inexperience of self-identified *décadents*, the presentiment of decay remained in place as the more enduring undercurrent at its time.[9] Accordingly, in another one of these pieces, he confesses his regret at the brief lifespan of the journal *Le Décadent* and explains it as the relative lack of savoir-faire in literary commerce when compared to the more seasoned *symbolistes*.[10] Nonetheless, both as a reason and a result of this history, in "the Symbolist version of events" that become the dominant story, "Symbolism attains the status of a theory," as McGuinness correctly puts it, "whereas Decadence is perceived as a mood."[11]

Further to these characterizations: as a "philosophy" or "theory," symbolism tends to live somewhat independently of the actual poems associated with it, and so encodes a sense of creative possibility for a new literature, which, in existing literary histories, becomes a formative force for the modernism of the subsequent century. Contrarily, in the certain and concrete terms of Symons's own critical tropes, decadence centers a declaratively emphatic "mood," one that captures a sense of endings rather than beginnings, and so needs to be separated from those legends of potentiality that attend the understandings of modernism. As an overview of the Parisian fin de siècle suggests, however, decadence and symbolism need to be understood as categories of literary polemic rather than adversarial characters in the actual practice of writing. This is to say: there was an intense sense of possibility and novelty in the air, but it was not detachable from the feeling of current civilization being at its end and a concomitant sense of dissolution in norms ranging from the literary to the moral. And if, underwriting a theory of novelty, the sensibility identified with the term *symbolisme* has dominated the origin story of modernism, an alternate story comes with an emphasis on the equally important mood of decadence. This needs to be seen as an equal contributor to the inventiveness of modernism, but it has been written out of our account of these developments by the victory symbolism enjoyed in that original local struggle. Recovering the substantial force and enduring importance of this mood in literary modernism is the project of this book, which, to begin with, needs to acknowledge and account for the extraordinary power that the term "symbolism" has been given in the literary history of modernism following Symons.

This power comes out of certain readings of the term "symbol," which, from the beginning, provided a capacious indicator indeed. As the artists originally associated with symbolism usually insisted, the operative sense of "symbol" veered away from and even defied the idea of a restrictive sense in the act of symbolization. Verlaine's famous saying – *De la musique avant toute chose*, "Music first and foremost!"[12] – takes the action of poetic language to be not the representation of some prior reference, but the direct presentation of the poem's own sensations and impressions. The poet handles the verbal counters as centers of immediate sensory experience, as material of musical plastic, where the acoustic token prompts those imaginative associations which encompass the multiplicity of possible meanings that "symbol" claims as namesake for the school. A different and in fact contrary quality is posited for the symbol by Symons. Following Yeats's own developing interest in occultism, Symons elaborates an imaginative understanding out of a Swedenborgian system of *correspondances*, where natural details are perceived as a mirror or echo of a supernal metaphysical order. This is no system of misty indeterminateness for Symons. Incorporating this quotation from Carlyle's *Sartor Resartus*, Symons demands "some embodiment and revelation of the Infinite; the Infinite is made to blend itself with the Finite, to stand visible, and as it were, attainable there."[13] Symons goes on to invoke this "doctrine" of symbolic embodiment of spiritual essences for a number of his authors, most notably for Baudelaire (included in a 1919 edition) and Gérard de Nerval and Verlaine.[14] As any focused reading of this literature will reveal, however, and as Walter Benjamin pointed out in his writings on Baudelaire, a Swedenborgian scheme reads in practice more like a system *manqué*.[15] It affords a rhetorical opportunity most often for the representation of the *loss* of symbolic meaning in the poetic imaginary, where the barrenness of natural fact is all the more poignantly lyricized.

Given such an open range of application, the term "symbolism" acquires a remarkably adaptive power in the subsequent history of literary criticism. As we will see in a number of key instances, symbolism becomes a marker of possibility, an invocatory concept, all in all, an explanatory paradigm for nothing less than the immense inventiveness of modernism itself. It is assisted in this wise by the mystic significance Symons has imputed to it, which is unhindered by the doctrine he tries otherwise to turn it into. So, where *décadence* once enjoyed an equal share with *symbolisme* in the making of the inventiveness of fin-de-siècle literature, subsequent constructions tend to disaggregate the pair. They attach the inventiveness of modernism to the theory of novelty in symbolism and detach it from the mood of decadence as the more powerful undercurrent of that time. For reasons that range from the political to the moral, as we will see, they elaborate and in fact radicalize the difference, turning *symbolisme* into the better angel of its erstwhile twin, its increasingly disapproved double.

The token power of *symbolisme* may be accounted for in good part, moreover, by the pressure of the term it is attempting to suppress. An advance indicator of this threat, and an early example of the process of subverting it by renaming it, comes in the first years of the decade ending with the first publication of Symons's book. It appears already in the set of revisions that Oscar Wilde performed on the first published edition of *The Picture of Dorian Gray* (1890, 1891). Wittily, certainly cynically, Wilde is already manipulating the sensitivities that attend the term *decadence*, which owned a signal role in the first version. He is responding to reviews, which turned their dislike of his particular story into a more explicit and intense contempt for the general sensibility of decadence, of which the novel was designated a most objectionable representative. Thus, in referencing the literary convention that lies behind the infamous "yellow book" that Lord Henry has given Dorian (as guide to his downfall), he changes "the French school of *Décadents*" to "the French school of *Symbolistes*." In descriptive details that make this fatal book indistinguishable from Huysmans' *À Rebours*, the work Symons would call "the breviary of the Decadence,"[16] the language is otherwise substantially unaltered across a long paragraph of rich depiction. Wilde then complements this shift from "*Décadents*" to "*Symbolistes*" with another winking change, which alters a "dangerous novel" in 1890 to a "wonderful novel" in 1891.[17] The change of the keyword alone makes for an absolute difference in the attributed value and assigned character of its referent.

In his uniquely guileful way, however, Wilde takes back more than he gives away in this exchange. The chapters he adds for the later version surround that now missing word with an array of evidence as readily assignable to "decadence" as that word itself remains persistently unsaid. In doing so, he reveals the subsidiary power and heavier menace of the "decadence" that "symbolism" nominally, but only nominally, overrules. And so Wilde establishes in advance the character of the enemy and threat which Symons – and later critics – will be suppressing in that term.

In the first of those added chapters (III in the 1891 edition), Wilde offers "the story of Dorian Gray's parentage," which features a mother of aristocratic lineage fallen into a marriage of low and mean degree (*PDG*, 31–34).

This genealogy provides a genetic determination for the narrative fiction of the book, specifically, for the de*cad*ence (the middle syllable preserves the Latin etymology for "fall") Dorian will have fallen into (and through) by the end. Thus the story becomes one of those determinist fictions that subsequent critics will take as the evidence of the undue pessimism of decadence, which marks its own special extremity to the literary school and behavioral laboratory of naturalism.

In these added chapters there are also extensive references to the melodrama and music hall venues of Dorian's one-time romantic interest, Sybil Vane. Here is the living theater of English "decadence" in the conventional sense of behavioral practices and scandalous characters (Symons will have furthered these associations considerably in his personal life). This is a turn for the worse that Wilde stages in this scene, where the sentimental connection we expect between the musical heroine Sybil and her faithful brother James suggests something rather different, as forbidden indeed as incestuous love: "In Sybil's own room they parted. There was jealousy in the lad's heart, and a fierce murderous hatred of the stranger who, as it seemed to him, had come between them. Yet, when her arms were flung round his neck, and her fingers strayed through his hair, he softened, and kissed her with real affection" (*PDG*, 61). The usually coyly moralizing voice of Wilde's narrator dissolves ultimately into an indulgence of this underworld. Its density of presence in the revised text is significant. Its supposedly subsidiary place in the moral economy of the culture Wilde is representing in this supposedly cleaned-up version becomes something more of a majority power through the added volume it occupies.

Then, in the third of the four chapters added in 1891, a conversation between Lord Henry and the Duchess of Monmouth on the condition of England demonstrates the evidence of the "decadence" which, as a word, appears in a form as truncated as the reference is abrupt:

> She shook her head. "I believe in the race," she cried.
> "It represents the survival of the pushing."
> "It has development."
> "Decay fascinates me more."
> "What of Art?" she asked.
> "It is a malady." (*PDG*, 162)

Parodying the now familiar language of the "survival of the fittest," Henry objects to the ethic of social Darwinism in a fashion characteristic of decadents, who, in all accounts, would opt out of that none-too-artful struggle. Thus the conversation moves toward its signal word and characterizing value in "decay." Thus, too, Henry finishes into a reference to the "malady" of art – a reference to *Les Fleurs du Mal*, the older testament of poetic *décadence*, which Baudelaire had provided.

The critical and interpretive question is not the presence of these references. It is the oddly angled, somewhat erratic, but still mechanical character of the exchange in which they appear. They are the verbal signals of a sensibility at once uninvited and irresistible. They connect as points in a conversation that exhibits none of the fluency in dramatic dialogue for which the later plays of Wilde will be rightly famed. If the word that dare not speak its name is the silence that subtends this exchange, its cognates and references are nonetheless surfacing with the interest of the forbidden, and with something of its contorted force. It is an augury of the force this word will exert even – or especially – as it is omitted or replaced in the public intellectual culture of England at the end of the century and, as it turns out, in most of the literary criticism of the next century. Here symbolism[e] will do the concerted work of trumping decadence as a sign of critical power and major value in the literary histories of modernism.

This critical legacy is responsible for a restriction in our understanding of the historical origins of literary modernism. Its work may be discerned most tellingly where its consequences are also most demonstrable: in mid-century, when the canon of literary modernism was being formed and its critical understandings were being formulated. This development is epitomized in some of the major scholarship on early modernism in particular, which takes up specifically the poetics of Imagism and its turn-of-the-century backgrounds.

An early representative is Glenn Hughes's 1931 book, *Imagism and the Imagists*. "From 1885 until 1900," his literary history begins, "'symbolism' was the dominant force in French poetry, and practically every poet of ability who wrote during those years came under the influence of its ideals. There were parallel movements, that of the so-called *décadents* being one, but all these overlapped with and were submerged by 'symbolism.'" Hughes not only overrides the idea of *décadence* as influential background. He needs to sweep it away, at once magnifying "symbolism" as the term of all-inclusive reference (it was not) and reducing "decadence" to the sheerest name: the poets grouped under this counter are merely "so-called."[18] "Decadence" is the wrong word, in other words, because that other word, "symbolism," is telling the right story of origins – but through the sort of critical swerve that bespeaks the nervousness in that replacement, that suppression.

This story continues in *Romantic Image* (1957), where Frank Kermode sets out to establish the developmental continuity of the Image from early nineteenth- to mid-twentieth-century poetics. He takes Symons's book as a crucial link in the chain. Not only does he accept Symons's changed term, without interrogating the shift, he also uses the advantaged word "symbolism" to disadvantage "decadence," which is dubbed an "inferior forerunner of Symbolism." He continues in a rhetoric of value-graded comparisons, merging his own words into Symons's, which provide the intoners of strongest value: "But in any case, Symbolism was much more, nothing less than 'an attempt to spiritualise literature, to evade the old bondage of rhetoric, the old bondage of exteriority ... Description is banished that beautiful things may be evoked, magically'. It is by the Symbol that 'the soul of things can be made visible.'"[19] This joined language shows Kermode as a co-believer – in every relevant sense of that term. For he is availing himself of those overtones of spirituality in Swedenborg's scheme and applying them as a moralizing force in his critical project of converting decadence into symbolism. Not only is "symbolism" being substituted for "decadence," but there is a peculiar virulence, a sometimes judgmental vehemence, that shows substitution as judgment, as suppression. It shows symbolism as a denial, in code, of some disapproved, even loathed, original.

The consummate instance of this critical tradition is Hugh Kenner's *The Pound Era* (1971), which, to begin with, positions Imagism as a riposte to "the decadence of a tradition."[20] The negative judgment in Kenner's phrase comes with the chiastic reversal it irresistibly implies: "the tradition of decadence." This predecessor needs to be suppressed, cleansed, coded or recoded, in Kenner's professed attempt to explain how, under Pound's aegis, "our epoch was extricated from the *fin de siècle*."[21] This is rescue or salvage work, not an extension or refinement. And although the antipathy to decadence is general and intense, the need to write it out of the account reveals the strenuousness of its effort most particularly in the exceptional complexity attending his appropriation of symbolism. Insofar as symbolism gains any specificity of understanding, Kenner does not admire it, but because it must do the work of getting rid of decadence, he needs to keep it in place as the antithetical and dominant power.

In his account of literary history over the turn of the century, Kenner follows the progress across the channel of what he calls "Post-Symbolist poetry," where "post" is the interestingly unfixed, ambivalent prefix. "Post," as "after," means latter-day, *unoriginal*, and is negatively assessed. At other moments, it suggests a matured, developed, and approved practice. Thus

Kenner uses "Post-Symbolism" to invoke equally a poetry that is decadent (late, decaying, unoriginal) and a poetry whose particular interest in painting, shared by French *décadents* from the time of Baudelaire, carries the seed of Imagism across the British Channel in a narrative of purifying transit, when it will be implanted as the growing point of a new, otherwise identifiably modernist project. This is the ambiguity of code, where the substitute word reveals that which it is suppressing. And as Kenner's account proceeds, the rhetoric of invective and judgment ramps up to do the work of suppressing that contested referent. The literary history thus becomes a sort of *moral story* for Kenner, where the technical hygiene that Imagism performs on the painterly poetry of *décadence* comprises but far exceeds any expedient function. It takes on the words and import of an ethical correction, which the emphases added here are not needed to reveal: "For it was an English post-Symbolist verse that Pound's Imagism set out to *reform*, by deleting its *self-indulgences*, intensifying its *virtues*, and elevating the glimpse into *the vision*."[22]

This suppression and conversion of *décadence* will come to its exemplary demonstration as Kenner moves to his comprehensive account of modernist poetics. "It was the post-Symbolists of the 1890s who brought pictorial images into short poems: theirs was the dead end we are frequently told Imagism was. Imagism on the other hand made possible the *Cantos* and *Paterson*, long works that with the work of T. S. Eliot are the Symbolist heritage in English."[23] The word "Symbolist" in this last phrase exerts an odd dominance indeed. There is the obvious inconsistency of a literary history moving forward by going back, progressing from post-symbolism to symbolism. More subtly, more tellingly, there is the fact that Kenner has spent little time on his resolving note here – on "Symbolism" without the "Post," that is, symbolism per se, which, in itself, touches the edges of decadence all too obviously, and so moves into usefulness for him otherwise in the posterior time that "post" confers. These several tenses of literary history nonetheless demonstrate one salient point in the history of modernist criticism. The hero in Kenner's story of modernist poetics appears as a kind of symbolism *ex machina*. It is a counter and code word into which those contested predecessors have been resolved of all the trouble they present.

So, what is the trouble? The word suppressed in these once official histories of literary modernism is a complex and potent signifier, one that opposes received notions of social modernity as well as developed conceptions of artistic modernism. I want to reclaim that adversarial sense, which is manifold, and insert it into a new history of literary modernism. This includes decadence, not as an incidental but a constitutive identity, which it will be the work of this book to regain.

Not as a term in a ready-made binary, however, where the degeneration sometimes synonymized with "decadence" provides a spur for the work of modernist renovation. That is a story for which the modernists themselves have already authored a script, sometimes in livid imagery. "For an old bitch gone in the teeth, / For a botched civilization": thus Pound sardonically characterizes the cultural circumstance of his work as poet and critic and agent provocateur in the literary London of the prewar years, where the disintegration of contemporary civilization provides the ground and warrant for his adversarial campaigns.[24] "My house is a decayed house," T. S. Eliot echoes in the same year (1919) in "Gerontion," drawing the disintegration of the English national circumstance into a domestic figure that indexes the intimacy of this experience of decay, a condition that provides the target for his own responsive novelty in poetry.[25] The relation between this historical sense and the emergent poetics of Eliot and Pound is a good deal more complex, however, than the one critics customarily understand as an opposition between the decadent condition of history and the renovating work of modernism. That is the operative rhetorical dichotomy for critics such as Kermode and Kenner, who, major intellects as they were, provide an indicative measure of the power of this scholarly mythology.

This critical construction relies on the establishing value of "novelty," that is, on the resolving power and absolute validity of the "make it new" slogan for literary modernism. This motto, as Michael North has recently demonstrated, has been accorded a wholly unwarranted authority in the understanding of modernist poetics. Not concocted until 1934, and targeted to the work of translation primarily, "make it new" was not the ordaining precept it has become, now, in the regular refrains of critical appreciation for the major instigations of literary modernism.[26] A presumptive understanding, as the heavier efforts of Kermode and Kenner suggest, newness has been constructed in good part as an occlusion of the power and presence of its nominal opposite: of decadence, which the supposed or conferred novelty of *symbolisme* first replaced in the proto-modernist environs of fin-de-siècle Paris. This series of displacements, in other words, owns a depth of precedent. Opening this critical archive not only reveals a lengthened memory of suppression; it will also point to some of the major issues at stake with these substitute names, these codes.

2.   Edmund Wilson, or Walter Benjamin

The labor of displacement in the mid-century criticism of modernism draws in its distant memory on *The Symbolist Movement in Literature*, but Symons's influence has been renewed along the way and reinforced by a work that stands as the first major literary history of modernism. This is Edmund Wilson's *Axel's Castle: A Study in the Imaginative Literature of 1870–1930*. Published in 1931, it merged into the first generation of the academic scholarship of modernism in figures such as Lionel Trilling, Alfred Kazin, Irving Howe, and Harry Levin, who were manifestly and often admittedly in his debt. Although it may now appear more often in the bibliography than in the list of works cited in our contemporary modernist scholarship, it remains in place in the study of modernist literatures as a kind of buried cornerstone; sometimes, in fact, it is visible by name and stands as the weight-bearing wall in the structured history of modernism. Where this book recycles the vocabulary of Symons's *Symbolist Movement in Literature*, it provides a substantial understanding for the uses "symbolism" performs in this critical tradition. It is not merely a polite word for "decadence"; it is a replacement with political implications and ideological content. This frame of reference may come into view through the social context of its production, which involves Wilson's personal part in the story.

When he wrote to Max Perkins at Scribner's in November 1928 to propose the book-length project that would become *Axel's Castle*, Wilson had already logged nearly a decade in New York literary and cultural journalism. By the end of the 1920s, he had become a sort of "cultural man-of-all-work," writing on subjects that ranged from burlesque shows to Stravinsky, Charlie Chaplin to Georgia O'Keeffe.[27] Where his field of view was broadly and identifiably "democratic," it provides a background for the political orientation he would follow into the next decade, when, in the Great Depression, he turned toward Marxism and produced *To the Finland Station*, which, arguably, is his most important book. Earlier in 1929, however, his aesthetic values remained traditional in a somewhat restrictive, exclusionary way. He wished to make the work of literary modernism available to a wide audience, but it was obvious that the authors in his table of contents belonged to a private and acquired taste. Besides the poetry of Eliot and Yeats, who may have entered a zone of general recognition by 1930, there were the highly recherché interests of Proust, Stein, and Valery, and, most notably, the mysterious scandal of the officially unpublished, still forbidden *Ulysses*. His title, moreover, readily admits the distance between his broadly gauged audience and the literary sensibility he sequesters in its domain: "Axel's Castle" is the fortress to which the aesthetic hero of Villiers de L'Isle Adam's (appropriately) closet drama withdraws from every sordid compulsion of everyday existence. And while the opposition of private life and public value does not provide an overt rhetorical dichotomy in the book, it is operative in ways equally subtle and substantial.

These pressures are evidenced in the work he performs through "Symbolism," which provides the title for his opening chapter. This classificatory category brings together a set of otherwise various talents, gathering the main developments of French and Irish and American modernism under this heading as their literary faith and establishing value.[28] On one hand, and most obviously, "symbolism" denotes the imaginative attitudes and practices of the literary clerisy he situates as the habitués of his title figure. To this retreat his writers have decamped, leaving behind the realities of other people and the claims of a generally understandable, let alone socially ameliorative, poetry and fiction: *la poèsie pure*, all in all, a poetry dense with musical content and semantic suggestion (rather than definition), in the phrase Stéphane Mallarmé provided as a directive for his own salon coterie of French *Symbolisme*.[29] This is a sensibility, however, that Wilson needs to turn away from any identification with symbolist retreat. To this end he will be availing himself of the specifically French inflection of his title word. *Symbolisme* summoned a range of associations that linked his authors with a national literary culture which, some time before the currency of our English "modernism," was seen as the most advanced and daring in Europe. This connection with the progressive carries a lot of ideological weight for Wilson. It will allow him to broker an identity acceptable to his emergent social conscience and, in effect, to cleanse the sensibility of affiliations unacceptable to that conscience. What he is leaving out of the account of the story of symbolism is that aspect whose absence is at once most motivated and most consequential: this is the erstwhile fellow traveler but now identifiable enemy of *symbolisme*: this is *décadence*.

Wilson thus extends the Symons precedent without questioning it, allowing "symbolism" to stand wherever it can in place of the disapproved "decadence." When he first names the "decadents," then, he lifts them out of his text on the tweezers of those inverted commas, holding them at an arm's-length safety zone. Putting them in the company of their sometimes better brethren, the English "aesthetics," he can say ... well, that there's nothing much to say: those "English 'aesthetics' and 'decadents' ... for the most part imitated the French without very much originality."[30] Whatever "originality" may mean in Wilson's account – this word and concept are interrogated by key figures in the longer literary history I will be telling – Wilson presumes that those decadents have failed in their aspiration to attain it, while the symbolists somehow, but certainly, had it. For these attributed deficiencies and gifts, there is a framework of explanation that, in being unexplained by Wilson, reveals its powers of presumption all the more strongly. Here the association of the decadents with an historical time of late or last days precludes their participation in a literary mythology of "origins," whereas the symbolists seem to exercise this originality as the birthright of a new age, existing as they do on the brink of the "modern" century, serving all in all as ancestors in a mythology of novelty that will remain most powerfully in place in the scholarship of modernism.

Wilson reveals these presumed values in the place he makes for symbolism in a longer literary history, which he begins in the earlier century in a pan-European and trans-Atlantic romanticism. This critical project entails a reading of romanticism as somehow always and everywhere the same sensibility, which, for Wilson, is instinct already and first of all with those values of originality and freshness that are the attributed significance of symbolism. If, however, we recognize romanticism at the earlier end of the century as a sensibility of developing and mutating phases, we may understand its advancement into the early-mid and mid-late nineteenth century, so that, at the end, a later and assignably "decayed" version of an earlier romanticism is showing up in the literary productions of symbolism, which will be better named as decadence. A sustained analysis to the point of this claim will be developed in my first chapter, but the story it records may be typified in one of its early iterations by Thomas De Quincey, who, in *Confessions of an English Opium-Eater*, recasts passages of Coleridge and Wordsworth, turning the natural happiness that was framed as aim and value in the earlier poetry to the somber impossibility of this latter, later day. This sense of historical time ramifies into the temporal imaginary of literature in fashions equally intricate and significant, as will be seen in readings of a wide variety of writers. It endures most tellingly in De Quincey's devoted reader Baudelaire, who provides a tuning fork for a poetics of decadence as the music of melancholy in urban modernity, which occurs in an imaginatively late historical time. This sense of time will abide as one of the most powerful imaginative tenses in literary modernism.

None of this lateness or lastness, however, none of this aftermath imaginary, for Wilson. His symbolism, which finds its inaugural figure in Baudelaire, is not the last gasp or dying fall of romanticism. It is a second wind, pumped up already in the second paragraph of his book: "the movement of which in our own day we are witnessing the mature development is not merely a degeneration or an elaboration of Romanticism, but rather a counterpart to it, a second flood of the same tide."[31] "Not merely a degeneration": this dismissal targets an irresistible synonym of "decadence," which takes the sense of decline and maps it onto a process of regression in biological history. Here, in a counter-evolutionary direction, and under the strains of the civilization it has generated, humankind is seen to be reverting increasingly into less evolved types. This is simply inadmissible to Wilson as the social progressive, and the force of his rejoinder to this "degeneration" of romanticism suggests how, in the literary history under review, decadence is the power needing to be driven away.

As the category of dominant value, the combined idea of the "new" and the "original" reveals its compulsive quality through the most striking, and indeed startling, maneuver in his argument. Here Wilson takes the origin of "symbolism" away from its ostensible center, the Parisian capital of a European order beginning to feel its age under the presentiments of entropy and the attendant sense of an ending. He relocates it in the New World, in his own America. Here, as he avers, "it was in general true that, by the middle of the century, the Romantic writers in the United States – Poe, Hawthorne, Melville, Whitman and even Emerson – were, for reasons which it would be interesting to determine, developing in the direction of Symbolism."[32] Indeed, "it would be interesting to determine" the reasons for this (reverse) direction in his literary history, but the more relevant task is to see the ends to which this need of the new compels Wilson. Where his relocation of the movement to the New World confers a lease of new life on it, he follows through on this motive in a declamatory passage that is as remarkable as it is revealing. "The Symbolist Movement proper was first largely confined to France and principally limited to poetry of rather an esoteric kind," he has first to concede, "but it was destined, as time went on, to spread to the whole western world and its principles to be applied on a scale which the most enthusiastic of its founders could scarcely have foreseen."[33] Not only is the phenomenon of symbolism given the status of a forward movement, it is accorded a destined force and authority that, in the context of an America-centric literary history, reads as its own version of American Manifest Destiny.

These extreme measures – symbolism as literary jingoism, its development a triumphalist progress of New World energies – reveal a compelled and compelling need to inscribe the poetics of modernism with the values of novelty, of energetic direction most of all. And Wilson's progressivism is writing its ideology into literary history with a remarkable degree of success. In effect, his own rhetorical mastery could be seen as the force that helped him overcome his initial reservations about the social progressiveness, and so the political worthiness, of the work of literary reference.[34] As Robert Spiller indicated in 1958, *Axel's Castle* created an intellectual environment in which "a love of Eliot, Joyce, Proust, and Yeats seemed compatible with radical politics."[35] So that, independently and virtually simultaneously in their reviews of the book, Allen Tate and F. O. Matthiessen could identify an expression of that "economic determinism of literature" in which "*all* poetry is only an inferior kind of social will"[36] and a treasuring of the "the private imagination in isolation from the life of society."[37] These are the oppositions reconciled in the tonic chord of Wilson's symbolism.

If that harmonic quality bespeaks the appeal of coherence in his version of literary history, we do well to remember that this appeal requires the muting of that discordant note of decadence. Indeed, this is the omission that F. R. Leavis insists on as the one thing needful for his appreciation of the book. Even as "*Axel's Castle* is a book not only to read, but to buy," Leavis advises a readership struggling to put pennies together in these early years of the Great Depression, one must eliminate the figure of "Axel, a kind of personification of the aesthetic Nineties," since "there is nothing *fin de siècle* about [Leavis's favored authors'] maladjustment with the modern world."[38] The French end of the century attaches its sense of an ending to "the aesthetic Nineties" and so summons those associations with lateness and aftermath that provide the negative edge of decadence. All will be well, Leavis is saying, once we eliminate those associations in Wilson's title figure with the so-called decade of "decadence," the word that has already been pushed out of substantial account. And it was the spirit of progressivism in Wilson's particular and idiosyncratic understanding of "symbolism" – in lieu of the opposite qualities denominated by even a standard sense of decadence – that gained the strong hand in the critical story. As one of the book's earliest readers, Robert Adams, remarked in a retrospect in 1948: Wilson "became largely responsible, by the publication of *Axel's Castle* alone, for the advent and widespread acceptance in America of what had been almost entirely a foreign or expatriate movement. Symbolism and its associated techniques are today firmly ensconced in our poetical repertory."[39]

The long-standing power of "symbolism" in this critical narrative of modernism testifies to the appeal it exerts, as I suggested earlier, as a counter of possibility. As an invocatory concept, it summons a set of technical incentives and imaginative ambitions in the greatening range of modernism itself.[40] Its tendency in this respect is demonstrated already and first of all in the transit between Symons and Wilson, where the different interests and aims of the two critics are equally well served by the plastic, variable senses of this term: alternately, the far-sounding counter of an acoustically induced spirituality and the historically directed engine of progressive political change. Where this critical tradition has lived forward into the present through Kermode and Kenner, "symbolism" carries these usually promissory qualities of progressive innovation as an almost entirely nominal power.

So, in 2010, Robert Scholes can claim without hesitation that "the French little reviews – especially those associated with the symbolist movement – are the real breeding grounds of international modernism," whereupon he proceeds without any indication of what "the French symbolist movement" actually contributed in the way of genetic material for this breeding. So, three years earlier, also in *Modernism/modernity*, Morag Shiach finds the "symbolist presence within modernism" to be the most important point of reference for innovation in the language of modernist poetry, which, as she proceeds in this valuable analysis, leaves any stipulated sense of symbolism behind. So, in 2000, in *ELH*, Andrew John Miller takes the "poetic professionalism" of Eliot and his companion talents back to French symbolism, which he specifies as the "professional ethos of the symbolist avant-garde": the otherwise unlikely combination of the avant-garde, professionalism, and symbolism suggests the unconsidered, ready-made, automatic character of the "symbolist" reference in the origins of literary modernism. More discerningly, in 2005, in "Symbolism at the Periphery: Yeats, Maeterlinck, and Cultural Nationalism," Raphael Ingelbien modifies the customary understanding of "symbolism" as a universal poetic language, showing how it forms differently in different cultural locales. If Ingelbien qualifies the content of symbolism, however, he does not challenge its dominance as a counter in the story he is otherwise attempting to complicate, citing and accepting "Edmund Wilson's groundbreaking study *Axel's Castle*" as the work that "set the tone as early as 1931" for the critical tradition in which "the terms 'symbolism' and 'modernism' are often virtually synonymous."[41]

Misnomer or misprision, the dominance of "symbolism" in these literary histories of modernism may be for the most part unmotivated, even automatic. Though it might serve as a kind of academic shorthand, it also makes short shrift of that "mood" of decadence with which "symbolism" was once inextricably intertwined. Terms that are automatically applied, after all, serve to provide ordinal points of reference. And the most important, long-standing effect of the prevalence of "symbolism" in this story of modernism has been to remove "decadence" from any determining force in the background story. "Decadence" was – and is – a word for some of the most disturbing and tradition-shaking qualities in modernism, which "symbolism" has muted, but which we will see in detail and at length throughout this book.

The import of this challenge may be invoked through consideration of a work of criticism that was published only three years before Wilson's: Walter Benjamin's *Origin of German Tragic Drama* (*Ursprung des Deutschen Trauerspiels*, 1928). Although this subject obviously lies on the far side of time to the literary history of Wilson's interest, Benjamin's first book clearly anticipates his own subsequent work on the sensibility of literary decadence. The occlusion of decadence from the critical understanding of modernism may explain the fact that Benjamin's study owns no place in a bibliography of modernist scholarship (with a signal exception, noted in the last inter-chapter of this book). Nonetheless, *Origin* offers a new sense of connection between some of the most important works of nineteenth- and twentieth-century literatures, which is the area of literary history within which Benjamin's intelligence operates so characteristically and incisively. In the full context of its endeavor, *Origin* illustrates the menace decadence presents to a modernism for which the critical fiction of Wilson's symbolism has provided the explanatory paradigm.

In addressing false conceptions of his historical subject, Benjamin's greatest vehemence is reserved for the set of values that are incorporated in "the symbol." Here "the symbol" provides a unification of aesthetic experience in a manner analogous to that of "the tragic," a term which, in its classical sense, he exchanges freely for the "symbol." This is a literary practice and critical concept that he understands in its ideal or aspirant form in the same way as Paul de Man, who takes the construction and understanding of the Romantic symbol back to the intellectual culture of Enlightenment and post-Enlightenment Europe. Here, even as the linguistic ground and epistemological warrant for symbolic embodiment in language was being taken away, the appeal of the possibility of organic synthesis or natural totality in verbal representation was exerted all the more strongly.[42] For Benjamin, the symbol reveals this nostalgic quality already and first of all as the bygone of the Early Modern. And he criticizes this conception of "the symbol," especially of its falsely promissory value, with a rare and fierce intensity. What draws fire most strongly and revealingly, however, is not the notion of the symbol that may have existed in his field of primary historical reference.

> The striving on the part of the romantic aestheticians after a resplendent but ultimately non-committal knowledge of an absolute has secured a place in the most elementary theoretical debates about art for a notion of the symbol

which has nothing more than the name in common with the genuine notion. This latter, which is the one used in the field of theology, could never have shed that sentimental twilight over the philosophy of beauty which has become more and more impenetrable since the end of early romanticism. But it is precisely this illegitimate talk of the symbolic which permits the examination of every artistic form 'in depth', and has an immeasurably comforting effect on the practice of investigation into the arts.[43]

This intensity comes not from a passion for the Early Modern archive but, most closely and urgently, from Benjamin's interests in the poet associated with romanticism in the late or decayed phases of its "twilight" time: Baudelaire. It expresses concerns emerging concurrently with his ongoing work on the French poet, which had started in the 1910s and continued through the early 1920s with an increasingly heavy immersion in the texts of Les Fleurs du Mal, which he was translating as well as writing about in the late 1920s; this project moved to culmination in a series of essays on Baudelaire in the 1930s.[44] Benjamin's endeavor represents his study of another set of origins, the origins of the décadence which, identified with Baudelaire from the start, was being brought under the coded misnomer of symbolism. This critical concept is the appropriate target and the intended referent in this jeremiad. And the value to be gained from this identification is an understanding that a poetics of decadence is being worked out in the otherwise unlikely context of the Early Modern setting of this first critical book. The sensibility he is outlining under the unwritten word "decadence" emerges not as the same thing as symbolism under another name but as a wholly antithetical power, an antagonist so deadly it must otherwise be coated – and coded – in that antonym.

In place of the impossibility of symbolic embodiment, Benjamin provides the idea of "allegory." While this concept gains clear relevance to the historical subject of baroque German theater, it comports strongly also with the Baudelairean context and oeuvre. As the obverse of the symbolic, moreover, Benjamin's "allegory" reads in its detailed features as a virtual breviary for a poetics of decadence. Here the separation of the sign and the signified in the arbitrary language of allegorical signification provides a primary instance of the fall from unitary significance in literary representation; this fall will be reenacted as the paradigmatic action of decadence.[45] This formative idea will be reiterated in Benjamin's subsequent work on the allegorical in Baudelaire's poetry as well as later in this book, where we will see it developing from the poetics of décadence into a poetics of modernism. And an anticipation of its major points may spell out the substantial challenge it presents to the appeal of Wilson's "symbolism."

Working with the remains of the unitary symbol, where the gods of antiquity once fabulously lived in the images depicting them, the verbal concepts of Early Modern allegory are relics or, in poetic effect, the dead bodies of those gods, who are now detached from the language representing them as the sheerest of spectral entities. The undead afterward is one of the primary imaginative tenses of decadence, and it is configured in Benjamin's account of the dramatic imagination of the Baroque in ways consistent with the actions of allegory in his later writings on Baudelaire.[46] This is a literary taxonomy that de Man describes in "The Rhetoric of Temporality," where, without specific reference to the literary history we are working through, "symbol" and "allegory" are vividly counterpoised. Instead of the symbol and symbolized living in the simultaneous unity of the numinous body, de Man notes that allegory is an art in and of a broken time: the succession of words in a text establishes the frame of verbal reference and sets the work of poetic representation as a backward action of ever more phantasmal character.[47] This condition generates an extensive lexicon of tropes and images particular to its temporal imaginary, most vividly in Benjamin's account of the Early Modern, as the effigy. This frequently iterated figure presents a poignantly failed attempt to revive the disincarnate meaning in the form of a death mask, which appears again in the dramatis personae of decadence as the effigy human, the puppet or marionette, which serves as an image and icon of an historical time that has outlived its natural or organic term and so petrified into a mask.[48] In anticipation of his later analysis of Baudelaire, Benjamin's persistent emphasis on allegory offers a form of the musical refrain to match Wilson's symbolism, to which it offers also the riposte of a counter-poetics point for point. It is an oblique but severe critique, if not of Wilson himself, certainly of the critical tradition preceding (and following) him. The difference he draws between the symbolic and the allegorical is the same difference that exists between symbolism and decadence as theme words for the background values and character of modernist poetics. The difference it indexes also explains the intensity of resistance that was long evident in the mainstream traditions of modernist criticism.

3. A Queerer Tense

Whereas Benjamin reveals what is at stake in writing "decadence" so forcibly out of the account of the origins of modernism in histories such as Wilson's, Oscar Wilde would be as notable an absence in subsequent understandings of literary modernism as he was a conspicuous presence in the contemporary scene of English "decadence." The queerness with which he and decadence were both associated accounts in some measure for the exclusion of his influence in those formative accounts of modernism. This exclusion has been removed in the best work of the last twenty-five or so years. From Eve Sedgwick's *Epistemology of the Closet* (1990) to Rita Felski's *The Gender of Modernity* (1995) and beyond, literary history has included the trials of Wilde as a new orienting point for the precedent-upsetting energies of artistic modernism.[49] That 1895 spectacle offered a sort of *tableau vivant* for the sexual dreads of a generation and, in the disturbances it stirred, provided an opening into new gender imaginaries. This development coincided and reciprocated with an experimental aesthetic temper, all in all, with new imaginative attitudes and fresh technical incentives which, in retrospect, may be seen as one expression of a nascent literary modernism. The connection between the artistic ferment of modernism and the insti-gating figure of Wilde, whose proscribed sexuality provides the strongest point of reference, is occasionally made under the heading of "decadence." This identification works to some extent to redress the omission of deca-dence from the modernism under construction in the scholarship of the mid-century.

In many of these accounts, there is an advancement narrative of cultural history, where, looking back from the present, the commentator emphasizes a sense of destined progression on these issues of sexual freedom and so pulls the story of the historical subject into line with the progress ideology of mainstream liberalism.[50] This is the thematic narrative in the literary history mapped by Ann Ardis in *Modernism and Cultural Conflict, 1880–1922* (2002), where the moment of the Wilde trial comes into signal focus. Ardis demonstrates how, among others, Ezra Pound and T. S. Eliot continued to play away from the major dare of that figure of celebrity decadence and, in their literary and cultural criticism, to move toward formal positions more traditionalist, in fact, than their work manifested in actual practice. In the evaluative language of her critique, the literary attitudes of this mainstream modernism are contracting into a conservative and reactionary stance in relation to the alternative, emancipatory sexuality that Wilde represents.[51] With an understanding of the history of the criticism of literary modernism, we can see how Wilde is being read forward into modernism and into the progress narratives of a traditional modernism in a way that displaces its former representatives and replaces these with figures whose difference does not challenge the standard of progressivity as the establishing value. Conversely, then, in the literary-political history of these newer modernisms, the old (and long-ignored) decadence is being recovered in its convention-dismaying character as a source and center of essentially progressive energy. Its manifestations include the figure of the New Woman, who emerges from the decadent temperament of the fin de siècle as the chief icon of an advancement narrative that ranges in its centers of interest and value from social position to sexual experience, where an experimental energy on these several fronts expresses the temper of progressivity and futurity above all.[52]

In a field of modernism far larger and more populous than the one once dominated by those identifiably straight "Men of 1914," the queer radical chic of Wilde assumes due prominence. If the scholarship of literary modernism long abjured or ignored this connection, however, the absence it leaves in the formative narratives of Wilson and Kenner has never been filled in with the import it originally owns. So, the emphasis in my account goes to what has been erased as critics representing the newer modernism have replaced the figures of an older modernism – but without challenging the standard of progressive value that led Wilson to put them there in the first place. What this development leaves out of the story is the considerable, significant pressure of the adverse orientation. This backward track takes its interests and values not in terms of some necessarily atavistic political attitude, but as an expressive disenchantment with the cultural construction of forwardness, an orientation that situates its representatives in the positions of a queerness that has also not yet been taken into account. This is the sensibility whose presence and pressure we need still to understand in those figures for whom it was earlier – and is still – supposed to be antithetical.

A first point of reference in this critical field is Lee Edelman's *No Future: Queer Theory and the Death Drive* (2004). For Edelman, the threat that queerness presents to the premises of conventional heterosexuality comprises but exceeds the category of some assignably "deviant" sexuality. Queerness challenges a modern ideology of progressive time in general; it defies most particularly the underlying values of futurity; it denies the Child, as image and emblem of the Future, with the non-reproductive condition of homosexuality. In this contrary campaign, Edelman theorizes queerness to unmake and remake those assumptions whose comfortableness disguises the extent to which life in the present has been mortgaged to those promissory mythologies of reproductive futurity. More specifically, the "death drive" that he takes as the provocative motto for his title is working to relocate the energies of sexuality to those centers which, following Freud's observations on the behaviors that demonstrate this compulsion, manifest "its insistence on repetition, its stubborn denial of teleology, ... and, above all, its rejection of spiritualization through marriage to reproductive futurism."[53]

These are the behaviors – reiterative, non-reproductive, obsessive to no end – that Edelman sees with an increasing frequency in Victorian fiction particularly, most vividly in the figures of Dickens's Scrooge and George Eliot's Silas Marner. He finds the culture of reproductive futurity clearly exemplified and possibly instigated earlier in that century in the Romantic cult of the child, but his interest does not lie in historicizing these developments.[54] Putting those attitudes in the context of mid-late-nineteenth- and early-twentieth-century literary history, however, will reveal new dimensions of understanding. In following their development over this longer period, we will see the non-reproductive compulsion being taken to new and revealing extremes, where an erotics of disembodiment rewrites some of the stereotyped versions of queer sexuality and recasts its standard character in a framework of more powerfully adversary values. This is an account I will be following into the poetics of modernism through the intellectual and literary history of decadence.

What I am suggesting, then, is that there is a fundamental connection between queerness, which has been assigned to decadence as its most vivid interest (its most livid identity), and the denial of futurity, that is, with the imaginative circumstance of aftermath. This is the sensibility in which the temporal imaginary of decadence pronounces its profoundest, certainly its most unsettling, poetry. There is a kind of nervy courage in Edelman's book that verges at times on the perverse. Excesses in this direction are not so much an oddity of personal or preferential style; they are the demonstration of an argumentative challenge: the whole performance provides one measure of the daring it takes to address the system and episteme of reproductive futurity. And while Edelman's formulations have already generated a countercurrent in subsequent discussions, which attempt to bring back a sense of futurity in models of the queer utopia and a prerogative for embodiment in the possession of queer sexuality,[55] there is something specific in Edelman's argument and arguing that locates a temper special to the temporal imaginary of decadence a hundred years earlier. Queerness may have been the subject of heavy suppression over the long turn of that century, but the denial of progressive time and reproductive growth presents the most substantial challenge to established standards now as well as then. This is a challenge that Heather Love reframes eloquently in *Feeling Backward: Loss and the Politics of Queer History* (2007), where she contests the co-optation of queerness in those mythologies of liberal history that feature tolerance of this kind as the emblematic accomplishments of progress, which, she is saying, queerness so painfully upsets: "In this book I have tried to resist the affirmative turn in queer studies in order to dwell at length on the 'dark side' of modern queer representation. It is not clear how such dark representations from the past will lead toward a brighter future for queers. Still, it may be necessary to check the impulse to turn these representations to good use in order to see them at all."[56] The imaginative tense of decadence is queerer than that.

Resisting the tendencies of temporal progressiveness in some of the value structures of recent queer studies, Love identifies the more important temper of negativity within modernism first of all. This is a sensibility she associates with the impact of homophobia in particular and locates most indicatively in a modernism populated with "modernity's others" (her chief figures are Radclyffe Hall and Willa Cather, Walter Pater and Sylvia Townsend Warner), who demonstrate most specifically that "backwardness is a feature of even the most forward-looking modernist literature." "This historical ambivalence is particularly charged, I want to suggest, in the works of minority or marginal modernists . . . Reading for backwardness is a way of calling attention to the temporal splitting at the heart of all modernism," so that, "even when modernist authors are making it new," she concedes and emphasizes, "they are inevitably grappling with the old."[57] These writers are working from positions of estrangement to the mythologies of progressive time in general and the ideologies of reproductive futurity most specifically, but the queerness of Love's modernism should be understood not just as an orphans' asylum within the societal norm of productive time. It stands, I wish in turn to suggest as strongly as possible, as the presentiment of exceptionality in the feeling of time left behind, not a powerlessness – or powerfulness – but a possession of the temporal remnant as an all in all; a stopping of the time of progress and an inhabiting of this circumstance, not with despair necessarily but neither with hope. This is a condition I will be identifying as one of the most powerful of the establishing categories in the temporal imaginary of modernism, and I will be connecting it in a more widely working way to the legacy and temperament of decadence. Here, the current of influence that Ardis has charted otherwise helpfully needs to be reversed so that, beyond reading the fin de siècle forward, we learn to read modernism backward, both historically and attitudinally, into the sensibility of decadence and, among other things, into those backward orientations manifested most apparently (but not only) in queer temporalities. This reverse continuity may be seen not only in the figures of the "marginal" modernism that Love focuses on, but also in some of the major modernist fiction of the period and, especially, in the poetries of Pound and Eliot, whose defining inventions are often a reinvention of decadence.

Projecting some of the consequences of her model of queer temporality in her "Epilogue: The Politics of Refusal," Love centers her meditations on Walter Benjamin's "angel of history." This is the figure he conjures, in his "Theses on the Philosophy of History," as an imaginative gloss on Paul Klee's painting *Angelus Novus*. The intensity of intellectual and imaginative apprehension in this characterization is manifest in the difference it witnesses to the original, which shows a figure with the expression Benjamin delineates but with none of the circumstantial detail he fills in. Benjamin sees

> an angel looking as though he is about to move away from something he is fixedly contemplating. His eyes are staring, his mouth is open, his wings are spread. This is how one pictures the angel of history. His face is turned toward the past. Where we perceive a chain of events, he sees one single catastrophe which keeps piling wreckage upon wreckage and hurls it in front of his feet. The angel would like to stay, awaken the dead, and make whole what has been smashed. But a storm is blowing from Paradise; it has got caught in his wings with such violence that the angel can no longer close them. This storm irresistibly propels him into the future to which his back is turned, while the pile of debris before him grows skyward. This storm is what we call progress.[58]

For Love, Benjamin's figure provides "an emblem of resistance to the forward march of progress" and, in a subtler and more ambitious understanding, synthesizes the backward-oriented force of its attention with an alternative model of progress, one that is advanced by "modernity's others" and represented by an openness to the value and even the necessity of the detritus of official, that is, progressive history. Whatever value is attributed to the putatively "new" in literary and cultural history, there is something unprecedentedly significant about this attitude as an establishing orientation. Its novelty may lie in the recognition of the impossibility of novelty, which, in one of the sardonic responses of his *Minima Moralia*, Theodor Adorno offers as his understanding of the "cult of the new" that provides one of the formative recognitions of modernism.[59] This is the vanguard awareness of the modernism I wish to return to the technical experimentation as well as temperamental adventuring of literary and cultural decadence. This is a precedent sensibility for those vagabonds of progress in Love's formulations, and it provides a longer memory and more extensive reference for the queerness she presents so compellingly.

Benjamin opens a path to this understanding. Compositing his "angel of history" with *Origin of German Tragic Drama*, we can see how the emphases of queer temporality are not only corroborated in that earlier work but extended and developed in a more comprehensive model, one that reclaims "decadence" from "symbolism" and so regains the place of this long abjured sensibility within the literary history of modernism. An acknowledgment of anti-futurity in early modernism, however, takes nothing away from the force of its technical inventiveness. It remains as daring as the challenge to productive and reproductive futurity in conventional attitudes; as defiant as the imaginative temporalities of queerness and decadence; as experimentally adventurous as the greater menace of inconsequential time. Indeed, it is about time: it is about time to write this more complex sense of decadence into an account of modernism; and it is about time that these two words are most crucially concerned.

4. "Decadence," "Modernism"

"Certain words of a moral or behavioral kind, judgmental words, continue to insinuate themselves into contexts where they injure meaning and bring about confusion, since they carry with them a *previousness*, something once true, something, that is to say, once applicable. There are words in use now that are no longer applicable." Thus Richard Gilman writes emphatically in the first paragraph of *Decadence: The Strange Life of an Epithet* (1979).[60] He is underscoring the importance of an always earlier validity in the significance of the word in his main title. Granted, there is a difference between earlier and later uses of "decadence." "The word 'decadence' has come down to us partly through writers such as Verlaine and Flaubert," he continues, discerning a crucial "difference between their use of the word and ours. For all their hyperbole, they were serious about it, staking something on their interest. You would not find them toying with 'decadence' the way nearly all of us do these days, using it glibly, offhandedly, having encountered it in the Zeitgeist."[61] Despite that slide to a looseness of designation, "decadence" maintains a meaningful reference where it centers an experience of historical time in a sort of posterior tense. The observation to which Gilman returns repeatedly in his book is the perception of the pastness of the present; of a perennial *afterwardness* as the imaginative time zone of decadence. This perception allows us to understand the sense of unreality that often gathers around the frame of designated reference for the word. It opens a realm of possibilities, all in all, a world of the permissible forbidden, where the unreality of pastness at once stimulates and absolves the prurient interest it focuses in the present. This verbal dynamic explains the colloquial association of "decadence" with notorious characters and scandalous behaviors, which are often more than slightly tinted with the sepia of a former age. The most important aspect of this understanding, however, lies in the temporal imaginary of decadence. This feeling of a declining afterward has recurred as a dominant quality of consciousness at different moments of world history – ancient Rome, Alexandria, and Byzantium are entries in Gilman's catalogue – but the sense of a late historical day or an aftermath circumstance is concentrated with particular intensity in European cultural history in the mid-late nineteenth century. This *décadence* finds one of its strongest expressions in this time in France, most of all in the Paris of *la belle époque*, but it was coextensive through the cultural capitals of Europe: a decaying aristocracy, an entropic cosmos, an imperial outlook losing moral confidence even as it was gaining terrain, and the emergence of "the crowd" as a randomizing force in the experience of urban modernity.

These features may be seen equally as evidence of "degeneration," the word and concept that massed substantially as well in the cultural imaginary of the second half of the century. As Daniel Pick has demonstrated in his defining study of this subject, "degeneration" represents the focal point of a new "medico-psychiatric" framework of understanding for social stratification as well as human character and group behavior. Demonstrating the tendency of certain populations to revert to more "primitive" stages of development for the species, degeneration theory offered a paradigm of value as well as a framework of analysis.[62] Degeneration discourse thus tends to emphasize the evidence of regression from the normative values of historical advance in moral warnings and cautionary tales, and on this tonal and attitudinal point we may more narrowly specify its relation to artistic and cultural decadence, which, instead, most often flaunts its difference to those standards in stylized practices, vaunted attitudes. If the methods were obviously different, the message was more or less the same. The worried screeds of degeneration and the triumphal legends of decadence were rewriting the promissory mythologies of Progress, now in a reverse script, turning the narratives of "the new" – a category of developing and intensifying value over the long nineteenth century, as Gilman helpfully points out[63] – on a backward track in degeneration and into an aftermath circumstance in decadence. Here progress has stopped and afterward supplies the tense of imaginative interest and value. This antagonism speaks for long submerged but always growing apprehensions about the value of novelty and progress and, to bring in Edelman's word, futurity in world-cultural and world-historical prospects. It is the claiming, heightening, and stylizing of this circumstance in decadence that I am recovering in this book and regaining as one of the origin stories for literary modernism.

These developments represent the circumstantial history within which the sensibility of decadence reveals its timely content and historical depth, but a pressure specific to literary history helps to make literature – British literature especially, as Walter Jackson Bate would have it in *The Burden of the Past and the English Poet* – the most particular and indicative register for this sensibility. Here the great surge of inventive work in verse in the English Renaissance is seen as the challenge that establishes a kind of impossible novelty as the new category of interest and exertion in subsequent centuries. Various negotiations, compromises, and countermeasures are followed by Bate into the early years of English romanticism. Now the imaginative concept of originality is fostered and reinforced in ways we may track adequately in the next chapter. What Bate's account provides most immediately and helpfully is an understanding that the gravitational drag of the past is no invention of the decadent sensibility of the later nineteenth century, which serves instead to gather these long-standing apprehensions to their moment of climacteric and climax at the end of the nineteenth century. Here, in reaction to an ever-proliferating culture of commercial, mass-consumed, and mass-advertised modernity, the cult of "the new" presents a newly substantial challenge and so focuses and intensifies a reaction in the temporal imaginary of the literature most alert to this circumstance. This is the literature of decadence, and it draws upon the extensive precedent Bate has documented in England in particular.[64]

It is on this particular point of the historical place and time of the most recent decadence that Gilman, in attempting to periodize his subject, makes a most revealing move in conclusion. "Apart from Wilde and Beardsley," he motions in closing his book, "the Decadent/Aesthetic period in England had little effect on the subsequent course of her art and literature."[65] In taking the historical location of decadence in late-nineteenth-century England as the end of the story (he does not follow the legacy of Wilde or Beardsley in any detail), Gilman submits to the still prevalent conception that decadence does not extend in any meaningful way – only in the ways of an increasingly meaningless moral and judgmental epithet – into the cultural production and artistic history of the twentieth century, that is, with the locating circumstance of modernism. This restriction repeats the exclusion evidenced in the scholarship forming the canon of modernist literature through the middle of the century, and, where it comes from the earlier side of the dividing line of the century's end, it points all the more strongly to the predisposition in the received understanding of modernism to resist this affiliation. Much of this critical tradition may be read accordingly as a history committed to a rejection of the anti-progressive sensibility of decadence within the namesake value of a modernism that exists primarily, in its own signature cliché, as an art of the new, even though, it is important to remember again, Pound's own forging of the "Make It New" slogan did not occur until 1934.

A number of major modernists also contested their connections with decadence as a sensibility. They usually staged the confrontation as a battle between the old and the new. In the oppositional logic of these campaigns, however, there is a sense of complicity with the antagonist, where the resistance they exhibit also demonstrates the sort of reciprocity Pound modeled in his 1914 piece. For this particular complexity there may be any number of historical explanations. If the accelerating pace of change in early twentieth-century modernity puts an increasing pressure on the value of the new, for instance, the modernists' invention of the novelty of themselves shows a compliance with that sense of the times, which they also subvert, claiming in that resistance some sense of historical autonomy. This resistance maintains a connection to the imaginative temperament as well as technical conventions of decadence. A range of reasons such as this provides for the importance of the story, which is the literary history of modernism in England that I want to tell. And while the classificatory label we apply as "modernism" is, unlike "decadence," a terminological convenience of a time later than the era to which it refers, there is something in the literature we bring into this classificatory category that confirms an interior meaning in the term. For the root of this word links its most radical concept to the exact sense of its otherwise contested counterpart in "decadence."

Modern*ism*: the suffix adds the special intensity of a faith or belief to the root sense of the Latin "modo" – "today," "now," or, most accurately, "just now." "Modernism," accordingly, suggests an acute awareness of a temporal present, all in all, an empowering awareness of living in a Now distinctly different from a Then. This brink-instant sensibility is associated understandably but loosely with the ever-accelerating conditions of change in the material and social circumstances of urban modernity. It is essential nonetheless to maintain the difference between "modern" (or "modernization") and "modernism," which, in turn, refer to the chronological location of the twentieth century (with its accelerating dynamic of change) and a special, ramifying self-consciousness about living in this particular moment in time, that is, of living in this brink instant of the ultra-Present and working within the apprehension of this charged condition of constant change. A literary impulse that takes its own moment as its empowering occasion – the special present, the radical Now – is inscribed with the impermanence that is the condition of its existence. So, if we think of modernism in the simplest terms as a poetics of the new, as the record of the next day of Now, decadence presents an aesthetic of the old, as the register of the last day of

Then. In the most intense experience of Now in the radical time of modernism, however, Now is already going over into Then – into the temporal imaginary of decadence.

This double measure provides a dimension of understanding that is missing, crucially, in the model of imaginative temporality that Karl Heinz Bohrer maps in *Suddenness* [*Plotzlichkeit*]: *On the Moment of Aesthetic Appearance* (1994), which, in its emphasis on the dominance of an autonomous moment in aesthetic perception, Fredric Jameson rightly objects to as a form of avoiding and indeed voiding historical time in art.[66] In its double measure, however, the temporal imaginary of modernism is bound up profoundly with the experience of passing time. With this emphasis, it lies close to the establishing concept of modernism in the understanding that Raymond Williams offers in 1987 in "When *Was* Modernism?" "Very quickly," he notes, following the progress of the word "modern" from its etymology through the sixteenth to twentieth centuries, " 'modern' shifts its reference from 'now' to 'just now' or even 'then', and for some time has been a designation always going into the past with which 'contemporary' may be contrasted for its presentness."[67]

This understanding is one that de Man reiterates and augments in "Literary History and Literary Modernity." While de Man routinely resists and sometimes attacks the notion of a special time in twentieth- and even nineteenth-century modernity, he develops ideas of an exceptional temporality within the experience of reading and writing literature, where, in effect, we realize the meaning of the modern most significantly: in the feeling of being divided against time, more particularly, of being put into productive estrangement from any feeling of a consecutive present, all in all, from the pleasures of progressivity. This is, in effect, the most complex sense of modernist time, and, despite himself, de Man locates this sensibility with remarkable historical specificity. He takes this sense of modernist time back to the ur-moment of European decadence (without using that term). He finds it in its most charged form in Baudelaire, whose characteristically "modern" sense of the "present," as expressed in "The Painter of Modern Life," frames the Absolute Present or Radical Now as the signature frustration of urban modernity, recording at once its extraordinary appeal and its ultimate impossibility. Baudelaire writes (in de Man's English): "The pleasure we derive from the *representation of the present* (*la représentation du présent*) is not merely due to the beauty it may display, but also to the essential 'present-ness' of the present." But de Man follows, concentrating on the contradiction between "the present" and its written "representation," a *re*presentation that is keyed especially for Baudelaire to aesthetic pleasure, to the experience of beauty in this second iteration of the written afterward, and, in the reference frame of Baudelaire's essay, of urban modernity most generally:

> The paradox of the problem is potentially contained in the formula "*représentation du présent*," which combines a repetitive with an instantaneous pattern without apparent awareness of the incompatibility. Yet this latent tension governs the development of the entire essay. Baudelaire remains faithful throughout to the seduction of the present: any temporal awareness is so closely tied for him to the present moment that memory comes to apply more naturally to the present than it does to the past . . . . The same temporal ambivalence prompts Baudelaire to couple any evocation of the present with terms such as "représentation," "mémoire," or even "temps," all opening perspectives of distance and difference within the apparent uniqueness of the instant.[68]

This sense of the present moment being written as the memory of its possibilities of presence takes the radical meaning of modernism, or Just-Now-ism, and ties it to the root sense of *décadence* (de-*cad*-ere), to *fall* away. These conditions join under the apprehension of time always already falling away from its ideal imaginary, the instantaneous whole in the present moment. This is an understanding that helps us to reconstitute one of the original provocations and defining crises of modernism, which involves the raising of the absolute instant to a value it cannot realize or sustain. The moment of ultra-modernity, which is experienced as the ultimate Now in the temporal self-consciousness of modernism, is constantly sought and always lost. This condition differs from the experience of reading and writing in that temporal imaginary of post-structuralism which, with the differences of his exceptional individual intelligence, de Man is also representing here. It is an awareness that is specific to the temporal imaginary of the long turn of the century. Whether a chronological numerology is arbitrary or not, this moment receives the pressure of a joint sense of endings and beginnings; it registers the empty dread of endings and empty expectations of beginnings and correlates these presentiments to the events of one long historical day, which extends from the ongoing end of the age of European revolution into the immediate aftermath of the First World War. Decadence and modernism are dual names for this joint condition, and it is the aim of this book to follow the history of its literary representation within an understanding of cultural and political history.[69]

This critical story involves a literary history, then, with an extended frame of reference. The developments I am following begin with a turn I locate at the junction of first- and second-generation romanticism. Here the disappointments of an earlier revolutionary enthusiasm are registered in changes being made on one of the primary structures of first-generation romanticism, an ideal imaginary of time. The vision of historical loss that this development records lives forward as the substantial content and effective memory of a poetics of decadence, which develops a technical repertoire to represent this sense of temporal dispossession. This is the critical narrative of my first chapter, whose account turns into a consideration of the place that this sensibility of decadence maintains in the history of modernism. This is a consciousness which, connected now to that longer story of nineteenth-century political and cultural as well as literary history, presents a deepening challenge to cultural norms that have not taken the measure of the failure of the value of futurity. The remains of that ideal have been left in place as the poetic material of literary decadence. And where decadence registers this sense of a time not renewed, or not even capable of renewal, it locates the moment of an exceptional present, which provides at once the local time and the root sense of modern*ism*. The suffix, suggesting a self-conscious involvement in the modern moment, in a radical "today-ism," fixes the site of a temporal dispossession which decadence not only inhabits but stylizes. Although the Progress mythologies of Enlightenment and post-Enlightenment eras have been contested before, even by adherents to otherwise dominant values of empirical reason and instrumental logic, the exception defined by decadence represents a fundamental opposition, one that is based on the loss of its primary possibility in progressive revolution. Modernism goes on reliving this condition as its first circumstance and reinventing as one of its most substantial imaginative challenges, which, despite the disclaimers the sensibility of decadence may make about the impossibility of novelty or renewal, also produces technical inventions of the most exceptional kind. This is the reinvention of decadence that I am centering on as the theme word of this book.

This sensibility is demonstrated in the range of historical fiction I read in the second chapter. Here an array of major novelists, who sometimes stand in an uncertain relation to modernism, will become more coherent in this connection by virtue of the decadence we can now see them demonstrating, aesthetically as well as imaginatively, as they extend and adapt a poetics of decadence, which I will have constructed in the first chapter. And so, in the second half of the book, to a reading of two of the primary poets of Anglo-American modernism, Ezra Pound and T. S. Eliot, through an interlude on Imagism, which prepares an understanding of the decisive role that a poetics of decadence plays in the formation of modernist poetry. Pound and Eliot are obviously not the only modernist poets. My concentration on their work narrows an access to the comprehensive identity of the modernism I am using them to exemplify, and it also draws the otherwise extensive legacy of decadence into formations particular to its consequence in their work. This restriction may serve in turn to magnify and so clarify the presence of decadence within the hallmark work of literary modernism – in the *anni mirabiles* of the 1920s (and beyond). For the story moves through the poetry and prose of early modernism into a confirming of the worst worries in the historical pessimism of decadence: into critical mass in the Great War of 1914–1918. This event will be met by a sensibility that, on the evidence of the texts we will have read, has been readied by an extensive preparation in a literary history untold until now.

CHAPTER I

The Time of Decadence

If a consensus understanding of English literary history represents decadence as a "late" or "decayed" romanticism, both adjectives claim their status as relational. When does "late" begin, after all, and what specifically has "decayed" from an earlier, presumably better state? The readiest answers to these questions represent understandings that are durable but presumptive. The major developments are regularly seen as occurring in the generation of Swinburne and Rossetti, extending in one direction back to De Quincey and forward in the other to the poets of the English fin de siècle, most notably Ernest Dowson, Lionel Johnson, and Symons. The sense of decay is usually attributed to those aspects of character and activity that are manifestly counterconventional, sometimes scandalous and sometimes tragic, in these latter-day figures. While those metrics of calibrating literary time are obviously inexact, the categories for sorting poetic identity are equally rough, and the understanding of the relation between the lateness of historical time and the presentiment of moral loss is also undeveloped. In the effort of drawing out a longer story of literary generations, I will refine this consideration by shifting the frame of reference from the external instances and typical figures of a standard literary history. I will focus instead on the internal record of temporality, on the imaginative apprehension and literary representation of time itself – in one of its most meaningful and influential configurations in poetic romanticism.

This is the "spot of time," which may be tracked from its inception and consolidation in early romanticism. Here, as we know from familiar formulations in Wordsworth's autobiographical *Prelude*, the spot of time represents an integration of the various times of the poet's ongoing life, joining the present thoughts of the adult to the remembered experiences of the child.[1] The tasks and possibilities that are centered in this act of imaginative memory are complex, and so their accomplishment is far from assured. The spot of time thus provides the occasion for a major drama of consciousness:

> The days gone by
> Return upon me almost from the dawn
> Of life: the hiding-places of man's power
> Open; I would approach them, but they close.
> I see by glimpses now; when age comes on,
> May scarcely see at all . . .

Nonetheless, it is essential to note, those possibilities are not contradicted in principle, as this last passage continues:

> . . . and I would give,
> While yet we may, as far as words can give,
> Substance and life to what I feel, enshrining,
> Such is my hope, the spirit of the Past,
> For future restoration.

"– Yet another / Of these memorials . . .," the poet immediately continues, proving the truth of that constant and unflagging "hope" of "future restoration" of that "spirit of the Past."[2]

In the longer course of literary history, however, this optimism dissolves. The temporal imaginary of decadence acknowledges the motive interest in this fusion but accepts and even embraces its necessary failure. Not that this experience of disconnection is special or new: Augustine, for one, struggles in the feeling of being stretched between a past and a future he cannot integrate. What is new in the nineteenth century is the deliberate intensification of this failure. This is a development I want to follow across this chapter. In the work of explanation, I will be turning in a summary way from literary to political history, which will help to connect the sensibility of decadence to later phases of an earlier romanticism on one side and to the early moments of modernism on the other.

As an imaginative means of renewing a mature sensibility with the energy of younger times, the "renovating virtue" and "efficacious spirit" that Wordsworth proclaims in his classic passages on the spot of time in *The Prelude* suggest applications that he invokes in a nearby passage. Here, in more discursive measures, he summons the potentials of this imaginative experience:

> Oh! mystery of man, from what a depth
> Proceed thy honours. I am lost, but see
> In simple childhood something of the base
> On which thy greatness stands . . .[3]

As the spot of time redeems the experience of an adult poet with a remembered incident of childhood, it contributes the incipient energies and confident promise of that earlier time to the historical as well as personal present of the poet. Without reducing the poetic means of auguring this "mystery of man" to specified uses, we can see that the romantic spot of time presents a template for auguring the forces of new possibility in contemporary political history, too. It affords a literary corroboration, at once a poetic source and imaginative echo, for aspirations working in France and America, especially in the early age of revolutionary romanticism. As Lee Edelman notes in his cultural history of the cult of the child and the politics of futurity, it is the potency the romantic poets attributed to the figure of youth that underlies the promissory mythologies of revolution in the earlier age.[4] Most important, as James Chandler has demonstrated, the youth with which the mature poet is connecting in the moment of imaginative memory cannot be disconnected from the adult's historical and social experience, which provides the lens through which the past is remembered, and which may be restored accordingly through the benefits the poet attributes so demonstratively to this imaginative transaction.[5] As conceived and practiced, the spot of time is homologous with the cultural structuring and imaginative production of a renewal of historical time, which appears as the profoundest imaginative possibility of revolution. This promise of transformative power is epitomized in the new calendar of revolutionary France, whose innovative nomenclature spells out the same sense of history beginning anew that the spot of time models among its most consequential promises.

An identification of the political complement to this poetic figure also helps to refine the otherwise blocky chronologies of literary history. For an analysis of the imaginative practice of the spot of time opens a gap between first- and second-generation romanticism. The earlier poets, Wordsworth and Coleridge most notably, were sufficiently young to have undergone their poetic formations at a time when the optimism of Continental possibilities was still in the ascendant, and their work with the imaginative temporality that is evident in the spot-of-time consciousness reflects the possibilities of this earlier circumstance. These conditions shift for poets of the second generation, for Shelley most representatively, where the spot of time loses its integral force and so foregoes its transformative power. To follow the evolving morphology of the spot of time will be to connect literary and political history in a way that not only gives the novel content of political implication to the sensibility that technique encapsulates. It also provides a record of literary history that is sufficient to account for the consequences that follow. In the end, the remnants of this early romantic poetic possibility constitute some of the primary poetic material of modernism, which retains its declined ideal as a kind of primary disembodiment, a foregoneness that gains its affective depth and expressive power as an ongoing conversation of loss. It is a loss sustained and magnified in the catastrophic downturn of a first world war, as we shall see at greater length in later chapters, but it is expressed already and decisively in responses to the ongoing failure of European revolution through the middle years of the nineteenth century. It is in this period, in standard cultural histories, that the phenomena of decadence begin to be perceptible. Its literary culture, I am proposing, is related internally and essentially to the political history of failed revolution, which provides an underlying and ramifying influence into and through the modernism of the following century.

To follow that progress along this particular line of inquiry is to rediscover and reclaim the middle and turning term in the literary history bridging romanticism and modernism. This is "decadence," which represents a sense of historical loss that was experienced first in second-generation romanticism but then accepted and subsequently reified, stylized, by the writers affiliated with this term. This is the decadence that Edmund Wilson, Frank Kermode, and others have most emphatically and categorically written out of the account. Reinserted in the medial position and mediating role it properly occupies, decadence returns to alter our fundamental sense of this legacy, drawing a new volume and resonance from the political history we may restore to its developing and changing iterations.

In this chapter I will follow the turns this sensibility takes, from Wordsworth to De Quincey through Mary Wollstonecraft as well as Percy Bysshe Shelley and Byron and their companion talent Anna Barbauld, on to Baudelaire through Marx and back to Poe and Coleridge, and so ahead to Swinburne and Rossetti and the poets of the English fin de siècle. The original experience of revolutionary confusion in the 1790s is renewed in the ongoing failure of emancipatory ideals through the middle of the next century, as Marx's account reminds us. So this legacy will have become a literary memory, a developing convention, which evolves the attitudes and practices of the literary sensibility we call "decadence," as Marx's account also remarkably presages. This sensibility eventuates into the poems of the English fin de siècle. Those now recognizably "decadent" literary attitudes and practices look to the internal record of the spot of time as their literary memory, while the long story of its absconded possibilities in political history provides one of the more indicative measures of the import of this development.

1. **Spotted Time**

"Oh! youthful benefactress! How often in succeeding years, standing in solitary places, and thinking of thee with grief of heart and perfect love, how often have I wished that, as in ancient times . . ." Wordsworth's rhythms and diction are recognizable even in the prose of this passage. The benignity of the female figure recalls the familiar presence of the poet's sister. And the retrospect from the time indefinite of a dreary present to the alternative possibilities of time past includes the situation that promises, in an atmosphere drenched with that romantic's poetic spirit, the sort of inclusive emotional moment Wordsworth has focused in the expansive spot of time. Not Wordsworth, however, but De Quincey. Not a romantic nature idyll, but a portion of the story that makes up *The Confessions of an English Opium-Eater* (1821). And not Dorothy Wordsworth, but a young woman whose future includes her descent into a London brothel. "I do not often weep," De Quincey goes on to say as he rounds off this vignette in memory, "for not only do my thoughts on subjects connected with the chief interests of man daily, nay hourly, descend a thousand fathoms 'too deep for tears.'"[6] The echoing of "Intimations of Immortality" in this last phrase underwrites our expectation of a Wordsworthian feeling as conclusive as the spot of time. This is a possibility that is invoked most purposively, however, to be disclaimed.

Consider the rhythm of disenchantment that builds into the final *mise-en-scène* of this first part of the book, where an attempt to recover another memory brings the writer to this conclusion:

> I think that, though blind indeed, and scattered to the winds of late, the promptings of my heart may yet have had reference to a remoter time, and may be justified if read in another meaning: – and, if I could allow myself to descend again to the impotent wishes of childhood, I should again say to myself, as I look to the north, "Oh, that I had the wings of a dove" – and with how just a confidence in thy good and gracious nature might I add the other half of my early ejaculation – "And *that* way I would fly for comfort."[7]

Given the already intensive sense of the locative "remote," it is unusual to find the adjective in this comparative form of "remoter." And so, in a sequence so dense with echoes of Wordsworth, "remoter" cannot help but call up the memory of its appearance in "Lines Composed a Few Miles above Tintern Abbey," where, in comparing the pleasures of sensual childhood to the more abstract values of adulthood, the poet remembers the simplicity of experiences that "had no need of a remoter charm."[8] The sense of the adjective in De Quincey's text is working within the temporal dimensions of the spot-of-time consciousness: in his current distress, De Quincey is attempting to connect these "promptings of my heart" to some restorative source in boyhood, but that memory remains in the "remoter" zone of the unclaimed, indeed the disclaimed, where the "impotent wishes" with which the child is featured so strikingly serve to match the incapacity of the man's own imaginative powers. The Wordsworthian voice is resonating in plaintive reverse in this recessional echo, saying farewell to the several possibilities that the spot of time comprises.

De Quincey brings this sense of temporal dispossession to a more suggestive consequence through its strategic placement in his text. Those last words come just above a vertical break on the page that includes the title of the next section: "The Pleasures of Opium." Here he is to find the "comfort" left unfound in the last word of the preceding section. Opium is indeed the medicinal for the sickness of time. The drug is a substitute for the otherwise unaccomplished possibilities, the aims unmet by the redemptive temporalities of the spot-of-time consciousness.[9]

In the transition between the two sections of De Quincey's text, we see a transaction that marks a major turn in literary history. The romantic temporal imaginary is swapped for the narcotic that is at once the icon, prop, and cliché of the sensibility of decadence. This transmission is particular to the temporality theme, since, after all, drugs are not unknown to romanticism (we recall the provocation of Coleridge's "Kubla Khan"). And decadence is far more interesting and substantial than those commonplaces of bad behavior, those truisms of scandalous character, which are recycled and pasted over the profounder disturbance it represents. It is the disturbance of ideal time. That grand romantic adagio of harmonized and reconciled times, which holds the moments of childhood and adulthood in a single continuum of imaginatively coherent feeling, has decayed.

The intent that is evidenced in this set of strategic juxtapositions suggests not just a self-consciousness on De Quincey's part, it also shows a motive pressure to explore the resources of loss. This interest is exhibited best as this next section ends. Here he engages at length with the possibilities of Wordsworth's now foregone ideal. To establish the magnitude of this loss, De Quincey sets up the expectation of another moment of romantic memory. So, for the "reverie" he experiences in looking over a country town, he brings an especially heavy concentration of Wordsworthian echoes to provide the background sound of promissory accomplishment, all of which leads to an indented quotation from Wordsworth's "Excursion":

For it seemed to me as if then first I stood at a distance, and aloof from the uproar of life, as if the tumult, the fever, and the strife, were suspended; a respite granted from the secret burthens of the heart; a Sabbath of repose; a resting from human labours. Here were the hopes which blossom in the paths of life, reconciled with the peace which is in the grave; motions of the intellect as unwearied as the heavens, yet for all anxieties a halcyon calm: a tranquillity that seemed no product of inertia, but as if resulting from mighty and equal antagonisms; infinite activities, infinite repose.

Oh! just, subtle, and mighty opium! that to the hearts of poor and rich alike, for the wounds that will never heal, and for "the pangs that tempt the spirit to rebel," bringest an assuaging balm; eloquent opium! that with thy potent rhetoric stealest away the purposes of wrath; and to the guilty man, for one night givest back the hopes of his youth, and hands washed pure from blood; and to the proud man, a brief oblivion for
    Wrongs unredress'd, and insults unavenged;
that summonest to the chancery of dreams . . .[10]

Not only a quotation from Wordsworth but also a Wordsworthian phraseology – "aloof from the uproar of life, as if the tumult, the fever, and the strife, were suspended; a respite granted from the secret burthens of the heart . . . motions of the intellect as unwearied as the heavens" – provide a tuning fork for the alternate music of this sequence, which plays *against* the temporal imaginary of these Wordsworthian tempos. Quoting Wordsworth against Wordsworth, invoking the *dis*satisfactions of time in those figures of "Wrongs *un*redress'd, and insults *un*avenged," De Quincey turns the more benignly expansive and ideally comprehensive temporality down into the diminished instants of limited, explicitly temporary, reprieve: "a respite," "a Sabbath of repose," "for one night," "a brief oblivion." These are the markers of a fractured totality. The now foregone hopes of a comprehensive temporal presence are invoked even as they are given up in these fragmented pieces of totalized time, which, in turn, serve as the source of an expressive distress: the "infinite repose" promised in the integrated instant of the romantic temporal imaginary has turned into the record of "the wounds that will never heal." The inversion of the Wordsworthian ideal of time is at once exactly pointed and systematically complete.

The influence of Wordsworth on De Quincey has been studied revealingly by Margaret Russett, who follows De Quincey's rewriting of his Wordsworthian models in the imaginative vocabulary of the Gothic. Russett also maps the relation of these two writers onto the ongoing history in post-revolutionary France, where she uses the incident of their collaboration on a political pamphlet – *The Convention of Cintra* (1809), composed by Wordsworth but edited substantially by De Quincey – as the most indicative witness of an already changing politics of revolution. The differences she attributes to this "second age of romanticism," which witnessed a considerable diminishment of revolutionary aspiration, are convincing, and, in her apt summary of the significance of De Quincey's intervention, "embodied history's revenge on idealism."[11] This is a process that lives in De Quincey's later prose in *Confessions*, but not as an explicit history or any narrative of change that would be manifest in official record. It is a record of political history lived as it were from the inside out, most closely and expressively, as we shall see, as a chronicle of the lost possibilities of the spot of time, that temporal signature of revolutionary literary politics.

This complex of literary and political history is lived indeed from the inside out in the imaginative drama of the spot-of-time possibility in Shelley's "The Triumph of Life" (1822). Here, in the form of a medieval dream vision, and in the dramatic scenario of a Roman triumphal march, the figure of Life appears as nothing less, or more, than physical life. This Life is depicted as the force victorious over the many representatives of history's various ideals, beliefs, and ideologies. Chief among these is Rousseau, who speaks in the heightened language of the dream vision as he provides an intellectual and imaginative autobiography that reads, in effect, as a story of the failure of revolutionary romanticism. Key to this account is the visionary figure of a "Shape All Light," which, in Rousseau's narrative, emerged as his guiding ideal as it crystallized out of his youthful experience of nature. This incandescent "shape" appears as a consolidation of the possibilities of a natural millenarianism as well as a natural supernaturalism, and the impossibility of these ideals is told boldly and conspicuously in the figure of a disgraced Napoleon in the parade of Life's captives. It is revealed most movingly and consequentially in Rousseau's own recited history, however, in the story of the overtaking of the Shape All Light by the figure of Life. While Shelley stages this process as a reenactment of the biblical fall from the garden of original innocence, his narrative emphatically dramatizes this lapse as the incapacity of the imagination of the adult to be connected to and revived by that memory of childhood – in effect, as an undoing of the reciprocities of the spot of time in the Wordsworthian ideal.

Rousseau represents this experience of disconnection between youth and maturity with high affect as the waning of that "light from Heaven whose half-extinguished beam // 'Through the sick day in which we wake to weep / Glimmers, forever sought, forever lost.'" This loss has been hypostasized in the story in the single incident in which the Shape is overtaken by Life, as "the new Vision, and its cold bright car, / With savage music, stunning music, crossed // 'The forest'" of original innocence and so displaced the Shape. And if Shelley negotiates the loss this replacement represents with an otherwise light irony by referring to the figure of Life in the triumphal car three times as a "Shape" (variously upper and lower case), there is no minimizing the import of the exchange and, so, of lessening the imaginative failure he represents in Rousseau's narrative.[12]

The sense of disconnection between the glowing memory of childhood and the present experience of the adult leaves the condition of contemporary history unimproved by the renewing energies of youth, so dissolving the promise of its relevant brand of revolutionary romanticism. The images of this dispossession appear in epic perspectives through the poem, especially in the figures arrayed in parade behind the triumphal car: they are aged, decrepit, and dying.

> Old men, and women foully disarrayed
>   Shake their grey hair in the insulting wind,
>
> Limp in the dance and strain with limbs decayed
>   To reach the car of light which leaves them still
> Farther behind and deeper in the shade.[13]

And so, as the poem concludes, in the hypostasized state of an ever-fading and decaying youth:

>   "after brief space,
> From every form the beauty slowly waned,
>
>   "From every firmest limb and fairest face
> The strength and freshness fell like dust, and left
>   The action and the shape without the grace
>
> "Of life; the marble brow of youth was cleft
>   With care, and in those eyes where once hope shone,
> Desire like a lioness bereft
>
>   "Of its last cub, glared ere it died."[14]

These figures are depicted reiteratively as the fate of a natural Life that is unimproved by the restorative powers of the temporal imaginary of the spot of time and, thus, subordinated entirely to the fate of decline through linear time.

This loss of rejuvenating force in the temporal imaginary of early romanticism is bound up inextricably with the absconded possibilities of revolution. In aftermath, this loss accounts for the feeling of oldness that is the dominant emotional quality. It is one of the most powerful of the imaginative tenses of decadence. The predecessor to this mid-late nineteenth-century sensibility is visible already and first of all in the failure of romantic revolutionary time. And the recognition of this connection brings explanatory coherence to a range of books written in the England of second-generation romanticism.

Chief among these is Mary Shelley's 1826 novel *The Last Man*. As its title suggests, and as a range of literature written in France as well as in Britain through the 1820s and 1830s witnesses, there is a powerful apprehension of a decay of futurity, in effect a confirmation of the loss of the promises of revolutionary romanticism.[15] In *The Last Man*, this future belongs to a crank astronomer, who prophecies an apocalypse to occur in a hundred thousand years. In the meanwhile, in what purports to be the history of the end of the twentieth century, the characters inhabit the remains of time, which represent a continuing diminishment, in a historical age whose resources have already been exhausted. They live in the final stage of a cosmically entropic process, which has eventuated in a universal plague. A "failing remnant" of humankind thus abides in Britain in "these latter days" and seeks some sort of endurance in the "last throes of time-worn nature."[16]

This eventuality is presented in the novel as the consequence of the failure of the romanticism that Mary Shelley demonstrates so extensively in the book. As a roman à clef, it features clearly the counterparts of Byron as well as her recently deceased husband. Despite some differences in their orientations to the value of equality, which has been established as a banner aim in events clearly modeled on the French Revolution, these personages are gathered variously as heroes and villains of that lost cause. "We were all equal now" is a phrase uttered in plaintive refrain in the time of the plague.[17] And while irony and satire enable her retrospect on the pains of recent literary and political history, there is also a prospective vision.

This prospect emerges in the denouement of the novel, where Shelley's "failing remnant" becomes an émigré population. The narrative of their journey offers a history in miniature and a record in advance of the political and literary stories joined across the century in the development of decadence out of later romanticism. The migration tracks across the sites of failed revolution in France, where, at Versailles, they relive the legacy of revolutionary events in an experience of internal dissent.[18] They move on then to Rome, a location which, in its current abandonment, recalls the desolate state of the late imperial capital, which, in turn, offers a first version and historical origin of the sensibility with which decadence will be routinely identified. Intentionally or not, and more interestingly because she cannot be working from a developed knowledge, Shelley connects the events and the legacy of failed revolution to the conventions of an incipient decadence, which she centers affectively in the register of the decrepitude and death that are her obsessive concerns.

Their journey goes thus through Venice, that island of decadence perennial, and brings those associations forward to their Roman destination alone now with the protagonist, who is the title character.[19] This Last Man writes a book for no one to read. Here is the conceit of a literary decadence that Pound would focus on in his diatribe nearly a century later: the deathliness of the silent page is realized in the dead readership of this Last Man. Equally revealingly, he writes while reading the poetry of Horace and Virgil, obviously not with the promise of a new republic but with the sense of the fate of an older empire, which, in its demise, provides one of the defining conditions of decadence. Fittingly, invoking "the murky night of the empire" as his own historical location, Shelley's protagonist inhabits the circumstance of an "old worn-out age" as he "ascended St Peter's, and carved on it topmost stone the aera 2100, last year of the world!"[20]

Rome is constructed thus in the historical imaginary of a later romanticism, where an ancient, ruined, imperial capital provides an image of the failure of the grand imaginative plan for the renewal of history in revolutionary romanticism. An empire that has declined provides not only the expressive metric of loss but, in the expansive hubris Napoleon has duplicated in assuming the title of emperor, an assignable cause of the fall. So Byron, in the fourth canto of *Childe Harold's Pilgrimage*, brings his poetic itinerary to Rome for an extended critique of Napoleon as the betrayer of revolutionary idealism.[21] Labeling him a "bastard Caesar" (XC), the poet indicts the illegitimacy of the imperial mission the new emperor has taken up (he may also be denigrating the infamously base-born Corsican, taking the populist quality of the revolution Napoleon has commandeered as collateral damage). Byron also mourns the source of these wrongs in the original instance of ancient Rome in apostrophizing the now fallen imperial capital as "Lone mother of dead empires" (LXXVIII). Developing this figure of the city as "lone mother," he images the condition of aloneness in a Rome that is "Childless" as well as "crownless" (LXXIX). Thus he depicts his vision of a future not renewed by youth, so representing the failure of the renewal of history in revolutionary romanticism and anticipating as well the condition of a childless futurity that will figure so largely in the temporal imaginary of decadence. Turning the current of historical maternity in yet another direction, he portrays the habitués of the Rome he has constructed from these various poetic emotions as "orphans of the heart" (LXXVIII). Parentless, the citizens of the history Byron is depicting in Rome live as denizens of a present that is unconnected productively to past or future. This is the most powerful of the affective tenses of literary decadence. Its imaginative temporality is characterized by advancing age alone, and this preoccupation reveals the literary memory of political history as its own inward continuity. Thus Shelley's poem anticipates its epic bleakness in depicting a vision of history that is missing the condition of renewing youth, and he presents this apprehension in that cavalcade of age and decrepitude and death that he arrays behind the triumphal car of sheer biological life. So Byron conveys the same understanding in strikingly similar figures, as he turns an image of successive generations into a vision of degeneration alone: "And thus they plod in sluggish misery, / Rotting from sire to son, and age to age" (XCIV).

Where Shelley's poem recasts the narrative of failed revolution in France in Rousseau's reliving of the legend of the biblical fall, so Byron represents the aftermath circumstance in post-revolutionary France as the site of "man's worst – his second fall" (XCVII). Not before but within history, this "second fall" coincides with the establishing circumstance and typifying condition of an historically situated "de*cad*ence." The lapse from the aspirational values and imaginative ambitions of revolution, from the restorative promise of romantic youth as from the former glory of a resplendent empire, records the loss that the authors of decadence take as the core of their imaginative sensibility.[22]

This transit – from the failure of the temporal imaginary of revolution to the emergence of the imaginative sensibility of decadence – is followed more particularly still by Anna Barbauld. In her book-length poem *Eighteen Hundred and Eleven* (1812), she presents Britain's part in the Napoleonic wars as a testament, written jointly and severally by Britain and France, of the loss of primary revolutionary possibility. And she maps this failure onto a vision of history that anticipates the major imaginative circumstances of literary decadence. There is first of all the now familiar image of the decline of empire, which, if it is not a necessary condition for the sensibility of decadence, provides a measure of the magnitude of the feeling of loss that it measures so grandly. Images of decayed futurity in Britain thus combine with a newer and moodier futurity accruing to the former colony of America, which, as the revolution that succeeded, is the young country draining the ever-older imperial parent of its native strength. English social and political history, which is linked also to the fading force of the mythologies of progress, lives on as a dwindling form of the remnant temporality which Mary Shelley will dwell on and which Barbauld memorializes thus:

> Perhaps some Briton, in whose musing mind
> Those ages live which Time has cast behind,
> To every spot shall lead his wondering guests
> On whose known site the beam of glory rests ...
> And when midst fallen London, they survey
> The stone where Alexander's ashes lay,
> Shall own with humbled pride the lesson just
> By Time's slow finger written in the dust ....[23]

This last image vividly depicts a poetics of literary decadence, where the themes of age and death find their figure and instrument in the dead-as-dust medium of a written page. The somewhat startling prescience with which Barbauld envisions the conditions and features of literary decadence continues:

> Then empires fall to dust, then arts decay,
> And wasted realms enfeebled despots sway;
> Even Nature's changed; without his fostering smile
> Ophir no gold, no plenty yields the Nile;
> The thirsty sand absorbs the useless rill,
> And spotted plagues from putrid fens distill.
> In desert solitudes then Tadmore sleeps,
> Stern Marius then o'er fallen Carthage weeps.[24]

Beginning with the circumstance of dying empire, Barbauld includes the counter-natural values – "Even Nature's changed" – which will be attached to literary and artistic decadence, for example, by J. K. Huysmans, who, in *À Rebours* (*Against Nature*), sets his hero (if that is what he is) within the counterclockwise life of sleeping by day and working (if that is what he is doing) by night. Barbauld thus takes the consequence of Britain's part in failed revolution into the historical narratives and temporal imaginaries of ancient – and future – decadence, which are realized and measured most grandly by the metric of fallen empire, both the Roman (in Marius) and the Carthaginian.

So, too, does De Quincey, who tells this development in *Suspiria de Profundis* (1845), the short book whose subtitle identifies it as *Sequel to the Confessions of an English Opium-Eater*. Here the energies of the first age of revolutionary romanticism turn into the attitudes and postures of a soon-to-be conventionalized *décadence*. "Already, in this year 1845," he gestures in this opening paragraph to frame his immediate present in connection with that longer political history,

> what by the procession through fifty years of mighty revolutions amongst the
> kingdoms of the earth, what by the continual development of vast physical

agencies – steam in all its applications, light getting under harness as a slave for man, powers from heaven descending upon education and acceleration of the press, powers from hell (as it might seem, but these also celestial) coming round upon artillery and the forces of destruction – the eye of the calmest observer is troubled . . . it becomes too evident that, unless the colossal pace of advance can be retarded, (a thing not to be expected,) or, which is happily more probable, can be met by counter-forces of corresponding magnitude . . . the natural tendency of so chaotic a tumult must be to evil; for some minds to lunacy, for others to a reagency of fleshly torpor . . . . The word *dissipation*, in one of its uses, expresses that effect; the action of thought and feeling is too much dissipated and squandered.[25]

The failure of this "procession through fifty years of mighty revolutions" is witnessed in his refusal to credit the success of the progress that these revolutions would serve in the generation of new and varied technologies, that "continual development of vast physical agencies" in the "colossal pace of advance" which history has demonstrated. This is the conceit of a progress against itself, of modernity against itself, which Max Nordau will develop in a more contentious objection in *Degeneration* (1892; trans. 1895), but it is already clear that the "eternal hurry" of this "colossal pace of advance" anticipates the super-evolution which, in Nordau's worried account, is spurring the reversion to the weaker strain of the species through the exceptional stress which these developments effect: it is in the circumstances of urban modernity, otherwise the destined end and symbolic embodiment of the advancement narratives of progressive evolution, that the reversion is most evident.[26] Images of the same kind of degeneration show thus in the "lunacy" to which these orphans of progress are declining in this present prospect, while this degeneration finds its complement in the manners of a *décadence* that, already and ahead of time, De Quincey features in "fleshly torpor" and emphasizes in "*dissipation*." This is a development which, as registered in images that typify its observable traits in visible signals, has been lived indeed from the inside out in De Quincey's earlier text: in the unmaking and remaking of that imaginative experience of the spot of time, whose integrations of childhood and adulthood offer the promise for a revolutionary renewal of the historical present. It will be the work of literary decadence to go on remaking it.

2.   Baudelaire, Marx, Poe

Les Paradis Artificiels represents Baudelaire's creative translation and adaptation of De Quincey's *Confessions* and *Suspiria*. And intensification. This may be attributed in part to the history of post-revolutionary France, which Baudelaire has lived as the formative circumstance of his earlier years. The complexity of this legacy has been adequately characterized by Walter Benjamin, who points out a constantly shifting division of allegiance in Baudelaire to the older echelons of *l'ancien regime* and the newer values of republican France.[27] This mixed condition is significant not as a confusion of social view so much as a crucible of historical record, which provides the acutest register of the tensions in literary and political history. Whether or not Baudelaire completely believed in the ideology of the revolution that failed, that is, and more indicative of the power and import of the legacy of failure if he did not, he is extending the expressive potential of the poetics of loss. The points of greatest imaginative stress in his work will witness the disintegration of the temporal imaginary of revolutionary romanticism. In the distress of the romantic "spot of time" in particular, as we shall see, he provides as it were the inside story of the failed renewal of historical time in the external dimensions of political and literary history.

This history eventuates in the later century into a *décadence* that, as a repertoire of attitudes and mannerisms, will look back to Baudelaire as an early if not instigating instance of its now conventionalized temperament. This convention, I am proposing, represents a generalization outward of that inside story of the failing ideal of romantic revolutionary time. This failure is now thrice told: from 1789 to 1815 and again, in a pan-European scope, in 1848, when, according to Georg Lukács's account in *The Historical Novel*, the final forsaking of revolutionary energies results in the avoidance of actual class struggle and a withdrawal of resources of cultural energy into compromises of a bourgeois "liberalism," which, in his terminology, expresses a "decadence" of general if not specifically literary reference ("decadence" tends to be hurled like the Olympian thunderbolt, from the highest plane of his Marxist historiography, at any slacker in the narratives of socialist advance). This understanding is reckoned in the categories of class warfare which, established as it may be in the history of political thinking, presumes the primacy of social history in the formation of the individual works of literary history. This assumption can be revealingly turned around, however, so to see the failure of the imaginative time of revolutionary romanticism working from the inside out into the poetics of a decadence much more inflected and interesting and consequential than the flatly reactionary attitudes imputed to it by Lukács.[28]

What is particularly revealing in this respect is the record Marx himself leaves in his 1852 report of the breakdown of revolutionary possibilities in France. *The Eighteenth Brumaire of Louis Bonaparte* invokes in its title the reinvention of historical time in the new revolutionary calendar. This promise is recorded as thwarted – if not in the idiom specific to the spot of time in romantic poetry, certainly in a language that takes the impact of the failure of that renewal in historical time that was promised in revolutionary romanticism. And this will provide the precedent for a poetics of decadence that he also anticipates in remarkably particular ways.

"Tradition from all the dead generations weighs like a nightmare on the brain of the living," he gestures already and first of all in his second paragraph. Here he is directing his sense of the energy of the present away from a revolutionary renewal of historical time in futurity. On the contrary, he motions forcefully, history operates under the inertial drag of the past, which he represents as weighing most oppressively on the present even – or especially – when the rousing motions of revolution are most strenuously felt. "And just when [the living] appear to be revolutionising themselves and their circumstances, in creating something unprecedented," he reports, "in just such epochs of revolutionary crisis, that is when they nervously summon up the spirits of the past, borrowing from them their names, marching orders, uniforms, in order to enact new scenes in world history, but in this time-honoured guise and with this borrowed language."[29] He images this unchangeably oppressive past in the remains of bygone time, more generally as a remnant temporality, which counterpoints the new time of revolution and, all in all, points up the failure of the renewable time of early romanticism.

In this catalogue of the "uniforms" which history imposes on the initiatives of the present, Marx takes the legacy of Roman history as the amplest wardrobe, in effect, the weightiest burden, as he repeatedly compares the progression of events in France with their Roman counterparts. And he follows the process of this history in a form that provides a de facto model for the vision of historical time in the temporal imaginary of decadence. This is a history in which the earlier ideals of republican Rome dissolve into their contradiction in the ambitions of the Roman Empire, whose Mediterranean and European extensions coincide with the distention of its moral authority and the dissipation of its political virtù. The historical fatalism in this account takes for granted not only that things will turn to the worst, but that this downward course follows the model already authored by Rome. "Wholly absorbed in the production of wealth and in peaceful competitive struggle," goes a retrospective warning to revolutionary France no less fatalistic for coming after the fact, "it could no longer comprehend that the spectres of Roman time had kept watch over its cradle."[30] This is the pessimism of an historical determinism that underlies a temporal sensibility akin in every meaningful way with the temperament of literary *décadence*, which its French authors will reference repeatedly to this version of Roman history.

Marx conjures this model almost obsessively in these opening and framing pages. References to the "Roman republic and the Roman empire" will be most salient for the understandings he offers for contemporary time. Despite the failure recent events may have witnessed in returning to the personages of ancient history, the protagonists of the early Roman republic provide an unquestionably estimable set of references for the efforts of those first French revolutionaries. These are "Camille Desmoulins, Danton, Robespierre, Saint-Just, Napoleon – these heroes of the former French revolution, as well as the political parties and massed crowds alike – accomplished the business of the day in Roman costumes and with Roman phrases," that is, in the manner and attitudes of the republican ideals that are fundamental to the values shared in those early days of republican France. Again and again he grafts the story of the last half-century in France onto a history in miniature of Rome, spanning the centuries from its legendary beginnings to the decline of empire. "Once the new social formation was established, the antediluvian colossi, and along with them the resurrected Romans – the Brutuses, the Graccuses, the Publicolas, the tribunes, the senators and Caesar himself – all vanished."[31] Here the movement from the mythologized precessions of republican Rome to the conspicuous figurehead of its distended empire moves swiftly within a single sentence, beginning in mythic antiquity and finishing in imperial Caesar. The same narrative occurs in the same paragraph, only more expansively, where the idealized energy of the early republicans turns down into the delusional pastimes of an imperial capital:

> But unheroic as bourgeois society is, it nevertheless required heroism, sacrifice, terror, civil war and national conflict to bring it into the world. And in the strict classical traditions of the Roman republic its gladiators found the ideals and art forms, the self-deceptions that they needed, in order to hide from themselves the constrained, bourgeois character of their struggles, and to keep themselves emotionally at the level of high historical tragedy.[32]

Or, more specifically and vividly, in this vignette: "The period 1848 to 1851 saw only the spectre of the old revolution on the move, from Marrast, Républicain en gants jaunes."[33] Where the former revolutionary is dressed now in yellow gloves, Marx updates and shifts the *dramatis personae* of Roman decline to the Paris of recent (and future) days. In the costume and color of the dandy, he features the most stylized image of the *décadence* that takes the existing conditions of declining ideals as its defining circumstance.

Whether or not the installation of Louis Bonaparte as emperor in 1852 augurs the imperial ambition that the French state would manifest in the latter half of the century, it is not the experience of the fall of empire per se that provides the instigating condition for the sensibility of *décadence*, which, in the standard historiography, is always attached to these circumstances as an establishing fact. The grand scale on which the ambition as well as the failure of empire is recorded may provide more an expressive metric than a material source for these feelings of loss. After all, the sensibility of decadence is moving into recognizable shape in the last third of the nineteenth century, in the age of massive imperial expanse, when the aggrandizement of terrain by France and Britain is so rapidly advancing. It is this ambition itself which may be registered as a failure, and it is an explicit and manifest contradiction of the dictates of early republican France.

In the context of this particular historical moment, it is the fate of that romantic ideal of revolutionary time that underlies those general presentiments of historical disappointment in the sensibility of decadence. Not the renewal of time in the promissory future of a new revolutionary calendar, as echoed in Marx's title and belied in his text, it is the lapsing of that chance that will live on as the historical memory and imaginative provocation for the sensibility of decadence later in the century. This is a development that is anticipated in Marx's account in his overview of recent events:

> A whole people, believing itself to have acquired a powerful revolutionary thrust, is suddenly forced back into a defunct era; and so that there is no mistake about the reversion, the old dates rise again, the old chronology, the old names, the old edicts, which had long declined to mere antiquarian interest, and the old functionaries, who had seemed long decayed.[34]

In this "powerful revolutionary thrust," an accelerated motion of history has apparently sped things ahead, but only to reverse its current and plunge history into a "reversion." As observed earlier in connection to the same reversal that De Quincey notes in *Suspiria*, this formula matches the disorder of the ideal historical time of Progress in Nordau's *Degeneration*. There, under the pressures of super-evolution, an all too rapid advance in the conditions of material progress reveals the inveterate weaknesses in the human species, which is reverting accordingly to primitive and inferior types.[35] Nordau's formulation may well represent a response to the frustration of revolutionary energies in the Germany of mid-century. Most important, he represents the failure of the evolutionary renewal of the species also as a reversion to older types, which accords exactly with the major points in Marx's litany of complaint: "defunct," "reversion," "old," "old," "old," "old," "declined," "antiquarian," "old," "decayed," where the reiteration provides one expressive measure of the sense of loss of revolutionary renewal. This is the failure of a rejuvenation for which the romantic spot of time, with its emphasis on the integration of youth and age, will have provided a formula of inspired instigation. As indexed in the grim and bitter eloquence of Marx's report, that temporal dispossession provides a model for an equally inspired despair – here, and in the poetics of decadence into which it will eventuate.

It is the inversion of the romantic ideal of the spot of time that Baudelaire records so expressively in his work. Consider the first section of "The Poem of Hashish" (not drawn specifically from De Quincey's text):

> It is this corruption of the sense of the infinite, I believe, that is the cause of all of man's guilty excesses, from the solitary, concentrated intoxication of the literary man who, obliged to seek in opium a relief from some physical affliction and having thus discovered a source of morbid pleasures, has gradually made of it his sole comfort, and the sun of his spiritual life, to the most common, vile drunkard . . .[36]

"A Taste for the Infinite," which is the subtitle of this opening section, suggests a connection between the inclusively expansive feeling of the Wordsworthian "spot of time" and "the sense of the infinite" which the "taste" of opium may provide for "the *literary* man" first of all. Political as well as literary history is in play here, reaching back to Wordsworth through De Quincey and registering the first reverberations of the failure of romantic revolutionary time which, in Baudelaire's version, will reveal that Wordsworthian ideal in its most expressive disintegration.

Where a density of recollection would be gathered into the one surcharged and radiant instant of the romantic spot of time, that possibility breaks down into a very spotted time indeed. Not the integral picture of the inclusive instant, a maculated canvas of separate, pseudo-infinitudes is painted here:

> that interminable fantasy lasts only one minute, as you observe when a lucid interval, which you won with great effort, gives you the chance to glance at the clock. But now you are borne off on a new current of ideas, which will toss you in its living whirlpool for yet another minute, and that minute too will seem an eternity. For the proportions of time and being are thoroughly disrupted by the multiform variety of your feelings and the intensity of your ideas.[37]

The expansive but integrated feeling of temporal possession has degenerated into a pattern of heterogeneous moments, each invoking the whole which each of them fails to include in his zigzag motion from one to the other. The passage recalls that particular catalogue of ersatz infinitudes that De Quincey recorded as the legacy of his own later romantic dispossession.

This loss represents an absconding from the possibilities of renewal in the time of political history most particularly and consequentially. A complex, manifold failure, it finds a representative moment in a passage that Baudelaire has taken from De Quincey, one which recounts an Armageddon-like battle at the end of time. In its expectation of temporal fulfillment, the apocalyptic quality of this fiction conveys the promise of some final revelation of history:

> "The dream commenced with a music which now I often heard in dreams – a music of preparation and of awakening suspense; a music like the opening of the Coronation Anthem, and which, like that, gave the feeling of a vast march – of infinite cavalcades filing off and the tread of innumerable armies. The morning was come of a mighty day, a day of crisis and of final hope for human nature, then suffering some mysterious eclipse and labouring in some dread extremity."[38]

The "dread extremity" and "crisis" of this moment of "final hope for human nature" provide at the moment of time's finale all the requisite energy of an apocalyptic change. Here we find the potential as well as the memory of those hopes of historical transformation in the revolutionary romanticism of Wordsworth, which accounts in part for the epic dimension of this prospect. In this framed moment of consummation, that tradition plays out now in its most voluble and expressive form to a feeling . . . well, to a feeling of lost consequence, all in all, to the evocative power of inconsequence and loss:

> "Then came sudden alarms: hurryings to and fro, trepidations of innumerable fugitives . . . and then – everlasting farewells! And with a sigh, such as the caves of hell sighed when the incestuous mother uttered the abhorred name of death, the sound was reverberated – everlasting farewells! And again, and yet again reverberated – everlasting farewells!"[39]

While this finale gains some of its volume and resonance through its echoing allusion to Book II of *Paradise Lost*, where Milton is configuring the unholy trinity of Satan, Sin, and Death, it gains its expressive strength from the voiding of the expectations which De Quincey and Baudelaire have raised from romantic as well as biblical sources. The fullness in and of time becomes by the end an emptiness, which makes an exclamatory language of absence. The plenum of time drains away into the poetry of kenosis, which takes the echo that fades as the tuning fork of this poetics of emptiness. And where the sense of the infinite that is the ingrained expectation of early romantic as well as biblical eschatology is preserved certainly in the *everlasting*ness of these "farewells," the last and lasting note of the passage is struck in an ongoing manifestation of absence, as heard in the dying fall that goes on dying.

The same note goes on sounding through Baudelaire's writings. "For the perfect flaneur," that is, "for the passionate spectator, it is an immense joy to set up house in the heart of the multitude, amid the ebb and flow of movement, in the midst of the fugitive and the infinite."[40] This fugitive infinitude may be suggestively connected to the "everlasting farewell" in the De Quincey passage, and it relocates this conceit in the circumstance of urban modernity that he invokes with the setting of this "multitude." It appears in "The Artist, Man of the World, Man of the Crowd, and Child," the third part of the longer essay *The Painter of Modern Life*, where Baudelaire argues the now famous case for the particularity (non-generality) of beauty in the art of the modern city. This is the terrible beauty he finds in the instant of time that is charged in its particularity in being so elusive, in being "fugitive." And while this conceit echoes to his well-known formulations of the conditions of modern city life, which he represents as the perceptual and sensual experience of ever-changing instantaneousness, this condition develops its expressive power most tellingly as a literary philology. It follows the unmaking and remaking of the romantic spot of time as a locus of poetic possibility, which has been powerfully modified by the eventualities of political history.

This is a history that works backward from Baudelaire to De Quincey but also, beforehand, forward from the English writer to Poe and so back to the French poet. "Man of the Crowd," one of the phrases in Baudelaire's title, appears earlier as the title "The Man of the Crowd," Poe's prose vignette on the modern city. It is widely recognized that Baudelaire is making a substantial allusion in this piece to the Poe story, but we also need to see how Poe is giving a significant reconfiguration to a romantic original, in this case Coleridge. The relation between this story and its source provides another parabolic account of the disintegration of the romantic spot of time.

"But, as the darkness came on," Poe's scene-setting narrator muses to open the story, "the throng *momently* increased; and, by the time lamps were well lighted, two dense and continuous tides of population were rushing past the door. At this particular period of the evening I had never before been in a similar situation, and the *tumult*uous sea of human heads filled me, therefore, with a delicious novelty of emotion."[41] The emphases added to that passage repeat these in "Kubla Khan":

> And from this chasm, with ceaseless turmoil seething,
> As if this earth with fast thick pants were breathing,
> A mighty fountain *momently* was forced:
> Amid whose swift half-intermitted burst
> Huge fragments vaulted like rebounding hail,
> Or chaffy grain beneath the thresher's flail:
> And mid these dancing rocks at once and ever
> It flung up *momently* the sacred river.
> Five miles meandering with a mazy motion
> Through wood and dale the sacred river ran,
> Then reached the caverns measureless to man,
> And sank in *tumult* to a lifeless ocean . . .[42]

Where the "tumult" of this sacred river resounds as the noise of Poe's "crowd," the most important point of connection between the two works shows in the unusual adverbial form, which occurs twice in Coleridge's poem: "momently." This temporal adverb can mean either "occurring at every moment" or "enduring for a moment." The ambiguity of temporal sense is augmented by that oddly concocted formulation of the "half-intermitted burst" – how can intermittency be halved? In this otherwise illogical way, Coleridge is stressing (halving here is doubling) the brevity of those intermittent bursts. Fleetingness is a moving target but here the center of attention. These ambiguities are indicative of the major tensions specific to the work of the romantic spot of time, which takes the once passing and now past moment as the expansive and inclusive site in memory, in the ongoing life of the older poet.

These tensions are amplified in the prose account of the genesis of the poem, whose moment of inspiration came and went too quickly to allow for its completion. In keeping with the possibilities available in first-generation romanticism, however, these problems are resolved in the prosodic and figurative art of the piece. The closely kept pattern of rhyme augments the force of closure and feeling of completion that Coleridge focuses in the major imaginative figure: the pleasure dome, mirror of the poem's own making and metaphor of an art of inclusive completion. Specifically, the poem's moment of inspiration springs up with the river of its sacred poesy "at once and ever," in an instant preserved in perpetuity, in the same way that the single instant of memory can serve to center a comprehensive and inclusive and continuous consciousness in Wordsworth's spot of time. The imaginative fiction of this early romantic convention finds in this particular poem an exemplary demonstration. And it is this established understanding that Poe is unmaking and remaking in a way that will live forward through Baudelaire.

The breakdown of this poetic ideal can be followed across a passage which represents the feelings that this change releases, here at climactic strength. This is the final paragraph of the story, where, to complete his retuning of the romantic original, Poe repeats one of the two keywords he struck earlier from Coleridge's poem: "momently." The long *moment* of the romantic spot of time, which takes the single instance of a special memory and extends it into the continuous fiction of satisfaction of the whole life it contains, has become the pursuit of a singularity as fugitive as this man in the crowd:

> It was something even more intense than despair that I then observed upon the countenance of the singular being whom I had watched so pertinaciously. Yet he did not hesitate in his career, but, with a mad energy, retraced his steps at once, to the heart of the mighty London. Long and swiftly he fled, while I followed him in the wildest amazement, resolute not to abandon a scrutiny in which I now felt an interest all-absorbing. The sun arose while we proceeded, and, when we had once again reached that most thronged mart of the populous town, the street of the D– Hotel, it presented an appearance of human bustle and activity scarcely inferior to what I had seen on the evening before. And here, long, amid the *momently* increasing confusion, did I persist in my pursuit of the stranger. But, as usual, he walked to and fro, and during the day did not pass from out the turmoil of that street.[43]

Where Poe's narrator stresses "the singular being" of his title character, he establishes in that radical particularity a quality consistent with the precious brevity of Baudelaire's fugitive instant. The eponymous figure of "The Man of the Crowd" may be seen as it were as a speck of fleeting time: he is in perpetual flight through the piece, at once compelling the pursuit of the narrator and eluding any form of fixed or finished understanding. Moving with a quicksilver slipperiness, he is the mercurial god of no graspable message at all – nothing, that is, except the now foregone possibility of comprehensive time, indeed, of temporal comprehension.

The loss of the integrating power of the spot of time recalls a forsaking of the model of renewal in political history. While this European experience is being echoed from afar by the American Poe, a vision that emphasizes the randomizing force of the crowd in the political condition of the modern city certainly and strongly recalls those historical origins. For the lost content of the fullness of time in the individual figure of the title character shows most noticeably in Poe's story in the peculiar elusiveness of "the crowd" en large, which features "*innumerable varieties* of figure, dress, air, gait, visage, and expression of countenance."[44] Across the ungraspable expanse of its multiple idiosyncrasies, Poe is multiplying the fugitive singularity of the spot of time he is chasing so unsuccessfully in his title character.

In the future memory of this literary and political history, "The Man of the Crowd" anticipates also the conventions of European decadence in some of its now recognizable features. These stand, as it were, as the externalized record of the temporal distress that is its inside story. There is an overwhelming experience of material decay, which dominates his sensory perception – "by the dim light of an accidental lamp, tall, antique, worm-eaten, wooden tenements were seen tottering to their fall" – and increases in intensity over the course of the story and focuses in the decrepit, ragged, and specifically "old man," who is the central obsession. There is the narrator's special sensitivity to "ennui." And there is a general hysteria of exhaustion in the tonal chord of this report. Unbalanced, assignably "unnatural" in its intensities, this voice echoes ahead to those antinatural aspects of decadence, which Huysmans will frame in his defining work. This quality of feeling is complemented already by the special extent to which Poe's story replaces nature with the conditions of artifice, as when "the rays of the gas-lamps, feeble at first in their struggle with the dying day, had now at length gained ascendancy, and threw over every thing a fitful and garish lustre."[45]

This miscellany of features, which is connected on one side of literary history to Coleridge and on the other to Baudelaire, reveals the span of a longer story in which decadence greatens out of a decaying early romanticism. This macro-narrative of cultural time may be retold most closely and meaningfully, as these readings demonstrate, in the micro-narratives of imaginative time itself: in the concentrated but broken moments of an ideal temporality, which Coleridge shared in its pristine form with Wordsworth and De Quincey gave to Poe and Baudelaire in its increasingly expressive distress. This sense of troublous time, which takes much of its volume and resonance from the failure of the renewal of historical time in revolutionary romanticism, extends suggestively into the feeling of declining times and exhausted time in the historical imaginary of decadence, which is strongly pronounced in the Poe story.

The literary history that folds out of the moment of the romantic spot of time might be extended to the sensibility of Walter Pater. Famously praising the moment glowing as it goes in the once infamous "Conclusion" to *The Renaissance*, where the precious brevity of this experience was taken as a counsel to late-days hedonism, Pater seems to take the breakdown of ideal romantic temporality as the defining circumstance of his aesthetic experience. "Analysis goes a step further still," he proposes in refining this consideration,

> and assures us that those impressions of the individual mind to which, for each one of us, experience dwindles down, are in perpetual flight; that each of them is limited by time, and that as time is infinitely divisible, each of them is infinitely divisible also; all that is actual in it being a single moment, gone while we try to apprehend it, of which it may ever be more truly said that it has ceased to be than that it is. To such a tremulous wisp constantly re-forming itself on the stream, to a single sharp impression, with a sense in it, a relic more or less fleeting, of such moments gone by, what is real in our life fines itself down. It is with this movement, with the passage and dissolution of impressions, images, sensations, that analysis leaves off – that continual vanishing away, that strange, perpetual, weaving and unweaving of ourselves.[46]

If one's own analysis goes a step further, however, one discerns that Pater does not really accept foregoneness as the condition of the aesthetic instant. He is opting instead for a model of aesthetic perception that is whole, if not in a specific instant, at least as a generic moment, which is constantly and indeed endlessly recurrent. Pater's moment goes away; it glows as, and perhaps because, it goes; but it is emphatically and categorically restorable or at least repeatable. This is not the imaginative circumstance of the aftermath, which is the establishing condition of decadent temporality. And it is Pater's model of restorable time that brings him more into line with the fictions of integrated, synthesizing time in early romanticism.

This is a positioning which Harold Bloom has insisted on in his construction of the longer romanticism of the nineteenth century, taking Pater as the hinging figure between the earlier-nineteenth and twentieth centuries. Bloom's model of literary history turns decisively on the experience of "belatedness." In Pater's relation to earlier romantics on one hand and later modernists on the other, in Bloom's most significant instance, an Oedipal desire to regain the paternal place turns into the fraught backward longing for the poetic origin. This is an origin whose presence is confirmed even or especially as it is contested – it is in this way most manifestly not missing – and which, just so, provides the substance of a long *durée* in which the latecomer is not stranded in a fragment of detached time but linked intensely indeed to the instigating instance.[47] The condition of belatedness differs categorically in this respect from that of aftermath, which draws its sense of a bereft temporality from historical sources, which serve in turn to reinforce the finality of time lost. In the aftermath, lateness is not experienced as a looking or yearning back but, in the most interesting and significant instance of this imaginative condition, taken as its own isolated and radicalized time. The condition crucial to the temporal imaginary of decadence is an embracing of the finality of loss, which offers the basis of its reification and stylization in the conventions which this sensibility will generate.

This imaginative awareness of discontinuous time was reinforced substantially by the more advanced understandings and experimental protocols of physical science in the later nineteenth century. There is the evolving technology and art of photography, which, as Siegfried Kracauer emphasizes in his cultural history of the impact of the photograph, tended to stress not the everlastingness of the recorded instant but its status as a lost original instant, which, undiminished otherwise before the viewer, tended to make the same effect on the viewing present.[48] The older models of an apparently "natural" time, which were based on sensory impressions of fluidity and continuity, were being dissolved by a chronometry that measured temporality in ever-finer demarcations as detachable fragments. Admittedly recherché, these interests ramified, gradually but inevitably, into public understandings. The summary import might be focused in the significance of a single figure in this new micro-science of time: the "after-image."

What medical technology was demonstrating was the lapse between the instant of sensory impression and the moment of conceptual recognition. This gap opened only instantaneously and so below the level of unaided human perception. Nonetheless, it was formative of a special tense for actual cognitive and emotional life: the always afterward. The term that developed for the instant of vision lost in actual time but preserved in present memory was "after-image." This term worked initially as a descriptor for a certain type of situation-based color blindness, where optical concentration on an object of one color could cause the appearance of another, spectrum-related shade (either while looking at that first color or in taking one's eyes away), but the reference for the term took the turn of its own idiomatic sense. It included the idea of a lag between visual stimulus and conceptual image and, with that, all the trouble – and interest – of the lost original instant of living experience. What was apparently present was actually a memory. This interval of the after-image remains neutral, at least in principle, in the discourses of science, but it is a site in which some major cultural values are being contested: chief among these are originality, presence, integral identity.[49] In the register of aesthetic perception, this interval is filled with feelings of foregoneness as the condition of artistic representation.

This is the written and remembered tempo of lost time, which, in its most radical understanding, is the lost *modern*ity of *today*, of the instantaneous Now. It is the poetics of afterward. It runs in counter-rhythm initially and particularly to an idea of beforehand, more grandly, to a value concept of originality. Walter Jackson Bate, as indicated earlier, has chronicled the longer story of the imaginative idea of originality. His account follows the reconstituting of the models of classical rhetoric, in particular the practices of *imitatio* and *inventio*, in England in the seventeenth and eighteenth centuries. The pressure to claim the autonomy of invention crests into the late-eighteenth and early-nineteenth centuries.[50] At this moment, it may be added, *inventio* participates in synergy with the opening of millenarian futurity, all in all, with the possibilities of inventing an historical present in a perfected future tense. It is the closure of one form of such possibility in the thwarting of revolutionary politics that marks a turn in this story. Some of its direct consequences are shown in the tempos, as in the whole temporal imaginary, of literary decadence, which registers a temporal dispossession of immense significance. A poetics of afterward is going against a notion of originality that is specific to early romanticism and that stands, accordingly, as the first term in the longer record of this literary history.

3.   Afterward: A Poetics

First of all, then, the attack on the early romantic first of all. Here is Poe in a letter of 1831 on Wordsworth's claim for the genius of experimental firsts. "The long wordy discussions by which he tries to reason us into admiration of his poetry," Poe complains, "are full of such assertions as this (I have opened one of his volumes at random) – 'Of genius the only proof is the act of doing well what is worthy to be done, and what was never done before' – indeed!" The exclamatory challenge to Wordsworth's first of all is expanded in the same letter in a passage on Coleridge, who "goes wrong by reason of his very profundity, and of his error we have a natural type in the contemplation of a star. He who regards it directly and intensely sees, it is true, the star, but it is the star without a ray – while he who surveys it less inquisitively is conscious of all for which the star is useful to us below – its brilliancy and its beauty."[51] Against early romanticism, and against the penchant Coleridge and Wordsworth share for the early moment (and its poetic retention), Poe's topos of poetic stargazing privileges not the original celestial body but the ray, the secondary emanation. Even if Poe's optical science is more than a little impressionistic, it shows an interest already consistent with the glimmering of the after-image later in this century, which, for Poe, is the surer subject of poetic beauty.

Afterward: it develops as a poetics in prose in this overture to "Ligeia," where the several first of alls of the story – its first paragraph, the first memory it purportedly recalls – are positioned at an unbridgeable distance, which provides the site and subject of Poe's special literary tense:

> Yet I believe that I met her first and most frequently in some large, old, decaying city near the Rhine. Of her family – I have surely heard her speak. That it is of a remotely ancient date cannot be doubted. Ligeia! Ligeia! Buried in studies of a nature more than all else adapted to deaden impressions of the outward world, it is by that sweet word alone – by Ligeia – that I bring before mine eyes in fancy the image of her who is no more.[52]

Out of the verbal stock of gothic novels and the rhetorical fiction of individual memory, Poe has compounded a tense in which to represent an original event that is at once as dimly perceived as distant literature and intensely felt as personal history. This is a temporal imaginary that generates the tonal mood of the passage, which can be tracked along the curve being followed in the assertion of truth for the memories being presented: "I believe," "I have surely," "cannot be doubted": the movement from uncertainty to willful surety shows the inverse ratio of a profounder doubtfulness, where that original exists only and most intensely in dubious refractions. This is the beguilingly uncertain first of all that Poe taunts us with in the linguistic riddle in the opening sentence, where "first and most frequently" presents at first view a kind of verbal absurdity: if it is "first" how can it, as such, recur? This uncertainty frames the puzzling moment, the "frequented first," of Poe's special temporal imaginary: an original which exists always in reiteration, a first that occurs only in repetition, which dims that original but also enhances its life with the fraught energy of the artificial, secondary emanation. Thus, in his "image of her who is no more," Poe anticipates the later century's interest in the after-image and fixes attention in a poetics of afterward, which he implements in the grammar and syntax of this passage. The aim shows most particularly in a repetition that spells out not the cresting presence and, so, repossession of the title figure but, instead, an intensifying sense of loss. Thus the triple repetition of "Ligeia" crests in its third occurrence into "her who is no more": not the intensification which repetition usually effects, it is the reverse intensity of absence that the passage is designed to convey. By its end the verbal recurrences have strengthened as the progressively diminished echo of a lost original. The absconded god of romantic first of alls rules most powerfully from an empty, or emptying, throne.

The individual memory the narrator purports to recall reads more clearly as the script of a literary tradition, gothic novel by its obvious markers, which, in representing the figure of "Ligeia," makes "her" as manifestly unoriginal as its syntax and diction are already vintage, its rhythms curial and quaint. The powers particular to this condition of a secondary literary tense are a special interest of Poe. He intimates this again in "Berenice," in another moment where the narrator's personal memory coalesces with references to texts. "The recollections of my earliest years are connected with that chamber, and with its volumes – of which latter I will say no more. Here died my mother. Herein was I born."[53] As in the assertion of the truth of memory in "Ligeia," the awkwardly forced quality of this disclaimer serves to strengthen the claim it is negating: the texts his memory is suppressing so strenuously are felt to be in play as strongly as the early events he is inscribing, or encrypting, in these curt and curtailed representations. The language of his own text appears indeed as the shadow script of an original existing in some ordinal but immemorial (a favorite Poe word) and inaccessible dimension – the sphere of foregone first of alls, from which an original Word exerts the forceful appeal of its dying fall. Not quietly, mind you. The fulsome over-doneness of literary language in general in Poe's fiction and poetry reveals the exertions of a writer working with an already posthumous idiolect in the literature he is refurbishing. The vocabulary and prosody of this secondary literary tense demonstrate the special intensities of the dead replica, of the weirdly living effigy. This is the figure whose interest for Poe comprises but exceeds the literary corpus and shows in his penchant otherwise and everywhere for revenants, for the spectral undead, those characters that are drawn from the cast of gothic fiction and that reveal the powers special to the condition of the repetition, in death, of the once living.

Poe's interest in this condition turns forward, not just in the fanciful elaborations of gothic horror conventions, but in the closer, more locally inventive work of poetics – the expression of the time of the secondary in the tempos of repetitiveness. This technical sensibility marks its importance in literary history by the reversal it turns on the effects connatural to repetition, which accrues usually to the redoubling of emphasis. The expectations of normal accumulative repetition are being reversed in the repetition that fades. As the expectations of furtherance are foreclosed, so too the idea and possibility of futurity: the most radical manifestation of the temporal imaginary of literary decadence may be found in those models of queer temporality that Edelman has outlined in his analysis. This is a technical sensibility that we will see featured with telling frequency in the literary history of decadence, where, with a mildly appropriate irony, it grows rather than wanes in its density. And whether or not he is interested in the condition of the original, Poe is probably its progenitor.

Take, for instance, his poem "The Coliseum," where the topos of the ruined monument provides the classic example of the original instance that is seconded now. This is the condition Poe reiterates in the figure of "Echo," which, in the imaginative and rhetorical fiction of the piece, goes on answering his speaker's plaintive question about time ravaging "all":

> "Not all" – the Echoes answer me – "not all!
> Prophetic sounds and loud, arise forever
> From us, and from all Ruin, unto the wise,
> As melody from Memnon to the Sun.
> We rule the hearts of mightiest men – we rule
> With a despotic sway all giant minds.
> We are not impotent – we pallid stones.
> Not all our power is gone – not all our fame –
> Not all the magic of our high renown –
> Not all the wonder that encircles us –
> Not all the mysteries that in us lie –
> Not all the memories that hang upon
> And cling around about us as a garment,
> Clothing us in a robe of more than glory."[54]

The power that the repetitions of his piece serve to augment shows, substantially, in what is "not" there. This *not* marks the intensity Poe is attributing to the seconded sound. It is indeed the power of the negative, where the now voided forms of the older building and all the august authority it recalls may gain the greater intensity of their disembodiment – the "more than glory" of those ghosted stones.

In the poetics of the decadence that emerges out of the undoing of the primary value of the romantic first of all, it is the technical incentive of repetition in this special sense that bears most attention. This is a repetition that echoes some putatively original moment into the effectiveness of a greater insubstantiality, where the shadow reality of the secondary locates the point of intensifying imaginative presence. This conceit encloses the concept that is the developmental point of this legacy.

In this tradition there is for signal instance Swinburne's ode to the defeat of one ideal of early romantic time, "The Triumph of Time." Here the demise of the idea of some integrating poetic moment – "Time, swift to fasten and swift to sever / Hand from hand, as we stand by the sea" – is presented in one grim inversion after another: "I will say no word that a man might say / Whose whole life's love goes down in a day."[55] This sense of temporal dispossession finds its expression in a prosody of recessive echo, which, to demonstrate the strength of the imaginative conception, works in consort and contrast with a rhythmical and affective fiction of resistance to the idea of depletion over time. Thus the seconded sounds in the second halves of these double-structured lines build a rhythm of a reiterative, two-step, call-and-respond prosody, which crests toward the crescendo expected at the end:

> Is it worth a tear, is it worth an hour,
>> To think of things that are well outworn?
> Of fruitless husk and fugitive flower,
>> The dream foregone and the deed foreborne?
> Though joy be done with and grief be vain,
> Time shall not sever us wholly in twain;
> Earth is not spoilt for a single shower;
>> But the rain has ruined the ungrown corn.[56]

How closely fingered and acoustically dense are the reiterations Swinburne works into the hemistichal pattern of these lines. After the phrasal repetition of "is it worth" in the first line, there is the near-homophonic echoing in the second of "think" and "things"; in the third, the repeat of adjective-noun phrases in "fruitless husk and fugitive flower" is reinforced with the alliteration; similarly, in the fourth, the phrasal repetition *cum* alliteration in "dream foregone" and "deed foreborne" while, in the next, there is the reiterative syntax of "joy be done" and "grief be vain." The first variant on this two-step pattern comes in the sixth line, where a continuous syntax glides smoothly through the caesura and provides, in effect, a signal of the reversal to come. Not in the seventh line, where the caesura splits the line perfectly between the alliteratively echoing "s"s, since the pattern must be resumed to have the effect of its reversal maximized, as happens in the final line, which also expresses the theme of temporal downturn most directly. Here Swinburne concentrates the alliteration and envelope rhyme of "rain" and "ruined" before the caesura and, besides making that internal break more strong accordingly, makes the rest of the line fall off into the void left by a recurrence that has already occurred, into a void of no echo at all – except perhaps the alliterative "r" sounds, which are embedded in the interstices of the words "ungrown" and "corn," and which whisper this appropriate diminishment. This terminus provides at once a reversal and a revelation, since there is in the reiterative two-step pattern of these hemistichal lines not the building rhythm of rhetorical redoubling but, after all (and after Poe), a falling effect, which turns on the especially echoic impression Swinburne achieves in the second half of each line. Each line falls away from its origin by its end and makes the disappointment that attends the theme of depletion as deep as the prosodic methodology of the stanza is consistent.

The effect of the fall and the fade in Swinburne's verse may be linked to a number of explanatory contexts in the literary history of the later Victorian period. In *Victorian Sappho*, Yopie Prins shows the powerful interaction between Swinburne's prosody and the culturally constructed understanding of the Sapphic legacy in English poetry, where the figure of the female poet in particular is submitted to a ritual of reiterative diminishment over time. So Swinburne writes this disappearance into a poetic cadence, Prins correctly and helpfully notes, that recalls the strong fall encoded in the literary and cultural history of "decadence."[57]

The effect of the fade away in the poetics of repetition is as intense as the grip on the poetic mind of the newly developed idea of entropy, which, with the residual memories of the failure of revolutionary futurity, is contributing substantially to the new allure of the feeling of things just running down. The gradual loss of solar energy, the inevitable diminishment of heat over the long course of cosmic history: the death of the universe is the plot of an old story renewed with special intensity in the latter half of the century, to which the poets of an incipient decadence are responding as the source of a new sublimity. As one measure of its power, these poets are generating a set of techniques especially calibrated to this disposition.

Dante Rossetti confirms the presence of this new temporal sensibility and the power of the visionary destitution it registers. As in this passage from his otherwise infamous "Jenny," where the threat comprises but exceeds the interest in the prostitute for which it would be scandalized in the equally notorious critique of Buchanan's "Fleshly School of Poetry." Here, in gazing at his title subject, Rossetti's speaker sees a "cipher of man's changeless sum / Of lust, past, present, and to come," and then projects this feeling of an unimproved human time into a stunning prospect of an entropic cosmos. He envisions cosmic history as the product of a sun unproductive from the start and so, in the shorter course of human history, as the sum of the nothing toward which it has always been running down – it is a destiny perennial, which,

> Like a toad within a stone [is]
> Seated while Time crumbles on;
> Which sits there since the earth was curs'd
> For Man's transgression at the first;
> Which, living through all centuries,

Not once has seen the sun arise;
Whose life, to its cold circle charmed,
The earth's whole summers have not warmed.[58]

The toad that images the history of postlapsarian Man also depicts those fears of regression that attend the legends of degeneration later in the century. These will be complemented by those mythologies of decadence that lay stress equally on the fall or "transgression" registered here. But it is most of all the degenerative direction, the downward trajectory of an entropic cosmic process, that poets are responding to. And they are finding the time for this incipient interest in the figure, intellectually conceived as well as rhythmically expressed, of the fading repetition.

This application shows in another poem by Rossetti, "The Morrow's Message." A sonnet in his *House of Life* sequence, it takes the succession of days as the basis for a poetics of repetition that Rossetti demonstrates in poetic practice. This speaker asks a question of "To-day" that is answered, supposedly by the personified character of the day, but, as analysis may show, as the repetitively fading echo of his own words:

> "Thou ghost," I said, "and is thy name To-day? –
> Yesterday's son, with such an abject brow! –
> And can To-morrow be more pale than thou?"
> While yet I spoke, the silence answered: "Yea,
> Henceforth our issue is all grieved and grey,
> And each beforehand makes such poor avow
> As of old leaves beneath the budding bough
> Or night-drift that the sundawn shreds away."[59]

The assonance of "day" and "yea," spaced to the greater length of the enclosure rhyme of the opening quatrain, sets up the second word as the echoing far away of the first, which the hyphen and dash, suspending "-day – " effectively at the end of that first line, isolate as the sound reverberating later. Consequently, in the second quatrain, the same rhyme sound in the same pattern may be heard as the extended echo of the speaker's entreaty. This echo specifically encloses the afterward in the already – "While yet I spoke, the silence answered" – and so locates the seconded state within this original instance. The instant oldness of things is the apprehension that will compel the controversy beginning a few years later around the "after-image." The uncanny quality of the seconded reflection will be admitted with a reticence that registers the threat this apprehension presents to established values, as of originality, of identity. So too, the oddly compounded "sundawn" cannot help but recall "sundown" and, in folding the afterward into the first of all once again, demonstrates the comprehensive coherence of the temporal imaginary that Rossetti is realizing in this piece. Where an event as primary as sunrise is seconded already in its first place, sounds are repetitive and fading echoes of themselves right from the start, just as those "old leaves *beneath* the budding bough" depict a reversal of the growth curve to put decay in the place of expected origin. It is the growing point of this new sensibility.

In establishing "newness" as a category of value for an imaginative apprehension of afterward, I recognize the somewhat paradoxical quality of the formulation. What newness includes here is the concerted and collected pressure of precedents stemming from the literary and political history of post-revolutionary Europe. This legacy crests into a substantial critical mass toward the century's end, which, if only by symbolic chronology, reinforces that imaginative apprehension. Here the condition of aftermath temporality acquires an importance of its own.[60] Seconded states in artistic practice comprise a new category of activity, which shows most notably in the aesthetics of echo and reflection and in a poetics of repetition, where the reiterative witnesses an interest not in redoubling but in fading. Its conceit may be focused to extend this consideration in a single poetic subgenre: the villanelle.

The importance of the villanelle to the poetics of decadence is manifest in the extensiveness of its record in the poetic bibliography, a review of which will reveal the special turn the poets of decadence work on its repeating structures: this is the fade-away. The reiterative refrains of their villanelles do not build or intensify but work inversely and, as such, exert the major appeal. This complex is invoked in the appreciation Ezra Pound offers in his 1915 introduction to a collection of the verse of another assignably "decadent" poet, Lionel Johnson. For Pound, Johnson's "villanelle, even, can at its best achieve the closest intensity, I mean when, as with Dowson, the refrains are an emotional fact, which the intellect, in the various gyrations of the poem, tries in vain and in vain to escape."[61] The repetitions of the decadent villanelle (Dowson's as well as Johnson's), in other words, are working away from the primary reality of the originating feeling, and, so, would constitute an ongoing and diminishing echo of that "emotional fact" – but how successfully? On the one hand, or on its first occurrence, "in vain" suggests that this escape fails but, on the other hand, or as the "in vain" phrase recurs, Pound not only mimics the reiterative structure of the villanelle but, in doing so, achieves a level of verbal attention that includes the etymological memory of the word: *vanus*, "empty." Not presence but emptiness: this is the impression that the poetry of this tradition achieves through the technique of the repetition that fades.

"Come hither, Child! and rest," goes the first line of Dowson's "Villanelle of Sunset," where the otherwise oddly compounded interests of an exclamatory appeal to the pleasures of rest do the work of defining the tensions and counter-rhythms special to this villanelle. Here the force-building reiterations one expects (before and after Dylan Thomas's exertions in this genre) turn to just the opposite ends, as registered in the tonal atmospherics of the third line of the first stanza, where an exclamation once again points up its opposite quality in fatigue: "Behold the weary west!" As these two lines comprise the refrain structure of the poem, the special effect of a strength fading against the greatening that is expected from a repetitive structure is an appreciation as fine as the tightly fingered work Dowson performs in the final line: "Behold, the weary west!"[62] The insertion of a comma offers this small pause as a stopping point; unexpected as it is in the otherwise strictly reiterative structure of the villanelle, this pause makes the rest of the line fall off track and lose the cumulative force of an uninterrupted form and, with that, the physical body, the material confirmation, of the expected effect. The small difference in the repetition leaves the poem falling and fading away at the end.

"Villanelle of Acheron," "Villanelle of His Lady's Treasures," "Villanelle of Marguerites," and "Villanelle of the Poet's Road": a census of Dowson's efforts in this form offers the opening invocation of the last – "Wine and woman and song" – as wording that has served as a virtual slogan of "decadent" behavior. Tellingly, this association has lost the memory of the poem's third verse, the other line of its structured refrains: "Yet is day over long." A day too long to sustain the momentary pleasure of the first line, of the original event: afterward is the poetic tense of the villanelle as Dowson elaborates this subgenre, where the refrain structure serves the impression of a fading and not a gaining strength of poetic declamation. Likewise, on that poet's road, by the time of the final couplet in this closing quatrain:

> Fruits and flowers among,
>> What is better than they:
> Wine and woman and song?
>> Yet is day over long.[63]

As it recurs in the third verse of this final stanza, the first line of the villanelle has changed its emotional as well as grammatical mood, fading from the declarative fact of immediate experience into an interrogative uncertainty.

In effect, this gesture questions the pleasurable first of all, the sensory immediacy, which the first line of the poem originally declaimed. Subtle as it may be, the minor note this change strikes also rhymes with the major feeling of the villanelle, whose final line locates the imaginative tense of afterward as its last and lasting note.

This condition of afterward is the main work of Dowson's efforts in the villanelle. This statement may be borne out, contrariwise, by the relative failure of a poem whose location hands him this condition to begin with. In "Villanelle of Acheron," the site of the classical afterlife has already prepared the place of aftermath. Its feeling is not sought for in the repetitive textures of the poem. The refrain lines – "By the pale marge of Acheron, / Beyond the scope of any sun" – do not vary; the feeling remains static.[64] What is not at work in this poem is that rhythm of diminishment, which provides the reiterative structures of his best villanelles with their signal interest.

What this composite record of Dowson's successes and failures may suggest is the imaginative challenge as well as the technical opportunity that this new apprehension of lost and fading time presents to writers. As such, it lives forward into some of the major initiatives of an identifiably modernist prosody, as we will see at length in the poems of Pound and Eliot, who, in this respect, will be reinventing the poetics of decadence in their own distinctive ways. This is a recognition that has been deflected in the history of modernist criticism in a substantial and ramifying fashion by Arthur Symons. So, in turning forward, a consideration of his "case" may provide some indication of the daunting import of the tradition he has so consequentially written out of the account – in the year ending the century whose legacy is a substantial part of the major modernist literature of the next.

4.   The Case of Symons

Symons's rewording of the title of "The Decadent Movement in Literature" (1893) into *The Symbolist Movement in Literature* (1899) may be put inside the record of the poems he composed over this decade. This narrative tells the inner history of the shift he registers with that change of title. It is a story of challenges framed and abandoned. It shows him testing and exploring the difficult initiatives of a poetics of decadence but giving these up in the end for the more ready-made measures of a symbolism that takes Yeats as its proximate model and a nostalgic notion of the symbolic as its primary refuge. Whether or not we characterize this progression as a failure of personal nerve, the reversal it represents offers a literary history in miniature and in advance. The reassurance that the poetics of the Symbol will exert as its appeal to later scholars of modernism is shown all too clearly in Symons's case, which also provides a living record of what is at stake in that trade.

In the early years of the decade, Symons is attempting to turn his new-found interest in the authors of French *décadence* into his own English practice. His interest shows in the opening moment of "On the Heath":

> Her face's wilful flash and glow
> Turned all its light upon my face
> One bright delirious moment's space,
> And then she passed.

The first line encloses the intense original instant of romantic temporality, but it is a fancy passing already by line four into the imaginative circumstance of the aftermath. This is the moment glowing as it goes in the temporal imaginary of Poe and Baudelaire. Where the poetics of decadence develops interest in the imaginative tense of the secondary, in the reiteration that diminishes, Symons does not or cannot grasp this major chance. He works instead to preserve and further that first moment in the narrative and imaginative fiction as he

> followed slow

> Across the heath, and up and round
> And watched the splendid death of day
> Upon the summits far away,
> And in her fateful beauty found

> The fierce wild beauty of the light
> That startles twilight on the hills,
> And lightens all the mountain rills,
> And flames before the feet of night.[65]

If the original moment in the spot-of-time consciousness is no longer available to the living imagination of the older poet, the visionary presence that Symons registers in this finale is displaced from its original location. It is transferred from the prompt of the woman's fading face to this alternative consequence in the apocalyptic sunset flush. And that is where the deflection may be registered: Symons does not yet in 1892 accept the secondary as a diminishment and reverts instead to fulsomeness as the language of customary power.

This is an exemplary swerve. It demonstrates not only the difficulty but the importance of the challenge which Baudelaire and others poeticized as the heroic despair of the transient. Symons does seem to get this sensibility (at least intermittently) right by the time of his third volume, *London Nights* (1895), which is commonly regarded as his most important poetic accomplishment. As in the sequence "Intermezzo: Pastoral," in the vignette "At Dieppe: Grey and Green." In this setting, the poem presents an almost inevitable echo of "Dover Beach," but the imaginative time of Symons's finale subsumes Arnold's Victorian melancholy into his special temporal dispossession:

> One stark monotony of stone,
> The long hotel, acutely white,
> Against the after-sunset light
> Withers grey-green, and takes the grass's tone.
>
> Listless and endless it outlies,
> And means, to you and me, no more
> Than any pebble on the shore,
> Or this indifferent moment as it dies.   (*PAS*, I, 104)

The "after-sunset light" of Symons's poem is indeed the after-image of an original event, which would be the sunset glorious he used in "On the Heath" as a substitute for the romantic first of all in that poem. Now, however, the poetic interest is not engaged in an effort to recover or reconstitute that foregone original. It is suspended instead in afterward as a steady-state condition, which is represented strikingly in the epic bleakness of each "*indifferent* moment as it dies." The word deserving stress reaches beyond the standard meaning of a lack of bias in attitude. In a radical sense appropriate to those roots of early poetic romanticism that Symons is disturbing, "indifferent" suggests an instant not different to any other, not special, not original. This recognition is registered in the apparently minimal condition – "no more / Than any pebble on the shore" – of the instant, which, in the micro-chronometry of imaginative time, is where the difference is told. The plangent despair of small things bespeaks the import of the difference this understanding of imaginative time makes in literary history as well as in Symons's own poetic development.

Symons demonstrates this sensibility already in the overture to *London Nights*. Here he doubles the opening moment of the volume with two poems under the same main title: "Prologue: Before the Curtain" and "Prologue: In the Stalls." Humorously or not, this redoubled opener offers the formal suggestion that the event original is impossible. Its truth nonetheless provides the burden of some serious discursive versifying in the first words of the first of these openers:

> We are the puppets of a shadow-play,
> We dream the plot is woven of our hearts,
> Passionately we play the self-same parts
> Our fathers have played passionately yesterday
> And our sons play to-morrow. There's no speech
> In all desire, nor any idle word,
> Men have not said and women have not heard;
> And when we lean and whisper each to each
> Until the silence quickens to a kiss,
> Even so the actor and the actress played
> The lovers yesterday . . . (*PAS*, I, 79)

The interest of the action unoriginal is of course not in the concept, hardly news in itself, and the regular and somewhat plonky pentameter of these verses certainly represents no major contribution to the history of prosody. The growing point of interest lies in the potential of the redoubled title, in the special technical incentive of the repetition that fades. Appropriately, an effort in this direction is evident in the second opener, where the echoic envelope of the poem's first and last lines frames the diminuendo he intends:

> My life is like a music-hall,
> Where, in the impotence of rage,
> Chained by enchantment to a stall,
> I see myself upon the stage
> Dance to amuse a music-hall . . . .
>
> The light flares in the music-hall,
> The light, the sound, that weary us;
> Hour follows hour, I count them all;
> Lagging, and loud, and riotous;
> My life is like a music-hall. (*PAS*, I, 80)

The emotional afflatus in the first stanza, the laconic observation in the last: the stock in poetic trade that Symons is working with – the vocabularies, roughly, of romanticism and decadence – leaves the language of the poem in a function of conventional description as unremarkable as each indifferent line as it dies. The interest lies instead in the return in the last line to the words of the first, where the visionary conclusion, such as the one he trumped up in "On the Heath," is missing. In depriving the poem of the transformational closure readers expect, Symons is also voiding its authority as a moment of vision, where an original experience is worked toward a representation of the difference it makes in the imaginative apprehension of the poet. The flattening effect he gains in the face of expectation is the accomplishment *manqué* of a novel prosody, which, wanly or not, bespeaks the considerable pressure of this emergent sensibility in English poetics. It is one which the modernists Pound and Eliot will reinvent and extend consequentially.

Not the furtherance of this sensibility but a turning away from it will be the most significant story in the development of Symons's verse. This development shows the influence above all of Yeats, whose importance in a longer literary history begins with the difference he made for Symons as poet and left as a record in the development of his verse through the decade. It shows in the poems of *Amoris Victima* (1897), where the intermittent echoing of Yeats's already distinctive manner becomes, by the time of "Stella Maligna," from *Images of Good and Evil* (1899), a virtual sound-alike in rhythm and diction:

> There, in the quietness of dreams, it broods
> Above untroubled moods . . .
> And thy passion shall release
> The secret light that in the lily glows,
> The miracle of the secret rose.   (*PAS*, II, 130)

Not just the Yeatsian moody-broody, the imaginative casting of this poem lays notable stress already on the epistemology of Yeats's symbolic world. The apprehension of an immanent, defining light in the mystery of individual things takes over Symons's earlier interest in the secondary or reflective quality of phenomena. A prosody of symbolic presence, where each line stands as a discernible entity of imaginative sense and sensation, defines the new measure of Symons's aspirational practice. This is a prosody that declines the imaginative challenge and task of disembodiment in the poetics of decadence.

This development is paralleled in the narrative of his literary criticism, which clarifies and magnifies its significance. Its import shows in Symons's renaming and recasting of "The Decadent Movement in Literature" (1893), which witnessed a driven attempt "[t]o fix the last fine shade, the quintessence of things; to fix it fleetingly; to be a disembodied voice" – as *The Symbolist Movement in Literature* (1899), where, among other changes, disembodiment turned into embodiment, turning the "mysticism" of an "unseen world" that "is no longer a dream" into a "doctrine" of such spiritual knowledge, which, following Symons's quotation of Carlyle's *Sartor Resartis*, demands "some embodiment and revelation of the Infinite; the Infinite is made to blend itself with the Finite, to stand visible, and as it were, attainable there."[66] In the largest sense, the symbolist turn that Symons takes also shows a poet turning away from the sense of history that is the establishing circumstance of the decadent imaginary – its apprehension of aftermath, of shadows, of after-images – and turning toward a poetic doctrine of symbolic presence and material realization, where, in the intense sense of creative potentiality that this doctrine encloses, the poem works in response to the appeal for realization in history of a not-yet, even a nonexistent. Yeats's intervention is crucial in this respect. The Irish poet offers this English one (Symons sometimes identified as Cornish or Welsh but his literary circumstance is really English) a change of poetic habitation and imaginative tense as well as conferred name. The site of Ireland locates the most intense sense of creative possibility for the poetic Symbol, which, in turn, becomes the counter of lasting power in the longer history of the literary criticism of modernism. This development can be augured and followed through Symons's imaginative negotiation in the poetry with a country which, to adapt some later phrasing of Yeats, does not exist (at least not yet or not officially), and which is still (especially for Symons) but a dream: Ireland.

The appeal the idea of a young Ireland exerts on a sensibility embedded in the decadence of contemporary Britain is demonstrated first by Yeats himself, and a brief reading of his early poetry may reveal the two cultural imaginaries in exchange in these poems. Much of Yeats's Nineties verse is indeed double spoken. It expresses a fatigue we can identify as the wan atmospheric of Britain's late imperial day, but also a vigor, which is sourced in the springs of the nascent state of Ireland. Recognition of this double tone also opens an understanding of the appeal the so-called Celtic Revival would exert not only to *Anglo*-Irish writers but even – and especially – to *English* poets. This was the dominant nationality of the Rhymers gathered around Yeats in the tavern on Cheshire Street in London, some of whom adopted mannerisms as caricatured as the Irish brogue put on by Lionel Johnson. In this configuration, Ireland stands as the complementary opposite to the decadence of England, and Yeats's Nineties verse shows this reciprocating duality consistently.

A representative example appears in his poem "Into the Twilight," whose opening invocation goes "Out-worn heart, in a time out-worn." That fatigued heart, recognizable as the conventionally postured sentiment of decadent weariness, is historicized as the condition of the "time." It is a ciphering of the internal as well as external circumstance of late empire. In this condition, Yeats turns to the tonic, resolving promise of an idealized Ireland: "Your mother Eire is always young, / Dew ever shining and twilight grey." Always, ever: these temporal adverbs suspend historical time in some ideally continuous present. It is a tense of infinite potential – the still untested promise of an Irish alternative to English diminishment. This is a relation whose actual historical adversity is resolved often in these poems in the way of the next two lines – "Laugh, heart, again in the grey twilight, / Sigh, heart, again in the dew of the morn": it is resolved into the pleasantly mingled measures of light and dark in this emotional chiaroscuro, this Celtic twilight.[67]

Like any poetry that is so richly informed by contemporary history, this work is tense with political oppositions as well as visionary possibilities. Here the optimal mood of the Irish subjunctive is spoken in a specifically English tense of decadence. This compound sensibility finds its signature rhythm in "The Valley of the Black Pig." The representation of an end-of-empire-days feeling appears as the dusky landscape of depletion, drawn from the palette of an English decadence, but this emotional weather opens and swells into an Irish prospect that is at once starkly prophetic and grandly visionary, more sharply and ominously or even sensationally drawn. "The dews drop slowly and dreams gather," this poem opens, turning down the lights to the mistiness of a Celtic Twilight. But then

> unknown spears
> Suddenly hurtle before my dream-awakened eyes,
> And then the clash of fallen horsemen and the cries
> Of unknown perishing armies beat about my ears.

And who, or where, is this speaker?

> We who still labour by the cromlech on the shore,
> The grey cairn on the hill, when day sinks drowned in dew,
> Being weary of the world's empires . . .[68]

The "We" through whom Yeats expresses this feeling of "being weary" are the largely Anglo-Irish and English recruit of the Celtic Revival, who represent a feeling of being tired of – in – the final days of "empires." It is this imperial fatigue that turns these writers to the Anglo-Hibernian dialect of the Revival, just as it turns Yeats's speakers and the speech of this poem to those Gaelic words – "We who still labour by the *cromlech* on the shore, / The grey *cairn* on the hill." These words offer their numinous otherness as a place of difference in imagined space and, on the verbal surface of the poem, as a measure of cleansing or even redemption for the English words of a worn out time, of a speech outworn.

And so the temporal adverb "still" presents its own concentration of complex sense. Not the no-time of ever-always in "Into the Twilight," "still" is the real time of a history which is lived in but from which, under the magic lighting of those Gaelic words, the historical prophecy of the poem's title is summoned. The Valley of the Black Pig locates the site of the ultimate battle between Ireland and its enemies, and it presents a remedy for the sickness of time in the English present in this mythic end of Irish time, which, in this circumstance, will also mark the beginning of a specifically Irish history. The Apocalypse it promises in Armageddon is configured thus in the very un-decadent, non-diminuendo finale, where the weary "we" of empire's final days now "bow down to you, / Master of the still stars and of the flaming door."[69] Since the end portended is only promissory, given the actualities of history, Yeats's incendiary imagery is only as urgent as it is uncertain about when it will ignite. The vatic rapture gives nothing away to that indeterminacy, however, which opens with the immensity of the appeal that Ireland may exert in this future perfect tense.

The appeal that Yeats's cultural nationalism exerts for Symons shows revealingly, then, in poems which also feature a trading away of the poetics of decadence. Predictably, the earnest words of personal conversion are spoken on a specifically Irish site, "By the Pool at the Third Rosses," which is the second piece in Symons's five-part sequence "In Ireland" (in *Images of Good and Evil*):

> I heard the sighing of the reeds
> Night after night, day after day,
> And I forgot old age, and dying,
> And youth that loves, and love's decay.

As important as the giving away of those obvious denominators of poetic decadence – "old age," "dying," especially "decay" – is the manner of their going. For these lines feature a technique of repetition that gains rather than fades in strength, declaiming its seconds as points of emphatic assertion in consecutive, cresting motion. "Night after night, day after day" repeats and strengthens the wording it inverts from the previous stanza – "Day after day, night after night" – and echoes as an answer of redoubled volume and power to the question he asks rhetorically in the poem's close:

> I hear the sighing of the reeds:
> Is it in vain, is it in vain
> That some old peace I had forgotten
> Is crying to come back again?   (*PAS*, II, 163)

In the now five-times repeated opening line of the stanza, the shift in tense at the end of the poem from past to present provides a sign of the final intention of presence, which extends to affirm the positive response the speaker expects to his question and appeal for the recovery now of past attitudes. This sense of presence gainsays the emptiness that stirs in the etymological memory of the "in *vain*" phrase, where Symons recalls in advance the counter Pound will deploy to sound the powers of voluble depletion in the repetitions of the villanelles of decadence. Not here, or, rather, *all* here, Symons is saying in his effort to reclaim the fullness of a presence which, in his representation of that final sound, is returning rather than receding.

Symons is trading away the poetic techniques and emotional themes and imaginative experiences of decadence in an Irish location which provides the establishing circumstance for this imaginative transaction. This point is borne out as he repeats the deal in two of the other poems in this sequence. In "Lough-na-Gar: Green Light," the "green light" of the title presents a color symbol configuring equally the ideas of hope, growth, and, of course, a young Ireland – a cluster of associations that works by the end of this short piece to transfigure the conditions of a poeticized decadence:

> The light of the world is of gold,
> But the light of the green earth fills
> The nestling heart of the hills;
> And the world's hours are old,
> And the world's thoughts are a dream,
> Here, in the ancient place
> Of peace, where old sorrows seem
> As the half-forgotten face
> Of flower-bright cities of gold
> That blossom beyond the height
> Seems in the earth-green light
> That is old as the earth is old.   (*PAS*, II, 165)

Under the golden color of sunset in the late-days imaginary of decadence, the "old" age of the world of "cities" and history begins to fade into the color of an earth as new, eternally, as the temporal framework of the final lines suggests, where the color of growth provides the inward light of this Irish place and stands in for its promissory nation. This immanent truth is the challenge and aspiration of a language adequate to that potential significance. It is the vocabulary of literary symbolism in the strictest sense. These words provide the representative signs of what they signify – even in prosody, and even in the soft enjambments, where the lines measure out integral units of verbal and referential sense and so offer a sense of integral embodiment.

Again, in the fifth and last poem of the sequence, "In the Wood of Finvara," the figure of green works symbolically as a tonic to resolve "the dust of the world in a soft green flood" and wash away the remains of that earlier "decay" in "a delicate wave-green solitude" (*PAS*, II, 166). The green wave that Symons is riding may bear this Englishman into no zone of consequences as politically specific as the obviously symbolic national color; indeed, it sends him in the opposite direction of "solitude." But this image of a current suggests the impetus of symbols like this in Yeats's early poetic practice and imaginative faith. The Irish poet's cultural nationalism brings with it a doctrine of the symbolic, which gives his poetic symbols an authenticity that is the register of his individual originality and, most important, a potency that is instinct with the generation of a nation state. Given the broad range of applications possible for the idea of the symbolic in the Parisian fin de siècle, it demonstrates the specialized register of Yeats's usage and, so, of Symons's derivation. Where it points to the singular and, arguably, restricted interest of one particular proto-national imaginary for Symons's English vantage, it also bespeaks the appeal in late imperial England of a "not-here" place; it reveals the attraction of the "not-yet" time of a national Ireland, which is more a promissory even than a young country.

While Symons is discarding the poetics of decadence in the name (or in the wake) of a political project that is not even his own, we may look to the case of Yeats as the most indicative record of the impasse between the imagining of a new Ireland and the remnants of an older decadence. Whatever political prepotency may (or may not) exist in the poetic tempos and temporal imaginary of decadence, the turn that Yeats took away from that sensibility for the developing purposes of his political commitments influenced more than his protégé. His own masterful example accounts in the end for nothing less than the supplanting of decadence by symbolism as the identity and category of major power in literary histories following Symons's. And so the record of Yeats's discarding of the poetics of decadence as the instrument of political use may serve not only to explain the motives and consequences of this change for himself and the furtherance of his own career. In view of the bigger picture of literary history, this story provides its parabolic and prophetic account of the turn away from decadence toward symbolism as the formative story of literary modernism.

5. Yeats's Prosaic Turn

"Did that play of mine send out / Certain men the English shot?" Yeats would ask, rhetorically. And he answered, not at all tentatively, but also rhetorically, in his famed declaration about the prepotency of literature in Irish political history: "The modern literature of Ireland, and indeed all that stir of thought that prepared for the Anglo-Irish war, began when Parnell fell from power in 1891."[70] Now that the procedures of parliament and the protocols of negotiation had been lost with their major agent and representative, Yeats is saying, the words of literature chartered a politics by other means. If it is customary to understand Yeats's understanding of this literary agency of the second wave of cultural nationalism as stemming from the Celtic Revival (from the incentives he attributed to its recovering the stuff of ancient Gaelic identity), another understanding comes from the historical circumstances that establish the attitudes and practices of literary decadence. Where the late moment of British imperial history locates the sensibility of decadence, the experience of exhaustion at the center of British culture turns the literary sensibility toward the Celtic fringe as the wellspring of a new energy. As observed in detail in the last section, the relationship between the late-empire-days feeling of the English Nineties and the nascent strengths of Irish cultural – specifically poetic – nationalism is clearly discernible in Yeats's early verse. This poetry does not explicitly address the question of the political applicability of art. This issue focuses attention most directly instead on a set of prose texts, where it reaches its furthest discursive elaboration. This is some of the most visionary and radical writing that Yeats did. It goes back to the roots of literary *décadence*, to Paris, which Yeats visited in 1894.

This was a city prepared for him by his new friend Symons. Literary Paris was shaded still with the memories of the greater *décadence* of the late mid-century, with the ghosts of Gautier and Baudelaire living still in the aging figures of Mallarmé and Verlaine and Huysmans. He kept company with representatives of this legacy of artistic *décadence*. Crossing the sometimes porous borders with *symbolisme*, these survivors were migrating also in the direction of the occultist studies that would provision some of the images of *symbolisme*, which would increasingly preoccupy Yeats. Here he also found the denizens of an émigré Irish nationalism, which was already forming its underground force toward the centenary of the Wolfe Tone Rebellion in 1898.[71] In this milieu, aesthetical *décadence* brought the machismo of hermetic research to the most pointed of political motivations. This is the force field which helps to generate the prose fables he collected several years later, in 1897, in *Rosa Alchemica*, of which "The Tables of the Law" is of first interest.

Yeats frames this story as a history of the relationship between his narrator, who is also his protagonist consciousness, and Owen Aherne. They had been students in Paris, the story goes, and what they studied in that cultural capital of decadence seems to have been a *décadent* primer for another revolution – this one being written by the French for the Irish. As beauty, which is a fundamental value in Yeats's understanding and practice at this time, art might indeed be revolutionarily useful. "When he and I had been students in Paris," this recollection goes,

> we had belonged to a little group which devoted itself to speculations about alchemy and mysticism. More orthodox in most of his beliefs than Michael Robartes, he had surpassed him in a fanciful hatred of all life, and this hatred had found expression in the curious paradox – half borrowed from some fanatical monk, half invented by himself – that *the beautiful arts* were sent into the world to *overthrow nations*, and finally life herself, by sowing everywhere unlimited desires, like torches thrown into a burning city.[72]

The "paradox" is "curious," but it drives the poetic and rhetorical energy of the prose: this art, whose apparent use is to be beautiful, is an instrument of revolutionary change. As the added emphases make clear, Yeats's representation has picked up the aestheticism that stems from the Baudelairean incentive of art for art's sake, and then weaponized it, flexing it in the hands of these adepts and protégés of the dark arts of *décadence* as the device to ignite that world-changing blaze. And it is indeed the Irish point of ignition that he locates as this passage continues, beginning with this strategic concession:

> This idea was not at the time, I believe, more than a paradox, a plume of the pride of youth; and it was only after his return to Ireland that he endured the fermentation of belief which is coming upon our people with the reawakening of their imaginative life.[73]

In other words, which are fighting words, it is Ireland that ripens the political prepotency of French *décadence* to real political uses, turning the beauty of art to the terrible beauty of an art bent upon some utter change. But what *actual political* use is this plume that Yeats has plucked from his pride of youth? Is it just the splendid beauty of the imaginative dare, the posturing of this *poète maudit* in the elegant menace of well-formed prose, or is there some imminent, more terribly beautiful deed poised within that aesthetic gesture?

The response to this question follows the fate of the "secret book" that Aherne brings with him from France to Ireland as the emblem of this continental influence, as the vessel of this French instigation. This "secret book" is kept in an inner chamber where it exerts its extraordinary powers, working its magic effects upon the title figure of Yeats's fable. It is said to have erased the tables on which the Commandments of the Old Testament were once inscribed. "'It has swept the commandments of the Father away,' [Aherne said], 'and displaced the commandments of the Son by the commandments of the Holy Spirit,'" which, as the evident condition of their great power, are unwritten. And, in Yeats's elaboration, the representatives of this New Covenant sing "the praise of *breakers* of the seventh day and *wasters* of the six days, who yet lived comely and pleasant days." These elegant outlaws are as well dressed and well mannered as they are inactive and indeed indolent. Like Oscar Wilde, after a fashion, they may be exaggerating manners in a way that parodies and even travesties manners and so presents the profounder challenge to the existing system. These *poètes maudits* are the artistic revolutionaries who take aestheticism back to *décadence*, reclaiming its radical character of defiance to the social as well as religious commandments of convention and so reconnecting their attitude to the roots of a revolutionary art. Where the disciples of this new indiscipline are seen "sitting throned in the blue deep of the air, and laughing aloud, with a laughter that was like the rustling of the wings of Time,"[74] we see the representation of their opposition to the normative clock of social convention as nothing less than a victory over conventional time itself – in the spirit of comic conquest that Yeats tropes in this figure of release and transcendence: "the *wings* of Time." So Yeats is positioning the sensibility of aesthetical decadence as the instrument of a redemptive, visionary difference to the real time of history. And there is the issue. How this change can be realized in the narrative of actual political history is the question Yeats frames and intensifies by leaving open a ten-year period between his narrator's first glimpse of the possibility and his return to the site of this provocation. This is the interval in which history, we feel, may actually happen.

When, a decade later in the fiction of this story, Aherne is seen again in Dublin, he takes the narrator back to the magic room, which witnesses this scene as the record of change in the interval of possibility. The narrator, looking into the inner chamber, can see

> that its corners were choked with dust and cobwebs; and that the pictures were grey with dust and shrouded with cobwebs; and that the dust and cobwebs which covered the ruby and sapphire of the saints on the window

had made it very dim. He pointed to where the ivory tablets glimmered faintly in the dimness, and I saw that they were covered with small writing, and went up to them and began to read the writing. It was in Latin, and was an elaborate casuistry, illustrated with many examples . . .[75]

What has happened to the tabula rasa of political, specifically revolutionary, possibility? The visionary but invisible script of the earlier incident has been replaced by actual writing; we recall that the possibilities of redemptive temporality were explicitly *sung*. It is the condition of written or printed words that is bound up with this charged and talismanic object, the pages of that "secret book."

This enigmatic figure opens into the underpinnings of the literature of decadence. The recurrences of the secret and mysterious and also lethal book – the instances range from Pater to Huysmans to Wilde, where, in the hands of Dorian Gray, it works its deleterious effects most famously – evince some of the assumptions that were fundamental to a contemporary science of language and, in turn, to the linguistics as well as the poetics of literary decadence. As Linda Dowling has demonstrated convincingly, a shift of interest in the study of language had relocated the developmental energy of words from their semantic roots to their phonological contents, which developed and changed according to the rules of the material science of sounds. In the imaginative understanding of these developments, the written page is left as a site for reliquaries only: printed words appeared as fossils of their former lives. This "dead language" factor ramifies throughout the poetics of decadence, informing the interest its authors exhibit in heightening the writerliness of their styles.[76] It is manifest in a more enigmatic aspect in this "secret book," whose lethal effects may be taken to represent the deathliness of the word written, of a letter that killeth. More, or more particularly in Yeats's version of this book, where the page is written in the signature script of dead language: in Latin. Where this figure also frames the Latinity in the idiolect of literary decadence, whose writers heighten their writerly style by interring it in the Latinate crypts of English, this practice included the notion, sometimes stated and sometimes not but always powerfully intimated, that the eventual fate of the Latin language and the Roman Empire was the immanent, and perhaps the imminent, destiny of the English language and the British Empire. And here is a riddle thicker in its iterations in Yeats's text even than that of this secret book. This is the puzzle embedded in the turn of the plot at this point in the story's narrative: those political initiatives, which the magic communications in the charged air of the chamber had earlier projected, have withered entirely. If the decline of empire is the fate to be ciphered from the mystery script, if this is the meaning written down in – or, in fact, as – the wording of that now long-gone imperial tongue, why does this eventuality not coincide in Yeats's text with a liberation of revolutionary possibility in his own imperial province?

Yeats provides a response in the contemporary, companion piece in *Rosa Alchemica*, "The Adoration of the Magi." He is taking up the question of the relation between literature and the contemporary "trembling of the veil," Mallarmé's figure for the unrest in history in the end of the century. From the standpoint of the erstwhile revolutionary, Yeats writes provocatively, but unpromisingly: "I have grown to believe that there is no dangerous idea which does not become less dangerous when written out in sincere and careful English." A use of the word "sincere" in the 1890s can hardly avoid an echo from Wilde's charming dismissal of "sincerity" as a category of value in *The Decay of Lying*, where honesty is the worst policy for an artist, since artifice is his one bounden duty. Yeats is so bound, too.[77] Where the double negatives combine with an adjective in the diminishing degree of a comparative, there is an identifiably arch kind of stylization that, in this case, becomes a type and model of artistic language itself, which certainly challenges ready and operative sense. The sentence thus provides an illustration of sensible *grammar* vanishing into poetic *glamour*, a double sense that Walter Scott first exploited in eliding the two terms and that Yeats invokes elsewhere in his prose fiction in playing the compound meaning, in "glamour," of magic knowledge or necromancy.[78] More specifically, a Wildean conceit turns the earnest grammar of those fastidious writers into the artistic glamour of Yeats's sentence: a formed and dense literary language can make nothing happen, and this inability is featured most characteristically, as in this sentence, in the stylized inconsequence that provides the logic and prosody, indeed the consummation, of a poetics of decadence.

He puts a finer point on this admission in the linguistic fiction of "The Tables of the Law." Here, in the passage excerpted, the language of the former empire occurs in a practice of "casuistry." In one sense, this word suggests a process of close verbal reasoning, like the "careful" usage imputed to those would-be revolutionary writers in "The Adoration of the Magi." In another, however, "casuistry" holds in its root the meaning of a *fall*: *casus*, step or fall, represents our understanding of a legal *case* as a fall from some ideal principle; it is also the nominative form of the past participle of *cad*-ere, as in *de-cad*-ere, which represents the *falling away* of "decadence." And casuistry shares in the poetics of decadence not only etymologically but temperamentally, affectively. After all, the practice of casuistry usually suggests an equivocation or a dubiety – "Jesuitical" and "speciously legal-istic" are the attributed synonyms – that is akin to the deceit that provides the poetics of Wilde's *Decay of Lying* with its contrarian value, its potentially agitating power. *Au contraire*, say the failed revolutionaries of "The Tables of the Law," whose uselessness, splendid or not, spells out the end of any millennial political extension of their aesthetic attitude and practice, which Yeats inters formally these several times in his prose. In the persistence with which he records its undoing, moreover, we may see all the more vividly the power which it maintains, even – or especially – as a promise undone. For him, it is a promise relocated in the imaginative capacity of the Symbol, and in a doctrine of the potency of the Symbolic in the national poetry of the Ireland, which it also helps to create. "[L]ike all who are preoccupied with intellectual symbols in our time," Yeats writes in "The Symbolism of Poetry" (1900), he sees his work of symbol-making as "a foreshadower of the new sacred book, of which all the arts, as somebody has said, are beginning to dream," so that, "whether it be but a little song made out of a moment of dreamy indolence, or some great epic made out of the dreams of one poet," his poetic symbol will seem to have come out "of a hundred generations whose hands were never weary of the sword."[79]

The political poetics of Yeats's Symbol also underwrites the power of this counter in the literary history of modernism, which his mentee Symons would shortly provide. Symons's own poetic development in this decade anticipates and, to some significant degree, helps to explain an ongoing swerve in the critical understanding of the genealogy of modernist poetics. Here the powerful lure of symbolism, which is bound up with the magisterial status of Yeats himself, has displaced the ethos of decadence as an explan-atory paradigm. What I want to underscore as forcefully as possible is the secondary, incidental quality of that intervention. Its appeal is keyed to the signal figure of Yeats, who draws in turn on the strong source of attraction Ireland can exert at that moment as a figure in political history.[80] Its significance has been increased by virtue of the attractiveness of its imagi-native program but, in view of the breadth with which a poetics of decadence has been presented in this chapter, it is a good deal narrower as an interest.

The restricted nature of this interest becomes clearer in the inter-chapter that follows, which surveys the work of some of the major figures of twentieth-century attitudes. This material reveals the comprehensive and gaining strength of an intellectual culture that features the new interest in an imaginative quality distinctly opposite to Yeats's – and Symons's – doctrine of the symbolic.

The Cultivation of Decay and the Prerogatives of Modernism

In this inter-chapter, I want to recover a dialect in cultural history that has not found its place in the critical language we have used in representing the tradition of literary modernism. In this language, the ostensibly progressive methods and advanced attitudes of modern art and science are working in the service of an observably antithetical force. It is not primitivism, whose synergy with modernist aesthetics has been well researched. What I am looking at comes instead under a heading that combines the methodologies of modernity and its designated representatives in modernism, which are routinely represented as forward-oriented in outlook and value, with its backward-tracking opposite, which, as it is imagined and conceived, exerts a reverse fascination: in a word, with decadence.

This term claims its use as a reference for the fundamental other of the modern, which is taken mainly as a synonym for advancement narratives, liberation fables, and progress mythologies. "Decadence" expresses not just a condition of being fallen from this increasingly mainstream value, as are the more unwitting representatives of the degeneration disclaimed in moralistic discourses of the later nineteenth century. "Decadence," instead, represents an enriching debility of loss. It bespeaks an empowering economy of exhaustion, which preoccupies the most developed intelligences as a sometimes unexpected and so troubling but usually emboldening and powerfully attractive discovery. This is a motive interest sufficiently compelling to generate not only the conversation I am recapturing, but the coherence of an intellectual history that is also a cultural memory. It is, ultimately, the form of an artistic consciousness I will present as the sensibility of a profounder modernism. This lost conversation may be reconstituted from a broad resource, and its wider ground might be surveyed at first from above, as it were, in writings by three of its loftiest personages: Nietzsche, Freud, and Poe, who stand respectively in the middle and end and beginning of the history I am following.

The Novelty of Decline

Beginning with Nietzsche, whose constant and voluble jeremiads against *décadence* (the French formation sometimes provides the target for his most vituperative attacks) have tended to deflect attention from his closer engagement with the sensibility he is referencing under this term – at least until recently. Among these contemporary critics, Rita Felski notes how Nietzsche participates in a turn "toward a decadent aesthetic of surface, style, and parody" in the "self-conscious textualism" underlying the strongly performative quality in his prose.[1] More particularly, in a more extended and consecutive analysis of the oeuvre, Eve Sedgwick sees the queerness of *décadence* as the suppressed source of his obsessive analysis and as the contested source of his complex, apparently contradictory pronouncements about it. Alternating between resistance and reciprocation, Nietzsche's characterizations of his relation to *décadence* are taken by Sedgwick as the record of a tortured binary of denial and admission, where the "homosexual attribution" that is the irresistible synonym of this French word is centering all the complication.[2] This reading regains much of the intensity and some of the density of Nietzsche's engagements with his purported enemy. What it leaves unappreciated is the obviously conscious, even voluntary quality in Nietzsche's involvement with *décadence* – not as the love that dare speak its name unbeknownst to him or only in the camouflage of this French term, but as a condition of history. It is most particularly his own version of Prospero's consciousness of some dark backward and abyss of time, where the moment of a self-consciously ultra-modernity, which is also the time of modernism, allows him to perceive and experience and exult in the imaginative attraction of its most powerful opposite.

"Need I say after all this that in questions of decadence I am *experienced*?" Nietzsche emphasizes in *Ecce Homo*, the retrospective apologia for his intellectual life that he was drafting in 1888: "I have spelled them forward and backward," he continues in the next sentence. On this last sentence, Sedgwick ends her quotation, taking the "forward and backward" trope as the figure of his now predictable ambivalence in his exchange with the unsaid.[3] But significantly more is actually said. Continuing into the next sentence, this trope of the double direction of "forward" and "backward" turns into a figure of upward and downward, better and worse, with Nietzsche's own emphases:

> Looking from the perspective of the sick toward *healthier* concepts and values and, conversely, looking again from the fullness and self-assurance of a *rich* life

> down into the secret work of the instinct of decadence – in this I have had the
> longest training, my truest experience; if in anything, I became master in *this*.[4]

The poetic intensity and schematic insistence in the language of this
"master" of decadence certainly ask for analysis. The most important
point to mark is the fact that this perspective on decadence includes the
viewer in the condition being seen and analyzed. As he looks "*down* into"
this "secret work of the instinct of decadence" from *above*, from "the fullness
and self-assurance of a *rich* life," he is positioning his perspective from the
side of one who has also been looking *up*, admittedly, from "the perspective
of the sick."[5] The spatial coordinates may also be taken as temporal markers,
standing in place as stations of a developmental history he graphs more
expansively in sentences immediately preceding these. Here he is account-
ing for the special faculty of perception that has opened his recognition of
that "secret work of the instinct of decadence":

> Even that filigree art of grasping and comprehending in general, those fingers
> for *nuances*, that psychology of "looking around the corner," and whatever
> else is characteristic of me, was learned only then, is the true present of those
> days in which everything in me became subtler – observation itself as well as
> all organs of observation.[6]

This developed sensibility appears as the fruit of an intellectual progress. As its
culminating awareness, it claims in that "secret work of the instinct of
decadence" its ultimate recognition. This involves the "nuances" he emphasizes here as the subject of his most intense inspection: these are the dark
recesses of natural time, this is the farthest abysm of human character. Here
we find the markers of a sensibility whose particularly developed and
advanced and so assignably "modern" quality of mind constitutes itself in
the "subtler" recognition of this condition of radical atavism, indeed, of some
ineradicable decadence. This is a recognition that, in being "learned only
then," and in speaking as "the *true present* of those days," makes a highly
indicative claim of the historicity of its understanding in the modern day,
which, by all the other evaluating markers in this extended passage, is the
modernity of developed awareness. Absolutely "true" or not, the modernity
that is its establishing condition is asserted most emphatically then as a
condition that is not only self-conscious, and so modern*ist*, but, in terms of
its dominant conventions of progress and refinement, also *lost*. This is the
apparent paradox that resolves into the profounder truth of a modernity
which takes the recognition of its ostensible opposite as its denominating
quality. This is a modernism that takes the awareness of decadence as its point
of most novel self-consciousness.

The quality of self-consciously modern novelty in this recognition of decadence is an awareness Nietzsche has maintained, sometimes under different words, all along in his work. It emerges already and first of all in 1872 in *The Birth of Tragedy*, where he imposes on classical antiquity the understanding he will have historicized in 1888 as the outcome of his own time. So, in this first work, he proposes that the newest and most important aspects of the sensibility of Euripides involve a consciousness in decay. An "audacious reasonableness," a "penetrating critical process": these are the features of a new intellectual virtù that is inseparable, for Nietzsche, from a "poetic deficiency and degeneration."[7] Minus the censure of "deficiency," this sense of degeneration encapsulates the essential other of the advanced imaginative rationality he attributes to the Greek dramatist. So, too, in "The Problem of Socrates," from *The Twilight of the Idols* (1889), where he writes emphatically: "Does wisdom perhaps appear on earth as a raven which is inspired by the smell of carrion? . . . This irreverent notion that the great sages are *declining types* first dawned on me in regard to just the case in which learned and unlearned prejudice is most strongly opposed to it. I recognized Socrates and Plato as symptoms of decay, agents of the dissolution of Greece, as pseudo-Greek, as anti-Greek (*Birth of Tragedy*, 1872)."[8] The qualifications for his own "irreverent" novelty as well as "learned" superiority as a philosopher involve this perception: decadence is at once the condition and recognition of the most important and innovative philosophers.

Resisted as well as reciprocated with, the new awareness centered in decadence shows in its quintessential complexity in *The Case of Wagner* (1888), where the music Nietzsche loathes also exerts the most powerful imaginative attraction. Stipulating the conditions of Wagner's music as "the sickness" that "goes deep," in a "decay" that "is universal," and even standing "horrified before this almost sudden downward motion, abyss-ward," he esteems the accomplishment of Wagner's case, his *fall* (the German word *fall* preserves the meaning of the Latin *casus* "fall," which is also the nominative participle of the Latin radical of the middle syllable in de*ca*dence), in a more subtle vocabulary of praise. "He had the naïveté of decadence: this was his superiority."[9] For an author who plays incessantly on the etymological resources of his title word, the original sense of "naïveté" (*Naivität* in German) – newly born – also enters the manifold of this sentence. Packing its semantic action down among the radicals of the words, Nietzsche expands the sense of "decadence" in the wholly positive direction of "superiority," so to suggest that this "decadence" is also and especially a "newborn thing," all in all, the wide-eyed wonder that reflects the quality of modern novelty in his recognition of it.

The pressure this recognition exerts on the sensibility of modern science, and on the progressiveness most readily identified with this discipline, may be discerned thirty years and a long turn of the century later in *Beyond the Pleasure Principle* (1920). Writing in the immediate aftermath of a first world war, Freud is working within a frame of urgent and immediate reference for the compulsions Nietzsche had attributed to "the instinct of decadence." Whether or not Freud was working within a specific realization of Nietzsche's phrase, it is not too much to say that history had realized its meaning all too strongly, having weighed out proof of this deathward instinct in dead bodies by the millions in that recent war and, so, occasioned the Freudian phrases that have been translated, interchangeably, as "the death instinct" and "the death drive." And whatever "secret work" that "instinct of decadence" had presented to Nietzsche, it is Freud's work to submit this occulted power now to the hard light of the scientist. It is this work that helps to animate the extraordinary rhetorical performance in this book, which, even in translation, witnesses a remarkable combination of intensity and reticence in his engagement with his theme.

Freud's analysis is compelled, yes, but compelled by a truth to which he must otherwise object. The idea of a primary death instinct certainly reverses the current of his major work to date, not only as a pioneering scientist but as a self-consciously modern intellectual, who has been committed to a scientific analysis of those *vital* instincts of desire and appetite and attainment that motivate his human subjects. The recognition of this death instinct thus slows the deliberation notably, and this halting pace takes the measure of the impact this new awareness has made on the conventional sensibility of scientific modernity. Following Darwin, of course, and in a sense attested to also by Nietzsche, it may be the irrationality of creaturely appetite that is driving the otherwise rational work of modern progress, but the standard language of this secondary elaboration acquires the status of primary human ontology and reality in its subsequent iterations in public culture, to which Freud is also manifestly bound. So, here, a language of rational progress pauses before its awful other, the intractable atavism enacted in this "death instinct," which, in any case, is made out of the anti-matter to those values of vitality which Freud has otherwise also served. His mixed idiom of appalled fascination provides one expressive measure of the impact of the awareness I am identifying as the chief conceit of that profounder modernism, which is constituted by this still shockingly novel consciousness of backwardness even – and especially – in its own modern day.

The tempo of this new understanding of the modern shows representatively in the following passage, whose consideration is at once hesitating and inexorable in pursuit of its unwelcome truth:

> It would be in contradiction to the conservative nature of the instincts if the goal of life were a state of things which had never yet been attained. On the contrary, it must be an *old* state of things, an initial state from which the living entity has at one time or other departed and to which it is striving to return by the circuitous paths along which its development leads. If we are to take it as a truth that knows no exception that everything living dies for *internal* reasons – becomes inorganic once again – then we shall be compelled to say that "the goal of all life is death" and, looking backwards, that "what was inanimate existed before what is living."[10]

The recognition of this death instinct has challenged a standard grammar of motives in scientific discourse; it has estranged the authority of the individual writer, whose deliberations have been drawn into a verbal logic that is determinist and impersonal: "It would be in contradiction," "On the contrary, it must be," "If we are to take it as a truth that knows no exception," "then we shall be compelled." Overmastered by a premise that has alienated the language of analysis into a machine of reason, Freud shows also a sort of mournful fascination with this darker other. This new truth of a death instinct emerges in a language equally remorseful and remorseless in its pursuit of this truth:

> The hypothesis of self-preservative instincts, such as we attribute to all living beings, stands in marked opposition to the idea that instinctual life as a whole serves to bring about death. Seen in this light, the theoretical importance of the instincts of self-preservation, of self-assertion and of mastery, greatly diminishes. They are component instincts whose function it is to assure that *the organism shall follow its own path to death*, and to ward off any possible ways of returning to inorganic existence other than those which are immanent to the organism itself . . . . What we are left with is the fact that the organism wishes to die only in its own fashion. Thus these guardians of life, too, were originally the myrmidons of death.[11]

As the scientist forces his reasoning into obedience to a belief he would not have approved beforehand, but cannot now disprove, we find the double measure of a conflict so fundamental that it generates its own counter-rhythm. This is the exceptional tonality of a modern empirical reasoning in despair of itself, as it finds itself "compelled" to abandon the vitality that has provided its elementary and establishing values. The concluding allusion to the Greek warriors obedient unto death offers this word "myrmidons" as the vocabulary of a special kind of mythopoeic grandeur, its own desolate grandiloquence.

In this English translation by James Strachey, "myrmidons" resonates with the depths of that classical antiquity from which it has been fetched, remaining as powerfully opaque as the nearly unspeakable quality of the premise in Freud's book. And it is this feature of the unspeakable in his thesis that is revealed so powerfully in Jacques Derrida's engagement with Freud's major point in *The Post Card: From Socrates to Freud and Beyond* (Derrida's own translator, Alan Bass, makes a special point of appreciating Strachey's choice of "myrmidons"). Derrida's commentary comes to the limits of his own language of interactive analysis. He is reduced in effect to a simple summary, which, by the comparative standards of his other writings, is remarkably transparent and, in his framing statement, urgently emphatic:

> The component drives are *destined* to *insure* that the organism dies *of its own death*, that it follows its own, proper path toward death. That it arrives by its own step at death (*eigenen Todesweg*). That are kept far from it (*weg!* we might say, *fernzuhalten* he says) all the possibilities of a return to the inorganic which would not be "immanent" to it. The step must occur within it, from it to it, between it and itself. Therefore one must send away the non-proper, reappropriate oneself, make oneself come back [*revenir*] (*da!*) until death. Send oneself [*s'envoyer*] the message of one's own death.[12]

It is as though Freud's claim has to be stated outright, and starkly, to be believed. And it is the challenge of Freud's concept that properly deserves emphasis, though for the novelty it still presents. Its challenge may be measured nearly a hundred years later, when, in his queering of the death instinct, Edelman needs to speak so stridently and defiantly in the face of those established values of reproductive futurity which, nearly a hundred years earlier, were still sufficiently (if precariously) in place to produce the baffled rationalism of Freud's confrontation with their atavistic other.

The expressiveness of Freud's entanglement with inexpressibility strikes a special note in the language of that cultural and literary history I am surveying in this inter-chapter. The thwarted idiom of progressive reason bespeaks its fascination with its shadow values. Where, from the height of a highly developed intellectual attitude, the modern Nietzsche peers down and back and grows engrossed by that "secret work of the instinct of decadence," the modern scientific mind of Freud is also compelled to open up that zone of regressive tendencies of the human species. Of course, Freud speaks the dialect of this site in a particularly emblematic fashion, and at a particularly indicative moment, when, after the novel technological horrors of the first world war of the modern century, this scientist could see the hitherto "secret work" of that "instinct of decadence" working in the laboratory – the abattoir – of modern Europe, in a public demonstration of hitherto unimaginable atrocity. That the engines of progressive science could drive death like the underlying and compelling instinct Freud now knows it to be is the grimmest iteration of the concept of a modernism that takes the backward shadow of its modern day as its most gripping interest. This is the "ism" of a "modern" that records the shock of its own moment as the provocation of its most self-conscious novelty. It is the modernism of a modernity against itself – a formulation, not a tautology at all, that expresses a generative tension in ways that will be outlined in due course and at length. And it is a modernism that claims the darker imaginary of *decadence*, not just as a temporal precedent but as a temporal imaginary, where, beyond the interests this term locates in the queering of the idealized times of futurity, it locates a *reversal* of the forward current of progressive thinking, claiming the loss of that mythology of the modern as the defining ideal of historical time. It is the constituting power of a modernism that takes the plangent despair of Freud's postwar thought as an establishing language.

The claim I am making for the exceptionality of this language may be strengthened in view of the issues Robert Pippin addresses in *Modernism as a Philosophical Problem*. This book retells the long story of modernity's debate with itself. A long-standing faith in the Enlightenment ideals of rational inquiry and empirical science has coincided with an equally long-lived tendency to question the premises of those practices. This skepticism extends at least as far back as Kant's *Critique of Pure Reason*, and it develops its own variant language in registers as various as the impassioned critiques of Rousseau and the disciplined, reciprocating exchanges of Hegel. For Pippin, this evidence is consistent with an ongoing, alternative line within the majority consciousness of Enlightenment (and post-Enlightenment) rationalism.[13] What Pippin builds into the official tradition is a critical and self-critical condition that makes its own claim on being a dominant consciousness. But the mainstay standard of logical methodology remains in place even – or especially – among these contrarians. This is the difference in the idiom I am identifying in the imaginative vocabulary of decadence, where the logical protocols connatural to the consciousness of modernity have despaired of themselves and animated instead in the imaginative attraction of their antimatter.

A requisite depth of historical memory and literary precedent may be recovered for this special language, this special tradition, so as to reclaim the power of the sensibility cresting at this later moment of 1920. It comes out of that longer history of imaginative time that takes its crucial turn with the recognition of the failure of revolutionary futurity. This is a crypto-history in the sense that it has not been charted as a consistent or consecutive record, let alone as a precedent memory of modernism. This sensibility finds an early instance in a figure seen variously but never concurrently as the first of the decadents and the first of the moderns: Poe.

In "The Imp of the Perverse," Poe anticipates the substance of Freud's discussion. While Freud does not connect perversity with the "death drive" per se, Poe develops his own version of "perversity" in relation to normative values of human reason, in counterpoint to normative (Enlightenment) discourses of human well-being. His "perversity" follows thus a contrary will to dissolution, which drives the human creature to the brink at which Freud's death instinct also fulfills itself. At this "precipice's edge," a primary excitement fills the human creature with "the idea of what would be our sensations during the sweeping precipitancy of a fall from such a height. And this fall – this rushing annihilation – for the very reason that it involves that one most ghastly and loathsome of all the most ghastly and loathsome images of death and suffering which have ever presented themselves to our imagination – for this very cause do we now the most vividly desire it."[14]

Granted, the sensationalism of Poe's account may represent an exaggeration of the surprising quality of the recognition that, in being repressed or understated in Freud's report, accounts for its particularly somber eloquence. But it is worth noting that Poe's piece returns again and again to the paradox which is primary to Freud's own mournful fascination. This contradiction includes the deathward drive of an instinctual force committed supposedly to a furtherance of its own life. As with Freud, this awareness is sufficiently counter-rational that Poe approaches it at first tentatively, gradually, in a rhetorical fiction of elaborate and exacting rationality. "Through its promptings we act without comprehensible object; or, if this shall be understood as a contradiction in terms, we may so far modify the proposition as to say, that through its promptings we act," he proposes, at first considering the transgression as an issue of moral behavior, "for the reason that we should *not*," where he emphasizes the force of the compulsion to go *against* conventional morality. Such conduct reaches into deeper regions for its motive power, however. "Nor will this overwhelming tendency to do wrong for the wrong's sake, admit of analysis, or resolution into ulterior elements. It is a radical, a primitive impulse – elementary."[15] Summarily, at this original or aboriginal level of instinctual existence, Poe sees this double rhythm of self-preservation and self-destruction working under the aegis of one rule of human nature.

In dealing with the apparent paradox of a deathward-oriented life, then, Poe is working in an idiom not significantly different from Freud's. And where the man of modern science expresses the despair of his creed of vitalism in the somewhat sotto voce manner of the despondent professional, leave it to Poe to speak the truth of consequence – the impact of this recognition on the standards and values of the scientist's progressive reasoning – in the skew of his own verbal perversity, his mock logic: "Induction, *à posteriori*, would have brought phrenology to admit, as an innate and primitive principle of human action, a paradoxical something, which we may call *perverseness*, for want of a more characteristic term. In the sense I intend, it is, in fact, a *mobile* without motive, a motive not *motivirt*."[16] Even if it is suppositious in its contents and oriented more to performance than ratiocination, in the ridiculous Latinity of his comic expostulations in face of this "paradoxical something," Poe's language is tuned to those values of empirical reason that provide the basis of Freud's eloquent distress.

This "paradoxical something" centers Poe's attention mainly to the purpose of the spoof that is his rhetorical opportunity, but the wit of this passage thickens interestingly through the implications and forward memory of the word "phrenology." The study of skull size was already a quack science, a status Poe complements with his jocosely serious pose, but his "paradoxical something" is also anticipating one of its most strenuous applications later in the century: by Nordau, in *Degeneration* (1892; 1895). Phrenology provided the evidence of the paradox that baffled even the redoubtable Nordau, who could see human evolution producing ever more backward types. This conundrum is not grasped in advance in detail by Poe, but the jest of this passage darkens with an equivalent wit. This prescience is manifest in the fabric of the language, in the conceit of its antic seriousness, which features a would-be modernity of scientific analysis sputtering in front of the revelation of its own intractable backwardness. The scientific magus is the creaturely fool; a comic Prospero bows before an all too serious Caliban.

The degenerate imp provides a weird but revealing mirror for the most evolved consciousness; this conceit reaches across the near-century-long tradition sampled here. It is the recognition that Nietzsche achieves in his representation of that double direction, in the "forward and backward" or upward and downward aspect of his relation to decadence, whose sickly face he saw beneath his own superior mien; that Freud understands as a function of his work on uncanny doubles and that provides the profounder ground of this modern scientist's dismay in his finding of the primal death drive, above all, in himself; and that Poe performs as the shamanic babble within that rhetorical fiction of analytical mastery. Its expressions vary from that exquisite buffoonery in Poe to Nietzsche's excited defiance of any progressive standard to Freud's plangent despair at its failure. And if that range measures the comprehensive power of this imaginative apprehension, we might identify the source of this power in the special substance of its understanding, in the material feeling generated by that collision of modern progressive method and ancient regressive content. The modern sensibility is drawn toward it with the force of the negative, the repressed, the inevitable. In every available sense, we might name this substantial feeling as the *dis*content of the modern.

Or, to change the emphasis, of modern*ism* – understanding the special sense of this suffix to involve a self-consciousness about being modern. This awareness is established and intensified by a recognition of its fundamental other, and it includes an oppositional relationship to the available ideologies and operative mythologies of progressive modernity. What I am proposing is that one of the major, constituting opportunities of the sensibility we call "modernist" is this acknowledgment of an opposite quality that is not just tolerated but recognized as essential – even if this recognition involves resistance, a contesting that confirms. In the relational nomenclature of its own day, over a turn of the century lengthening from the 1920s back to the 1870s or 1860s (Poe is one of the forerunners), this opposite quality came to be known most often as "decadence." In the struggle to enunciate and assert its self-consciousness, the sensibility of modernism sometimes denounces decadence as its opposite and putative enemy, but their connection comprises and meaningfully exceeds any ready, general formulation as the antagonism of parent and child, of generations in succession. Rather, in the enabling bleakness of Nietzsche's superior view, as anticipated by Poe and consummated by Freud, the most advanced awareness of the modern day entails this apprehension of its untoward other as its most self-conscious novelty, that is, its modernism.

Modernity against Itself

The imaginative dare of this understanding provides the impetus for a range of fiction that, normally classified as proto- or para- or even pseudo-modernist, may be understood without the apologetic qualifications of those hyphens. We may read it as the literature of a modernism that takes this consciousness of decay as the point of its most novel awareness. Not that modernism invented this sense of decline. The general preoccupation with the feeling of loss at the century's end has been amply demonstrated. In the most comprehensive of these accounts, *Fictions of Loss in the Victorian Fin de Siècle*, Stephen Arata provides a telling record of these "fictions of loss" and the extent to which this imaginative subgenre dominated the novelistic production of the period.[17] When, in a further turn, the protocols of "modern" progress lead to their opposites as conclusions: here is a modernity against itself, here is the modernist opportunity. For the dislocation between the methods of progress through modern technology and a reverse reality in current circumstance locates a moment of critical difference, an occasion for the sort of historical self-consciousness that is at the core of the modernist apprehension. This condition was especially intense in the 1890s, when temporal specificity is intensified by the otherwise arbitrary chronology of a century's end, which, as it approaches, and within the shrinking interval of the diminishing decade, sharpens the sense of the present. It also puts the immense pressure of final proof on the dominant mythologies of progress of the century now ending. If a deflection from the destined end marks the turn or downturn of decadence, the recognition of the difference this new understanding represents provides the circumstance of a literature that is modern*ist* by virtue of this pointed alertness to the moment of difference it occupies.

This awareness lies as the contextual sense of a signal phrase in Hardy's fiction. "The ache of modernism" comes as a narrative characterization of the special perception of time that the heroine of *Tess of the D'Urbervilles* expresses to her suitor Angel Clare – a vision specifically of time future, and of time future as time indefinite:

> "And you seem to see numbers of to-morrows just all in a line, the first of them the biggest and clearest, the others getting smaller and smaller as they stand farther away; but they all seem very fierce and cruel and as if they had said, 'I'm coming! Beware of me! Beware of me! . . . '"
>
> He was surprised to find this young woman – who though but a milkmaid had just that touch of rarity about her which might make her the envied of her housemates – shaping such sad imaginings. She was expressing in her own native phrases – assisted a little by her Sixth Standard training – feelings which might almost have been called those of the age – the ache of modernism.[18]

Tess's sense of "to-morrows" disconnects the future from new as well as old covenants of history. At odds with the outcomes projected by contemporary visions of progressive temporality, her future also reverses the older notions of tradition, which would find the solace of sameness in the assurance of continuity. Tess stands powerfully in the exceptionality of her own instant as a radical "modernist": in her own moment (her feelings are "those of the age") she is conscious of a time not accommodated by any explanation, and she shows the roots of this sensibility in the historical despair we have been recovering for it. Hers is a modernity against itself in a most exact sense, since it is the working of an applied ideology of Progress that has occasioned her main recognition. A "Sixth Standard training" has given this vision of time indeterminate to its exceptional student, who "had just that touch of rarity about her which might make her the envied of her housemates" or, indeed, her classmates. Tess is the favored, forward point of a widely working force of social modernization, of progressive general education, which has served to constitute in her the consciousness of its opposite – a forward abysm of time as dark as the backward chasm Nietzsche claims as the awareness of his own vanguard sensibility. Jointly, Hardy and Nietzsche reclaim the original intensity of their shared historical present in its most negative presentiment: this is a modernity at its self-conscious worst, this is the "modernism" that "aches."

Tess's recognition is lived out in the narrative of Hardy's other major novel of the decade, *Jude the Obscure* (1895). In particular: the protagonist plans his advance through education as the progressing mastery of dead languages, Latin most fervently. Where the cultivation of Latinity by writers of the English fin de siècle reflects the sense of the treasured deadness of that language, the anti-futurity that underlies this attraction to dead languages is the prevailing attitude here, too.[19] The future Jude foresees as the result of his study fails to materialize, but this is also and most of all a closing down of futurity in an expanded historical sense. This out-of-time feeling is extended into contemporary history, which maps the landscape of modern Britain closely onto the late and failing phase of the Roman Empire: again and again, Hardy shows the ancient, decaying remains of the old Roman roads as a virtual substructure of the English countryside. What awaits Britain, it is irresistibly suggested, is what happened to Rome. Thus, the subject of Jude's study does not lead to his advancement but, instead, to the realization of a negating fate as ancient and unchangeable as those paleographic days. The modernist consciousness of this book lives in the ache of the difference between his progressive expectations and the regressive direction of his experience.

That modernism constitutes itself as an awareness of the backward character of human history is more than an apparent paradox. It is an understanding realized in the most powerful moment of feeling in the novel: the incident of Jude's son's suicide and murder of his half-siblings. "*Done because we are too meny*":[20] the death message left by the boy presents the vestige of some terrible version of species self-protection. Beyond the mordant comedy of its misspelling, this written note recalls the all too obvious failures of a system of progressive general education to correct or redirect atavistic instincts. In this parabolic account, we read that lesson in the failing hand of its student: the methods of modern progress serve in the end to intensify the recognition of their opposite qualities, their reverse conclusions. The point is reiterated and developed in the oddly school-masterly attitude the older Jude assumes in his explanation of his son's action to Sue Bridehead (who has put the blame on herself):

> "No," said Jude, "It was in his nature to do it. The doctor says there are such boys springing up amongst us – boys of a sort unknown in the last gener-ation – the outcome of new views of life. They seem to see all its terrors before they are old enough to have staying power to resist them. He says it is the beginning of the coming universal wish not to live. He's an advanced man, the doctor."[21]

Hardy's speaker anticipates both the discovery and the conundrum that Freud unburdens in *Beyond the Pleasure Principle*. Like that "advanced man," the modern experts that Jude invokes provide a version of Freud's formulation of the death drive in their recognition of this "coming universal wish not to live." Where the recent war provided the background for Freud's recognition of a human reality antithetical in every sense to the mythology of progress, the foreground for Hardy's Jude shows in the manifestly unimproved, indeed retrograde, nature of the younger Jude's behavior, which, Hardy makes a strong point in observing, is "the outcome of *new* views of life." This apparent paradox – ultra-modernity encourages reversion, or at least clarifies and magnifies our understanding of it – is presented as an intellectual challenge that ties the tongue of Hardy's speaker most expressively. The combination of aphoristic dialect phrases – "boys of a sort," "in his nature to do it," "staying power" – and the words and rhythms of apocalyptic historiography – "the beginning of the coming universal wish not to live" – coalesces to a dissonance that is indicative on its own. The recognition Jude is expressing represents a novelty as complex and obdurate as the one that forced Freud, wrestling with the untoward truth of his own modern science, to turn his own vocabulary of scientific analysis into a parody rationality, so automatic it was.

This is a recognition whose difficulty provides one measure of its impor-tance, and not in 1895 only. In a centenary collection of critical articles on Hardy's novel in 1995, for example, Gillian Beer stakes the major claim of her essay "Hardy and Decadence" on the apparently surprise turn of linking this literary figure to that cultural phenomenon. Assessing "decadence" as a "withering of hope, of the will or capacity to live that expresses decay," Beer moves this condition of decadence a turn further, or, rather, turns it in reverse, as she makes its convention-challenging attitudes synonymous with the values of social modernization, which, in her understanding, finds its vanguard in the defiance decadence presents to the way things are. "But the Decadent movement is not concerned only with exploring sickness. It encompasses also limber play across the threshold between the normative and the monstrous, experimenting with fresh futures; it is preoccupied with new sound worlds; and it is closely involved with New Woman's Writing."[22] Although it is not untrue that there was an emancipating force in the anticonventional temperament of decadence, this new aware-ness represents an apprehension of a negative or unprogressive direction in human history and, as such, constitutes the novel consciousness of mod-ernism. This awareness tracks strongly against the progress ideology operat-ing still in a good deal of scholarly discourse. As for Beer, the composite quality of her decadent modernism serves mainly, in the end, to save decadence from itself: "We can hear, too, the degree to which new scientific ideas about sound-waves, survival, and the ether of the universe unexpect-edly gave Hardy ways out of the impasse of human mortality and decay."[23] As valuable and attractive as these ideas may be, we should not sidetrack the condition of Hardy's "decadence" into the optimism of modern progres-siveness. We should not lose the content and import of a view so new and unique it is, in the expressive instance of Jude's words to Sue, almost – but only almost – inexpressible.

The novel quality of this understanding is represented in other fiction of this moment with the expedient of the non-realist genres of science fiction and gothic horror. Claims to historical verisimilitude are being waived here so as to provide a space in which a most untimely idea can be represented. In these fictions, the force of scientific advance opens inexorably into recog-nitions of human regression. Turning modernity against itself, these novels claim the imaginative conceit that is also the formative concept of that profounder modernism, whose new awareness is constituted by this recog-nition of its unregenerate other.

Consider the familiar fiction of Wells's *The Time Machine* (also 1895), which advances through the serial, enumerated progress of the years as its narrative mechanism. Following a chronological sequence toward the promise of an improved future modernity, it heightens its self-consciousness about its own place in time, thus establishing the specifically modernist quality in its narrative fiction. The recognition that waits at the end of this modernist adventure is nothing less, or more, than the "deca-dence" of its own moment – the word is addressed in references and even dressed in images of the English fin de siècle.

"What strange developments of humanity," Wells's narrator exclaims in his approach to this land of the distant future, "what wonderful advances upon our rudimentary civilization, I thought, might not appear when I came to look nearly into the dim elusive world that raced and fluctuated before my eyes! I saw great and splendid architecture rising about me, more massive than any buildings of our own time, and yet, as it seemed, built of glimmer and mist."[24] The not so solid monuments of this prospect suggest an ephemeral element to the conventional sense of the embodi-ments of Progress that the time traveler has brought with him. This awareness is augmented by the view of a sun consuming itself constantly, and increasingly, in a parallel entropic process. He furthers this reversal of expectation with the double turn he takes in his first glimpse of the creatures of this strange new world, finding an image not of distant futurity but of his own familiar day: "He struck me as being a very beautiful and graceful creature, but indescribably frail. His flushed face reminded me of the more beautiful kind of consumptive – that hectic beauty of which we used to hear so much."[25] The winking reference is to the person of Aubrey Beardsley, who was being consumed by the tuber-culosis that would soon kill him, and to those "more beautiful kind of consumptive" features that distinguished the figures he was already draw-ing as the signature image of his decade. This fiction of the future thus spells out an intractable paradox: a progressive history, which is sped ahead by the engine of progress that is its narrative vehicle and so advanced to its imagined conclusion, reveals the face of contemporary decadence. This is the conundrum Wells's narrator pauses over and expands upon: "It seemed to me that I had happened upon humanity upon the wane. The ruddy sunset set me thinking of the sunset of mankind. For the first time I began to realize an odd consequence of the social effort in which we are at present engaged."[26] Assuming in "we" the pronoun of his fellow travelers in Fabian progressivism, Wells registers the perplexity of a social modern-ist who has discovered "the sunset of mankind" and a "humanity upon the wane" as the "odd consequence" of a "social effort" that was supposed to institutionalize those values of the new and youthful and futuristic with which it was otherwise synonymous. This reversal of expectation consti-tutes the consciousness of the profounder modernism, which takes a recognition of decay as its content and establishing awareness, knowing its particular day as a particularly late day.

Where the difficulty of this recognition establishes one measure of its importance, it provides the substance of the drama of consciousness in the book. "And yet," Wells's narrator continues in the sentence just following the last, "come to think, it is a logical consequence enough. Strength is the outcome of need; security sets a premium on feebleness." Wells's narrator-character is working within a Darwinian frame of reference and explanation, which understands the development of history as the record of successful adaptations to "need." He attempts thus to explain decadence away as the unintended consequence of progressive evolution, where greater strengths have created the condition in which others are relieved of the needs of the struggle and so may safely indulge their weaknesses: "Even in our own time certain tendencies and desires, once necessary to survival, are a constant source of failure .... For such a life, what we should call the weak are as well-equipped as the strong, are indeed no longer weak .... This has ever been the fate of energy in security; it takes to art and to eroticism, and then come languor and decay."[27] This explanation accommodates the behaviors and attitudes that were conventionally attributed to decadence: "art and eroticism," "languor and decay," and it explains these aspects of decadence away as exceptions to the rule of evolutionary improvement. But it cannot account for the other face of the decay that is otherwise stylized in artistic and behavioral decadence: not those exquisite Eloi but the obdurate Morlocks. These underground creatures provide an image of degeneration – a reversionary strain of the species that Nordau surveyed in the manic catalogue of *Degeneration* (1892), whose first English translation also appeared in 1895. These denizens of the nether spaces of futurity exhibit the evidence of a reverse evolution that is at once the opposite in look and the complement in outcome with contemporary decadence. And so the images of the decadence Wells is attempting to marginalize by his Darwinian reasoning keep returning to the evidence of degeneration as his greatest test, which, as he admits later, enjoins on him the necessity of revisionist thinking: "I must confess that my satisfaction with my first theories of an automatic civilisation and a decadent humanity did not long endure. Yet I could think of no other."[28] The human decay that is evidenced in the accrual of ruins at this far end of time is at once the "odd consequence" and the all too "logical consequence" of an evolutionary history that has produced such weakness – or, most crucially, the recognition of such weakness – as its anomalous product. The conclusion to the Fabian progressive's vision of history is the undeniable truth of human decadence, which impresses itself on his reasoning as an awareness so awful he can neither grasp it in one master plan nor let it go. Resolved or not and more important in being not resolvable, it is the problem that constitutes the consciousness of a modernism at the extreme: the recognition, which awaits the ultra-modern time traveler at the forward edge of his modernist history, of a perennial and inevitable decadence.

Bram Stoker presents a similar recognition, through a different fictional convention, in *Dracula* (1897). If the figure of the vampire represents the horror of human reversion already in the literature of gothic romanticism, the special end-of-the-century sensibility that Stoker shares with Wells puts this possibility of backward sliding in the context of technological modernity in particular. This is a progressive technology of writing. Writing is depicted in the successive stages of a development that, all in all, encompasses the progress mythology which the title figure of this book will belie. Beginning with the simple phonetic script of longhand, developing into the more complex code of shorthand dictations, rising into the relatively new-fangled mechanism of the typewriter, and crowned and focused in the manifestly magical apparatus of the "phono*graph*"(emphasis on the second part in the compound preserves the place the device holds in this series of *writing* instruments): there is a developmental history of writing in the novel that is modernist in the sense that it has crested into a present of which the narrative consciousness is aware as some ultimate present. While Stoker's book has gained a new importance in various contemporary scholarly contexts, ranging from the social and anthropological interests of the vampire to the political issues of women's history, one of the simplest and most easily missed configurations in the story is the dramatic opposition between the figure of Dracula and the act of writing, which involves the thematic confrontation of his reversionary character and the evolving technology of script.

The density of references to writing devices in this book may be sampled in a single episode, where the various protagonists are assembled to consider the fate of Dracula's most recent victim, Lucy Westenra. This dramatic exchange is framed by the identification of the source of the narrative in "Mina Harker's Journal," which, for the reader, reiterates the promise of writing as the one activity pooling these various and ever advancing resources of written record. "I have *read your letters* to Miss Lucy," opens Dr. Van Helsing, who has been brought in to direct the resistance. "She sometimes *kept a diary*," he continues, "and *in that diary*, she . . .," he reiterates with a repetition that signals a liturgy of faith in the powers writing will direct. "I *wrote it all down* at the time," Mina replies in a responsorial refrain keyed to the same liturgy of faith. "[S]o I *handed him the shorthand diary*," goes Mina's reported part in this service. "Alas! *I know not the shorthand*," Van

Helsing replies, prompting thus a further turn forward in the record of writing mechanisms, as Mina produces the sense of her shorthand now in typewritten copy: "I have *written it out on the typewriter* for you."

> "Oh, Madam Mina," he said, "how can I say what I owe to you? This *paper is as sunshine*. It opens the gate to me, I am daze, I am dazzle, with so much light; and yet clouds roll in behind the light every time. But that you do not, cannot, comprehend. Oh, but I am grateful to you, you so clever woman." ...
> "And I have *read your diary* that you have so goodly written to me, and which breathes out *truth in every line*."[29]

The character in voice of Dr. Van Helsing, a personage who might be identified as one of Hardy's "advanced men" of contemporary science, manifests the otherwise odd backwardness of a nonnative speaker. This irony includes more than the social comedy it provides in the novel. It touches upon the deeper conceit of the book. Here, insofar as the instruments of social modernization provide the technology of reconnaissance, these will become inseparable from their backward opposite and complement, their untoward other: the figure of that vampire.

This is the confrontation toward which the protagonists of the story and their mechanisms of script begin to converge in a subsequent episode, as recorded in "Dr Seward's Diary," which records, too, the extraordinary reliance on the written record:

> After lunch Harker and his wife went back to their own room, and as I passed a while ago I heard the click of the typewriter. They are hard at it. Mrs Harker says that they are knitting together in chronological order every scrap of evidence they have. Harker has got the letters between the consignee of the boxes at Whitby and the carriers in London who took charge of them. He is now reading his wife's typescript of my diary.[30]

"And so now, up to this very hour, all the records we have are complete and in order," Jonathan Seward summarizes in manifest satisfaction about the typewritten format. "The Professor took away one copy to study after dinner, and before our meeting, which is fixed for nine o'clock. The rest of us have read everything; so when we meet in the study we shall all be informed as to facts, and can arrange our plan of battle with this terrible and mysterious enemy."[31] Thus he gathers this written matter toward its destiny in the allegorical fiction of the book – an Armageddon with the atavistic character of Dracula.

In this war of Progress against Dracula, the most advanced apparatus is the phonograph. As the newest and most miraculous technology, it provokes a range of associations, which, in *Victorian Soundscapes*, John Picker catalogues and focuses most suggestively in his consideration of its appearance in *Dracula* as representations of an otherwise sublimated sexuality, which, in conjunction with some of the New Woman thematics in the novel, is emerging into a new recognition.[32] This understanding represents the phonograph as an emblem as well as an instrument of the progressive advance it demonstrates. It merits accordingly a nearly curial attention, which is evident in Stoker's fiction as soon as it is introduced in the cloistral atmosphere of this inner room: "To my intense surprise," Mina Harker remarks on her discovery of the phonograph in Dr. Seward's room,

> there was no one with him. He was quite alone, and on the table opposite him was what I knew at once from the description to be a phonograph. I had never seen one and was much interested . . . .
>
> "Your diary?" I asked him in surprise.
>
> "Yes," he answered. "I keep it in this." As he spoke he laid his hand on the phonograph. I felt quite excited over it, and blurted out: –
>
> "Why, this beats even shorthand. May I hear it say something?"[33]

As a latter-day form of the "diary" Dr. Seward identifies it with, as a device which "beats even shorthand," the phonograph emerges with the typewriter in Mina's account as the furthest version of advanced writing technology, intensifying the effect of the information it conveys in this ritualized setting as the device of most exceptional powers:

> After dinner I came with Dr Seward to his study. He brought back the phonograph from my room, and I took my typewriter. He placed me in a comfortable chair, and arranged the phonograph so that I could touch it without getting up, and showed me how to stop it in case I should want to pause . . . . I put the forked metal and listened.
>
> When the terrible story of Lucy's death, and – and all that followed – was done, I lay back in my chair powerless. Fortunately I am not of a fainting disposition. When Dr Seward saw me he jumped up with a horrified exclamation, and hurriedly taking a case-bottle from a cupboard, gave me some brandy, which in a few minutes somewhat restored me . . . . I took the cover off my typewriter, and said to Dr Seward: –
>
> "Let me write this all out now. We must be ready for Dr Van Helsing when he comes . . . . I think that if we get all our material ready, and have every item put in chronological order, we shall have done much . . . . Let us be able to tell them when they come." He accordingly set the phonograph at a slow pace, and I began to typewrite from the beginning of the seventh cylinder . . . . I did not feel so lonely whilst I worked.[34]

Whether or not this "seventh cylinder" is intended to reference the last of the seven seals to be opened at the end of time, in the Book of Revelation, the secular pieties of progressive technology in this book obviously imagine some apocalypse of technology as the destiny of contemporary time. Here the material advance of which the phonograph is emblem and instrument will speed the triumph over its reversionary other.

This is the conditioned expectation, all in all the consummation of a modern mythology of Progress, in which Stoker intervenes most mean-ingfully. The phonograph is instinct instead with the unspeakable, unto-ward horror of its opposite, which remains a secret at once undisclosed in the dramatic fiction of the book and inherent, in our imaginative under-standing, with the very device that preserves it. Notice first of all, when Mina Harker engages the phonograph, how the "terrible story of Lucy's death" it has told her is left as the unheard portion of the story – terrible for her but, for us, as readers who cannot hear or read it, a still more unac-countable horror as it remains inside that device. Again, when Mina's "mind was made up that the [phonographic] diary of a doctor who attended Lucy might have something to add to the sum of our knowledge of that terrible Being," the progressive sensibility she demonstrates in her expect-ation of the useful knowledge to be released from that novel device compels this stunning contretemps:

> "Then, Dr Seward, you had better let me copy it out for you on my typewriter." He grew to a positively deathly pallor as he said: –
> "No! no! no! For all the world, I wouldn't let you know that terrible story!"[35]

The "deathly pallor" of the man who keeps the secret the machine keeps puts him in a mirror relation with the victims of vampirism, just as the device becomes identified with the unaccountably dark backward of human history that the vampire configures. Like the time machine, that is, the latest invention of a super-modernity provides at once the instrument of the would-be progress of modernization and a method of recognizing its con-trary quality in a degeneration with which it is, here, substantially identified. In the unspoken story it encloses, which comprises the legend of a pro-gressive modernity inseparable from its reversionary other, it testifies to the power of a threat sufficiently daunting to be unspeakable.

This is the silence of that profounder modernism, where, in the moment of self-conscious difference to the ethos of its time, modernity speaks against itself in the recognitions which decadence features as its characterizing, establishing awareness. This literature looks ahead in the subsequent century to the poetics of a modernism that includes this awareness as a fully expressive dimension as well as an identifiably constitutive element. While the contrary quality of this consciousness still constitutes a shock in the novels of Hardy and Wells and Stoker, it is recognizable increasingly, in some of the most significant writing being done over the long turn of the century, as a coherent and comprehensive sensibility, which appropriates the recognizable conventions of literary record. Which is to say: if this contrary consciousness has been growing from the top of an intellectual culture, as featured in the figures of Nietzsche and Freud, it extends into a literature whose representativeness is as extensive as the sense of convention it features. It speaks for no coterie membership, no interest of minority quality or recherché placement. It is not nearly so particularized as Yeats's poetic nationalism, which, in being transmitted to his disciple Symons in the doctrine of poetic symbolism, has misled the understanding of the relation of literary modernism to its antecedents in the fin de siècle, to decadence above all, which, in the fiction of early modernism we are about to read, demonstrates the power of this evolving consciousness in a literature of major record.

CHAPTER II

The Demonstrable Decadence
of Modernist Novels

This chapter presents a range of writing that comes under the general heading of the novel of the historical present. This fiction works overtly to the purpose of representing its current circumstance, which is defined imaginatively as well as chronologically by the (lengthening) turn of the century. For the historical content of the novel as genre, it claims the temporal imaginary of late days as the present condition of England. This is the establishing circumstance of the "decadence" this literature represents as a matter of imagined contemporary fact.

These books are written by novelists who are not identifiable in any ready-made way, however, with the traditions of literary decadence, either individually or, certainly, as a group: Henry James, Joseph Conrad and G. K. Chesterton, D. H. Lawrence, Frederic Manning and Rebecca West. Not as the tag attached to the more infamous of the Nineties writers, the "decadence" in these books works in a more complex and important way. It provides a record of end feeling as an established, if uneasily assimilated, understanding, one that has already generated a set of literary conventions and so needs to be taken as the record of an essential stage in literary history. These novels complement the historical content of late or last days with a broad and resourceful implementation of those literary techniques we established in "Afterward: A Poetics," which, all in all, demonstrate the historical condition of decadence in a sort of poetics in prose.

Not that demonstrating decadence is the whole story in this prose, poetic or not. This is a literature that also often remonstrates with "decadence," either as a specific name or a presumed view. This resistance witnesses something different from an otherwise understandable challenge to the historical pessimism with which decadence is identified. It manifests a more interestingly unspecified anxiety. Beyond a demonstrable quality, that is, this decadence registers a presentiment of the contemporary that is edged with menace as well as fascination and so locates the growing points of a literary sensibility in this highly charged dimension of current unease.

The timeliness of this sensibility accords with the conventional sense of "modernism," which is the heading under which several of these authors are usually grouped. Like Hardy and Wells and Stoker, however, these writers also tend to attract the somewhat apologetic wobble of the hyphenated proto-, para-, semi-, or pseudo-. What I am proposing is that we come to understand them as radical modernists and the sensibility of decadence they demonstrate as one of the primary – earliest, most important – constituents of modernism. In this sense, modernism is marked not by the easier (and later) understandings of the "make it new" variety, but by the more timely, novel awareness that decadence centers in its historical unease, which includes and even features the elusively new, sometimes fearful but usually exciting, aspects of the time it apprehends. The novels to be discussed in this chapter reveal this sensibility in formation, not in the ready-made formulas of literary history but in the historical force fields of the long turn of the century, which the First World War will bring to a climacteric.

One of the values of the range of modernist novelists in the catalogue just provided is its breadth of coverage. The figures missing from this list, however, include writers as significant, in the context of modernist literatures in English, as Virginia Woolf and Ford Madox Ford, James Joyce and William Faulkner, and, in continental locations, Marcel Proust and Thomas Mann. For reasons specific to each of these authors, which include issues of national tradition, political affiliation, and the literary cultures of various individual interests, their engagements with the legacy of decadence show variations on the attitudes and practices that stem from the mainstream developments I have laid out in the previous chapter. The war tetralogy *Parade's End*, for example, shows Ford representing a general sense of historical decline in the "last of England" feeling he centers in his déclassé aristocrat Christopher Tietjens, but the sense of decadence in the imaginative experience of this war finds a more specific and intense focus in the imaginative temporalities and literary styles of the war novels of West and Manning. Such variations are important and are indicative of the ramifying power of decadence within modernism, but the constraints of space compel a focusing on novels that best illustrate the concerted work of this sensibility within British literary fiction specifically. This material also prepares the ground for the major work of the second half of this book, where I discuss the poetries of Ezra Pound and T. S. Eliot separately, and at major length; in their representation of the London experience of the First World War, they bring a specifically British tradition of decadent modernism to a definitive expression. The extent as well as the coherence of the sensibility they are extending is demonstrated through the range displayed in this chapter.

As a poetics in prose, indeed, this literary fiction witnesses the preponderance of poetry in the formation of the technical sensibility of decadence. Poems occupy the largest share of the literary space in the first chapter of this book, and not incidentally. The temporal imaginary that is fundamental to decadence may find its most explicit presentation in poetic tempo – and in its allied tonalities, which include the integration of rhythmic schemes and imaginative figures, so to coalesce the sense of affective time that is essential to this sensibility. Essential to the genre of poetry, yes, but not restricted to it. For a poetics of decadence is demonstrable in the prose of these early modernist novels. This sensibility emerges sometimes as a comprehensive whole, as in the works of Lawrence, Chesterton, and Manning, novelists who were also poets, and sometimes in modular parts, as in the works of James and Conrad, who were not poets; and while West was not a poet, her novella *The Return of the Soldier* presents a poetic compression that makes it an exemplary demonstration of this literary sensibility.

The compositing of genres stands in itself, moreover, as a record of the extensive connection between these two eras, these two sensibilities. After all, in the avowed practice by artists as well as the dismayed protest by critics, "decay" in generic purity was observed in literary decadence as the aim and consequence of some of its most experimental work. This sensibility extends into the novelistic poetry as well as the poetic novels of modernism, as, here, into the decadent poetics of these early modernist prose fictions.

1.   Henry James

In the same year in which Symons published *The Symbolist Movement in Literature*, Henry James models the possibility of an alternative prosody for the modernist literature of the subsequent century in *The Awkward Age*. He offers this sensibility out of the record of the decade now ending. Awkward, uncomfortable, disquieting: these qualities appear as the most intense register of change in the "Age" of this novel, which brings the sense of an ending so extensively conventionalized in the fiction of the turn of the century into configurations at once familiar and unsettling. These are the now recognizable conventions of literary decadence, which James arranges in ways that produce the impact of the difference they represent in a constant provocation of unease.

The most conspicuous of these is the Nineties figure of elderly youth, which reflects the feeling of a late age most powerfully where it touches the young. It occurs in this story in the unsettling connection between the older man Mr. Longdon, who in his own words lives "in the twilight of time," and Nanda, who is little more than a girl.[1] The strangeness between them is intensified as an experience of the uncanny, a weird and more than weird familiar, where Nanda's face presents the image of her grandmother Lady Julia, who was the romantic interest of Longdon's own youth. This is a double exposure that he appreciates as he delectates, emphatically if ghoulishly, "that she has just Lady Julia's expression. She absolutely *has* it . . . . She's much more like the dead than the living."[2] The older "age" of Mr. Longdon may be the most obviously "awkward" point of relevance for James's title, but it is the steady effort of this book to generalize this awkwardness as a condition of the historical "age," which, as the last decade of the last century before the last century of the millennium, grows into a steadily more awkward strangeness in its lateness.

The historicity of this particular sense of time may be appreciated through a comparison with the novel from which James has obviously taken his "romantic" plot: Hardy's 1897 novel *The Well-Beloved*, which represents a rewriting of a work he had serialized in 1892 as "The Pursuit of the Well-Beloved." If this novel is little known now, it was widely read in its own day, especially after the public débacle of *Jude the Obscure* in 1895 had charged its appearance with a considerable pressure of advance attention. Hardy models the May-December liaison of Nanda and Longdon for James, but in even odder form. Hardy's male protagonist is represented in a progression of chronological ages – 20, 40, 60 – in which he pursues women of increasingly younger years who are revealed not only to be related but, in series, to be grandmother, mother, and daughter.[3] Here lies one source of the image of Julia, Nanda's grandmother, which Longdon sees with amorous awkwardness in the young girl's visage. The successive configuration of increasingly odder couplings, however, is not set up in any revealing way as a representation of the times in which they occur. Even if Hardy might be credited in the earlier 1892 piece with an augury of the figure of the elderly youth of the Nineties, his interest does not lie in historicizing this figure, since, in his novel's chronology, the protagonist's behavior begins a good deal earlier in the century.

The sense of historical location is well pointed in James's novel, considering the historical reference in its title. Consider further this exchange between Mr. Mitchett and Mrs. Brookenham, where the dialogue invokes a bibliography of contemporary decadence with a reference to two of its recently published "French books." One of these is now singled out:

> "I rather liked the one in the pink cover – what's the confounded thing called? I thought it had a sort of something-or-other." He had cast his eye about as if for a glimpse of the forgotten title, and she caught the question as he vaguely and good-humouredly dropped it.
> "A kind of morbid modernity? There *is* that," she dimly conceded.
> "Is that what they call it? Awfully good name."[4]

Whether or not any color can be striking *après le débacle* of *The Yellow Book*, the "pink cover" of the more scintillating of these novels serves as a marker and blazon of the really interesting thing, which focuses this otherwise undirected conversation. This image of "morbid modernity" matches and exaggerates the familiar Nineties type of the elderly young man in a figure of decrepit dynamism. The ingredients of this figure comprise but exceed any individual reference and, whether or not the dim-witted Mitchett gets the implication (his incomprehension accentuates our interest), offer these as the distinguishing constituents of the awkwardness of James's own age.

Further, the phrase "morbid modernity" recurs nearby for a person (if that is what she is) of identifiably modern recurrence, the fashion-plated *ingénue manqué* "Beach Donner." She is "that charming child, who looks like one of the new-fashioned bill-posters, only, in the way of 'morbid modernity', as Mrs Brook would say, more extravagant and funny than any that have yet been risked."[5] The saying that Mrs. Brookenham has repeated from Mr. Mitchett is now being repeated with the diminishing return that Beach Donner represents. This figure's "more extravagant and funny" version is the humorous extreme of the witless reiterative, all in all, an involuntary parody of a mass type. Here we see an intersection between the age of mechanical reproduction and the interest in fading repetition in the poetics of decadence. The production of images and commodities en masse in the public culture of urban modernity may be seen as the fundamental and fostering analogue of the repetition that fades. This perception takes the status of the work of art in the age of mechanical reproduction, as discussed by Walter Benjamin, into an historically informed understanding of decadent repetitiveness. The loss of the aura in the reproduction of the original artistic work is an effect which is reiterated in the repetition that fades in the poetics of decadence.[6] An original now lost is being reiterated in a way that reveals not only its own diminishment, the effect now recognizable as standard in the poetics of decadence, but, in the circumstances in which it is recurring, something of the historical significance of the technique it features as it recurs for that figure of mass-produced culture. In the critical turn James is taking on these circumstances of commercial modernity, and in the self-consciousness he is demonstrating about this consequently "awkward age," he is claiming the condition of his own radical modernism in the "morbidity" that stands as the signal figure of cultural decadence.

Wings of the Dove (1902) is a novel that demonstrates the thematic aspects and technical conventions of decadence in a more extensive fashion. The plot is driven by a motive and stratagem that belong in that zone of moral dubiety readily identifiable with decadence as a custom of reprobate behavior: Kate Croy persuades her lover Merton Densher to befriend and woo a wealthy young American heiress, Milly Theale, a one-time friend now dying of consumption, in hopes of an inheritance. Our response to the ongoing provocation of this plot is the target of James's constant complication, which he stirs relentlessly through the aesthetic conventions of the decadence he is also demonstrating on the behavioral stage. He moves this discomfiting complexity toward critical mass as the novel approaches its close. In this climactic action, he takes the plot to the site that qualifies in any literary Baedeker as the isle of decadence perennial and, so, as the scene of its most exemplary demonstration: that ever-sinking city, Venice.[7]

In an early, establishing shot in the Venice section in the book, James sets up the figures of Milly and Kate in the prospect of a decadence equally comprehensive and self-conscious. The atmosphere in this ever-decaying city is of late and dying day. The two characters are staged explicitly as personages in a Maeterlinck drama, where the costumes and props of an assignably decadent theater, accentuated with the lighting and tone of the lengthening sunset, provide the atmospheric dimension of a sensibility that is working more deeply and influentially. The dying light of this late hour overshadows not just the visual prospect but the ethical question, which is engaged in a language whose opacity serves to obscure – and so accentuate – the moral problem in the plot motive:

> Certain aspects of the connexion of these young women show for us, such is the twilight that gathers about them, in the likeness of some dim scene in a Maeterlinck play; we have positively the image, in the delicate dusk, of the figures so associated and yet so opposed, so mutually watchful: that of the angular pale princess, ostrich-plumed, black-robed, hung about with amulets, reminders, relics, mainly seated, mainly still, and that of the upright restless slow-circling lady of her court who exchanges with her, across the black water streaked with evening gleams, fitful questions and answers . . . .

> ... It may be declared for Kate, at all events, that her sincerity about her friend, through this time, was deep, her compassionate imagination strong; and that these things gave her a virtue, a good conscience, a credibility for herself, so to speak, that were later to be precious to her. She grasped with her keen intelligence the logic of their common duplicity, went unassisted through the same ordeal as Milly's other hushed follower, easily saw that for the girl to be explicit was to betray divinations ...[8]

The ethical questions are being deflected through an art of perspective where, in free indirect speech, the self-exculpating motives of Kate are parleyed into the narrative voice. Its authority is suspended in a revealing propensity for assertions in the conditional mood or conjectural tense – "might well have," "it may be declared." In this grammar, issues of moral responsibility are reckoned in the "so to speak" fashion James's narrator names; they are being turned into questions of phraseology. So, by the end of this extraordinary verbal performance, where the beautiful shades of sunset are refracted in a language of moral opacity, the "duplicity" that is originally and actually Kate's alone (with Densher) is somehow "common" with these others, that is, normative; given the syntactical ambiguity here, it is shared even with Milly, who is otherwise its target and victim. The decorous presentation of the subject has tested and even contested its ethical reprehensibility.

The performance exemplifies the central premise of aesthetical ethics in *The Decay of Lying*. In this hallmark inscription of a poetics of decadence, Wilde proposes that an ingenuity of deception is the essence of art and so of beauty. No less archly than Wilde, but more boldly because more specifically, James is demonstrating the premise of the poetics of decadence in practice. It comes in an instance so particular that its aesthetic idea is not just disturbing, it is excruciating. This pain registers the acuter consciousness of a novelty, a disturbance that records a way of feeling as new as it is disconcerting and, in its very subtlety, more disconcerting once it is recognized. Here then is another discomfort of the same awkward age, where a decadence that is demonstrably in extremis causes an awkwardness that enforces this acuter self-consciousness of novelty, of the difference such novelty signifies.

This understanding of modernism – as the novelty of a decadence being demonstrated at an awkward extremity, thus with a specially heightened consciousness of its novelty – waits at the end of a reading of James's two novels, and especially near the end of *The Wings of the Dove*. Here the consummation of the plot presents the ultimate extension of the poetics of decadence he is demonstrating. Densher approaches and completes his

emotional connection with Milly – to his otherwise unspeakable purpose –
in a manner that takes the aesthetical ethics of Wilde to subtle extremes, to
the extremes of Densher's (James's) own subtlety. "He had however only
to cross again the threshold of Palazzo Leporelli," James's narrator motions
to put Densher on the track of his pursuit, which, as he continues, puts him
most suggestively in the role and attitude of a visual artist: "to see all the
elements of the business compose, as painters called it, differently."[9] The
"elements of the business," that extraordinarily coarse piece of mercantile
verbiage for the scheme underway, effects another one of those (now none
too) subtle discomforts that are special to the awkwardness of this age. This
discomfort comes from the all too obvious realization in practice (in
narrative) of that chief conceit of a decadent poetics, an aesthetical ethics,
as the phrase also enacts in language the capacity, as painters "compose"
their prospects, to see this business "differently." This is the difference
aesthetics can make in the ethics of the "business," which is transfigured
in this prospect into the last of all beautified views:

> This spectacle had for him an eloquence, an authority, a felicity – he scarce
> knew by what strange name to call it – for which he said to himself that he
> had not consciously bargained. Her welcome, her frankness, sweetness,
> sadness, brightness, her disconcerting poetry, as he made shift at moments
> to call it, helped as it was by the beauty of her whole setting and by the
> perception at the same time, on the observer's part, that this element gained
> from her, in a manner, for effect and harmony, as much as it gave – her whole
> attitude had, to his imagination, meanings that hung about it, waiting upon
> her, hovering, dropping and quavering forth again, like vague faint snatches,
> mere ghosts of sound, of old-fashioned melancholy music.[10]

As a character in voice compounded of his monologue and the monitor of
the narrator, Densher is talking his way into beautifying the objectionable.
In doing so, he is offering in evidence a most radical instance of the
aesthetical ethics James is identifying, demonstrating, as such. The "disconcerting poetry" that Densher attributes to Milly is "disconcerting," after
all, insofar as its aim and motive obviously go in the opposite direction: to a
soothing poeticizing of the alarming, distressing thing he is actually up to.
Once more, the somewhat subtle discomfort of his aesthetical ethics comes
in the disconcerting rightness of that adjective. In another signal word – "as
he made *shift*" to call it – James's narrator stirs our unease about the shifty
interest being served. But the ethical mess that is left by the cleansing
attempts of the aesthetics of decadence is being demonstrated for no morally
censorious purpose; there is no supporting framework of value or attitude.
The residue of some formally normative moral order serves mainly or only

to register and intensify the discomfort, the difference (it is the signifying difference of modernism), which the sensibility of this new, discomfiting age presents.

Far from moral censoriousness, the demonstration of decadence in this passage includes a poeticizing of James's own. It comes not just in the rhythmical filigree he achieves with the fining of stress and pace through his signature pauses in punctuation. It shows in a descriptive decoration that reflects his reciprocity with the methods and effects of the most particular- ized poetics of decadence. The repetition that fades, that serves the impres- sion of lost originals and foregone originality, is invoked in the troping of the "harmony" of Milly's demeanor as "ghosts of sound," the haunting of a "music" that is "melancholy" but most of all "old-fashioned" – the vibra- tions of her person are as sounds, which, outdated as music and disem- bodied as echoes, are lost now: the fade is the strength of this poetics. Thus the muse of the decadence being demonstrated is also the victim of its distortions of moral norms. The compound is as ethically unbearable as it is aesthetically irresistible. Not censure then but displeasure or, better, the guilty pleasure of enjoying a wrong, of enjoying awkwardly and so being involved self-consciously in the convention-disrupting novelty it presents: this is the awkwardness that James constitutes and reconstitutes, across the two major novels of his own turn of the century, as the special condition of this age.

"[A] pair of the children of a supercivilised age making the best of an awkwardness":[11] so James's narrator situates Kate and Merton historically and characterizes them attitudinally, repeating a conventional understand- ing of decadence as the later phases of an overripe culture. He is also indicating the discomfort that comes – with his special assistance – from the novelty it represents. Discomfort or not but mainly discomfort, the consciousness of novelty as a painful awareness operates to heighten self- awareness in the experience of this unprecedentedly specific circumstance. An identifiably modernist awareness is forged thereby.

2.   Conrad and Chesterton

One of the primary sites in cultural history on which the sensibility of decadence may be demonstrated is the turn-of-the-century European phe- nomenon of anarchism. The unlikelihood of this connection turns on the stereotyped figure of the decadent as a languorously bored, inactive char- acter. This preconception appears routinely in the scholarship that studies the subject of anarchism in relation to the literary history of this period.

What is striking in this criticism is the tendency to associate the aims and effects of anarchism with the sensibilities of the groups variously attached to or confused with decadence, but not with this temperament specifically. In "Anarchist Dandies, Dilettantes and Aesthetes of the *Fin de Siècle*," for example, Ali Nematollahy focuses on the literary and political culture of Nineties France, taking the artistic personalities named in this title and documenting their otherwise unlikely affinities with the emergent temper of anarchism. The decadents enter this calculus as peripheral figures, and then only as "Symbolists."[12] Where this counter performs its now predicable work of euphemizing an unacceptable temperament, this example provides a most striking indication of that general tendency: after all, "aesthetes" or "dandies" or "dilettantes" invoke artistic orientations no more readily mobilized in the anarchist effort; decadence is unacceptable, it seems, even to anarchists. Especially to anarchists, goes the argument in another study of Nineties France: Christopher Forth's "Nietzsche, Decadence, and Regeneration in France, 1891–95"; following the traditionally one-sided view of Nietzsche's opposition to *décadence*, Forth identifies that sensibility with the remnants of an older French order, against which the energies of a Nietzschean anarchism are directed.[13]

An exception to this general tendency and an opening for critical reconsideration comes in Adam Parkes' *A Sense of Shock: The Impact of Impressionism on Modern British and Irish Writing* (2011), which documents the synergies between impressionist aesthetics and the anarchist event. Parkes leaves decadence out of his account, though not to disclaim its connection to anarchism. He directs attention instead to the intricate linkage between the stated aesthetics and implicit politics of impressionist writing, which, he maintains, has been wrongly overborne by some facile associations with decadence.[14] This sensibility indeed needs to be separated from impressionism, and, in this wise, it may be reconnected to anarchism – through an imaginative understanding of history in which these two sensibilities are complicit.

A sense of late, last, and lost days tells the time of this linkage. Not that the poetics of the echoing fade shows up on the anarchists' placards. Nor that a program for declamatory action may be read into decadents' scripts. Instead, there is a representation of anarchism in the historical fiction of this period that demonstrates its connection to the imaginative apprehension of time winding down; this understanding is demonstrated extensively through the themes and techniques of literary decadence. Recovering this connection for decadence also adds an historical content and political depth to its sensibility; it gives warrant to decadence as a representation of the most urgent and consequential aspects of the contemporary historical imaginary. The linkage with anarchism also reinforces the shock of the novel that has already been consolidated for decadence, and, in the acuter consciousness of the modern day that this comprehension registers, it offers new ways of reading the modernist quality of these works.

The decadence that Conrad demonstrates in *The Secret Agent* (1907) begins with the initial depiction of his main character. Mr. Verloc

> generally arrived in London (like the influenza) from the Continent, only he arrived unheralded by the Press; and his visitations set in with great severity. He breakfasted in bed, and remained wallowing there with an air of quiet enjoyment till noon every day – sometimes even to a later hour . . . . He left it late, and returned to it early – as early as three or four in the morning; and on waking up at ten addressed Winnie, bringing in the breakfast tray, with jocular, exhausted civility, in the hoarse, failing tones of a man who had been talking vehemently for many hours together. His prominent, heavy-lidded eyes were rolled sideways amorously and languidly, the bedclothes were pulled up to his chin, and his dark smooth moustache covered his thick lips capable of much honeyed banter.[15]

An "exhausted civility," which represents both a civilization at its end and a stylization of this extremity; a voice that recalls a more vigorous original and rustles now as the echo of that lost sound; the counterclockwise habits of a character who operates *contra naturam*; and a presence that is registered as an infection, an "influenza" that has ostensibly come "from the Continent" but that may be traced, with its more specific literary source, to France: Mr. Verloc is the rumpled double of Des Esseintes, protagonist of Huysmans' *À Rebours* (*Against Nature*), the novel that Symons famously cited as "the breviary of the Decadence"[16] and that reappears in Conrad's abridgement with a special concision. This opening vignette presents an extended image of the conventions he will proceed to demonstrate in detail and at length.

An especially dense concentration of these motifs appears in the figure of Stevie, the mentally impaired brother of Verloc's wife Winnie and, in a pattern characteristic of the infertility theme in decadence, the only child of this otherwise unproductive couple. Stevie appears clearly as an example of "degeneration," a word that recurs in several synonyms and cognates throughout the novel,[17] but in the richer mixture already of this introductory portrait: "He was delicate and, in a frail way, good looking too, except for the vacant droop of his lower lip" (*TSA*, 13). This "delicate" trait is at one with an artistic proclivity, an aesthetic quality that Conrad depicts with a complementary physiognomy. "[A] growth of thin fluffy hair had come to blur, like a golden mist, the sharp line of his small lower jaw . . . . His spare time he occupied by drawing circles with compass and pencil on a piece of paper. He applied himself to that pastime with great industry" (*TSA*, 14): Stevie's visage is given the nimbus of an artist look with that growth of facial hair, which also soft-focuses the lineaments of his degeneration. He appears at once as the Caliban of the degeneration typology that was modeled by Nordau and the Ariel of the decadent artist who is exemplified in Beardsley, whose "frail way" is also Stevie's. This combination may not be resolvable into any demonstrable attitude on the part of Conrad, but it does provide an index of the comprehensiveness with which the conventions of decadence are being extended in his representation.

It is, all in all, the representation of one apprehension of contemporary history; as in this prospect of London in the first encompassing shot of his opening chapter:

> The very pavement under Mr Verloc's feet had an old-gold tinge in that diffused light, in which neither wall, nor tree, not beast, nor man cast a shadow. Mr Verloc was going westward through a town without shadows in an atmosphere of powdered old gold. There were red, coppery gleams on the roofs of houses, on the corners of walls, on the panels of carriages, on the very coats of the horses, and on the broad back of Mr Verloc's overcoat, where they produced a dull effect of rustiness. But Mr Verloc was not in the least conscious of having got rusty . . . . His idleness was not hygienic, but it suited him very well. He was in a manner devoted to it with a sort of inert fanaticism, or perhaps rather with a sort of fanatical inertness. (*TSA*, 15–16)

The "old-gold tinge" presents the burnished surface of a dusky time with an internal rhyme, which harmonizes the atmosphere of the dying day in the usual ways of the death beautiful in decadent aesthetics. The recurrence of the phrase in "powdered old gold" shows an artist working the verbal stock-in-trade of an existing convention, demonstrating it as such. The end-of-days feeling that is focused and intensified in this prospect represents a decadent atmospheric in general but also, in particular, the chronological imaginary of the Nineties (the action of the novel is set in the middle of the decade), that last decade of the last century before the last century of the millennium. This presentiment of endings is felt most acutely where it touches the young, who are depicted in Nineties typology as elderly before their time, and Conrad encapsulates that special conceit of ruined youth in this particular antinomy of "a sort of inert fanaticism, or perhaps rather with a sort of fanatical inertness."

This chiastic reversal of terms includes a peculiar sense of exactitude as the alternative conjunction produces that qualification of sense. The effect goes to a general knowingness in the demonstration of these conventions of decadence. This is also the sagacity of foreshadowing, for the controlling consciousness of the novel is predicting the specific turn that the story will take in the plot on the Greenwich Observatory. The inertia of the decadent is being mobilized and fanaticized and weaponized in anarchist programs. And it is Conrad's special interest to script the figures of contemporary political positions and the events of recent English history – the action of the novel is modeled on an actual attack by an anarchist on Greenwich in 1894 – into the attitudes and practices of decadence, which are demonstrated so obviously in these opening pages of the novel. The story that follows is framed accordingly as a history coincident with a literature.

It is a history pitched most particularly in that condition of lateness, even of aftermath, which Conrad is representing through his extensive demonstration of the conventions of decadence. Take this representation of the British Empire as a grand systemic organization. In line with general precedent in the conventions of decadence, this is a global and historical imaginary that, in its decline, registers the presentiment of downturn in history in its most indicative and consequential measure. Conrad records this condition as a function of a language otherwise deployed to support or celebrate its institutions. Here, in this vignette in the imperial capital, he plays with and overplays the idiolect of imperial order:

> The Assistant Commissioner, driven rapidly in a hansom from the neighbourhood of Soho in the direction of Westminster, got out at the very centre of the Empire on which the sun never sets. Some stalwart constables, who did not seem particularly impressed by the duty of watching the august spot, saluted him. Penetrating through a portal by no means lofty into the precincts of the House which is *the* House, *par excellence* in the minds of many millions of men, he was met at last by the volatile and revolutionary Toodles. (*TSA*, 162)

The intensives which Conrad scores into this passage and underscores on his own – "the very centre," "*the* House, *par excellence*" – raise the level of esteem in a mock-hyperbolic way and so destabilize the verbal surface as a record of credible value. The linguistic ritual of empire, which the narrative language seems to be serving so assiduously, is a verbal ceremony that goes wrong in the actual words. "The higher the slavery," Shaftesbury once aphorized, "the more exquisite the buffoonery."[18] The more strenuous the service to authority, Conrad is demonstrating in this verbal burlesque, the more authority is clowned and undone. A constantly sardonic verbal comedy, there is also a special entropic quality: a pomposity hollowing itself out in a tonal prosody of inflation and diminishment. In "the volatile and revolutionary Toodles," for most conspicuous instance, the polysyllabic Latinity dovetails into the diminutive name in a rhythm of expansion and contraction that also mimics the sense of a great political institution in decline. It is, all in all, an august inanity. Or, an Augustan inanity, insofar as the "august spot" provides a memory of the dynasty most closely associated with the turn in Roman history from Republic to Empire, the process that Marx memorializes as the first turn toward the decadence being replicated in mid-nineteenth-century France. That long story may be witnessed as a British history in miniature in this passage, where the linguistic wit formalizes the obsequies of imperial ambition in its extension and distention, swelling up and breaking down.

The global dominion of this imperial order is invoked by the Greenwich Observatory, which locates the Greenwich Meridian as the defining site of a new world order: a modern temporal rationalism.[19] So, the anarchists who have in view the primary site of Greenwich Mean Time are targeting not only the values but the measures by which those values of the rational are being implemented in a system of global modernization. All in all, they are attacking the Progress mythology for which the imperial plan was the promissory agent. Anarchism may be read in this novel then as a most vivid and specific instance of a crisis of modernization, which, in turn, defines the moment and opportunity of modernism. This, in a word, is a modernity that has become conscious of itself as such – here, at the special extremity of the threat being presented to it. The primary time of this novel is the imperiled time of modernity.

This is a circumstance inhabited and claimed by the sensibility of decadence. And so the difference anarchism and decadence and modernism make to the normative temporal order of modernity is realized in this novel, not in the success or failure of the anarchist plot itself, which implodes with the "degenerate" Stevie unwittingly carrying the bomb, but in the aftermath, which registers the temporal dispossession of a lost modernity. It is the primary imaginative tense of literary decadence. And Conrad fixes aftermath as the prime condition of contemporary time, in the closing motions of the novel, as he centers his representation in the signal tempo of decadent poetics: the repetition that fades.

In the long winding down of the story, Winnie murders Verloc in outrage at the death of her brother and enters a spontaneous liaison with Verlocs's anarchist companion, Comrade Ossipon, who promises her an escape to France and a new life but, deserting her on the way (having pocketed the savings she and Verloc had accumulated), leaves her to take her own life on the boat. Here, in the representations of Ossipon's reading and rereading of the newspaper account of her death, Conrad initiates a reiterative rhythm of his own:

> Before returning it to his pocket he stole a glance at the last lines of a paragraph. They ran thus: "*An impenetrable mystery seems destined to hang for ever over this act of madness or despair.*"
>   Such were the end words of an item of news headed: "Suicide of Lady Passenger from a cross-Channel Boat." Comrade Ossipon was familiar with the beauties of its journalistic style. "*An impenetrable mystery seems destined to hang for ever ....*" He knew every word by heart. "*An impenetrable mystery ....*" And the robust anarchist, hanging his head on his breast, fell into a long reverie. (*TSA*, 228)

The words emphasized by Conrad (the ellipses are also his) will be reiterated insistently across the closing sequence of the book – mostly as Ossipon's ruminations take over the narrative voice:

> Ossipon lowered his head slowly. He was alone. "*An impenetrable mystery ....*" It seemed to him that suspended in the air before him he saw his own brain pulsating to the rhythm of an impenetrable mystery. It was diseased clearly .... "*This act of madness or despair.*" ... and the paper with the report of the suicide of a lady was in his pocket. His heart was beating against it. The suicide of a lady – *this act of madness or despair.* (*TSA*, 230–31)

The refrain phrases are positioned tellingly in the dramatic fiction of reading. These reiterated words come from what is designated in the initially spare description of Conrad's narrative as "the last lines of a paragraph," then as "the end words of an item." We learn of an event through words that emerge first as an endpoint in an otherwise conventional, beginning-to-end process of finding out about the instigating event. The words surface in a moment of aftermath; they occlude their provocation from view as these phrases interlace with Ossipon's increasingly obsessive reiteration in the subsequent redaction. It is the original that goes missing in the repetitions of the poetics of decadence, a practice for which this finale provides a revealing example.

"An impenetrable mystery": what this "mystery" consists of becomes sufficiently clear, just as Ossipon's "much-folded newspaper" suggests he has pored over the story, remorsefully or not, and knows full well what has happened. And so the word "mystery" seems increasingly meaningless in its reiterative insistence, fading out of signifying presence in just the same way that the refrain phrases go in the poetics of repetition in decadence. It is a fade that is charged, if that is the word, with every implication and consequence of a novel positioned at the pivot point of a literary history of two centuries. In one direction this prosody echoes ironically back against the attitudes and practices in the poetries of Wordsworthian romanticism, which reclaim an original moment in the "mystery" of its poetic reiterations, in the rituals of a memory whose repetitions give it an ongoing, comprehensive, deepening significance. In the other direction, Conrad calls sardonically ahead to the circumstances of an urban modernity as the conditions of Ossipon's repetitions, which, in their increasingly automatic quality, are keyed to one of the instruments of art in the age of mechanical reproduction: "The mechanical piano near the door played through a *valse* cheekily, then fell silent all at once, as if gone grumpy" (*TSA*, 231). Grumpy but compulsive, Ossipon is running to the rhythms of a public culture typified by the mass production machine of the newspaper itself, whose phrases he has memorized and is now repeating in the mechanical fashion characteristic of that source:

> It was ruin. His revolutionary career, sustained by the sentiments and trust-fulness of many women, was menaced by an impenetrable mystery – the mystery of a human brain pulsating wrongfully to the rhythms of journalistic phrases. "... *Will hang for ever over this act* .... It was inclining towards the gutter ... *of madness or despair* ...." (*TSA*, 231)

Keying these repetitions so clearly to the machine of modern public culture, Conrad enjoins on his readers the kind of heightened self-consciousness of modern circumstance that is the occasion and opportunity of modernism, which he constitutes especially by those prosodies of diminishing repetition in the poetics of decadence. He is fixing the special, defining time of modernism in the late times and temporal dispossession of decadence.

A novel sometimes supposed to be "Conrad's reactionary satire of the late Victorian anarchist movement in London,"[20] written from the value standards of the British merchant seaman, thus reads very differently when, on the evidence of its textual practices, we understand its complicity with the materials and means of those reputed adversaries – an anarchism that finds its fellow traveler in the sensibility of decadence. While complicity on the level of textual practice is obviously not conscious partisanship, one consideration to emerge from this analysis involves the possibility of a specifically textual politics. How does the demonstrable decadence of this novel of early modernism position itself in relation to the political history of its own moment, and how may this negotiation inform our understanding of the relation between modernist aesthetics and modern politics in other modernist work?

Reading *The Secret Agent* with these questions of political position in mind, James English follows the operation in the text of Conrad's adaptation of the "joke," as understood in the more complex and ambitiously Freudian formula of "Witz," which usually involves combinations of contradictory quality. In English's formulation, this joke-work is typified and concentrated in the figure of "the fat anarchist," which, as "a witty construction," is "a complex and contradictory figure that is not reducible to the anarchist as such." This unlikely figure is "unthinkable outside the processes of joke-work" and so provides "not an alternative comic version or translation of a political thought but a particular moment within a politics that is itself, precisely, a witty negotiation of internalized but inassimilable contradictions in the social order."[21] These "inassimilable contradictions" include in particular the tensions between the residual allegiance of the man who had served in the British mercantile empire, as complicated as that memory may be in its fictional representations, and the intensifying pressure of the recognitions of the end-of-empire days. These tensions are released in the joke-work specific to this figure of a fat anarchist, which shifts the center of imaginative gravity in the novel from the framework of received political understandings and their otherwise single and restrictive ideologies. This joke-work provides a reprieve and so opens a dimension of possibility, where these otherwise antithetical political positions may coexist. This condition of possibility registers the novel shock of the awareness that produced it, that forced the otherwise pragmatic morality of the merchant mariner to adapt to it. This is the formative force that the sensibility of decadence represents in the historical imaginary of Conrad, who, in turn, is presenting the special-time consciousness of modernism through it.

A similar configuration appears just one year later in another novel of London anarchism, G. K. Chesterton's *The Man Who Was Thursday: A Nightmare*. As a work of social record, like Conrad's, this novel associates the anarchist movement with the sensibility of decadence, but in a more insistently juridical and vindictive way. While Chesterton's politics show a complexity of their own, offering a sort of vertical socialism in the neo-medievalism of his distributist economics, the rhetorical fiction of this novel features an authorial voice of Tory authority, which is committed ostensibly – and, from the range of Chesterton's other political writings, predictably – to a critique of anarchist activity and its fellow travelers in decadence. His novel evidences then a politics of explicit intention – a conservative's proscription – far more intense and directed than Conrad's. Like Conrad's, however, the political imagination of this book cannot be contained by a uniform political ideology. Like Conrad's, it is registering the immense pressure of the antithetical understanding that anarchism, as an extension of decadence, is presenting. And where Conrad releases this pressure through joke-work, using unlikely combinations as a means of exceeding the conceptions of fixed ideology, Chesterton's novel produces unlikely binaries of the same kind. These come from his favored genre of fable.

Chief among these is the pattern in which the supposed anarchists are in fact disguised authorities. With or without Chesterton's advocacy as an ideologue, and more significantly without it, his narrative gives the consciousness of its ideological opposite the right to exist, and so opens the verbal surface of the novel to an alternative idiom. In this created zone, the conventions of decadence demonstrate their validity in contemporary history as a language of equal if not greater explanatory power. The textual politics of this novel generate a force field of reorganized authority, of trivialized legitimacy, or, indeed, of legitimized triviality. Here political history submits to a new rule of reality as fundamentally strange and, as such, a place where the formerly alien and forbidden may assume a local habitation, a name. "Involuntary modernism": even if this term appears to be bound by its own impossible combination, its wit invokes the immense and seemingly irresistible pressure of the new reality that the conventions of decadence are encoding, which other authors are acknowledging self-consciously as the material of their early modernism.

The decadence Chesterton will be demonstrating in this novel is framed as its chief concern in a prefatory, dedicatory poem to Edmund Bentley. Here, ahead of fictional time, Chesterton draws the lines of moral order firmly, putting himself at declamatory odds with the cultivation of "decay" as he recalls the early moments of the fin-de-siècle world in which he and Bentley grew up:

> A cloud was on the mind of men
>> And wailing went the weather,
> Yea, a sick cloud upon the soul
>> When we were boys together.
> Science announced nonentity
>> And art admired decay;
> The world was old and ended:
>> But you and I were gay . . . .
> This is a tale of those old fears,
>> Even of those emptied hells,
> And none but you shall understand
>> The true thing that it tells – . . .

"And I may safely write it now, / And you may safely read," goes the closing motion in the poem that ends with the promise of a necessary corrective to decadence in the novel that follows.[22]

Given the intensity of conviction in this framing piece, at least some of the decadence being demonstrated in the novel will be remonstrated with – and usually in the form of a moralized binary. In its first chapter, for instance, "The Two Poets of Saffron Park," Chesterton opposes the persons of Lucian Gregory and Gabriel Syme as the angels of good and bad poetry in a political psychomachia of his own. These two poets demonstrate respectively the conventions of decadence as anarchism and the consensus of tradition as order: the first "serves up the old cant of the lawlessness of art and the art of lawlessness" and the other serves as "a poet of law, a poet of order ... a poet of respectability." And where Lucien combines in his profile the outline of "a pre-Raphaelite picture" and the "dark red hair" that recalls the burning menace that caricaturists such as Max Beerbohm fixed as the blazon of Swinburne's famous locks (*MWT*, 8–10), this representative of decadence is identified readily with its political extension in anarchism. Thus Lucian joins his fellow travelers in "The Anarchists' Council of Days," where the decadent temper of anarchism is depicted vividly in the presiding figure. He is "a very old man," this

> Professor de Worms, who still kept the chair of Friday, though every day it was expected that his death would leave it empty. Save for his intellect, he was in the last dissolution of senile decay. His face was grey as his long grey beard, his forehead was listed and fixed finally in a furrow of mild despair .... For the red flower in his buttonhole showed up against a face that was literally discoloured like lead; the whole hideous effect was as if some drunken dandies had put their clothes upon a corpse. (*MWT*, 57–58)

Where the totem animal of decay provides the name for this figure of decadence, Chesterton dresses this "de Worms" as one of its "dandies," but in a way that shows the morbidity of the sensibility as the subject of his moralized cartoon.

The principle of binary construction in the fabulous narrative begins to break down soon enough, however. The authorized agent of London law impersonates the agent provocateur of London anarchism, or, as it is the intention of narrative suspense if not authorial ideology to suggest, the opposite. These patterns of mutable opposition afford the recognition that decadence, like anarchism, is a quality that exists fundamentally in a condition of interdependent relation. If it needs its opposite to exist, so, in the wit or Witz of Chesterton's fable, its opposite needs it in order to exist itself. Under the glass shield of fantasy fiction, which is also a magnifying lens on historical reality in the contemporary imaginative understanding, Chesterton is admitting the otherwise inadmissible figures and ethics of decadence as a power equal to conventional law. The space he gives it appears in representative instance in this picture of a London sky at sunset. The declining time of day is the favored moment of decadence. Its ideological opponent should be lowering the atmospheric and imaginative pressure and not, as here, poetically heightening it:

> Over the whole landscape lay a luminous and unnatural discoloration, as of that disastrous twilight which Milton spoke of as shed by the sun in eclipse; so that Syme fell easily into his first thought, that he was actually on some other and emptier planet, which circled round some sadder star. But the more he felt this glittering desolation in the moonlit land, the more his own chivalric folly glowed in the night like a great fire . . . . The swordstick and the brandy-flask, though in themselves only the tools of morbid conspirators, became the expressions of his own more healthy romance. (*MWT*, 48)

Master of the crafty paradox, Chesterton deploys some "witty" antitheses to serve the purpose of his ideological opposition to the decadence emanating through this depiction, but the stronger force of a Freudian *Witz* is organizing a demonstration of decadence that gives it an equal if not greater status. The entropic process is scaled to a cosmic order of magnitude. Even as the dying light of the earth's sun is displaced in the comparative of "some sadder star," it is registered in the profounder power of its affective pathos. And the poetry of "desolation" that this perception generates is "glittering" with the incandescence of that other light, "a luminous and unnatural discoloration" in the juridical idiom of the ideologue but a "twilight" whose "disastrous" aspect glows with the power of a sublimity at least as strong as the force of this countermanding crusader. This "chivalric" character cannot avoid the "folly" of his own foolish company, just as the "tools of morbid conspirators" are made to work as the "expressions of his own more healthy romance," where the comparative degree of the value adjective carries the burden of an ideological will that has been met if not mastered otherwise in the passage by its opposite. The costume changes are of course the prop structure and mechanism of the fabulous adventure narrative, but the resistance that the Tory authority is offering as a forceful antithesis to the decadent temper is breaking down. It is coming undone under the power of a structure of representation whose organizational binary accords equal imaginative status to decadence. If this equity provides advantage to neither side in any objectively calculable fashion, it shows its greater import and consequence in the allowance it extends to the previously disapproved character.

This process is not just a function of some mechanical law within the grammar of ideas or the syntax of language: it is registering the pressure of a very heavy presence in the political history and historical imaginary of turn-of-the-century Britain specifically. This is the pressure of an end-of-empire-days feeling. Chesterton registers this presentiment in the codes of a spatial imaginary, in this visionary characterization of Syme's reaction to the Anarchist Council of Days:

> The sense of an unnatural symbolism settled back on him again. Each figure seemed to be, somehow, on the borderland of things, just as their theory was on the borderland of thought. He knew that each one of these men stood at the extreme end, so to speak, of some wild road of reasoning. He could only fancy, as in some old-world fable, that if a man went westward to the end of the world he would find something – say a tree – that was more or less than a tree, a tree possessed by a spirit; and that if he went east to the end of the world he would find something else that was now wholly itself – a tower, perhaps, of which the very shape was wicked. So these figures seemed to stand up, violent, and unaccountable against an ultimate horizon, visions from the verge. The ends of the earth were closing in. (*MWT*, 59)

Fredric Jameson has written on the effects of colonialism in the modern imperial metropolis, where the displacement of the main source of economic activity from the First to the Third World eventuates in a kind of ramifying absence in the imaginative apprehensions of urban modernity.[23] Chesterton is registering this condition in figures drawn from the lexicon of literary decadence, that is, in images depicting the critical state of empire. This final sentence images the shrinking dominion of imperial space. The failing command of distant places in the empire is apprehended in a presentiment of collapsed distances, warped proportions, erratic rationality (drawing on the etymon of *ratio*, scale or proportion), as here of "reason" on its "wild road." The prospect records a loss of the forming, ordering, and portioning authority of an imperial episteme, of British reasonableness supremely, as the means and scheme of mapping the world.

This is the pressure of an historical eventuality, which is registered also in the collapse of the moralized binaries otherwise asserted as the working force in the novel. Thus, while the negative prefix in "*un*natural" invokes a structure of binary opposition, which is intended to express a moral preference for the negated quality, this word serves instead as the tuning fork for a poetry of antithetical power. It sounds unmistakably through this passage in its depiction of the unnatural, the odd, the extreme. Its specific work shows most notably where this "wild road of reasoning" leads to the twin extremes of eastern and western "ends of the world." While an ideologue would use a binary of moral opposition to express a preference and not an equivalent distinction, the intellectual structure of that duality has lost its substance in this prospect. The "wicked" shape of the object on one side invokes a moral antithesis, but this judgment suffers the reduction of its admittedly conjectural existence – "perhaps" – and, besides, it is not borne out by any obvious quality of its opposite and complement on the other end. The wit of an ideological antithesis turns thus to the *Witz* of a poetic complexity.

Similarly, in Chesterton's representation of this extremity of London space:

> This particular evening, if it is remembered for nothing else, will be remembered in that place for its strange sunset. It looked like the end of the world. All the heaven seemed covered with a vivid and quite palpable plumage ... towards the west the whole grew past description, transparent and passionate, and the last red-hot plumes of it covered up the sun like something too good to be seen. The whole was so close about the earth as to express nothing but a violent secrecy. The very empyrean seemed to be a secret. It expressed that splendid smallness which is the soul of local patriotism. The very sky seemed small. (*MWT*, 9)

As a metonym for the imperial domain that its capital city centers, the London sky registers the pressure on the normative ideals of empire, here in equally spatial and temporal dimensions. Obviously apocalyptic in quality, this prospect represents a rushing ahead of the sense of destiny that has attended the extension of the imperial will into the world, which has turned back upon itself in the predominant feeling of spatial compression. This extremity of empire days, whether it is the establishing circumstance or expressive metric for the end feeling that is conventional to decadence, prompts a language as luridly heightened as any in the lexicon of poetic decadence.

Not that the ideological wars are called off. In the two concluding sentences, for example, the authorial will redeems the diminished space of the British Empire with that compensatory, vigorously insistent claim of the smaller, English, nation. What makes the verbal surface of the novel the accurate register of the realities of political history is the record of the struggle of ideologies that it reflects – with a complication that comprises and exceeds the unitary will of single ideology and belies the intention of any ideologue. This discrepancy measures the greater pressure of the new temporal imaginary of decadence, which, contested as it is, registers the power of the novelty of the consciousness it constitutes. Where this recognition constitutes the self-conscious novelty of modernism, its force and import may be shown all the more clearly where it comes to Chesterton inversely, involuntarily.

These tensions are resolved all too voluntarily in the finale to the novel. Here, as dawn breaks, Gabriel "saw the sister of Gregory, the girl with the gold-red hair, cutting lilacs before breakfast, with the great unconscious gravity of a girl" (MWT, 182). It is now revealed that the "nightmare" of the novel's subtitle is the occasion of its fiction. The erstwhile friendship of Gabriel and Lucian has been recovered; the contest of anarchism and order has passed with the other unrealities of the previous night. In this will to traditional order in the story, there is an ideology of plot, whereas, to the side of the mainstream account, a poetry of history speaks in a series of expansive asides. This is the poetry of a time out of conventional time. This sense of time is instinct with the feeling of an exceptional Present. It is the crisis and opportunity of modernism, and if Chesterton needs as it were to be backed into this vantage from his contrary position, the strain of that motion also shows something of the novel force of this new imaginative understanding.

The pressure of this imaginative apprehension cannot be assigned to or resolved into a politics as specific as anarchism. The major import of this recognition lies in its otherwise unresolved quality: it represents a menace that is, variously, quickened with and resisted. In all respects, as the shifting indicators of resistance and complicity indicate in Chesterton's fiction, it remains more powerful than the will to control its disturbance.

What is the economy of political ideology within which decadence exerts these disturbing effects? The literature of historical record that we are considering in this chapter provides the context and rationale for setting this question. To respond, it is necessary to turn from the representations of novelistic imagination to the writings of explicit politics. In this frame of reference, the word "decadence" may recover its power as a counter of profoundest disruption.

3.   The Political Chronicles of "Decadence"

Two books, published in the successive years of 1908 and 1909, may sample the work of the word "decadence" in the discourses of British political culture at this time. They are taken from opposing sides of the conventional political spectrum. Tory and Liberal interests alike present their antipathy to the references and implications of this fraught word. In the comprehensive opposition that "decadence" generates, a broad consensus center of resistance provides the most indicative measure of the present threat. In the public debate that "decadence" spurs, moreover, the censure being levied on the word helps indeed to sharpen its attraction. This is a fascination of the forbidden. And this is the context within which the particularly modernist novelty of decadence will assume the significance of its resistant shape.

From the conservative side of the political divide, the work of record is Arthur Balfour's *Decadence*, delivered on 25 January 1908 as the Henry Sidgwick Memorial Lecture at Newnham College, Cambridge, and published later that year at the university press. This is a full-dress event in print no less than in vive. Balfour, now the grey eminence of the Tory party (Chief Secretary for Ireland from 1887 to 1891, Prime Minister from 1902–1905), offers a view that has been taken from on high (if more than slightly to the right) on British life, looking retrospectively now across the chronological span of his political career. This is the period in which "decadence" will have emerged as the troubling word it still is. He looks prospectively, too, charting the relevance to the future of its expected references. For a political speaker as seasoned as Balfour, the instability the talk witnesses in relation to its title word is remarkable. In diagrammatic outline, this lecture follows a sort of parabolic curve, beginning and finishing with a resistance to the necessity of "decadence" as a descriptor for current conditions but succumbing in the middle to the powers and indeed the poetry of a counter whose relevance he is otherwise bound to challenge.

"My subject," the talk opens, "is Decadence," where the capitalized form of the noun sizes the referent to a dimensionality he sets out immediately in the second sentence to restrict, lowering the case of this "decadence" to its recognizably lesser representatives:

> I do not mean the sort of decadence often attributed to certain phases of artistic or literary development, in which an overwrought technique, straining to express sentiments too subtle or too morbid, is deemed to have supplanted the direct inspiration of an earlier and a simpler age. Whether these autumnal glories, these splendours touched with death, are recurring phenomena in the literary cycle: whether, if they be, they are connected with other forms of decadence, may be questions well worth asking and answering. But they are not the questions with which I am at present concerned. The decadence respecting which I wish to put questions is not literary or artistic, it is political and national. It is the decadence which attacks, or is alleged to attack, great communities and historic civilisations: which is to societies of men what senility is to man, and is often, like senility, the precursor and cause of final dissolution.[24]

Predictably, Balfour denigrates the poetics of decadence as he applies these judgmental adjectives to the now stereotypical traits of "overwrought technique" and "sentiments too subtle or too morbid." His representation of that morbidity is tinged nonetheless with no small portion of the "inspiration" he would otherwise deny his subject. He presents that sensibility with an inspired poetry of his own polysyllabic Latinity and English assonance: "these autumnal glories, these splendours touched with death . . . ." If he begins this talk with a predictable resistance, he already seems to be reciprocating with his expected enemy. This kind of resisted complicity will dominate the middle portions of the talk, which speaks against itself in strikingly particular ways.

As is evident from the overture, the effort to negate the reality of decadence as the destined end of British history goes to the truth of the biological cycle as a model for political and national life. This is the model he questions rhetorically and emphatically: "But why *should* civilisations wear out and great communities decay? and what evidence is there that in fact they do?" (*D*, 8). He then rejects this model in considering the fall of empires, the Spanish first of all: "There are misfortunes which in the sphere of sociology correspond to accident or disease in the sphere of biology" (*D*, 12). This "accident or disease" scheme is meant to intervene in the explanatory paradigm of the life cycle, where a once waxing and now waning imperial domain lives out its biological destiny. Subsequently, however, as he considers the long fall of the Roman Empire, his earlier words question themselves as an answer to the issues that "decadence" centers: "we are ignorant of the inner character of the cell changes which produce senescence. But should we be better fitted to form a correct conception of the life-history of complex organisms if we refused to recognise any cause of death but accident or disease?" (*D*, 32). More than rhetorical, this question reverses the current of his earlier objection as he reverses the sense of its signal words, so indicating the power of an imaginative understanding that is stronger than his will to resist it.

This instability around "decadence" and its attendant references increases measurably through the middle passages of the talk, especially when Balfour attempts (again) to discount the connection between the declining fortunes of the Roman Empire and the gathering gloom of a gradual, apparently natural process of decay: "Nor yet can we find an explanation of [the social decline] in the discouragement, the sense of impending doom, by which men's spirits were oppressed long before the Imperial power began to wane" (*D*, 24). The keyword is "discouragement." It recurs moments later with a striking reversal of contextual sense, which includes his openness now to "decadence" as a descriptor for an apparently natural and inevitable process of decay:

> And when through an ancient and still powerful state there spreads a mood of deep discouragement, when the reaction against recurring ills grows feebler, and the ship rises less buoyantly to each succeeding wave, when learning languishes, enterprise slackens, and vigour ebbs away, then, as I think, there is present some process of social degeneration, which we must perforce recognise, and which, pending a satisfactory analysis, may conveniently be distinguished by the name of "decadence." (*D*, 33–34)

Totalizing the scope of decline in late Rome, he uses "discouragement" as keynote and keyword for this whole symphony of concerted falls. He is taking the process of organic dissolution as tenor for the metaphors of the "decadence" he now also claims as a word and declaims indeed as a poetry of his own, which, like Chesterton's, is the more powerful poetry of the opponent, which he expresses through a poetic anaphora of palpable power. And could the poetry of the "decadence" Balfour intones really be written off to the utility "conveniently" invokes for his appropriation of the word? He is resisting its validity by belittling it even – or especially – when he is caught up most demonstrably in its evocative powers. This inconsistency witnesses a conflict between permissible ideas and impermissible words, a conflict that registers the darker power of the forbidden idiom.

This contradiction is all the more indicative insofar as it is framed by a high degree of self-awareness, on Balfour's part, about the character of political language. Just ahead of the last passage, in fact, he engages in a critique of official political lingo; he indicts that language specifically for the way it papers over the emergent recognition of an empire in decline. "The facile generalisations with which we so often season the study of dry historic fact; the habits of political discussion which induce us to catalogue for purposes of debate the outward signs that distinguish (as we are prone to think) the standing from the falling state, hide the obscurer, but more potent, forces which silently prepare the fate of empires" (*D*, 33). This hidden condition of decay (recalling the "secret work of the instinct of decadence" that Nietzsche so memorably phrased), which is a biological "fate" as "silent" as the verbiage of official record, may be understood as the truth that flows forth as an untrammeled power in the poetry of the subsequent sentences. How striking, then, as the parabola of the lecture swings upward (if that is the direction) and the political will of the career politician reasserts itself, to find the language of the talk turning a deaf ear to the eloquent cautions he has just expressed. This language is the blah blah of the policy wonk. It speaks the verbal absurdity of a mind taken over by the sheerest abstractions of schematic language:

> The flexible element in any society, that which is susceptible of progress or decadence, must therefore be looked for rather in the physical and psychical conditions affecting the life of its component units, than in their inherited constitution. This last rather supplies a limit to variations than an element which does itself vary .... But though the advance of each community is thus limited by its inherited aptitudes, I do not suppose that those limits have ever been reached by its unaided efforts. In the cases where a forward movement has died away, the pause must in part be due to arrested development in the variable, not to a fixed resistance in the unchanging factor of national character ... (*D*, 46–47)

Searching for an alternative to the "fate" of the "decadence" he has spoken in the earlier poetry, the official optimist returns to his designated senses (if that is the word). He seizes upon the saving "variable," that magic abstraction, which would make the equations of "progress" work in a model of society as highly abstracted as it is linguistically laughable. The involuntary comedy of this usage may stand as a grimly risible testament to the power of a conventional ideology to dominate the public culture of language. The stronger point, to be taken from the whole performance of the lecture, is the antithetical power which prohibition exerts, creating the contrary force and poetic import of the counter it outlaws; of "decadence."

The record of censure on "this dreadful word"[25] continues – with a variation that demonstrates the extent of suppression – in a book that comes from a public intellectual on the Liberal side in the next year (1909): C. F. G. Masterman's *The Condition of England*. Where Balfour worried most about the loss of imperial dominance, Masterman is troubled mainly by the deteriorating "condition" of English social life. As with Balfour, however, there is a fundamental struggle in the book to enunciate the causes of this condition. Does it come from "forces without" or "forces within"? One of the most vivid figures in the book – "seeds of futility and decay" – suggests that decline is indeed the growing point of the English condition, which is running down just as a function of its own life cycle.[26] More important as a question than an answer, however, a struggle for understanding in this book focuses most notably on one word, which, in his account of the English condition, is the word scanted: "decadence."

The virtual absence of this word is more remarkable in view of the fact that its cognate "decay" saturates the verbal fabric of this book. Out of those "seeds" of "decay" there grows "so tragic a decay" in British social life; "a kind of internal collapse and decay" is witnessed within the political infrastructure of the country, leaving behind "every day's record of that long autumn of decay" (*TCE*, 29, 62, 46). Then there is this mournful litany of decay in just one chapter, "The Countryside" (chapter VI), where the referent of the title word is seen

> ... everywhere hastening to decay. (*TCE*, 190)
> The houses tumbling into decay, no new houses built, apathy settling down like a grey cloud over all ... (192)
> Village after village, in which no new cottages have been built for a hundred years; crumbling walls, falling into decay ... (193)
> [There was] a richness and variety almost incredible to those who to-day see but the last guttering flame of parochial life, the attempt by parish councils, guilds of village players, and all the enterprise of occasional vigorous resistance, to combat the spreading atrophy of decay. (200)
> Here the estates are encumbered or falling into decay. (203)
> Over all which vision of a secular decay Nature still flings the splendour of her dawns and sunsets upon a land of radiant beauty. (208)

The expressive power in these passages, where "decay" is augmented in its descriptive force by a virtual thesaurus of available synonyms, suggests a level of linguistic self-consciousness that makes the omission of "decadence" all the more striking and significant.

In the then current *OED* entry for "decadence," there is this primary meaning: "I. the process of falling away or declining from a prior state of excellence, vitality, prosperity etc; decay; impaired or deteriorated condition." Not much different, it would seem, from "decay": "I. the process of falling off from a prosperous or thriving condition; progressive decline; the condition of one who has thus fallen off or declined." A change in connotation comes with the suffix "ence," however, an addition that also brings with it a difference of referential sense. As this same *OED* notes, "ence" forms abstract substantives, usually of quality, rarely of action, but its examples also show how often "ence" turns verbs of action into words of quality – no more strikingly than when "decay" becomes "decadence," that is, when the action of decaying, which is understood as a concrete phenomenon in a local and specific instance, leads to a "decadence" that is the consequence of that action and the quality of a far more comprehensive "condition." In managing the content of that title word, Masterman is obviously choosing to keep the decaying of the state local, keep it specific. For him, the process of decay is still underway and so is probably not irreversible to Liberal intervention. Decay may be as vivid and particular as it is to the presentiments of his social conscience, but he will not admit it as the finished condition and qualitative state which "decadence" suggests.

His aversion to "decadence" as the term for the social condition of England opens as an absence, too, in his account of a contemporary decadence in English literary culture.

> The change is becoming manifest as comfort increases and wealth accumulates, which has been manifest in all similar transformations. Literature loses its ardour and its inspiration. It becomes critical rather than invigorating: sceptical, questioning, sometimes with an appearance of frivolity, sometimes torturing itself with angers and despairs. The note to-day is that of a time of disenchantment ... a conviction that the zest and sparkle has gone from a society which suddenly feels itself growing old. (*TCE*, 230)

"Decadence" is the one word missing in this record of a sensibility already clearly identified with it in England by 1909 – its attitudes and mannerisms are as clearly established as this catalogue of disreputable traits is apparently ready-made. That word has been often deployed in the summary judgments Masterman is recycling in the practices he inventories here, and their targets have also taken the term of attack as the badge of their own defiant value. Predictably, but tellingly, "decadence" surfaces in his account in reference to a "decadent French play" (*TCE*, 45), where the condition is placed at that alien distance, and only twice more (150, 232), each time in distancing quotations. As the word estranged in his story of "the condition of England," "decadence" demonstrates again its power as a counter for the unspeakable, centering a range of omissions as irrepressibly evident as they are interesting and indeed compelling in being forbidden.

From their respectively conservative and liberal vantages, the accounts of Balfour and Masterman may take exception to each other even as they provide a unified view on the state of the public language in England. This is an economy in which "decadence" centers a range of evocations as powerful as they are unwanted. Unspoken, or spoken against itself in a poetry as unanticipated and uninvited as it is significant, the word "decadence" serves as a tuning fork for a poetics that registers the pressure of the previously impermissible and unsaid on the language of available record. "Decadence" opens thus into a zone of novelty as important as the defining qualities of a modernism whose special self-consciousness about this novelty is demonstrable, too, in the friction exhibited around it.

4.   D. H. Lawrence

The special poetic powers which "decadence" exhibits in the public record of political England turn us back to the critical heuristic of poetry and plot that we followed in Chesterton's novel. This formula provides a way of understanding the imaginative and ideological work in several more novels of major record of this time. Here the contrary provocations of decadence are negotiated in relation to the conventional forms of narrative fiction. To a Progress mythology and its imaginative analogue in the progressiveness of novelistic plot, the sense of an ending already realized in the temporal sensibility of aftermath presents a manifest challenge. The poetic aside abides thus in a kind of time-out-of-narrative time. It pronounces an alternative temporality in a tempo of exception, which registers a sense of modernity lost now as a living current. It speaks a poetry of antithetical power to the ideological will of the conventional story, which requires it thus to be sidelined from the progressive destination. This critical heuristic opens up an understanding of the struggle to enunciate an awareness whose self-conscious novelty is evidenced in the exceptional present, the modernist moment, of its poetic intervention in a normative order of plot time.

These tensions are brought to an exemplary demonstration in D. H. Lawrence's *Women in Love*, which represents a defining extension of the methods and patterns evident in the novels of an earlier modernism. The contributing conditions of this sensibility have been brought to critical mass in the historical circumstance of the novel's composition. Although not published until 1920, it was written and finished in the first half of 1916, that is, in the dead middle of the Great War. This already long moment of the national ordeal is evident in no explicit reference to the war but elsewhere and everywhere in an historical pessimism, a temperament Lawrence grounds in those conventions of decadence he is demonstrating so extensively. He puts it categorically and emphatically in a letter of November 1915, responding to the suppression of *The Rainbow* (1915) in particular but evoking the circumstance of the Great War in general: "I think there is no future for England: only a decline and fall. This is the dreadful and unbearable part of it: to have been born into a decadent era, a decline of life, a collapsing civilisation."[27]

In the more textured representation of this apprehension of "a decadent era" in literary form, Lawrence generates a poetry of history that operates in a special tension with the plot of his story, which involves a version of romantic comedy that is as complex as Lawrence's notions of heterosexual love. This story moves, if not to the marriage conclusion of generic convention, at least toward the perfection of Lawrence's own version of a normative union. In this wise, he refashions the pattern manifest in Chesterton's novel, since the comic resolution is more complicated now. The "decadence" so evident in contemporary history, in wartime, is too substantial to be so manipulated by imaginative fiction, and, in this augmented condition, provides a newly powerful resistance to any traditional will toward a former order. Those plot motives are blocked, the perfection of the heterosexual relationship is stalled. The friction of resistance to this comic plot comes as it were from the sidelines of the story, where it is voiced as the poetry of history in the poetics of decadence, which echoes and augments the demonstration of decadence in the historical fiction.

This demonstration of decadence also provides a parable of the circumstances of a developing modernism. The self-conscious novelty of modernity, which is the establishing awareness of modernism, comes with the blunt-force trauma of this unprecedented, this conspicuously modern, war. So intense is its impact, as I have suggested, it is deflected and diffused through the tonal atmospherics of the book. It is the novelty of this horror that this book marks as its chief point of difference to its erstwhile companion volume, *The Rainbow*, from which Lawrence detached the material of *Women in Love* early in 1915 for an autonomous work.[28] This separation indexes formally some of the difference the war made. It involves a novelty of awareness so awful in its historical as well as imaginative circumstance that it establishes its own literary reality.

This is the condition for which the book may be read, in every sense of a complex phrase, as an apology for modernism. Like its early contemporaries, it is a modernism that is constituted by the sense of its special present. This condition has been raised to the climactic state of an utterly unprecedented war. Its daily atrocities (spelled out in the casualty lists of the London *Times*) constitute the awful novelty of its every day and, as an apocalypse of modern technology especially, also provide the final but daily disproof of the Progress mythology of the modern. This is the special day of a modernism to which Lawrence responds with an apology that forgives little, or nothing, insofar as it is constituted by those conventions of decadence that are new, too, in the intensity and extensiveness of the deathliness they reflect. This is the extreme context in which the decadence he is demonstrating prompts a sort of appalled fascination, where the novelist is drawn most powerfully to the novelty that he also, with equal intensity, deplores and resents.

There is, to begin with, the force field centered in Hermione Roddice. This is the figure with whom the artist Rupert Birkin, Lawrence's sometime double in the novel, is fixed in a contested but long-unshakeable liaison. The relationship bespeaks Lawrence's fixated interest in the deadly novelty she represents. Modeled on Ottoline Morrell, patron and convener at Garsington Manor of some of the most "advanced" painters and writers of the day (including T. S. Eliot and Virginia Woolf, Lytton Strachey and Bertrand Russell), Hermione is depicted by Birkin as "more decadent than the most hide-bound intellectualism" (*WIL*, 40). This "intellectualism" situates the "decadent" temper of Hermione on the advanced-guard end of the contemporary cultural identity spectrum. Accordingly, Hermione exemplifies this decadence as a demonstrative novelty, which is identifiable in every evident way with the self-conscious novelty of modernism. This is the compound Lawrence depicts reiteratively in the figure of the fashionable cadaver. As in this next passage, where he dresses "decadence" on her person in the color that *The Yellow Book* had raised as the blazon of decadence and the hue of extreme chic, though, as one would expect, here overlabored. Hermione

> came along, with her head held up, balancing an enormous flat hat of pale yellow velvet, on which were streaks of ostrich feathers ... She wore a dress of silky, frail velvet, of pale yellow colour ... she drifted along with a peculiar fixity of the hips ... She was impressive, in her lovely pale-yellow and brownish-rose, yet macabre, something repulsive .... Her long, pale face, that she carried lifted up, somewhat in the Rossetti fashion, seemed almost drugged ... she was a woman of the new school, full of intellectuality, and heavy, nerve-worn with consciousness. She was passionately interested in reform ... (*WIL*, 13–14)

Combining the reference to the Pre-Raphaelite Rossetti with a "woman of the new school," Lawrence is projecting a character who compounds a figure of the New Woman, who is intent on the "reform" of women's social and marital roles and so exemplifies the temper of some of the major movements of social modernization, with one of the chief antecedents of "decadence" in cultural as well as literary history. Here then is the femme fatale of European *décadence*, turned toward the work of progressive modernity. Whether or not these efforts represent one of the offshoots of the change in consciousness that decadence also embodies, as subsequent commentators such as Gillian Beer would argue for the women in Hardy's world, none of these possibilities is going to be realized as social consequence in Lawrence's fiction. The modernizing impulse is subordinated always in Lawrence's representations to its place in the double structure of a particularly modernist decadence. For the self-conscious novelty Hermione embodies, variously in costume and politics, is inseparable from the decay he fixes in her person and intensifies in the aspects of fashion as well as physiology.

The conception of Hermione as a figure is compounded of the same stuff as a modernism constituted by the conditions of decadence in earlier novels, but this book provides an instance of that idea at a revealing extreme. For Lawrence's response to this concept is informed and intensified by the extremity of the current historical circumstance he is depicting through her. His antagonism to the "new woman" represents a displacement of apprehensions enjoined on him by the current war. As Sandra Gilbert and Susan Gubar have pointed out so thoroughly, the war economy reversed former roles of women and men in making the males the passive sufferers on the front and the females the industrious agents of work at home.[29] More than an expected resentment, however, is reflected in Lawrence's representations of Hermione. The novelty of the horror of technological apocalypse is traveling into the grimly thrilling aspect of this female character. Here the conventions of decadence are reflecting a decay that has been raised to an order of magnitude that the page-after-page display of the names of the war dead on the London *Times* was daily registering – even, in the sort of diptych one could see so often on these pages, in close juxtaposition to the images of the most contemporary fashion. Hermione is a reflection in extremis of the historical imaginary of decadence as modernism. As a historically constituted figure, she realizes that conceit of "morbid modernity" which James's turn-of-the-century phrase had echoed ahead of this time so presciently.

Hermione's character also represents a sensibility adversely disposed to the proposed interest of the plot of the novel – the perfection of the union of Rupert and Ursula. She is thus sidelined from the working out of the plot ideology. Even as the interest of this romantic story is privileged consistently in the manipulation of readers' sympathies, however, its advance in the narrative is challenged from the margins, as in Chesterton's novel, by a poetry of history and a poetics of decadence.

The division between the romantic plot of the story and the decadent poetry of history is working most clearly in the relationship between Ursula and Rupert. The conflict is hypostatized as erotic tension, sublimated as romantic attraction. Expressing belief in the purest form of Lawrence's sexual mythology, Ursula provides a binary complement for the dramatizing of ideas. She represents the interests of the normative order of romantic comedy, which, in the dramatic fiction of their exchange, serves as the spur to stimulate the resistance that Rupert voices into the story as the poetry of history, in the poetics of decadence, which, in consummate effect, owns the deeper truth of a reality borne into the story by the circumstances of the current war.

In this sequence, then, Ursula defends the presumptions of the highest kind of natural romance and so resists the conditions of decadence, which Rupert intensifies in a demonstrably poetic response:

"We always consider the silver river of life, rolling on and quickening all the world to a brightness, on and on to heaven, flowing into a bright eternal sea, a heaven of angels thronging. – But the other is our real reality –"

"But what other? I don't see any other," said Ursula.

"It is your reality, nevertheless," he said, "the dark river of dissolution. – You see it rolls in us just as the other rolls – the black river of corruption. And our flowers are of this – our sea-born Aphrodite, all our white phosphorescent flowers of sensuous perfection, all our reality, nowadays."

"You mean that Aphrodite is really deathly?" asked Ursula.

"I mean she is the flowering mystery of the death-process, yes," he replied . . . .

"And you and me –?" she asked.

"Probably," he replied. "In part, certainly. Whether we are that, in toto, I don't yet know."

"You mean we are flowers of dissolution – *fleurs du mal?* – I don't feel as if I were," she protested.

He was silent for a time. (*WIL*, 177)

The passage reveals a knowledge of the poetry of decadence on the part of its author that is both obvious and recondite: the reference to Baudelaire's *Fleurs du Mal* by name should not obscure Rupert's more knowing allusion to the "phosphorescent" glow that is the most favored shade for that premier poet of *décadence*. And while Rupert admits to not knowing if the condition of decadence that he is poeticizing represents an existence "in toto," it is worth noting the especially heavy pressure that the sensibility of decadence is exerting on the work of its poetry here.

This is the chapter (XIV, "Water-Party") in which two young people, following an annual party that Rupert and Ursula are also attending, die by drowning in the lake of the girl's familial estate. Ruined youth, as the signature image of Nineties decadence, has registered the sense of a century then ending most intensely where it touched the young. This imaginative concept has been transferred en masse from the more exquisite and specialized conceit of the young artists of Nineties decadence to the circumstance of this modern mass war, whose dead included an especially high census of youth, and whose heavy presence in the imaginary of contemporary history Lawrence is refracting throughout his novel. Dying young is a narrative of counter-natural aspect that also carries the inverted values of decadence most ostensibly and, in this passage, locates the apparent point of tension with the sensibility Lawrence locates in Ursula. It carries the most powerful impact of difference to the naturalistic myths that the references to Aphrodite otherwise suggest – Ursula seems ready to defend the goddess of natural love against this unnatural, this unexpected, deathliness. If, in the imagery of the "flowering mystery of the death-process," Rupert seems to be recuperating a naturalistic understanding of human mortality, his language is otherwise heightened in a way that measures its very contemporary reference and valence: it evokes the whole phenomenon, the process as well as the end and aim, of the Freudian death drive – a concept powerfully reinforced in the context of the same war which Lawrence is refracting so expansively through this book.

In Lawrence's novel, this poetry of history is sidelined by the plot of a story that turns its interest away from the decadence of contemporary England and toward a continental setting that works as a pastoral alternative. This is an alpine retreat which, in a composition of symbolic space, offers aloft a potential refuge from the lower turmoil of the otherwise unnamed Great War (the same composition of symbolic space appears in Hemingway's later war novel, *A Farewell to Arms*). Lawrence registers some of the heavier pressure being exerted by the conditions and sensibility of decadence in the counter-pressure he applies to it. In a compensatory and evidently self-defensive gesture, he impacts its poetics in parody. The *disjecta membra* of its literary conventions strew the path of ascent to the Alps. Turning the poetics of decadence into the zoology of degeneration is one of the favored tactics in projects of this kind, and Lawrence follows that familiar plan at the first turn of the climb, in the town that outfits his characters for the ascent. He populates the Pompadour Café with a "menagerie of apish degraded souls" (*WIL*, 396); in this topos of degeneration, the poetics of decadence is performed at its original, or aboriginal, worst. One of the habitués of this café thus offers his demeaning version of Rupert's earlier apologia for the poetics of decadence – "We're all flowers of mud – *Fleurs* – hic! *du mal*! – It's perfectly wonderful, Birkin harrowing Hell – harrowing the Pompadour – *Hic!*" (*WIL*, 400). The indignity to which the poet laureate of *décadence* is submitted here includes the antic excitement with which the French poet's favored shade is presented:

> "Do let me go on! Oh, this is a perfectly wonderful piece! But do listen to this. 'And in the great retrogression, the reducing back of the created body of life, we get knowledge, and beyond knowledge, the *phosphorescent* ecstasy of acute sensation.'" (*WIL*, 399)

The ridicule in Lawrence's remonstrations with decadence mounts to a final focus in the German artist Loerke, whom the English couples meet at the top of their climb in the ski chalet. This is the figure whom David Trotter has accurately characterized as "Lawrence's best shot at a degenerate," one who fulfills "to an almost parodic degree the requirements of stereotype."[30]

Here the symbiotic quality of the relationship between "degeneration" and "decadence" is most obvious, as in Conrad's compounding of the image of the decadent artist Beardsley in the simian lineaments of Stevie's lip and chin: the fear that is evidenced in response to decadence as a regression from progressive norms is taken to a ridiculing extreme in the degenerative type, as, here, in the degenerate artist Loerke. And although Herr Loerke was already one of Lawrence's characters in the draft he was working on when *Women in Love* and *The Rainbow* were one book, that is, before the war, the German identity now provides a timelier side to the negativity he is directing through the caricatures of decadence he is assembling in the closing motions of the book.

Loerke serves the purposes of the novel's discursive work in typifying most lividly the conditions of contemporary history, whose degenerative direction the war is all too strongly reinforcing in the decadent sensibility to which Lawrence otherwise objects. These are the historical circumstances that the plot of the story intends to leave behind, for the sake of the perfection of the union between Rupert and Ursula. This promissory ideal, however, is not realized. Attention is distracted at the end to the complications of the romantic subplot, which follows the wayward intentions of Ursula's sister Gudrun, who runs off with the otherwise despised Loerke and whose former lover, the wealthy industrialist Gerald Crich, dies of despair in the snows. This confusion comes out of a profounder impasse between the intention of the romantic story and the poetry of a circumstantial history, which, despite the plot to demean and disable it, reveals the power of the historical imaginary of the poetics of decadence even – or especially – in this frustration.

This impasse is visualized in the closing paragraphs of the novel in Rupert's double-turning view of the Alps. Upward, the direction of escape is no longer available. Downward, Rupert

> might have gone on, down the steep, steep fall of the south-side, down into the dark valley with its pines, on to the great Imperial road leading south to Italy.
>
> He might! And what then? The Imperial road! The south? Italy? What then? Was it a way out? – It was only a way in again. Birkin stood high in the painful air, looking at the peaks, and the way south. Was it any good going south, to Italy? Down the old, old Imperial road? (*WIL*, 496)

The route "down" follows a road that would lead Rupert back into history – to a history that Lawrence images in the condition of decadence. This relict of the now long-gone Roman Empire, which is seen in an image of the expansion that brought Rome down, presents in the example of a fallen greatness the prime instance of an original and in fact perennial decadence. Its conditions are as present and impending as the obsession Lawrence registers in the reiteration of that iconic phrase, "the Imperial road" – as present indeed as the memory of the poetry of history and the poetics of decadence that have been spoken from the sidelines of the story, whose romantic plot is now stalled.

This is the poetry whose closing notes sound the interment ceremony for Gerald's body, now removed to the lodge. Rupert

> went into the room, and sat down on the bed. Dead, dead and cold!
>
> > "Imperial Caesar dead, and turned to clay
> > Would stop a hole to keep the wind away."
>
> There was no response from that which had been Gerald. (*WIL*, 497)

These verses from the graveyard scene in *Hamlet* (V.1) put Rupert in the position of a Hamlet reflecting on the skull of Yorick. Where the doggerel prosody in the Shakespearean original echoes the forced indifference of Hamlet to the death with which he has been obsessed throughout the play, so too for Rupert, who can be heard to be defending against the homoerotic attachment to Gerald, which has run as a narrative parallel in the novel to the straighter line development of his romantic union with Ursula. Where the queer interest associated with decadence has been sidelined by the plot, it is emerging again at the end in a poetry whose contorted form reflects all of the pressure that the ideology of the romantic plot has brought to bear on the sensibility of decadence. This roughing up of the verbal surface, however, should not obscure the special poignancy of the poetics of decadence in its dying fall. Indeed, the reference to the "*imperial* Caesar" – it is "imperious" in the folio version of the play, and so Lawrence's choice goes to a more explicitly historical frame of reference[31] – transfers the mantle of the figure of the emperor in an original decadence to this industrial baron; across the two historical eras, he is keeping the metric of decadence consistent in the conditions of great things lost. Indeed, Gerald is a figure of the social and economic establishment of a nineteenth-century progressivism now in spiritual and emotional dissolution. This downfall includes the remains of a Fabian socialism, which his father has preserved in the form of a noblesse oblige with his workers, but which Gerald has disclaimed in the interest of a new efficiency; his economic rationalism has proven only as economically successful as it is interpersonally ruthless and personally ruinous. Gerald's family enterprise offers an image in miniature and in particular of a new industrial imperialism that has lost moral authority even as it has gained terrain. These are the conditions of the decadence that has proven more endurable in the poetry of historical despair than the wishes of the plot in the romantic comedy, from which the novel has now so obviously absconded.

The circumstances of the war still going on have brought the demonstrations of decadence in the novels of an early and developing modernism to this state of exemplary tension and revelation. The destructive novelty of an altogether modern war is being received, recycled, and represented in Lawrence's book in the images and sentiments of literary decadence, which provides as it were a dark mirror or negative space of that event's extreme modernity. In his moments of poetic exception, in this otherwise sidelined poetry of decadence, Lawrence is representing the exceptional moment of a modernity against itself and so providing for a more self-conscious relation to the circumstance of modernity. He is writing out the poetics in prose of his own radical modernism.

5. The Middle Parts of Modernism: Manning and West – Wartime

The fiction that deals explicitly with the war reveals a similar difficulty with the force of conventional story. The war challenges the narratives of personal development that go into story and plot. In fact, it attacks the establishing rationales for these narratives, for the stories of progressive development in characters and between characters stand as micro-narratives of the grander progressions of national time in the ideologies of English liberalism. This is the myth that was given the lie to in the war – most profoundly, in the plot of perfectibility in English liberal historiography, which was hardly resounding in triumphant coda in these years. The technology hitherto associated with Progress was coming to its appallingly inverse apocalypse and revelation in the day-by-day mayhem of the several fronts. The stalemated progress of armies, where the technology of each side provided the obstacle to that of the other, represented the failure of that idea in staggering human toll. These are the circumstances which help to explain why the narratives that suborn their representations of the war to some order of consecutive end-driven event, as some continuous fiction of motive and consequence, appear so forced and false. There were a good number of these, in a war where so many things were undone.[32]

Those increasingly untenable fictions of continuous time leave the temporal remnant as the most indicative record of wartime. This is the moment remaindered, the interval left out of the series of sequence and consequence.

In fiction that registers this temporal apprehension most directly, we can find the consciousness of modernism performing its most exemplary, definitive work. Modernism, I am saying, works most indicatively within an imaginative concept of time interrupted – whether this interruption is the end of consecutive and progressive temporality in the finality of last days, as in the representations of James and Conrad, Lawrence and Chesterton, or, as in the fiction representing the temporal imaginary specific to wartime, of historical pause. Stalled, registered with a self-consciousness about the difference this time out of time represents: here is the definitive moment, the signal condition, of modernism. This difference has been demonstrated already in the interventions that the poetry of decadence has entered into the progressive plots of late-nineteenth- and early-twentieth-century fiction. So, the literary history of decadence provides some of the most important writing of the war with an interior history, a literary memory, a resonating form. In this exacting sense, where the war is the manifestly central and generative event of the narrative fiction, there are two great modernist novels of the war. And the representation of the war in each of these reveals a powerful recycling of the sensibility of literary decadence.

Frederic Manning's *The Middle Parts of Fortune*, or *Her Privates We*, shows the situation of the temporal stalemate already in the punning bawdry of its alternative titles. These are drawn from the phrases Rosencrantz and Guildenstern trade off in *Hamlet* to locate themselves in their relevant parts of the goddess Fortuna's body.[33] Life in the middest is the condition of the stalled story of this war; on page after page, Manning offers a ruefully humorous vision of the non-eventuating events of infantryman's time. The story begins *in medias res* and ends *per medias res* (the death of its protagonist marks no conclusion) and continues with remarkable adequacy to the absent eventuality of this experience, to the sheer plod of the chronically indeterminate plot. Instead of any consecutive story, the writer occupies the stopped moment, where he offers a poetry of philosophical content and implication as profoundly moving as the plot itself seems unmoved, even inert. For the following passage, representatively, Manning has taken the chronicle of inconsequence that is the daily story of the war and, as a trained and published philosopher as well as an accomplished poet, converted this state of suspension into the metaphysical void he poeticizes so finely. His human subjects are suspended in a condition he takes over as the moment of philosophical poetry:

> These apparently rude and brutal natures comforted, encouraged, and
> reconciled each other to fate, with a tenderness and tact which was more

moving than anything in life. They had nothing; not even their own bodies, which had become mere implements of warfare. They turned from the wreckage and misery of life to an empty heaven, and from an empty heaven to the silence of their own hearts. They had been brought to the last extremity of hope, and yet they put their hands on each other's shoulders and said with a passionate conviction that it would be all right, though they had faith in nothing, but in themselves and in each other.[34]

The repetition that fades in the poetics of decadence is replicated in this emotional fiction in the call for an answer that is not answered. More concretely, in the language of this passage, the pattern of the fading repetition shows in the lengthened and increasingly fainter echoes of sub-merged rhymes, internal assonances: "rude and brutal," "natures . . . fate," "wreckage . . . empty . . . empty . . . extremity." This is the highly refined register of a vintage poetics of decadence, which poets have been fining down over the long turn of the century into this representation, where, in effect, the poetics of remnant temporality emerges in these personages as the human remains of some former ideal time. Leftovers, moments of exception to the prevalent conceptions of progressive modernity, these figures have no faith in any destiny of time and so bespeak the feeling of the middle parts of history. They exist in the perpetual middest of a story that has lost the sense of its aim and end as well as origin but, just so, in Manning's hands, provided the defining occasion of modernism in a sense of time as acutely self-conscious as its expression here is heightened, stylized, poeticized.

The status Manning enjoyed in the coterie modernism of prewar and postwar London – an elusive personage, this independently wealthy Australian was often regarded as a fellow traveler and companion talent, sometimes in fact as a leading-edge figure – may help to frame the attitudes and practices of his book as an example, even a parable, of modernism in its time.[35] This signature moment of poetic pause, at once the acutest form of temporal self-consciousness in modernism and sharpest instance of Progress Interrupted in decadence, provides the defining occasion of the other great modernist novel of the war, which may be read now as its complement: Rebecca West's *The Return of the Soldier*.

In West's story, a shell-shocked infantry officer returns from the present mid-war years (West wrote it in winter 1916–1917) to the year 1901, which, in his dissociated condition, he has reentered as current reality and is attempting to recover in the form of a romantic relationship from that earlier day. The experience of dissociation or fugue (flight from reality) was extensive among the officer class in the war, as recorded in the exploratory research and experimental therapy of W. H. R. Rivers, who followed a number of cases and catalogued the alternative identities they forged, often out of fantasy, sometimes out of past experiences.[36] This design of psychological time, where the present folds back into the past, provides a version of the suspended temporality in Manning's fiction, but the pause is backward-oriented in West's novel in a way that is historically specific and, accordingly, significant.

It is the last year of Queen Victoria's life and reign that her protagonist takes as his point of return and moment of solace. This was also the first year of the new and, in the promissory calculus of that chronological day, ever more progressive century. The nineteenth-century mythology of historical Progress finds its pivot point in this instant, swinging forward into the year 1916 as its moment of forward proof. The difference this interval of 1901–1916 marks in any conventional reckoning of political time, however, is one of loss and fall. And as the narrative fails to conform to fictions of Progress, it tells the story of a decadence that West builds into a sense of British history, shaping the narrative fiction and back story for her protagonist Chris Baldry.

The dimension of national mythological history in this account appears in the public status of the family estate, Baldry Court. Familiar in this fiction from pictures in popular magazines, it establishes its picturesque perspective on Albion's green and pleasant land. This is the "dear old place" from which "the eye drops to miles of emerald pastureland lying wet and brilliant under a westward line of sleek hills blue with distance and distant woods," which has provided the "matter of innumerable photographs in the illustrated papers."[37]

Into this larger dimension of national history West fits the change that this specifically "modern" war has meant. It coincides with the shift in register in the narrative language of this next passage. West's narrator turns from the ingenuous domesticity of her usual report into a range of different tonalities, beginning with a formed rhetorical question about the difference between 1901 and now:

> Why had modern life brought forth these horrors that make the old tragedies seem no more than nursery shows? Perhaps it is that adventurous men have too greatly changed the outward world which is life's engenderment. There are towns now, and even the trees and flowers are not as they were; the crocuses on the lawn, whose blades showed white in the wide beam let out by the window Chris had opened, should have pierced turf on Mediterranean cliffs; the golden larch beyond should have cast its long shadows on little yellow men as they crossed a Chinese plain. And the sky also is different. Behind Chris' head, as he halted at the open window, a searchlight turned all ways in the night like a sword brandished among the stars. (*RS*, 30)

The former world order, where things were somehow held in their proper places, has been defamiliarized now – under the strange light that Chris has brought home as his own war-related estrangement and that the war has shed on the Baldry Court (and Britain) of the present. The remains of an imperial imaginary are also estranged, insofar as the material brought in from abroad appears now to have forsaken its proper place in Britain. Its landscape has lost a sense of customary order, in the same way that Chesterton's London prospects recorded a loss of world-geographical proportion and so provided the incipient sign of empire under stress. It is now in manifest and expressive distress. The main grammatical mood and dominant imaginative tense lies in the reiterated "should have," emphasizing what is missing, now, in what is left behind. Recalling the remaindered time of Manning, the remaindered moment of this altered and evacuated present locates the point of expressive poetic power, which registers its difference in the shift of idiom in this passage, in the manifestly heightened quality of its imagery and diction.

Again, in the descriptive positioning of Baldry Court in a dusky twilit time: this public English place appears in the atmospheric time of a decadence that West complements by shifting her narrator's voice into poetically heightened diction:

> I was left alone with the dusk and the familiar things. The dusk flowed in wet and cool from the garden as if to put out the fire of confusion lit on our hearthstone, and the furniture, very visible through the soft evening opacity with the observant brightness of old well-polished wood, seemed terribly aware. Strangeness had come into the house and everything was appalled by it, even time. For the moments dragged. It seemed to me, half an hour later, that I had been standing for an infinite period in the drawing-room, remembering that in the old days the blinds had never been drawn in this room because old Mrs Baldry had liked to see the night gathering like a pool in the valley while the day lingered as a white streak above the farthest hills . . . (*RS*, 25–26)

The feeling of the old place, sponsored by and associated with Mrs. Baldry, Chris's mother, provides the memory of the conventionally languorous prosperity of late Victoriana. The new influence comes as the *terrible awareness* associated with Chris's return from the war, which makes the formerly comfortable and familiar into something strange and unknown. The discomfiting force of the war occurs on the level of fundamental awareness: it has changed "even time," that is, it has altered the conventional understanding of cultural temporality as it has voided it of its assurances and continuities. The present thus concentrates a poetry of loss in the *dragg*ing time, the suspended temporality, of decadence, which, in the affective register Manning will have likewise poeticized, has dilated into the experience of an "infinite period." It is an interval charged with the emptiness of the fugitive infinity Baudelaire, following De Quincey, has inscribed as the emptying of the fullness of the romantic spot of time and registered as the temporal imaginary in the poetic tempos of decadence, in these dregs and drags of time. It is a condition whose historical import grows out of this passage into the one examined before it, which follows it in narrative series in West's book.

The inwardness West reveals with the historical imaginary of decadence may be evidenced in the special connection she demonstrates with the novel that stands as one of the hallmark works of its literary tradition: Wilde's *The Picture of Dorian Gray*. Most obviously, there is the reminder through the married name of Chris's former paramour, now Mrs. Grey.[38] The graying that Wilde fables in the fall of his title character is certainly redoubled in Chris's loss of the green world of romantic youth. The mixing of color symbols in West's depiction of the varying shades in Chris's hair – "I cried out, because I had seen that his hair was of three colours now – brown and gold and silver" (*RS*, 23), in the changed aspect of Chris's return from the war – also strongly recalls the chiaroscuro Wilde paints into the changing aspect of Dorian's. Most of all, the double panel of Dorian's person and picture reappears as the dual coordinates of Chris's psychic life: one the unchanging aspect of a youth whose sempiternity is an illusion and the other a *memento mori*, made no less gruesome in the work of war in West's novel than it is in the aging of Wilde's protagonist's picture. In historicizing Wilde's fiction so explicitly, moreover, West extends those premonitions of "fin-de-globe" into the contemporary reality of this first world war.

The historical truth of decadence is being perceived and represented within a specific, identifiable sense of modernist narrative time. The fall from the illusion of 1901 to the disillusion of 1916, when the "soldier," now cured, will "return" to the war: those two temporal coordinates in the longer story are present as a constant simultaneity of feeling. From the endpoint of 1916, we as readers experience the appeal of the foretime of 1901, which, for the reader, is no forgotten circumstance. This compound moment might be seen as a version of the palimpsest that Hugh Kenner has appraised as the characteristically modernist apprehension of instantaneous time, where, as a function of increasing speed in the machines of information storage and retrieval, present and past are taken into a single manifold, as one layered imaginative totality.[39]

These modern conditions are as important in being resisted as recipro-cated with, however. The experience of an increasing swiftness of change and its replication in the concentrated times of the aesthetic present may include the pleroma of an expanded and intensified moment. As deter-mined in our earlier consideration of de Man's understanding of the imagination of modern temporality, however, it just as surely adduces a second-by-second feeling of kenosis, of depletion – the sense of a present ever emptying itself into the next instant and, with that feeling of loss, an equally chronic experience of regret. As in the quickening tempo of a modernity whose "accelerated grimace," in Pound's livid depiction, "demanded an image" of its "age," of itself.[40] This condition leaves the poet to work within the cadence of a fugitive and decaying Now, a decadence, which, as the register also of that special modernist instant, leads us back to an understanding of modernism as the representation of a modernity constantly sought, always lost.

How wartime charges this particular compound of decadent and mod-ernist sensibilities may be illustrated through a comparison of West's narrative with an earlier representation of the idea of declining time, H. G. Wells's *The Time Machine*. Even as fantastical scientific experiment, Wells's novel follows the history of entropy, or entropy as history, through a strict regimen of regulated temporal progression. It is a vision of the disintegration of history, but this is occurring on the old, linear, gradual, rationalistic calendar of time: on the chronometer the novel follows, the years fly by – and back – in numerical series. If Wells and West are both responding to and representing the reversal of the Progress mythology of high Victoriana, the difference the war made in this respect shows in their different ways of telling the imaginative time of its undoing. The earlier novel delivers its theme in a linear narrative of consecutive representation, whereas the later book speaks the truth of historical feeling in a concentrated apocalyptic present, in a revelatory poetry of loss. The fact that West was living in 1916 with (the much older) Wells puts the fine point of biograph-ical parable on this difference, which, in the end, is not a discontinuity. In the longer story of cultural and literary history that this lengthened turn of the century comprises, we may find an underlying continuity between the phenomena we know under the headings of decadence and modernism – not as types or slogans, not as old perversions or new tricks, but as one sensibility developing in two of its acutest registers.

Whether or not the representatives of the decadent sensibility of the English fin de siècle could be credibly understood as prophets of the war of 1914–1918, this is the historical location in which the literature of Anglo-

American modernism will take the legacy of decadence to its consummate expression. I will be following this trajectory into the war poetry of Pound and Eliot in the next two chapters. This is not an ad hoc accomplishment, however; it is not some appliqué version of decadence for the moment. These are writers whose experience of historical loss begins in family histories of lost dominance and extends to the ordeal of that Great War, which both underwent in London. The depth and drive of this work comes as well from a literary history that is more or less continuous. One episode may be singled out for consideration in an inter-chapter, where an identifiably nineteenth-century poetic decadence turns into a discernibly modernist poetics.

Imagism

On the evening of 17 July 1914, Ezra Pound and Amy Lowell faced each other from opposite ends of a long dinner table in the Dieu-donné restaurant in London. The occasion brought together most of the poets included earlier that year in the anthology Pound had titled (in pseudo-French) *Des Imagistes*: H.D., Richard Aldington, F. S. Flint, Allen Upward, and Ford Madox Hueffer (Ford), among others. The celebratory feeling turned to ritual toasts, but the accomplishments of Imagism(e) gave way in short course to questions about its identity. Hueffer confessed that he was ignorant of what an Imagist was, or could possibly be (even so, he professed his doubts that Lowell qualified as one). Upward joked that all it took to be an Imagist was to be named one by Pound. Then Aldington objected that Imagism certainly existed, but only in the signal instance of H.D. (also his wife), whose work discovered its proper company, not among the representatives of the contemporary avant-garde (vorticism had also gathered its members in the Dieu-donné), but with a classical prosody, with archaic Greek poetry in particular.[1]

The scene survives as an emblem of Imagism and, as a narrative for literary history, its parabolic fable. Here Pound and Lowell, sometimes behaving politely in public but usually not, face off in a test of strength for control over an initiative whose defining quality remains indeterminate. Any representative anthology of Imagism would reflect this uncertainty, showing more as a miscellaneous array than a coherent school. Even within the (assignably) Imagist oeuvre of individual poets, the inconsistency is striking. Hueffer alternates a verse of horrible doggerel with poems of exquisite urban impressionism. Aldington shifts from the songs of a neo-Hellenic ritual myth, which are remarkably adequate to a feeling of "primitive" simplicity and impersonality, to lyrics of the sheerest personal grievance only a few rhythmic beats away from prosaic complaint. A vatic minimalism in H.D. is incandescent with vision in some poems; small, uninteresting things clot the prosody in others. Even the term "Imagism," which frames a visual picture as the likely center of poetic attention, fails to define the emphasis in much of the verse actually written under its name.

This sundry production may provide a sign, however, of the experimental temper of Imagism, which, in the trial-and-error spirit of a novel prosody, generated a good deal of surplus work. Of course "surplus" is a term we impose retrospectively, as we read literary history backward and exercise a principle of exclusion on writing that we judge to be less significant in relation to those heuristic devices we call "subsequent developments." Even as Imagism is correctly seen as a development contributing to the nascent poetics of a supposedly High Modernism, the forward-looking bias in this story has left an understanding of its formative influences out of consideration. Imagism, it will be seen, defines a site of continuity as well as change, locating an obvious point of consolidation between the modernism of the new century and one of the major legacies of late Victoriana, with the sensibility of literary decadence in particular. If it is unsurprising that the story of this involvement has gone untold, in view of the sometimes concerted efforts to write decadence out of the account in the history of modernist poetics, a recovery of this tense but eventful exchange may restore some of the original, generative complexities in poetic modernism.[2]

By a rough-but-ready critical consensus, the most representative statement of Imagist poetics comes in the March 1913 issue of *Poetry* (Chicago). A variously descriptive and polemical essay titled "Imagisme," which is attributed to F. S. Flint but was composed jointly with Pound, features these three injunctions:

1.   Direct treatment of the "thing," whether subjective or objective.
2.   To use absolutely no word that did not contribute to the presentation.
3.   As regarding rhythm: to compose in the sequence of the musical phrase, not of the metronome.[3]

Then comes the famous set of advisory mottoes, gathered under Pound's name as "A Few Don'ts by an Imagiste," which, it turns out, he drafted originally as a rejection slip for the magazine's editors. That editorial function might encourage a misunderstanding of the principles of Imagism, in one critical reduction, as just some editorial cleansing action, that is, as a manual to good (old) writing. But these "Don'ts," which are more than a few,[4] exceed negation as they reiterate and develop the three points just listed. In this discursive synthesis, Pound projects the new ideals toward which Imagist poetry might aspire, offering the triple principle of "direct musical presentation." These three words, the weight-bearing elements in the structure of significance that Imagism is, represent the extension of initiatives undertaken by a nineteenth-century poetics whose identity – whose name, whose defining value – has provided all the trouble in literary history. This trouble begins with the Imagists themselves and extends into and through some of those early commentators on modernism.

Restoring Decadence

The most frequently credited precedent for Imagism is the *symbolisme* of fin-de-siècle France. These critical accounts follow the model set up by Wilson in *Axel's Castle*, which provides the points of particular emphasis in the poetics Imagisme shares with *symbolisme*, which was represented variously by Mallarmé and Verlaine and typified by their well-known statements about the musical essence of poetry, where the acoustic experience is providing the medium of sensual impression and association.[5] Although Wilson was not studying *symbolisme* as a precedent for Imagism specifically, the power of this counter to supplant "decadence" in the account is all too evident in the critical legacy of Imagism, which, at first sorting, appears to be a poetry composed around the appeal of "direct musical presentation." This poetic principle and practice might easily have been seen as an extension of "decadence," which lends the negative valence of its term to the degraded, nominally decayed romanticism that the indulgence of sheer musicality in language encodes. The long occluded term exerts no influence in the critical tradition of Imagism, however, as we saw in the scholarship of the subject that we surveyed in the Introduction.[6]

The heavy suppression of "decadence" in these accounts also suggests, in its own inverted way, the power of this counter in the reckonings of cultural history. This resistance is significant insofar as it extends a tension in the relation between Imagists and decadence – right, or wrong, from the start. In the negativity attributed to "decay," that is, decadence stands as the pole opposing the nominally fresher energies of the "modern" image, but the Imagists' actual negotiation with this precedent reveals a resisting reciprocity – a genealogy, a line of descent, where the derivation, if it comes with a difference, shows an outlook now identifiable as an early modernism extending important developments of the previous period even – or especially – as it attempts to establish its independence. If "modernism" signifies the *ism* of the modern, the self-consciousness of the new, and "decadence" invokes the old age of the world in its last stage of decay, the gravitational drag of this former century measures some of the historically determined content of modernism, right from the start. This legacy is contested, but confirmed as it is contested, in one of the orienting documents in this chapter of literary history, Flint's 1912 essay "Contemporary French Poetry."

This essay gathers under its title a substantial (sixty-page) analytical anthology, which Flint ranges as a history of French poetry from Baudelaire to the present. The poetics he frames through the verse he admires clearly anticipates the codes he will co-sign with Pound: a poetry not of statement but of direct, musical, sensual, evocation. Although he does not use the term "imagist," let alone "imagiste," the task of naming is perhaps the most significant and certainly the most strenuous effort in this piece, where Flint attempts to find a word for the precedents he favors. "Symbolism," as a comprehensive category, offers him a default term – with various prefixes attached to it or its representatives as partial apologies for the inexactness of the classification. Counters as lumpy as "neo-Mallarméism" make do, but will not do.[7]

The most conspicuous word is the one Flint takes great pains to exclude: "decadence," which he pushes out of the account in two signal positions. First, after opening with a census of poets writing in the aftermath of Baudelaire, and recognizing that the most significant "new spirit" to have "found a voice ... was called decadent," he relegates this designation immediately, in the next sentence, to the status of a remainder: "It chose the designation *symbolist* as an alternative."[8] The swiftness with which Flint accepts this alternative term, whose different significance is not provided for in any meaningful way, bespeaks a nervousness; the jerkiness of the turn suggests something too true to be good in the displaced counter. And second, in his conclusion, he addresses futurism as the extreme type of the convention-dismaying energies of his chosen poets: "[T]o those who cry out against a great wind for its destructiveness, one must answer that great winds are the necessary sanitation of the earth. Degeneration? Rubbish!"[9] The judgment that Nordau attached to "decadence" as the sometime synonym for his title word *Degeneration* all too evidently haunts the identity of the poetry Flint admires. The nearly spasmodic quality in this rejection provides a further expression of that nervous concern which, now twice-told, and evidenced in the conspicuous positions of overture and closure to the essay, provides a testament in reverse to the power – disturbing, interesting, significant – of the connection he otherwise denies.

This connection with decadence is the presumptive understanding of a contemporary analysis of Imagism by (Margaret) Storm Jameson in *The Egoist*, which ran a "Special Imagist Number" on 1 May 1915. It informs the essay in substance and style. Although she does not name "decadence" as such, she does not need to; the literary history she traces for Imagism emphasizes just those themes of decline and decay that were attached to the sensibility of decadence in polemics for and against it. That culture of controversy clings still to her own rather archly mannered rhetorical postures: "Pray regard again the *degradation* of literature ... the *descent* is prettily ordered," she remarks knowingly on the movement from Renaissance to post-Victorian art. Within this literary history of decline, she places Imagism as the last installment of a long process beginning with Shelley and extending through Swinburne. This downward trajectory, which is inscribed specifically as the long dying fall in the Romantic poets' call for response to an ideal of nature that has faded, provides a map of literary history through the nineteenth and into the twentieth centuries. Here Imagism fits into place as a late or decayed romanticism, that is, as the otherwise unnamed phenomenon of decadence.[10]

The rhetorical complexity in Jameson's invocations of this process of decay extends even to this tersely hortatory subjunctive: "Let us lament the decay of ridicule,"[11] she exhorts tauntingly near the end of the essay. Her wording contains an irrepressible memory of *The Decay of Lying*, the tract in which Wilde embodies a poetics of decadence in its signature expression: he rues the loss of untruth as the necessary condition of artifice (in the moralistic culture of late Victoriana) with a sort of moralistic probity, thus sampling the decay of any standard of moral accountability in art. Whether Jameson disapproves or approves of Imagist poetry, then, appears as a question not as important as the literary history she frames to explain it and the tone she adopts to respond to it: as a decayed romanticism on one hand, as a prompt to the signal postures of a celebrity decadence on the other. The dense involutions in her rhetorical pose provide one measure – even in jest – of the tensions evident in the decadent identity of Imagism. Suppressed, expressed in deflected gestures, it is a truth as unexpected and uncomfortable as it is important, above all, for the Imagists themselves.

Decadence appears in these suitably complex representations in one of the primary prose documents of Imagism, T. E. Hulme's "Lecture on Modern Poetry." (He first delivered it in 1908, the year he and Flint founded the "Poets' Club"; although Hulme stopped writing poems in 1909, when his interests shifted toward formal philosophy, he remained in contact with Flint as well as Pound and delivered the "Lecture" again in 1914, as *Des Imagistes* was moving through press.[12]) Like Jameson, Hulme features decay as the underlying force in the literary history he traces to frame his title subject. "It must be admitted that verse forms, like manners, and like individuals, develop and die. They evolve from their initial freedom to decay and finally to virtuosity." He then repeats "decay" in refrain as a *memento mori* for the major phases of English literary history: "after the decay of Elizabethan poetic drama came the heroic couplet, after the decay of the couplet came the new lyrical poetry that has lasted until now." In the previous paragraph, he has presented "decay" not as a descriptor of general principle but as the token word of a literary sensibility close to his own historical day: "The latter stages in the decay of an art form are very interesting and worth study because they are particularly applicable to the state of poetry at the present day." He expatiates: "[poetry at the present day] resembles the latter stages in the decay of religion where the spirit has gone and there is a meaningless reverence for formalities and ritual. The carcass is dead, and the flies are upon it. Imitative poetry springs up like weeds, and women whimper and whine of you and I alas, and roses, roses all the way. It becomes the expression of sentimentality rather than of virile thought."[13] From the effeminacy routinely attributed to decadence in the attitudinized case of Wilde, to those tropes of overgrowth, which feature an overdoing of Romantic attitudes as a form of decay, the poetics and ethics of literary decadence are evident in the strong caricature of this polemical negative. Accordingly, in the subsequent constructions of the "Lecture," Hulme presents his proto-Imagist poetry as an intervention in those conditions. The poetry he favors is to be pruned of those excesses of decadent verbiage; it is to be attuned to a new range of sensory reference, including the visual; it will resist in particular a poetics of decadent music, music all the way, of music above everything else.[14] If the poetry he extols clearly witnesses an interest in the possibilities of visualizing through language, however, the visual is not the exclusive or even primary sensory register for him.[15] What is primary is his obsession with musicality, which, in turn, registers the primacy of a poetics of decadence in this attempt to charter a new movement. And there is in this respect a generative tension, one that we may resolve into a larger formulation after a review of the evidence in the record of his own poetry.

Consider the instrumentation of syntax in "The Embankment (The fantasia of a fallen gentleman on a cold, bitter night)":

> Once, in finesse of fiddles found I ecstasy,
> In the flash of gold heels on the hard pavement.
> Now see I
> That warmth's the very stuff of poesy.
> Oh, God, make small
> The old star-eaten blanket of the sky,
> That I may fold it round me and in comfort lie.[16]

Normal word order is inverted several times, most strikingly in the first line. The words may thus function outside the constructive logic of normative grammatical statement. They are working as prompts, not only semantically but acoustically. And so the references to musical instruments, the conspicuous alliteration in the first line, the subtler consonance in the second between the feeling of the "hard pavement" and the hard vowels of "gold" and "heels": the irregular syntax suppresses a consecutive logical sense in favor of the finer audition of imagined sound. The direct presentation of associative sensation like this, as the review of those 1913 documents has suggested, establishes the method and directive of Imagist poetics. This aim is clearly realized as the syntax in "The Embankment" orchestrates its images to a poetic whole that is, in every available sense of the term, musical, musical above everything else, musical all the way. Like the modernism that will emerge as a reinvention of decadence and not just a riposte to it, there is a new music and novel prosody already detectable here, most notably, in the focusing and intensification of the individual register of imagined sensation.

The affiliations of Hulme's proto-modernist poetry with the poetics of decadence are strengthened and clarified by the contextual sense of their first collected appearance, in 1912, in an appendix to Pound's volume *Ripostes*, which Pound frames amusingly, but instructively. He titles Hulme's *petit oeuvre* (there are five poems in all, none longer than nine lines) *The Complete Poetical Works of T. E. Hulme*, and then observes the quietly sardonic chronology of an author "publishing his *Complete Poetical Works* at thirty."[17] The posthumous gesture in that title inters a young author's career virtually at its start, repeating a conceit that was played so pointedly across the English Nineties – the decade of genius dying young, the so-called Tragic Generation of Aubrey Beardsley, Lionel Johnson, Ernest Dowson (even the somewhat older Wilde). More specifically, Pound is remembering the label on the signal document of that literary decade, *The Works of Max Beerbohm*, a title which, in 1896, lowered the diminutive production (all *short* stories and essays) of a then twenty-four-year-old into an early crypt, a jest that Pound enlarges with his addition of "*Complete*."[18]

Invoking this decade as the framework of reference in literary history for Hulme's poems, Pound suggests the continued relevance of the sensibility of decadence, which Imagism reciprocates with as much as resists. Indeed, it discovers its substance in the struggle, confirming the pressure of this identification even – or especially – in contesting it. Whereas, for instance, the end-of-empire-days feeling that grew through the English Nineties called up comparisons with the late age of imperial Rome, often in an ominously Latinate diction, the first anthology of Imagism will offer an answer to the Latinity of English literary "decadence" in an alternative classicism, one that nonetheless reinforces the truth of the Roman analogy.

Imagistes, and Other Greeks

"It's straight talk, straight as the Greek!" Pound wrote of the H.D. poems he was sending to Harriet Monroe at *Poetry* in October 1912.[19] "It will be seen from these that *Imagism* is not necessarily associated with Hellenic subjects," Monroe countered in her "Editor's Note" to "Imagisme" in the March 1913 issue,[20] where the Hellenic element was in fact so strong that Monroe, presenting herself as spokesperson for the "modern" quality Pound had claimed for H.D.'s verse, felt obliged to issue this disclaimer about antique material. Together, Pound and Monroe frame the significant countermeasure of this verse: its directness and intensity are associated with living speech but worked out in reference to, often in rhythmic mimicry of, the antique measures of archaic Greek. "And she also was of Sikilia and was gay in the valleys of Aetna, and knew the Doric singing": this is the translation of the Greek script that is provided as epigraph to *Des Imagistes*,[21] which, if it presents Hellenic song as the tuning fork for the poems to come, does so as writing on a page, the medium and register for the otherwise (to most readers) unspeakable Greek: we are, after all, just *looking at* these printed forms.

This tension goes to a question in the aesthetic identity of the initiative being fabled here. A myth of origins, of a song performed in the morning of the world, locates the revolutionary (going in a circle) impulse in Imagism, which is seeking the immediacy and directness of first words for its poetics of direct sensual experience. But the record of this incentive is overwritten with – as – a series of scripts. The Greek recedes from speaking immediacy even further as the language of English translation overshadows it. On this first page of Imagism, then, the palimpsestuous record of *litera*ture (letters, on a page) locates the moment of its own writing at a late, an always later, day of history.

In the oblique but revealing light of this identification, this page provides a testament to the ongoing pressures of the poetics of decadence. As Linda Dowling has demonstrated, and as we noted earlier, the highly writerly style of literary decadence develops in significant part as a response to a shift from etymology to phonology as the model of under-standing for the history of the language. Words on the page are regarded as the remnants of the energy of phonetics, which dies as soon as it hits the page; the letters of literature are left behind as the shells or reliquaries of their extinguished acoustic quick.[22] This is the dead matter of language that the sensibility of decadence takes hold of as carvable stuff, accepting the written condition of literature as its necessary state. What ensues is a shaping and stylizing of writing in ways that Beerbohm made famous for Pater's practice, performed as it were in the mortuary of the page: "that sedulous ritual wherewith he laid out every sentence as in a shroud."[23] Highly stylized as Beerbohm's appreciation may be, it expresses a presentiment strongly underscored by the general sense of an aftermath circumstance in the English language, whose longevity as well as importance has been tied to the history and life cycle of empire. These are lasting apprehensions in English literary history as well as in the national imaginary of 1914. And if the developmental energy of a new poetics of Imagism is in some ways attempting to pull against those precedents and conventions, it is also being directed by them. There is an accommodation, which is interesting and significant as an integration of the sensibility of decadence in an aggressively and self-consciously novel prosody.

"The ancient songs / Pass deathward mournfully," Aldington writes in the first lines of "Choricos." Pound placed this poem as overture to the collection, and fittingly. Its mythos, its rhetorical fiction, commemorates the passing of that ancient music,

> From the green land
> Which lies upon the waves as a leaf
> On the flowers of hyacinth;
> And they pass from the waters,
> The manifold winds and the dim moon,
> And they come . . .
> In the silver days of the earth's dawning –
> Proserpina, daughter of Zeus.   (*DI*, 7)

If the Imagist attempts to intervene in the dying fall of speech onto the page, thus to restore a sense of the music of spoken words in the reader's "inner ear," this artistry works within the admitted condition of print; that is, it abjures the sort of acoustic bombast that might otherwise work to outdo the limiting condition of a written word. Restraint of this kind is the defining measure of this verse. Thus the parallelism of prepositional phrases – "in the silver days of the earth's dawning" – offers a rhythmic quality that is sensed more as an intimation, even a dim intimation, than a heavily affected sensation. Similarly, by placing "manifold" and "moon" at far ends of a line, he spaces out the alliteration, and, in the same line, submerges the vowel rhyme to the internal assonance of "wind" and "dim." It is a dense but hidden music, emerging as it were as the second intention within this secondhand – or second-voice – condition of print. Heard – or overheard – again in the next poem of the anthology, it appears once more in the precincts of Hellenic legend, in "To a Greek Marble":

> When the fragile pipes
> Ceased in the cypress shade,
> And the brown fingers of the shepherd
> Moved over slim shoulders;
> And only the cicada sang. (*DI*, 10)

While the "fragile" character of those pipes matches the secondary intensity of imagined and *re*presented sound, Aldington also recomposes the moment and theme of Keats's "Ode on a Grecian Urn" in his own Greek location to stress the value of the secondary. Thus the transient character of sensation in Keats's poem appears in the passing away of the sound of the pipes, which, in the dramatic fiction and represented scene of the lyric, obviously occupies the foreground, whereas it is the background sound of the cicadas that is valued for its lastingness. This is a standard that this verse paragraph emulates in the consistent diminution of sound in the reader's imaginative hearing, spreading the slant internal assonance of "fragile pipes" and "cicada sang" across its span and concentrating the intensity of "hard" vowels in "Ceased in the cypress shade" only by varying those hard vowels and so undoing any sense of concerted mass. This is a reinvention of a poetics of decadence, with its emphasis on the finality of the page, which is far more than a riposte or even just an accommodation.

Similarly in "Sitalkas," H.D.'s first poem in the collection, the Hellenic site provides the ground for another ritual myth of poesis. She observes it in the curial manner of a formulaic repetition, working to purposes and effects similar to Aldington's:

> Thou art come at length
> More beautiful
> Than any cool god
> In a chamber under
> Lycia's far coast,
> Than any high god
> Who touches us not
> Here in the seeded grass.
> Aye, than Argestes
> Scattering the broken leaves. (*DI*, 20)

Where the repetitions – "Than any cool god," "Than any high god," "than Argestes" – serve the rhetorical fiction of a liturgical refrain, the speaking presence that is necessary to that fiction is not really claimed. It is resisted by the syntax and lineation. Phrase by phrase, line by line, the language of the poem is shaped to a go-and-stop pattern that pauses always at the line breaks, where the ritual plea – cresting, directed, momentous – would push it ahead. This effect may be taken as the result of the Imagist's well-known attention to the individual line as the unit of composition, but the severing of the momentum at the end of the line is also a function of lineation composed for and registered from the page, which forces a counter-rhythm to the cadences of speech. And so this Imagist prosody – underplaying the musical effect as it undercuts the speakerly presence – works in the service once again of the finer audition of the reader's inner ear, that subtler music.

The subtler music that Aldington and H.D. jointly produce is of course scored against those patterns of appliqué sound that Pound abjured as the Imagist resistance to fixed patterns of mechanical meter (the ignominious "metronome") and the rushed compulsion of necessary end rhyme. In its studied faintness, however, it is designed fundamentally to resist the temptation to out-shout the resistant medium of the page. Indeed, it may be heard as music *for the page.* On this point, in fact, Hulme's "Lecture" is adamant: he insists on a verse that is "intended to be read in the study. I wish this to be remembered in the criticisms that are made on me."[24] Understood as the afterward of speech, the poetics of Imagism claims its medium in the necessarily and admittedly secondary dimension of the page. And what Hulme stipulated in 1909 and 1911 was really borne out in 1914 on the pages of *Des Imagistes*, as, most emblematically, on its first page: where the poetic word in English appears as the visual echo of a lost sound in archaic Greek. This is the character in which the experience of acoustic is most often represented as well as replicated in the textures of the verse.

This secondariness is the first condition of a poetics of decadence, which takes the after-image as the signal instance of sensual perception and matches this condition in a prosody of afterward, of the reiteration that diminishes, of the repetition that fades. Where adversity marks true friend-ship, English Imagism finds in the legacy of the decadence it otherwise contests its own strange familiar, its own precedent for reinvention, its own profounder continuity. And this is the deeper literary history that may explain the opportunistic interest in those otherwise recherché measures of Hellenic song. Recherché, indeed, and mainly forgotten nowadays both in themselves and in their import: once the initiatives of Imagism moved dramatically onto the wider plain of a movement phenomenon, most obviously as a response to the great success of futurism, Hellenism took its place as a counter in a less conspicuous cultural war. Largely forgotten now, it nonetheless provided an authenticating classicism to oppose the

Latinity in which the language of English literary decadence was so heavily invested.

Aldington reveals this conflict of classicisms clearly in another poem in *Des Imagistes*, "In the Via Sestina." He opposes the goddess of his Grecian muse to the Rome of the decadence:

> O daughter of Isis,
> Thou standest beside the wet highway
> Of this decayed Rome,
> A manifest harlot.   (*DI*, 15)

This invective is surprising, first of all, in being unmotivated in the immediate fiction of its dramatic lyric. More telling is the dissonance its volubility marks to the customarily restrained measures of the Imagist literary persona. This protest gives a good deal away in being too much: the rhythms and counter-rhythms of this short moment are indeed reve-latory of the pressures and counter-pressures of English literary history. What the poetics of Imagism may be contesting in the Latinity of deca-dence, after all, Aldington is confirming in his own words: the Latinate diction of the final line, where the blunt judgment goes to a moral category in an abstract language, is utterly unlike the more intimate particularity that Imagism depicts in the subtler music of overheard sounds, all in all, in the fainter acoustic that is, elsewhere, the better register of the reinvention of the legacy of decadence.

This legacy extends in ways that can be followed to one of its major consequences through the work of a significant but overlooked contributor: in the poetry of F. S. Flint. His position in the literary history of Imagism has been eclipsed, predictably but unfortunately, by the more powerful personalities of Pound and H.D., even by Lowell and Aldington. The word to which his importance may be rightly scored is "cadence." The term appears as the title of his 1915 volume, *Cadences*. He glosses it in his portion of the group-authored introduction to the second number of the now annual *Some Imagist Poets* anthologies, where it offers a sort of free-verse answer to conventional metrics.[25] If the impoverished Flint had less Greek than H.D. and Aldington and Pound, he did have a little Latin, and the root his chosen word shares with that otherwise disputed name of de-cadence goes to a radical understanding indeed, a deep complicity that insures the return of this repressed term. At his best, as his most defining measure, his verse reenacts the poetics of afterward in the repetition that fades as he features a "falling away" as his signature rhythm.

His first poem in *Des Imagistes* shows this characteristic action in its master cadence. Its rhythm, which rises and falls precipitously over its three verse paragraphs, is built up and let down through a skillful manipulation of syntax and line break. It opens with a lyric appeal to the apostrophized subject of London:

> London, my beautiful,
> it is not the sunset
> nor the pale green sky
> shimmering through the curtain
> of the silver birch,
> nor the quietness;
> it is not the hopping
> of birds
> upon the lawn,
> nor the darkness
> stealing over all things
> that moves me.

Flint maintains the feeling of a rising rhythm as he leads this series of rhetorical negatives toward a positive outcome. He reinforces this sense of forward-oriented expectation through the fluid continuities of soft enjambments: here is the subtler artistry of a page-based music in the poetics of decadence. Dramatically, then, in the second of the three verse paragraphs, he suspends this directionality with a medial hiatus. He expands this moment of dramatic waiting with emotions of longing and expectation –

> But as the moon creeps slowly
> over the tree-tops
> among the stars,
> I think of her
> and the glow her passing
> sheds on men,

– so that, having paused and gathered and concentrated the forward orientation of the first verse paragraph in the second, Flint reaches a consummation in this third:

> London, my beautiful,
> I will climb
> into the branches
> to the moonlit tree-tops,
> that my blood may be cooled
> by the wind.   (*DI*, 31)

The build-up and letting-go are not dissimilar to the structural rhythm of the Petrarchan sonnet, which accumulates the tension of the problem octave toward the "turn" and release into the resolving sestet. In fact, Flint also cast this poem into sonnet form where, however, he loses its dramatic cadence, which becomes indistinct as the generic rhythm of the sonnet form.[26] The contrast reveals the deeper conceit in his free-verse Imagism, especially in this climax. Just here, in the very last line, as it were at the top of the wave, the rhythm comes to an exquisitely minimal figuration of, well, just the wind, and a cooling wind at that. This *falling off* conforms to "cadence" in the radical sense – in the specific, technical sense that is instinct with his own appropriation of the precedent legacy of decadence. This tradition provides the primary point of negotiation and remaking for the most important poems in this collection.[27]

Although Flint has no recourse to the Hellenic measures informing the work of his companion talents Pound and H.D., his poem consorts as well as contrasts with the Latinity of a more standard classicism and, in that, it invokes a shared sense of living in a late historical age. This presentiment helps to explain a presence in *Des Imagistes* that is otherwise hard to figure. It is James Joyce, who, as a poet, might appear as a rather incongruous accomplice among these Imagists. In his single contribution to this anthology, however, Joyce locates one of the primary historical circumstances of literary decadence as the most substantial point of contact with the sensibility gathered in the volume:

> I hear an army charging upon the land,
> And the thunder of horses plunging; foam about their knees:
> Arrogant, in black armour, behind them stand,
> Disdaining the rains [reins] with fluttering whips, the Charioteers.
>
> They cry into the night their battle name:
> I moan in sleep when I hear afar their whirling laughter.
> They cleave the gloom of dreams, a blinding flame,
> Clanging, clanging, upon the heart as upon an anvil.
> They come shaking in triumph their long grey hair:
> They come out of the sea and run shouting by the shore.   (*DI*, 40)

This epic perspective of historical catastrophe focuses an end-of-empire-days feeling most of all. It envisions those northern European wastes, the channel- and battleground of fierce migrant tribes at the end of some perennially failing imperial reign. That is the establishing condition of a perennial decadence. And if an Irish political interest informs this imaginative prospect most particularly, Joyce scores his poetic acoustic in accord with the work of those Anglo-Americans. The subtler music in their joint Imagism is attuned to the precedents of the literary decadence they are extending and reinventing. This quality shows most strikingly in relation to the cacophony of sound in the descriptive report of the historical scene: a "thunder of horses plunging" sets the decibel level for the represented acoustic. All the more striking, then, is the way Joyce turns the volume down in the music his words actually present. This finer audition of poetic sound shows in the alternating pattern of end rhyme, where the muting effect of that sparer pattern is complemented by the concentration of *internal* assonance – internal both to the lines and to the words themselves, where the inner syllables form a recessed, a more distant, resonance to the reader's inner ear. The dainty hand Joyce displays in this versification, otherwise surprising in a representation of such a clamorous prospect, may gesture back to his earlier immersion in the preciosities of fin-de-siècle verse. In its pearled forms and vintage diction, though, Joyce's early poetry (a minor note in his whole oeuvre, one which strikes a distinctive difference to his prose) provides his version of the burnished verbal surfaces of Dowson and Johnson and, in a more complex way, the early Yeats. This is one of the background sounds to Imagist poetics, I am saying, and it indicates as well the continuity between the decades of late decadence and early modernism. Not that Joyce knew in Trieste that he was a London Imagist in this deep sense. His editor knew it. Including this poem, Pound builds out an understanding of the profounder historicity of Imagism, which includes the historical imaginary of decadence.

Pound, moreover, follows Joyce in *Des Imagistes*. His pairing of their two poems on face-to-face pages recalls the famous face-off with Lowell in the *Dieu-donné*, but he offers something more instructive in the conjunction here:

> Be in me as the eternal moods
>   of the bleak wind, and not
> As transient things are –
>   gaiety of flowers.
> Have me in the strong loneliness
>   of sunless cliffs
> And of grey waters.
>   Let the gods speak softly of us
> In days hereafter,
>   The shadowy flowers of Orcus
> Remember thee.   (*DI*, 41)

This is "Δώρια" ("Doria") – a title which echoes to the call for the "Doric singing" that Pound inscribed as legend and motto for his anthology. In republishing the poem in this collection and in this place, he provides one more example of the role and intention that Imagism assumes in its neo-Hellenic register: as a response, a riposte, to the Latinity of the decadence that Joyce's poem references in its historical fiction of falling empire, Roman as well as British. But the two poems may reveal a consonance profounder than opposition. The atmospheric aspect of this bleak season clearly mirrors the feeling of the late historical day in Joyce's poem. And the recognition of "transient things" in Pound's piece takes the sense of decline and decay in Joyce's as the establishing circumstance for this poem's dramatic location and thematic affect.

It is the poetics as much as the atmospherics of decadence that is essential to the work of Imagism in this piece. The carefully spare details that Imagism typically features also rhyme with the favored register of faintness on the prosodic palette of decadence. This is a poetics of the page, which silences the acoustic affect in the sound effect of the printed word. The lineation consistently breaks the sentence against the line and, for the movement of the reading eye, establishes the silent music of the fall from verse to verse.

In this piece of definitive Imagism, the Hellenic identity of Pound's invoked muse consorts more than contrasts with the god of that other denomination, a decadence of Roman reference. Indeed, Pound invokes the legacy of this other line of classical antiquity summarily in the figure of Orcus, the god of the Roman underworld. In its shadowy insubstantiality, that necropolis provides a local Roman habitation as well as a Latin name for the poetics of a decadence that renews Hellenism to its own purposes. This reinvention of decadence is the major imaginative challenge and task of Pound's early modernist verse.

A similar negotiation with the new Hellenism occurs in another poem Pound republished in *Des Imagistes*, "The Return," which, in its poetic fiction of lyric rapture, stages a rebirth of ancient deities:

> See, they return; ah, see the tentative
> Movements, and the slow feet,
> The trouble in the pace and the uncertain
> Wavering!   (*DI*, 42)

The feeling of these gods' "return" – hopeful but tentative, go-and-stop with the syntax breaking against the line ends – is as convincing as the rhythm is splendidly expressive. Our experience of this sensual dimension, however, is not keyed to syllable count, nor to the pacing or concentration of similar or related "sounds." The feeling of rhythm comes mainly through the enjambment, which serves at once to break the momentum of conventional syntax and, in the cadence of this disrupted expectation, generate the sense of a fall from line to line. It is music on the page for the eye of the reader. It exemplifies the visual prosody that Imagism has taken as the rule of its necessarily literary existence (as letters on the page) from that precedent legacy of decadence, whose Roman deities abide more tellingly within (Pound's) Homer's.

The tension evident in the contesting identities of classical antiquity may be seen now as the most intense register of the difference between an admission of derivation and a desire for self-invention in Imagism. This tension is resolved in one sense in the act of *re*invention, that is, in the renaming of its tutelary gods in repatriating them from Rome to Athens. The effort may be read also as an attempt to resist the late- or last-days situation that the sensibility of decadence enshrined in its Roman pantheon and conventionalized in its attitudes and practices. That aftermath imaginary asserts its pressures all the more strongly, however, where the poetics of decadence continue to echo and fine themselves down in the dying falls of the Imagist cadences. The sense of last days is about to be borne out, moreover, and in a way that will serve at once to reinforce the apprehension of afterward in the historical imaginary of decadence and to undermine the integrity of Imagism as a poetic school.

The Imagist Moment

The scene in the Dieu-donné may be located historically in the high pathos of that particular moment, mid-July 1914. This is the Last Supper of Imagists, already in their early season. Within several weeks, the war approaching from eastern Europe will dissolve their bonds and shift their center, which will not hold, to neutral America, where the somewhat compelled production of annual anthologies of Imagism (*Some Imagist Poets*, 1915, 1916, 1917) witnesses the mechanization of original energy. Some of the reasons for disintegration may have to do with the life cycle of any literary movement. The circumstances of immediate history also factor in strongly, however. The political and public culture of the war can be seen to exert the strongest force in the unmaking of the poetics of Imagism.

If Imagism is a poetics (at least by Hulme's intention) of the private readerly space, the public Word of the war locates an antithetical register for the language of verse. Already by early 1915, the difference is told. It occurs most notably in the wording of Aldington's references to archaic Greece – the verbal material that has grounded the distant music of the Imagist page. Those sound effects belong to a different order entirely now:

> Zeus,
> Brazen-thunder-hurler,
> Cloud-whirler, son-of-Kronos,
> Send vengeance on these Oreads
> Who strew . . .[28]

Aldington is turning up the volume of imagined sound in a way that echoes most notably to the gigantism of mass war. He records this feature of the imaginative experience in the graphic, phantasmagoric prospect of "1915": "A vast breast moves slowly, / The great thighs shift, / The stone eyelids rise."[29] The colossus of Total War overwhelms the perceptual content of the Imagist poem, whose specificity of feeling is at odds with the generality and ideology of political language in mass war. There is no Word for the small things of Imagism; there is no Imagist word for the big things of this war.

This is a literary and political history that Aldington tells in the parable he merges into the imaginative prospect of "Whitechapel":

> Noise;
> Iron hoofs, iron wheels, iron din
> Of drays and trams and feet passing;
> Iron
>
> Beaten to a vast mad cacophony.
> *In vain the shrill, far cry*
> *Of swallows sweeping by;*
> *In vain the silence and green*
> *Of meadows Apriline;*
> *In vain the clear white rain . . .*
>
> Noise, iron, smoke;
> Iron, iron, iron.[30]

Where the "*clear white rain*" presents the Imagist particular with exemplary specificity, the war impinges on this specialist language in a way that Aldington recognizes and reflects. The italics register the difference of this particular, and particularizing, idiom. Here the "*shrill, far cry*" of the swallows also echoes to the distant music in the poetics of decadence, inscribed for the silence of the page in the idiolect of Imagism just as much as it is accentuated in relation to the "*silence and green* / *Of meadows*" in the background prospect of this poem. As an exception to the historical moment of war in the imaginative fiction of this piece, however, the dialect of Imagism is threatened. The poem must take its language back to that sphere of historical experience where "Iron, iron, iron" reads as the one sound history is making. The One Word utters the generality of mass war, unspeakable in verse other than as a decimal recurring in the epic bleakness of its own barren magnitude. And so Aldington offers the parabolic truth of this signal piece, where the moment of Imagism is enclosed by the war that closes the moment of Imagism in literary history.

The "*green / Of meadows*" in this fated interlude reflects the color code of youth in the story being told of literary history. Imagism, as for the other young "men [and women] of 1914," is a victim of its short historical day. And so Imagism enters the chronological mythology of genius dying young. This is an experience which the casualty lists of the Great War are turning now into a commonplace, not reserved for geniuses surely, but taken up by young men most of all. The artist dying young was the singular and exceptional figure of a specialized feeling in the 1890s; the sense of an ending in contemporary history (reinforced by otherwise arbitrary chronological symbols) was registered most strongly as it touched the young. This fable is being restored now as it is realized with an authenticity as terrible – as extensive – as the dimensionality of mass war. This imaginative paradigm is returning as the historical imaginary of wartime, as potentially powerful for poetry now as its apocalyptic quality suggests. There are other ways of developing this precedent sensibility of decadence, as in the case of H.D., who, in the critical narrative Cassandra Laity has ably supplied, follows the counterconventional sexualities of figures such as Pater and Swinburne into a new fashioning of the female voice for modernist poetics.[31] It is the historical imaginary of last days, such a powerful coadjutor in the consciousness of Pound's and Eliot's early poetry, that provides the main line of development in my account, which follows this sensibility to its climax and conclusion in the poems they wrote out of their historical experience of a catastrophic war.

These major poets of Anglo-American modernism are working out of the sensibility of the decadence they will have developed, over the long turn of the century, as the main line of their literary legacy. The fact that this literary record is extending most consequentially in the work of poets deriving from an American historical background is certainly worthy of note. In its own way, it serves as a measure of the extent and power of the historical imaginary of decadence. Indeed, the apprehension of historical decline was familiar to them from the start. We may discern the workings of its historical sensibility within their particular cultural class of Anglo-Saxon Protestant American males, which, in their individual and different ways, they experienced as a threatened eminence, a dominance about to be (or already) lost. Theirs were families who felt the authority of their superior condition as a connection to some earlier, purer modus of American life, which, in their perception, whether in fancy or fact, was declining in time. This presentiment of lost dominance was strongly reinforced as it was constituted, historically and materially, by the immigrant waves of the later nineteenth century.[32] As T. J. Jackson Lears demonstrates in *No Place of Grace: Antimodernism and the Transformation of American Culture, 1880–1920*, moreover, a growing enervation in the governing and patrician classes in the years he frames in his title seemed to bear out a presentiment he identifies in a Puritan (radical Calvinist) mythology of history. This, in essence, represents the waxing and waning of virtue in ways more than roughly analogous with the historical models of cultural decadence.[33]

It is customarily acknowledged, then, that both poets toyed with the legacy of decadence in their poetic youths but, it is also strongly asserted, they *outgrew* this influence as they matured into the modernist poets they became. I propose a contrary understanding. Pound and Eliot *grew into* the poetics of decadence as an ongoing response to the truth history would be giving to the conditions on which the temporal imaginary of decadence was founded. That apprehension had been established in its own way in their American experience, which led each of them when young to dedicated readings of decadent poets, but it had not been corroborated and magnified by any event as momentous as that Great War. The war provides a formal conclusion to a process of maturation that shows their inwardness with the conditions of literary and cultural decadence. It is a story that needs, for the first time, to be followed through. It reveals the formative importance of the poetics of decadence in early modernist poetry as, here, in the record of these two major poets.

CHAPTER III

Ezra Pound: 1906–1920

Writing a roundup review of Ezra Pound's *Personae* and *Exultations* in the London *Daily News* in 1909, R. E. Scott-James praises a poetry that shows "no eking out of thin sentiment." This is a verse that "suggests virility in action combined with fierceness, eagerness, tenderness," demonstrating an admirable capacity for "passionate conviction." If, accordingly, Pound sometimes "writes out of an exuberance of incontinently struggling ideas," the youthful poet eludes any censure by this measure: "exuberance," it turns out, is the temperament Scott-James has established as the major category of value a year earlier in *Modernism and Romance*.[1] He is now romancing a modernity of vital energy and optimistic progress in Pound, whose youth and New World background may suit him especially to the agenda of that critical book. In Pound's early poems, Scott-James is finding the qualities of the literature that, in his critical conception, expresses best the temper of the new century.

Writing about the same poet in the same year in the *English Review*, Edward Thomas takes a different tack. "To say what this poet has not is not difficult; it will help to define him. He has no obvious grace, no sweetness, hardly any of the superficial good qualities of modern versifiers."[2] In a review that seeks at least – or at most – to be not uncomplimentary, Thomas offers a set of negative definitions to the positive qualities Scott-James appreciates in his account. These two reviews may be seen as oppositional complements. They reveal the qualities the two critics would unite in opposing, and they join as representatives of a consensus center in English literary culture at this moment.

This negative assessment coalesces in a set of traits that is identifiable as literary "decadence." This word, unspoken in Scott-James's review, echoes ahead from his critical book of the year before, where it centered the most intense rhetoric of objection in his early effort at consolidating a concept of "modernism." At that moment, in the same year that brought the author of the "make it new" slogan to England, we can see a modernism of the new, indeed, a modernism that romances novelty, as a reaction formation. This "modernism" sets the values of progressive energy as the defining mark of modernity. This quality, however, is under steady and increasing threat from its nominal opposite, "decadence," which, if he ostensibly deplores it, he does so at revealingly great lengths. There is a multi-front, several-chaptered counterattack on this "decadence," which seems to be not merely the most fearful but also the most prepossessing and interesting of new things, and which, accordingly, actually vies for pride of place in the emergent sensibility of this "modernism."[3] So, in this review, it stirs as the contested but all-too-present negative in his fulsome praise of fulsomeness.

Thomas, in order to find anything so positive in Pound's technique, has to note that the poet at least shows nothing of the "wavering uncertain languor of the new." The apparent insubstantiality of language recalls the prosodies of disembodiment in the poetics of decadence, where, say, the repetition that fades also diminishes the physical body of language on the page. Not only in tempo but in temper: Thomas's Pound "has not the current melancholy or resignation or unwillingness to live," and so avoids the worst proclivities of the disposition Scott-James has harangued as the "fin-du-globe" defeatism of the fin de siècle.[4] The "currency" of the temperament Pound most admirably lacks, moreover, matches the "new"-ness of the music Thomas is otherwise glad not to find.

The energy these two reviewers are expending to leave "decadence" out of the critical story may serve as a measure of the importance this sensibility represents in the literary culture from which they are speaking. It exhibits the presence of the overwritten, the energy and fascination of the forbidden. It retains the import and value of the still unaccommodated novelty it has represented over the long turn of the century. It emerges with a requisite complexity in those early volumes of Pound's poetry, where he engages this sensibility as a new but developed convention, one which presents itself with just the sort of timeliness that most urgently worries Thomas. Moreover, and most important, Pound apprehends in this sensibility the potential of some kind of breakthrough recognition, all in all, the consciousness of a critical present which includes that special sense of the contemporary that we properly denominate as "modernism."

The sensibility of decadence may constitute the special consciousness of modernism: this is the recognition resisted in a critical tradition which Scott-James is anticipating if not instigating, extending as it does from Symons through Wilson into Kermode and Kenner and beyond. It is a critical story we will begin to rewrite with a reading of Pound's early volumes. Here the exclusionary will in those two reviews of 1909 may be revealed for what it is: an attempt to suppress what is most disturbing – and significant – in this verse. These readings will demonstrate and engage the representations Pound is giving this sensibility of decadence concurrently, variously, in poetry that was published but not subsequently collected, beginning with some of the work (prose as well as poetry) that appeared in American venues before his departure for Europe in 1908.

Two prose pieces (published in the *Book News Monthly* in Philadelphia) show Pound scanning a period of literary history of signal interest in the poetics of literary decadence: late medieval Latin. In "Raphaelite Latin," in 1906, and "M. Antonius Flamininus and John Keats," in early 1908, he appreciates the expressions of a Latinity which, in this late medieval vintage particularly, was no longer a spoken tongue and, so, emphasizes the "dead language" interest that turns up so frequently in the working attitudes of literary decadents. This Latin fixes a feeling of afterward, a presentiment of being overtime, which the decadents experienced in their own day and, in its most extreme and telling iterations, put into practice in a literary language compatible with that of fifteenth-century scribes. In effect, they take the life cycle of the Latin tongue as the *memento mori* they inscribe in English words that stir – or, rather, do not stir – around their Latin roots, their dead radicals, on the silent page. The morbidity of contemporary civilization, which is bound also to organic cycles in analogous models of cultural time, is the testament that waits as the dying fall at the end of the Latinate sentence.

This sensibility provokes the lyric poetry in prose of Pound's 1908 report. It is an appreciation of just those qualities that Scott-James and Thomas would oppose in their polemical accounts, and, accordingly, it opposes the poetic values championed by Scott-James most significantly. To the full-throated vocalese of Browning's "vital" poetry, which exhibits the sort of "strong optimism" Scott-James might hope for, Pound retorts – "No, if you want such battle cry, or song of the day's work, go elsewhere" – and then expatiates:

> for here, in our classicists, whose tones are as Whistler's when he paints the mist at moth hour, is no strong, vivifying power to uphold us; but when we rest for a moment from the contest, what beauty can we find for our ease like to this evanescent yet ever returning classicism, that is warm without burning ... a beauty that is of autumn as Browning's is of summer and the day's heat. It is not the intense, surcharged beauty of blood and ivory that we find in Rossetti, but a beauty of the half-light of Hesper and Aurora, of twilight and the hours between the false dawn and the true.[5]

In savoring this sensibility, Pound locates the colors of appreciation in the seasonal mythos of autumn and the diurnal round of twilight. The prime time of the poetic imagination lies in this moment of afterward. "Warm without burning," the embers of this once living tongue stir as the *materia poetica* of Pound's preference. A medieval Latinity, after all, is an after-the-fact language, and it shows a quality "some of us fail to find . . . in the older Latinity,"[6] then, as its fundamental point of appeal: dead from the start to its practitioners, it is a speech now faded to a visual echo on the page, all in all, an imaginative language of afterward. This is a poetics of lessening that echoes once again in "half-," the familiar adverb of quantitative depletion in the lexicon of decadence. And the visual music of Whistler's "evanescent" nocturnes, which image those qualities of insubstantiality that the poetics of decadence will have enhanced in its various prosodies of disembodiment, appears in the equally familiar technique of the repetition that fades: "a beauty" repeats in this passage through references which, by the end, have lost all material density as they finish into a "beauty of the half-light."

Possessed by the poetics of decadence even in this belletristic prose, the young poet suggests the extent of this prepossession in a poem he published a month earlier, also in *Book News Monthly*. It appears under the title of the first essay on this subject, summoning those personages now as his dedicatees: "To the Raphaelite Latinists." Signing himself "Weston Llewmys," Ezra Weston Loomis Pound offers a pseudonym that does nothing to disguise his identity, since his proper name had come above the essay of (nearly) the same title in the same venue little more than a year earlier.[7] Comic or preposterous as it may seem, this alias provides a signature more interesting in the principle it illustrates so vividly. Whereas the imagined sound of the doubled vowel in "Loomis" allows this formation to move smoothly and fluently in an imagined speech, the consonants clustered in "Llewmys" clot as an obstacle to that effect. The discrepancy evidences the primary reality of literary language as lexical rather than phonetic, as letters not sounds. Unspeakable, Pound's written pseudonym presents the truth of the primary condition in the imaginative apprehension of language in decadence and stands as the measure of an intensity – a prepossession – not so readily left behind.

It already informs a demonstration of the poetics of decadence in the poem of like title shortly afterward. Apostrophizing his subject in the first words, "Ye fellowship," Pound is already doing antique in a way that displaces the speech he feigns on the page, in this rhetorical fiction, to a faraway time. Antiquity is the ramifying imaginative value in this poem. "[W]ine of old time myth and vintaging" provides the inspirational drink of his poetic praise. "Take of our praise one cup," he continues, particularizing his interest more suggestively in the concession, and the negatives, that follow: "though thin the wine / That Bacchus may not bless nor Pan out-pour." This is a wine that has been worn down now by time to an insub-stantiality he elaborates further, in imaging the instruments of a once living sound: "Though reed pipe and the lyre be names upon / The wind." This is the "wind" of the aphoristic "winds of time," and upon it the "names," along with the musical sounds of those ancient implements, have dematerialized. In the imaginative understanding of these manifold processes of disintegrating time, the words of poetry have been turned into a language whose interest and value lie in this condition of afterward. It is the establishing circumstance of the poetic dialect of decadence, and it appears strikingly in the images of the final, testimonial line. "One wreath from ashes of your song we twine!" (*CEPEP*, 205). The cinders of a once living sound appear as the primary material of a poetry that takes the unliving afterward of life as well as of language as its principal occasion.

If the extent of Pound's early synergy with the poetics of decadence has not been recognized in the critical account, this is an omission for which he is partly responsible. The choices he made in compiling his shorter and middle-length poems for the "definitive" collection he intended in 1926, *Personae: The Collected Poems of Ezra Pound*, witness a consistent interest in excluding the poems that show his formative connection with decadence. The turns of his poetic development, working in consort with forces both historical and aesthetic, move him into positions whose opposition to the poetics of his earlier career may be assessed later in this book. What remains to be told in the interim, however, is a great deal.

This new account begins with the recovery of some of the poems he omitted from the collection that would subsequently define his early career. This body of excluded work reveals not only the presence but the intensity and coherence of the sensibility of literary decadence. His early work provides a new vantage on the presence of decadence within his subsequent career, in the poems of modernist record in the late 1910s, and we may gauge its changing pressures and follow its variations as a primary line of his poetic development.

Understandably, insofar as the youthful Pound is a major poet in the making, there is in his early work a contesting of the legacy of decadence. Derivativeness and defiance combine to generate the force field in which the growth of this poet's mind occurs and in which it can be followed. Jejune or not in its first iterations, this sensibility grows consistently and is privileged ultimately with the difficult enrichment of a history that would make real, in 1914, the profounder pessimism of its historical imaginary. It is around that historical realization that this account will take its narrative turn.

1. Remnants of Decadence

Pound is capable of displaying a relative superficiality in his engagement with the conventions of literary decadence in his earliest verse. Intentionally or not, his attitude amounts to a kind of poetic pragmatism that, once identified as such, allows us to discern the substantial share this sensibility actually owns in his developing literary consciousness. In those conventions, Pound finds a set of thematic tensions which provide, in turn, a whole set of operative rhetorical dichotomies that a young poet, learning the tune of his poetic times, may take up as a set of five-finger exercises. While a novice quality attends some of this poetic production and may account as such for Pound's leaving some of it behind, he moves through the lesson book with fluency and aptitude. The more than occasional breakthroughs and developments in the exercise of this sensibility clearly suggest that there are powerful growing points within it. At the cellular poetic level, he knows that this is the imaginative language for him to work in.

The opportunism of youth shows in a pair of poems published in *A Lume Spento* (1908), neither of which would reappear in *Personae*: "In Tempore Senectutis" and "In Tempore Senectutis (An Anti-stave for Dowson)." The Latin titles ostentatiously recall the working vocabulary of literary decadence, while the sense of a late historical day that is evoked by the now dead language is reinforced by the meaning of the repeated words: in the time of old age. The engagement is revealingly insincere, for the young poet shows no compunction about arguing opposite attitudes to the decaying strengths of age – in the same volume. "But we grew never weary . . . And yet we twain are never weary . . . For our wonder that grows not old . . ." goes the poetic assertion in the first of these poems, while the second counters with the feeling of an older man seeing his image blown away in the wind (*CEPEP*, 21, 50). The condition of age is grist for the younger Pound's poetic mill; it is all about the grinding.

A pair of poems (the second of which was unpublished by Pound) of 1907–1908 reveals a similar inconsistency in more finely grained detail. In "Occidit," the poetic topos of the western horizon locates the site of the "sun-set herds" which, in turn, stirs a premonition of "the waning god" within this prospect of sunset color:

> Hung on the rafters of the effulgent west,
> Their tufted splendour shields his decadence . . .   (*CEPEP*, 82–83)

The chromatics of the declining sun are matched by a verse music of internal or buried assonance, linking "effulgent" to "tufted" across the line break in that finer audition of imagined sound that is the register of a page-bound music in the poetics of the "decadence" he names here. For now, this is a promissory accomplishment only. For "Autumnus (To Dowson – Antistave)," which is the poetic complement to "Occidit" in the notebook, swerves from the sensibility it invokes in the title and dedication. Switching his register as well as the season – "Yet the Spring of the Soul, the Spring of the Soul / Claimeth its own in thee and me" – he lurches into a sort of hurdy gurdy rhythm and rigmarole music in these refrain lines to shout over the somber Latinity of Dowson's declining year, as over a "decadence" that remains mostly a name (*CEPEP*, 249).

Those points of finer engagement stand as examples of the growing points Pound could find for his more particular poetic development within the conventions of literary decadence. Unsurprisingly, where the historical imaginary of late days is sensed most powerfully where it touches the young, a poet in his early twenties invests heavily in the figure of the elderly youth. He knew this from its particularly Nineties vintage. In a poem in *A Quinzaine for This Yule* (1908), for instance, he focuses that familiar conceit with the concision of a single figure – for sundown at daybreak, he promises this sunset song in the morning: "Aube of the West Dawn. Venetian June" (*CEPEP*, 63), where the island of decadence perennial complements those associations. Similarly, in presenting the figure of genius force-ripened and prematurely reaped in "In Epitaphium," the grammar of poetic aphorism provides the assurance of its two-line turn: "Write me when this geste, our life is done: / 'He tired of fame before the fame was won'" (*CEPEP*, 205). Like "Aube of the West Dawn," and also unpublished subsequently, this apothegm provides a record of an imaginative understanding that is possessed as powerfully, indeed, as it is tersely phrased. Moreover, the marks of quotation that Pound applies to this phrase, which in fact represents his own words, provide the feeling of a seasoned adage, which is compatible with an otherwise unlikely senescence in this youthful poet. This is a tactic he matches in the second section of "Und Drang" (only the later sections of this 1911 sequence would reappear in 1926 in *Personae*): "And what I loved in me hath died too soon, / Yea I have seen the 'gray above the green'" (*CEPEP*, 168). The tonal mix of the colors of youth and age on the visual palette is complemented by this young poet's assumption of some inveterate understanding as he puts his own words within those quotation marks. These finer points of punctuation show an engagement with the conventions of decadence which, in being so finely tuned, so particular, suggests that the growing points for his developing career within this sensibility are not so small as they are specific.

Of the larger figures impinging from this tradition, the most specific influence comes not from Swinburne, whom Pound names in the titles of two poems and imitates, usually rather badly, in a number of others. The main figure is Nietzsche, whom Pound cites as a vivid figure of his reading as early as 1911.[8] Some of his bearing on Pound has been formulated by Kathryn Lindberg, who focuses the connection in terms of a forward-looking, "modernist" quality in the philosophy.[9] It is in the direction of a nineteenth-century *décadence* that another line of interest may be discerned.

The poet shares the philosopher's understanding of the importance decadence owns in a map of cultural history. This goes to the quality of novelty in the consciousness of decadence. For Nietzsche, as we saw, a forward point of human inquiry and discovery lies in the affective time of decadence. The degenerative condition of humankind may be an understanding as inveterate as it is presumptive, but it is for Nietzsche an awareness special to his own historical day. It provides the most thrilling recognition of present and future history for him. Given the appropriate degree of self-awareness, this timely excitement constitutes the consciousness of modernism in an equally radical fashion. So Pound, in a section of "Und Drang" that would not be republished in the 1926 *Personae*, gives expression to a sense of "modernity" which, so named, frames a specially heightened awareness of the present time, which he apprehends in ways reminiscent of a Nietzschean decadence in particular:

> How our modernity,
> Nerve-wracked and broken, turns
> Against time's way and all the way of things,
> Crying with weak and egoistic cries!
>
> All things are given over,
> Only the restless will
> Surges amid the stars
> Seeking new moods of life,
> New permutations.
>
> See, and the very sense of what we know
> Dodges and hides as in a sombre curtain
> Bright threads leap forth, and hide, and leave no pattern.
>
>   (*CEPEP*, 169–70)

What is pushing human history ahead is also wearing us down, it may be unsurprising to learn, but, inversely and more interestingly proposed, the force of decay is inseparable from the energy of invention. Any forward-looking inventiveness is instinct with a debility – "nerve-wracked and broken" – that defines a counter-positive quality in the understanding of this "modernity": "Against time's way and all the way of things." This is a modernity against itself, which is the placarded attitude of a particularly modern*ist* decadence, where the decadent turn from the progress narrative of modernity locates the special time of modern*ism*. This sense of temporal exception is expressed most intensely in presentiments of being "nerve-wracked and broken," that is, by the affective aspects of decadence, which has provided the most novel and timely consciousness for Nietzsche.

If this formulation seems ready-made, something of individual interest and substantial value comes of it already, here, in the last verse paragraph, which expresses the terrible novelty of decay in a remarkably adequate fashion. It shows in the visual chiaroscuro, even in imagist miniature, of "bright threads" in the "sombre curtain." The visionary sublimity, mixing the conditions of beauty and fearfulness, presents a striking performance for a poet no older than twenty-five. Even so, the quality of accomplished finality attests in its own way to the *pre*condition of an awareness that has been taken already, in an earlier moment of this historical phase, by Nietzsche, who calls forward to Pound in ways that this youthful poet can already be heard to answer.

Other echoes of Nietzsche in those earlier and subsequently unpublished sections of "Und Drang" – "The winds of good and evil / blind me with dust," "There is no comfort being over-man" (*CEPEP*, 167) – witness an interest in the heroic codes of that philosophy, where the over-man vaunts his anti-morality. What is interesting and significant in Pound's engagement with that heroic ethos is the fact that, for him, it is constituted largely by the attitudes and values of decadence. Thus he grafts a warrior persona, masculinist to a fault, on the expressions of a decadence that has otherwise narrowed in the critical retrospect to the example of a feminized Wilde. Incongruous as Pound's combination may seem to a view limited in retrospect to that conspicuous figure, it anticipates the more regrettable exercise of a macho modernism in the later work. In this earlier verse, however, these vaunts show more interestingly as the poetic extension of a particularly Nietzschean decadence, which accounts for the counterconventional nerve of an emergent modernism, too.

"Thersites: On the Surviving Zeus" was published just once, in April 1910, in Ford Madox Hueffer's (Ford's) *English Review*, a journal of English modernism in its nascent day that would feature fiction by Conrad and Lewis as well as himself (and Thomas's review of his earlier poetry). Like some of their work, Pound's poem seems experimental in temper, testing the expressiveness of the attitudes of decadence in a manner indicating the challenge and dare this sensibility represented. Thus it takes the apostrophized and dramatized subject of "Ennui" into the otherwise unlikely register of heroic poetry, addressing it as the muse of warrior attitudes, spur of potent deeds:

> Immortal Ennui, that hath driven men
> To mightier deeds and actions than e'er Love
> With all his comfit kisses brought to be,
> Thee only of the gods out-tiring Time,
> That weariest man to glory ere the grave,
> Thee do we laud within thy greyest courts!   (*CEPEP*, 206)

Shifting the "Ennui" of this address into the surprisingly active attitude of his own character in voice, this speaker is attempting to act in the condition of history that boredom typifies – the era of decadence – not only as given or determined but as selected and, as emphasized, possessed. This is a struggle for control that goes to the younger poet's attempt to own the sensibility which history has given him. It offers the expressive measure of its own excess, this overdoing of affective volume, this surcharge of his own heroic poetic power, as the vocal measure of his superior possession. This ambition, which matches the "out-tiring" of "Time" through his surplus "ennui," extends this sensibility of decadence to imagine a special time, all in all, an exceptional present, which is the self-conscious novelty we otherwise denominate as modernism.

Exceptionality appears again in "The Decadence" (which did not reappear after *A Lume Spento*), here in the figures of the artists associated with the title. The members of this group wear the scandal with which they have been tagged as their badge, their blazon, of value. "Tarnished we!" goes Pound's vaunting identification with the proscribed group, "Tarnished! Wastrels all! / And yet the art goes on, goes on"; "And yet the *art* goes on," he emphasizes in reiteration, "goes on" (*CEPEP*, 44). In the extended temporal moment of "the *art*" that "goes on, goes on," we see an alternative version of mainstream cultural history: the sustaining value of useful continuities in progressive time is being challenged by an "*art*" which, as stressed by Pound, emphasizes its existence for its own sake. In the moment of exception that this *art* of decadence inscribes, Pound is again claiming the special time of modernism through the personage of the excepted "we" of "The Decadence."

The heroic tenor of this sensibility is again a point to mark. Resounding in the exclamatory mood of the preceding lines, it repeats as the speaker calls his companion talents to a vigorous consumption of the "sunset" age of decadence, first in the imperative and then once more in the exclamatory mood: "Drink of our hearts the sunset and the cry / 'Io Triumphe!'" Even in defeat, in the rising rhythm of his refrain line (the repetition that fades in the poetics of decadence does not work to Pound's purpose here), the "broken" persona of poetic decadence – "Broken our strength, yea as crushed reeds we fall" – is, in cadence at least, unbroken: "Broken our manhood for the wrack and strain" (*CEPEP*, 44). Note that the association with the "broken ... *man*hood" of an otherwise assignably effeminate decadence gives Pound no pause, either. So powerful is the machismo of this particular sensibility that it deafens him to the subtler implication of what is, seemingly, the most suggestive phrase. Was this homosexual element less important in the sensibility of a contemporary decadence than the great figure of Wilde would make it appear in critical retrospect? Was Pound inattentive to such controversy because, in 1908, he was still working mainly from an American frame of reference? However these questions may be answered, it is clear that this concern of sexual orientation is subordinate to the major claim he is making in placing this "decadence" in the cultural and historical imaginary of the poem. For him, the most compelling elements lie in the exceptionality decadence marks – in relation to norms, of course, but also in the excess all too evident in his expression of it. Announcing itself in this voluble character in voice, it is as self-consciously novel as modern*ism* can be.

Where, in Nietzsche's memorable phrase, the "secret work of the instinct of decadence" signals the reversionary attitude within this sensibility, it also locates for him the focal point of his most advanced awareness. So Pound, in another poem in which he observes his reading of Nietzsche (the unpublished "Redondillas, or something of that sort"), also observes his profounder consciousness of the riddle of this sensibility, finding it in Nietzsche's sometime fellow traveler:

> Schopenhauer's a gloomy decadent,
> Somewhat chewed by the worms of his wisdom.   (*CEPEP*, 221)

In Nietzschean particulars: the "secret work of the instinct of decadence" comes in the workings of these "worms" of Schopenhauer. Natural atavism that this image depicts in an otherwise sophisticated philosopher, this is also the figure of an instrumental "wisdom," advanced as the vanguard awareness Schopenhauer was understood to claim. This is a "gloomy decadent," whose "instinct" has brought him to the apprehension of the gloom of decadence as his most developed understanding, and that is a formula for the profounder modernism that Pound is also evolving.

This conceit reveals a motive concept in much of Pound's other early poetry, which would in fact be republished subsequently. Contextualized now by the recovery of those remnants of poetic decadence, some of this work may come into new critical perspective. These are poems that include references to some of the major personages of literary decadence. Not in the tradition of Hugh Kenner's literary modernism, which saw a young poet committed to the project through which "our epoch was extricated from the *fin de siècle*" and the "decadence of a tradition,"[10] we can now see how carefully and specifically these pieces do in fact imbricate themselves into this precedent tradition of decadent poetics.

Consider "Satiemus": the Latin providing the one-word title for Pound's poem is taken from this phrase of the Roman poet Propertius, "Dum nos fata sinunt, oculos satiemus Amore," which one of the most conspicuous poets of English decadence, Ernest Dowson, would appropriate in the sense of its translation – While the fates are with us, let us glut our eyes with love – as theme as well as title for a poem of the carpe diem type.[11] If this interest typifies the usual view of the sensibility of decadence as sexual excess or culinary surfeit, this poem shows the profounder reorientation in Pound's work. Here the echoes of those other two decadences, of late Rome and a later Victoriana, combine under the sign of a perpetually decadent time, the tense of afterward, which provides the imaginative time of Pound's primary interest:

> What if I know thy speeches word by word?
> And if thou knew'st I knew them wouldst thou speak?
> What if I know thy speeches word by word,
> And all the time thou sayest them o'er I said,
> "Lo, one there was who bent her fair bright head,
> Sighing as thou dost through the golden speech."[12]

Characterizing the "word by word" increments of his lover's talk as "speeches," Pound's persona casts those words as rehearsed, performed beforehand in the time of the poem's emotional fiction and so heard in the affective present as a seconded echo of themselves. And where the wording of the first line is repeated in the third, the language of the poem also moves into this extended register of the reiterative. This emphasis on the decadent secondary is so extensive it even casts the figure of his present lover as the echoing after-image of her predecessor, that "one there was who bent her fair bright head, / Sighing as thou dost," where this tense of aftermath is further stylized in the speaker's own self-quotation. So extensively imagined and represented, this condition of the secondary is consummated as it is dramatized in the figure of the rhetorical apostrophe, which, as Christine Froula has found, is a dominant manner in the early

poetry.[13] Here, the invocation of the woman who is not there is a representation, like her own "speeches," of an original now absent, and that condition
of decadence centers the affective and imaginative interest of the poem.

The point of heaviest technical work in this poem lies in its grammatical
imagination, in the manipulation in particular of the conditional mood.
"What if," Pound's persona repeats for the third time by the ninth line
(*P*, 41). In its first two iterations, the conditional does not come in its
usual tense, the simple past, which serves customarily to signal the distance
between the possibility that the conditional frames and the actuality of the
speaker's circumstance. Instead, the mood of the conditional is realized in
the twice-told present tense of "I know," which leaves the poem in its actual
time, its affective present, as a circumstance suspended in the conjecture and
divested of definitiveness. It is its own shadow reality, or its own substantial
unreality, and as such measures the extent of Pound's inventiveness with
the condition of a disembodied present in the sensibility of decadence.

Likewise in sound effects: in the hearing of those words "murmured
overhead." There is an indistinctness which the conjectured etymology of
"murmur" – the nonsense syllable "mur" is reiterated to intensify the sense,
the nonsense, of the indecipherable – offers as the exemplary case of the
repetition that fades in the poetics of decadence. Faint sounds, fainter
echoes, the secondary intensity of the repetitively meaningless syllable: in
these various forms, the single register of the indistinct organizes the sonic
prospect of the poem's conclusion around that radical sense of "murmur":

> How if the low dear sound within thy throat
> Hath as faint lute-strings in its dim accord
> Dim tales that blind me, running one by one
> With times told over as well by rote;
> What if I know thy laughter word by word
> Nor find aught novel in thy merriment? (*P*, 42)

The conditional that provides the prevailing mood of the poem returns
at the opening and closing of this passage and, in each instance, turns the
verb in its clause into the unusual tense of the present, thus suspending
the circumstance of the poem's delivered speech in the special time of its
conjecture. A present divested of actuality but not of intensity, this is the
affective tense of a decadence that lives in the divestment of presence – in
the temporal dimension of the secondary, in the insubstantial afterward of
a now foregone original time. These ideas provide a conceptual anatomy
for the alternate body of decadent aesthetics, which responds with greater
imaginative interest to physical stimuli of secondary charge – "low," "faint,"

"dim," and again "dim," where the repetition that fades in the poetics of decadence may in its second iteration claim "dimming" as the sense of its now customary effect. And where the poem actually performs the "rote" nature of the behaviors being observed, the rhetorical fiction of the complaint might be aligned with the kind of protest a poetic elegist usually indulges: an assertion of the inability to express grief moves in effective tension with the conventions of its expression. So the objection to the repetitive in this poem provides the license for an exercise in the rhythms of the reiterative, which, if there is "[n]aught novel" in that exercise of the poetics of decadence, shows nonetheless a masterful adaptation, an extension and reinvention, of the attitudes and practices already established in that sensibility.

Similarly, in Pound's appropriation of Lionel Johnson's poem "Mystic and Cavalier" in his 1912 sonnet "A Virginal": "No, no! Go from me" – the exclamatory negative is added to the wording of the imperative phrase Pound has taken directly from Johnson's poem, which continues: "I am one of those, who fall." Johnson's speaker is developing the radical truth of a decadence in which this experience of *fall* – moral, physical, attitudinal – is embellished in a standard vocabulary of decadent poetic affect: "in a mourning gloom, / I rest in clouds of doom," etc.[14] This is the tradition Pound begins to claim for himself in the second half of his first line with the insistence of the particular figure of apostrophe, which, already in play in his first phrase, explains the otherwise odd pronominal turn he now takes: "I have left her lately." Where "her" absence is the condition of conventional apostrophe, the woman he has addressed in the apostrophe of the phrase he has taken from Johnson is now put out of direct sight as well as at the official linguistic distance of the third-person pronoun. For a poet imbued with the prosodies of disembodiment and the poetics of the secondary in the conventions of literary decadence, this distance is the establishing circumstance of his most intense poetic affection. This "she" thus becomes the figure of the ethereal eros he limns in "Slight are her arms" and, in this appreciation, the subject of a poetic embrace that emphasizes the immaterial in the attraction: this "she" has "left me cloaked as with a gauze of aether," where the figure of shadow physicality describes an aura of erotic disembodiment. "To sheathe me half in half the things that sheathe her," the octet continues in its eighth line, reaching completion on the rhyme with "aether" and on that note formalizing and finalizing the attractions of the insubstantiality it features. The quantitative adverb of depletion, "half," goes through the lessening effect of repetition not only in the regular ways of that formulary in the poetics of decadence but also, and especially, in the harder quantitative analysis, where the second half is indeed half of the first. This sense of lessening enters into a sense of exquisite diminishment in the visual effect of the final line, "As white their bark, so white this lady's hours" (*P*, 67): the effect of the fade into the secondary in the now familiar measures of decadent repetition is finely pointed in the repetition of "white," which marks the washing out of other primary colors in the spectrum.

Any casual, idiomatic associations of "decadence" with sensual indulgence are challenged thus by an informed understanding of the importance of incorporeal love. It is an erotic of *dis*embodiment that Pound claims as his inwardness with this sensibility, which he continues to emphasize as the sexual appeal of the immaterial. While this conceit is reinforced by some of the concepts of the occult, in which Pound was a sometimes eager adept, there is the longer legacy of decadent poetics as its formative precedent.

This is the decadence Pound extends in his own early practice, then, in the dominance he gives to the prosodies as well as the images of fall, of loss, of disembodiment: in the art of the *cad*ence – of the repetition that *falls* and fades – and in his address to the apostrophized other as the beloved, in that otherwise odd erotic of disembodiment, in a sort of apostrophilia. This is a decadence against its every convention of facile characterization. It shows the profounder understanding of those foundational ideas of the secondary and the entropic. And it establishes an understanding of the reality of decline that history will soon realize in his own experience.

2. Wartime

"London," Pound wrote in 1913, "is like Rome of the decadence, so far, at least, as letters are concerned. She is a main and vortex drawing strength from the peripheries." If Pound advantages himself in this circumstance with the livelier identity of the vital barbarian, he quickly civilizes that likeness by drawing it into company with extra-territorials of already established repute: "Thus the finest authors, in my judgment –Yeats, James, Hudson, and Conrad – are all foreigners, and among the prominent English writers vigour of thought, as in the case of Wells and Bennett, is found only in conjunction with a consummate vulgarity."[15] In this imaginative configuration of literary history, Pound can take on both stances of barbarian yawper and the civilized writer-stylist. It is a comprehensive understanding, and it is constituted by the residual form of an imperial ideology that has drawn Pound to the metropolitan center of the British Empire to begin with. To that imperial capital, in this account, the writers of a farther-flung elsewhere-community are drawn, where they offer their untoward otherness as the source of fortification, shoring up a cultural order that has fallen into the "vulgarity" which its erstwhile representatives would assign to the edge. This is a model of literary as well as political history that comports exactly with the one traced for the Roman Empire by the writers of a second European decadence, French most of all, and most notably by Huysmans in the account of *À Rebours*. Here the exhaustion of the Roman source of linguistic as well as political order is matched by the rising prominence in the literary capital of the tongues of formerly colonized peoples.[16] The fall this version of history records is the one that provides the opportunity of the colonial subject, and it is a mythology as well as ideology that has compelled Pound from the outset.

This is not to say that Pound's relation to the imperial ideal is wholly from the outsider's side. Nor to pretend that he can identify with its assignably higher mission of civilizing the barbarian. Rather, it locates an historically enriched possibility of imaginative feeling, which replicates and magnifies the reality of Pound's specifically American experience. This is the feeling of historical loss. Claiming descent in various levels of credibility and even sincerity from the forebears of an American colonial foretime, this story gives him a primacy and authenticity in cultural and political history that is threatened, reactively but insistently through the nineteenth century, by the ongoing flood of new immigrants.[17] And he shows his reaction often in an appropriation of the history of the Roman Empire as his imaginative language of feeling. As, in 1912, in "Patria mia," where he presents the high dream of empire as always foregone: "All the fine dreams of empire, of a universal empire, Rome, the imperium restored, and so on, came to little. The dream, nevertheless, had its value, it set a model for emulation, a model of orderly procedure, and it was used as a spur through every awakening from the eighth century to the sixteenth. Yet it came to no sort of civic reality."[18] This emphasis on the elegiac measure of an always-falling imperial ideal is the stress of decadence, indeed of decadence as a steady state condition of Pound's literary-historical imagination.

This is the sensibility that has informed his appropriation, sometimes wholesale but often individualized, of the poetics and ethics of the sensibility of literary decadence. It reveals its ongoing and developing import as Pound lives it forward into the reality of the war he did not yet know was imminent. Here the two frames of imperial reference, one Roman and the other British, move between their recessive and dominant positions to capture and amplify the understandings of the massive downturn in human history that this Great War represents. The prose record of this ongoing development shows Pound turning and expanding "decadence" from a sensibility in literature to a condition of history, and, in this section, it provides a journalistic ground for the poetic extension of this sensibility we will follow in the next.

Already in early 1915, in "Affirmations VI," Pound expresses a relation to literary Latin that is significantly different to the appreciation he made in that long-before-war moment of 1908, when, in the gloaming of Whistler's moth hour, he had swollen on Latin words that could signify any- or everything he might make them mean. Returning in 1915 to late medieval and early Renaissance Latin, he abjures vagueness of that kind as the cause of decline. He does so in a way that says a good deal about the present historical moment, about the manipulations of political discourse in the current war, and about the feeling of history really disintegrating in the contemporary circumstance:

> And in the midst of these awakenings Italy went to rot, destroyed by rhetoric, destroyed by the periodic sentence and by the flowing paragraph, as the Roman Empire had been destroyed before her. For when words cease to cling close to things, kingdoms fall, empires wane and diminish.[19]

Silently but unmistakably, perhaps all the more powerfully for being unidentified, the historical institution of the British Empire is entering the calculation through its presumptive double, the Roman Empire. Of course it was doing so in the contemporary record of monitions to the British public, who were being warned that the same end which the former empire had met was awaiting theirs, if resolve was not conscripted for the current war. A powerful coadjutor in the productions of literary decadence, this end-of-empire-days feeling is borne out even in the short compass of this prose passage. In this model of cultural and political history, it is the grandiosity of an imperial ideology that establishes Grandness as the size, as the metric that measures the magnitude of the imminent fall. And in the grandiosity of Pound's own wording at the end of this passage we can read him taking the measure of the current circumstance with an embittered eloquence. In this grandiloquence, Pound testifies to his apprehension of something very large at stake, something estimable really being lost.

It is in this rhetorical tenor of embittered eloquence that the word "decadence" resonates through his critical and discursive prose in the war years. In one register, it crackles as a reactive word, one that is charged with the angry courage of his defiance of the historical reality it signifies. In another, however, it is registering the stronger apprehension of a difficult truth: this circumstance of historical "decadence" is as incontrovertible now as the ready descriptor this word provides. "Decadence" is the sign of the current times; it establishes the reality of his life as a writer.

"An age may be said to be decadent, or a generation may be said to be in a state of prone senility," he reports early in 1915, "when its creative minds are dead and when its survivors maintain a mental dignity – to wit, the dignity or stationariness of a corpse in its cerements. Excess or even absinthe is not the sure sign of decadence."[20] While absinthe goes back to the café culture of Verlaine's Paris as the emblem of an artistic decadence, the range of reference and implication for this word is also, and most significantly for Pound, not confined to an association with aesthetics: "decadence" characterizes a whole historical "age" and takes on the magnitude of that reality. The same recognition answers the rhetorical question he asks, again in 1915: "Has any one yet answered the query: why is it that in other times artists went on getting more and more powerful as they grew older, whereas now they decline after the first outburst, or at least after the first successes?"[21] The exception that the Nineties figure of genius dying young marks to natural law and historical norms is now no longer so: it describes the fate of *Blast* – its "outburst" would be limited to two issues, the last of which, the "War Number," identifies the circumstance of its fall – and also the rule of the new era, that comprehensive historical present he invokes in the temporal adverbial conjunction of "whereas now." The most conspicuous figure of decadence now configures the age.[22]

Under this apprehension, he can write of an apparently inevitable stage in the history of every civilization as "Roman and later decadence."[23] Consequently, the noun "decadence" gets attached to either the indefinite or definite article. In this variation it ranges from a suppositious condition to an historical reality, gathering the comprehensive sense that its potential threat is being registered as an established fact. If "French neo-Catholicism is a decadence" and if "a Chinese decadence" is different from a Japanese one and if later ancient Greek dramatists represent "a decadence from Homer," there is "the Roman decadence" in antiquity and, shifting the frame of reference to modern drama, "the decadence" of which George Bernard Shaw is "a stage."[24] This condition manifests the reality of decadence as general and contemporary as it is pan-historical and recurrent.

Pound's generalization of this condition across historical time provides one measure of the intensity of his apprehension of it in his own present. As, here, in February 1917: "the mush of the German sentence, the straddling of the verb out to the end, are just as much a part of the befoozlement of Kultur and the consequent hell, as was the rhetoric of later Rome the seed and the symptom of the Roman Empire's decadence."[25] Rome and Germany, antiquity and modernity, recurrent and urgent: the age of this decadence is now as general and inevitable as its precedents seem to make it.

By the early postwar moment of 1920, this understanding is as presump-tive as it is, at least ruefully, humorous. "A quarter of an hour's talk with anyone knowing the south-east corner of Europe is enough to remind one that modern 'civilisation' is no more securely perched on its pinnacle than was the Roman civilisation."[26] His twentieth-century reality has moved into that frame of a recurring historical present, which he phrased earlier as "Roman and later decadence."

The reality of decadence as the main characteristic of the historical present: this understanding shows some of its impact in his apprehension of the fate of his own "generation" and the "decade" it represents, centrally, in himself. These two words, moving into cognate forms and mutating into variant senses as *degeneration* and *decadence*, provide verbal touchstones for Pound's developing sense of the character and conditions specific to his close contemporaries. This is the generation of modernists for whom, in the severe light of his extreme perspective, the "decadence" of the Nineties "decade" (the force of Pound's feeling pushes him to overlook the fact that these two words are not etymologically related) has become the renewed and intensified reality of their own decade, of their time, of wartime.

This understanding finds a central reference in the record of a now little-known project Pound undertook in mid-decade. He refers to it in a letter to Wyndham Lewis in May 1916, where he cites "a book by me called 'This Generation' dealing with contemporary events in the woild-uv-letters, with passing reference of about 3500 words on vorticism. including my original essays on you and Edward [Wadsworth]."[27] With a title and cast of characters that recall the volatile force of his *Blast* collaborators, "This Generation" went astray in transatlantic passage, and its manuscript was for a long time lost. It is now in the Beinecke archive at Yale, although its contents – older material recycled with some prolix interconnecting passages – represent less of a breakthrough document than Pound's first words seem to be claiming for it; this disparity provides its own version of the decline in the fortunes of a younger generation that is the presentiment of this moment. It appears consistent with the several major reversals of this year, all in all, in the circumstances engulfing the personnel of this generation at mid-decade. Pound's companion talents Hulme and Lewis have gone to the front, Eliot has gone silent poetically, and, as of 5 June 1915, his great friend Gaudier is gone altogether, *mort pour la patrie* in the words of the testimonial eulogy in the second, the final, *Blast*.[28] For those now older "men of 1914," whose aging has been accelerated like their Nineties prototypes but by the experience of actual war, there is a new rubric, a new tone. Pound signals something of this difference in the change he rings on the keyword in the subtitle of that projected book. "The Spirit of the Half-Decade," in the original script, becomes – in the grimly funny instructions he provides his American patron John Quinn – "Am. humorists please copy 'half-decayed.'"[29] A "decade" now "decayed," this altered keyword is hinged on the quantitative adverb so familiar from the lexicon of decadence, which plays out its sense of lessening in this somber comedy of mispronunciation. A nervy courage in the face of these adversities, this is the tone of a modernism that takes its identity from a self-conscious relation to the current circumstance, honing its expression of this declining time not on the explosive moment of the prewar avant-garde in *Blast*, but in the extended epoch of the wreckage left to – and of – "this generation."

Not that Pound controls the atrocities of modern history through some Nietzschean laughter at catastrophe. There is an engagement with the circumstance of the war through the poetics of decadence, a literary sensibility that extends and refines the representation of its historical imaginary. Most notably, first of all, in one of the first pieces of verse to represent the war and its import in a coherent way, in "The Coming of War: Actaeon."[30]

> An image of Lethe,
>   and the fields
> Full of faint light
>   but golden,
> Gray cliffs,
>   and beneath them
> A sea
> Harsher than granite,
>   unstill, never ceasing;
> High forms
>   with the movement of gods,
> Perilous aspect;
>   And one said:
> "This is Actaeon."
>   Actaeon of golden greaves!
> Over fair meadows,
> Over the cool face of that field,
> Unstill, ever moving
> Hosts of an ancient people,
> The silent cortège.   (*P*, 109–10)

With the exception of the moment enclosed by the dramatic reference to Actaeon, the poem lacks a main verb. Instead of a comprehensive syntax, there is a series of paratactic units, like the hemistiches of oral-formulaic poetry, where the prosody of the two-part line operates across a caesura. Here, however, wobblingly: the halving effect of the hemistichal units is not being complemented by the accomplishment of a full and integral line. While the poem pauses abruptly on those strongly end-stopped verses, it progresses on pauses, but without the satisfaction of completed thoughts. It is a rhythm of abruption in sense as well as sensation, suspending the tempo of consecutive development in favor of this rhythm of glimpses, featuring these little intaglios of discreet details. When these details coalesce, as they seem to do in the epic perspective of the closing section, they resolve into the atmospheric prospect of a silence as defining as Pound's own variations on the prosodic models of oral-formulaic poetry, which, all in all, remind us that we are experiencing this poem not as actual sound but under the conditions of print on the page.

On the page: where print is the shadow of language, a visual echo of a once spoken word, the condition with which Pound is so visibly reciprocating in this poem provides the most conspicuous sign of a poetics of the secondary that is at work here. This precedent sensibility of decadence is being reinvented in wartime, in this defining moment of modernism, and the extent of its presence in Pound's poetic temperament is suggested by the manifold character of secondary temporality in the poem. Afterward shows indeed in the condition in which contemporary history is being envisioned – in the opening line, in the classical site of the afterlife. In being framed and distanced as an "image," which, we know from a scientifically informed understanding in popular culture, is also always an "*after-*image," "Lethe" appears moreover not as itself but as a picture, a secondary representation. All *literary* depiction is by the necessity of *letters* on the page a seconded state, and Pound's imagistic details do all they can to emphasize the impression of a secondary level of intensity: in the "*faint* light" of the prospect, in the opacity of the "granite" color of the sea, in the "high" remoteness of the gods, in the "*cool* face of that field," etc. This sense of the secondary extends then from the historical imaginary to the poetic technique. As essential a dimension in the sensibility of literary decadence as it is in this poem, it presents this manifold poetic moment as the record of the pressure of decadence in the lived sensibility of Pound's wartime.

3.   "Decadence" in the Major Poems of Postwar Modernism

Responding to an essay by Frederic Manning on Remy de Gourmont's concept of aesthetic beauty, in an editorial footnote in an early 1919 number of the *little review*, Pound plays the word "decadent" through several misprisions. "On writing to Mr. Manning that one of his phrases was likely to be misunderstood by a public to which the term decadent (dee-kay-d'nt) conveys an impression of a young man doped with opium in the act of dyeing his finger nails with green ink . . . ."[31] Admittedly slippery at this time, the pronunciation of "decadent" could vary its stresses between the first and second syllables, shifting into a hard vowel in the middle if that syllable were being emphasized. There is no evidence to suggest that both of those first two syllables could carry the stresses of the two hard vowels Pound scores into this parenthetical version – a gesture he complements by deleting the vowel in the suffix and bunching it thus into an unpronounceable sound. "Dee-kay-d'nt" gets the "decadent" just as wrong, it is the subtler point of this obvious comedy to suggest, as this image of scandalously bad habits and unmanly behavior (the color of his nail varnish recalls Wilde's flamboyantly green carnation) is a caricature misapprehension, where the serious meaning of "decadence" will be "misunderstood" as usual by a "public" subject to sensational figures such as this. The stronger point lies in the understanding Pound has evolved as the truth of a war just ending, where "decadence" has been invested with the sense of a downturn in history as real as his experience and as massive in its consequences as the scale of that European catastrophe.

Several months later in 1919, in a review of the Russian Ballet's version of *La Boutique Fantasque*, Pound centers his appreciation in his perception of a "decadent" quality that, once again, he provides with the cautionary marks of those inverted commas. It is a defensive gesture. For he must defend a decadence that has been renewed by recent history and intensified in contemporary import against the legacy that has been left as the record of that other decade of decadence, the Nineties, which he reduces, accordingly, to a museum of clichéd attitudes and outdated practices. "[T]he age that went in for Beardsley because he was wicked and because 'wickedness was so delightful'; the period that swallowed Wilde's false doctrine that 'art is mensonge'"[32]: if that is all there is to decadence, Pound is saying, the Russian production could not have come from it. No, he stipulates, "this superfetation of cultures is 'decadent,'" where the inverted commas may be read contextually not as a dismissal of the word but as a framing and attitudinizing of the several phenomena he has catalogued as the census of its stereotyped, now outlived, associations. Accordingly, he moves immediately in the next phrase to reclaim the power of that signifier. Labeling it "that much-abused aesthetic term," he opens the obvious possibility of uses better attuned to current circumstances.[33] And this is a currency he discerns in his most searching interpretation of the contemporary Russian production.

What Pound appreciates most intensely in this *Boutique* is its featuring of the figures of the "super-marionette."[34] Both terms in this verbal compound are relevant. The "marionette" is familiar from the dramatis personae of decadence, where the "resembling *unlikeness*" (the emphasis in Pound's report) of the puppet human presents a figure as though living in the deadness of the effigy and so represents not only the cult of artifice in the sensibility of decadence but, fundamentally, the loss of organic vitality recorded across its historical and cultural imaginary. It is the totem figure in this aftermath age of present history. More specifically: a mechanical character in humankind is an apprehension that has been magnified to unprecedented proportions by the new "super" dimensions of mass technological warfare. Here, in the popular as well as poetic imaginary, individual humans have become the moving parts of a war machine as immense and inexorable as the economy of this long unstoppable conflict. These are the circumstances Pound is reflecting in his appreciation of the timely relevance of this production, which he is depicting in images that draw on his experience of the first film versions of the conflict, especially the documentary footage. Where soldier figures go reeling en masse in those jerky and uncertain movements as human marionettes on screen, they are being translated to the stage by Pound and invested with feelings as intense and poignant as those highly timely associations may bring. He now affiliates these with a decadence specific to this time: "Every gesture of these new puppets is infinitely more intense and significant by reason of its jerky restraint than were the languors of the Swinburnian dances."[35] These "Swinburnian dances" reach back to the gesture circling "decadent" with those superciliously inverted commas. As the clichéd languorousness of the dances of a now foregone decadence is updated to the "frenzy and impotence" of its modern complement, as Pound notes in the same passage, we may see the mechanical character in the decadent imaginary being restaged and reinvented – rediscovered – with the revelatory intensities of contemporary history.

"An age may be said to be decadent ...": the truth of that 1915 supposition has been confirmed by the evidence of a decadence renewed for his own age – in images variously ghastly and uncanny. If this truth has been weighed out in dead bodies by the millions, it has also been piled up in the many more millions of artificial limbs being manipulated, in the first of these postwar years, as though they still had life. Human corpse, human puppet: the effigy figure of decadence is one of the dominant and

most powerful signs of these new times. It is the pressure of this decadence, as renewed in the historical imaginary of his own time and realized
in the artistic forms of this production, that underlies the exceptional
strength in Pound's final commendation: "There has been more intelligence, more intellect, used in this ballet than in any other six ballets I can
remember."[36]

"Six years ago the Russians tried to 'modernise,'" Pound recalls in this
same report, where he is remembering his attendance at the 1913 production
of Stravinsky's *Le Sacre du Printemps*.[37] That earlier work fails the standard
he circles with those inverted commas in the same sense that *Boutique*
achieves it: this is the "new birth" which he otherwise denies the Stravinsky
piece. The difference is the intervening event of that "modern" war, as
notoriously inhuman already as the character reflected in the mechanical
quality of this ballet. Where Pound is pronging "modernise" with inverted
commas, he is turning the referent of this term into an example of a self-
consciously modern, that is, modern*ist* art. So the aesthetic that represents
this sensibility belongs to the other word he has circled for self-interrogation,
"decadent," which he has released from the dubiety of clichéd and now
outdated meanings. In the discursive work of this review, he has reconstituted an understanding of modernism with the substantial urgency that
"decadence" confers on current circumstances. Decadence provides the
poetics as well as the content of a most timely modernism. And it is the
concerted work of the poems he writes out of the longer historical moment
of the war to bear out the import of this understanding.

In this light we may reconsider *Homage to Sextus Propertius*, the creative
translation of the Roman poet that Pound was at work on through the last
half of the war. Or, more simply, just consider it. For this middle-length
sequence presents a number of obvious anomalies that have provided the
points on which scholarly commentary has stopped short. It is a poem that
comes out of the circumstances of an overwhelmingly "modern" war, but
it is rooted in distant antiquity both imaginatively and linguistically. Its
vocabulary features the kind of Latinate abstractions which Pound abjured
as one of the defining objections of his earlier modernism; also, the
rhythmical periods of a frequently hypotactic artifice are antipathetic to
those prosodies of free direct speech, which he has extolled in his opening
manifesto in the first issue of *The Egoist*. In a larger sense, the problem with
the *Homage* is the difficulty of its critical placement in a literary history that
has denied decadence as a constitutive force in the forming of modernist
poetry. This is a restriction that a reading of Pound's sequence may begin to
lift. Identifying the poetics and temper of decadence in this work may

provide one of the most vivid and conspicuous indicators of the timeliest of modernisms.

Beginning in retrospect, in 1931, when Pound quips jokingly, but help-fully: the *Homage* "presents certain emotions as vital to me in 1917, faced with the infinite and ineffable imbecility of the British Empire, as they were to Propertius some centuries earlier, when faced with the infinite and ineffable imbecility of the Roman Empire."[38] With the Roman poet Pound shares a late moment in the history of empire, which, in the grandiosity of its fall, locates the most substantial of the establishing circumstances of literary decadence. In the longer view of literary history, the temper of decadence shows most evidently in the Roman poet's ingenious retreat from the mission and vocabulary of high Augustan martial verse, of which he makes a masterfully subversive play. Propertius regularly runs a Virgilian cadence into dead-end metrics, for instance, clogging the imperial sweep of an epic prosody in rhythms that twist away from any sense of destined endings – of history as of verse lines – just as he turns the themes of imperial conquest into the sexual adventures of the paramour's bed. On an equally obvious level, a lack of reverence for the national duty of the day shows still in Pound's 1931 comment, which echoes back to a poetic register of antic Latinity fifteen years earlier, as we will see. Here, his dereliction of duty appears most clearly in the choice of subject and its complement in poetic language: this is no story of native British fortitude in war, parleyed through an English rooted in the usage of Old English heroic poetry, which was the historical mythology being purveyed by and for the poetry of the British cause. It features a Roman history of late empire days that is conveyed in a diction weighted with outlandish Latinisms. The Latinity of the current day, a Propoundius in the midst of the English war: this is the conceit of a second and present decadence, undertaken in the imaginative tense of a modernism whose self-consciousness about its own time shows above all in its manipulation of contemporary idiom.

This current slang is juxtaposed in the linguistic wit of the sequence to extravagantly Latinate English. Pound is compositing the talky poet of the modern day with the antipodal time and manner of distant antiquity, where the sometimes tedious exactitude of Roman legal documents or chronicle prose serves to characterize that written record:

> Celebrities from the Trans-Caucasus will belaud Roman celebrities
> And expound the distentions of Empire,
> But for something to read in normal circumstances?
> For a few pages brought down from the forked hill unsullied?
> I ask a wreath which will not crush my head.

> And there is no hurry about it;
> I shall have, doubtless, a boom after my funeral,
> Seeing that long standing increases all things
>   regardless of quality.   (P, 205)

Who might "ex*pound* the distention of Empire" more cannily than Pound in his own time? This unmistakable signature takes ownership of the main conceit of this passage, as of this poem's whole historical imaginary. In this time of late empire, *redivivus*, the sense of a present being ghosted by a past shows as the words of a most contemporary sensibility are overshadowed by those background Latinisms. The *anachronistic* or (literally, etymologically) *backward time* of this poetic idiolect presents a supreme iteration of the poetics of afterward in literary decadence, where, in effect, the most contemporary expressions are being presented in and as the long aftertime of a primary foretime in linguistic history. The slang Pound dubs in reminds us where we are in present history, but its loquacious moment, which contributes to the fiction of living voice in literature, fades by dint of the smaller share it has in this passage (as of the whole sequence) into the archival silence of a longer gone but greater Latinity. This is the Latinity that waits at the end of every sentence as the *memento mori* of itself, of the empire that left these verbal remnants to English to begin with, and of a British empire winding down on the fading voice of its own day.

Not without comedy, sepulchral or not: Latinity impinges on the rhythms and diction of this poem in the fashion of verbal farce. Polysyllabic Latinisms are forced into cadences as willfully congested as these:

> Jove, be merciful to that unfortunate woman
>   Or an ornamental death will be held to your debit,
> The time is come, the air heaves in torridity,
> The dry earth pants against the canicular heat,
> But this heat is not the root of the matter . . .   (P, 217)

Recherché as it may be, "torridity" *is* an English word, deriving from the Latin root that gives us "torrid," but "canicular"? From "canis," recalling the English "canine," and so calling up the dog days of summer? Well. A nonword or, more accurately, a nonce-Latinism, it is amplified through the rhythmical rhyme with the four-syllable "torridity" into the affective volume of a comprehensive verbal comedy. The whole concoction recalls a practice familiar in the history of literary decadence, the sometimes overdone Latinity of *Marius the Epicurean*, but Pound out-patters the Pater of Latinate Victoriana with the extremity of his verbal sport. And the difference goes to the modernist quality of this production.

Pound is "making it new," but in a way that runs around or even against the accustomed sense of that overused phrase for modernism in general and modernist translation in particular. The verbal surface certainly presents a poetic language that is freed from any literalism in the construal. But this "creative" translation shows a practice that actually "keeps it old" as its boldest motive. An overdoing of the Latinity of his poetic English is the most evident incentive in the translation that the whole sequence features. Overdone or not, and excess is the measure of invention, here of a modernist reinvention of decadence, this surplus comes from the same hand that provides those occasional touches of Pound's verbal modernity as a character in voice in the poem. A minor character, and the sign of a minority time in the profounder depth of its historical imaginary, this voice of verbal modernity shows also as the manifest sign of the poem's consciousness of its own time, that is, of the modernist quality in this whole production.

As one of its now obvious consequences, this linguistic initiative features the recovery of Latinity itself as a poetic and expressive language. The idiolect of the poem is so full of Latinate terms, the language so drenched in Latinisms, that Pound's own poetic English seems like the dead language. This is the great conceit of the sequence. It is the range of innovation that is most intense with implication, as one other example may suggest.

This three-line vignette begins by framing a romantic encounter from the poetic fiction of Propertius:

> She was veiled in the midst of that place,
> Damp woolly handkerchiefs were stuffed into her undryable eyes,
> And a querulous noise responded to our solicitous reprobations.   (*P*, 211)

"She was *veiled* in the *midst* of that *place*": sufficiently inconspicuous to require the additional emphases, a trimeter rhythm is spaced through the passage in syntactic patterns apparently natural to speech. It is indeed the speech of an Imagist, joining the details of sensory perception to the expressive measures of imagined voice. It is an absolutely modern prosody, elegantly and intelligently of Pound's moment in recent literary history. By the next line, however, the diction has begun to turn, going into the oddly concocted "undryable." And so it goes, as comically Latinate as wholly antique, by the third: "And a querulous noise responded to our solicitous reprobations." From the modern to the unfamiliar to the distantly archival or recherché, from the living to the dead: this is a circuit that is traversed throughout the sequence as a feat of sensibility. It is the loop of wit that takes a modern consciousness, recognizable often through comedy, particularly through anachronistic impositions on the historical fiction of Roman

Empire days, and parleys this contemporary sensibility through an ever denser matrix of Latinate English. This is the darker matter, the tragic backdrop to the high jinks of the poem's verbal surface, its performative foreground, so that, all in all, in a sort of tonal chiaroscuro, the rising rhythm of Pound's verbalist humor includes the dying fall of a former (and present) empire. The modernist, who is definably conscious of his own time, has claimed the establishing circumstance of this poem's verbal and imaginative work in that decadent presentiment of an imminent (and immanent) end.

What this verbal comedy cannot accommodate or reconcile is also obvious. "There died a myriad, / And of the best, among them" (*P*, 188). In this second of the two war lyrics in the fictional autobiography of *Hugh Selwyn Mauberley* (1920), Pound's phrasing recalls not only the massive scale of casualties but more particular, more intimate, deaths. Those "best" include his good friends and companion talents in 1910s London: the poet turned critic T. E. Hulme, who was killed in 1917 and, two years earlier, the sculptor Henri Gaudier, who, dead at 23, provides the unidentified but irresistible center of reference for his commemoration of many other early deaths:

> Young blood and high blood,
> fair cheeks and fine bodies; . . .
> hysterias, trench confessions,
> laughter out of dead bodies.   (*P*, 188)

Ruined youth is not just a literary conceit. The legend of decadence has been realized, made real in the historical experience of the generation Pound has identified with himself. And he re-inscribes this history in the narrative motive and conceptual plan of his two-part sequence, which, being written into this fictional autobiography as the story of the generation ending with the decade now ending, follows the narrative of genius dying young.

There has been a large amount of fine critical work done on this poem, usually analyzing the identities of the speaking characters in the two parts of the sequence, but we can read the poem anew in the context of the literary history we have recovered as the biography of his early career. We can go to some of the fundamental principles of design in its imaginative narrative and affective elaboration. And here we may discern the extent to which he has assimilated the story of genius dying young, that foundational myth of literary decadence.

At its own foundations, to begin with, in November 1919, when, as Pound is beginning to compose the poems of the sequence and design its comprehensive shape, Max Beerbohm brings out a small volume of short stories, *Seven Men*. This collection contains a tale, "Hilary Maltby and Stephen Braxton," which will prove especially resonant for the author of *Hugh Selwyn Mauberley*. In the otherwise unplaced origin of this fictional character's family name, "Mauberley" picks up an echo in "Maltby." This is the most typical and obvious correspondence in the profounder consonance that Pound's sequence reveals with Beerbohm's tale, which retells the Nineties fable in paradigmatic fashion.

In Beerbohm's story, the two young authors Maltby and Braxton produce their "firstlings" in the spring of 1895. Both of these literary works find immediate success, stimulating each other's renown by competing for the fame of the day. Their nearly concurrent second efforts – Braxton's published in autumn 1895, Maltby's in spring 1896 – are instantaneous failures. "Maltby might once more have been compared with Braxton," the narrator muses with mock ruefulness, "but Braxton was now forgotten. So was Maltby."[39] Their high moment, after all, has been the decade's: 1895. This is the year, in most of the subsequent legends and commemorations of the decade, as in Holbrook Jackson's,[40] when the turn for the worst begins to occur; indeed, in the affective memory of the Nineties, it is in the spring of that year, which is of course the season of Wilde's extended trial and incipient fall. Beerbohm's personages are enacting the myth of fin de siècle, then, at its climacteric: in the brief compass of that single literary year, they die nearly as they are born.

"We presume it is harder to write straight comedy like Wilde or like Maltby than to . . . ."[41] So, in March 1920, just after completing the sequence, Pound reveals his awareness of the title character in the Beerbohm story and brings him into company with the other icon of the decade, Oscar Wilde. This perception of the representative value of Beerbohm's creation is sufficiently intense to be repeated in expansive fashion more than a decade and a half later, in a now little known enterprise of 1936, when the poet responded to the initiatives of the literary agent Montgomery Butchart and deliberated for nearly six months on the possibility of writing *The Life and Times of Max Beerbohm*. In fact, Beerbohm is the exemplary figure of his decade for Pound, as he attests in unpublished correspondence about the project: "as to Max: from my pt./ of v, there AINT any one of LIKE standing" in the Nineties. In declining the assignment, he pays Beerbohm the ultimate compliment by deferring to this writer's work as the only true mirror "of the period": "nothing but Max own work deals with the surface in a possible way."[42] Pitch-perfect to the period for Pound, Beerbohm demonstrates his inwardness with the myth of the Nineties in the story that the poet will appropriate for the story of his own poetic decade.

This appropriation is witnessed in the multiple correspondences to be found between the characters as well as the narrative of Beerbohm's story and those of Pound's sequence, which, despite an elliptical fiction, does follow a roughly sequential narrative pattern. Here the two personages of the poem's two major parts, "E.P." and "Mauberley," represent respectively if roughly the earlier and later parts of Pound's career. These characters, like Beerbohm's, come to one and the same early end. Where E.P. "passed from men's memory in *l'an trentuniesme / De son age*" (*P*, 185), and, in the larger imaginative design of the sequence, begets his double Mauberley simultaneously out of – and as – that failure, so the protagonists in Beerbohm's story experience their meteoric rise and fall at the shared age of thirty, that is, in the thirty-first year of their age.

Resemblance extends to the individual characteristics of the counterpart figures. "[B]orn / In a half savage country," (*P*, 185), that is, Hailey, Idaho, E.P. emerges from the American version of the English background of Braxton, who was "born and bred among his rustics" ("HMSB," 42). They are both characters of vigorous literary independence. Likening E.P. to Capaneus, one of the Seven Against Thebes struck down for his defiant impiety, Pound mythologizes the same trait that Beerbohm notes, more drolly, in Braxton, who "had distinction, I admit it; the distinction of one who steadfastly refuses to adapt himself to surroundings. He stood out" ("HMSB," 40). This is the distinction of an E.P. who, in the other mythological likeness to the heroic voyager Odysseus, "fished by obstinate isles" (*P*, 185) – that is, refused to adapt himself to the surroundings of the British Isles and the hebetude of its insular poetic clime. It is equally easy now to see the similarity between Mauberley and his namesake in Beerbohm's story. The title of Maltby's first book, *Ariel in Mayfair*, catches the effete, lighter-than-air affect of an aesthete who has refined himself out of bodily existence. All too evidently sexless, this Maltby has taken to elaborate rituals of artifice in his obsessive attention to costume, to the secondary skins of clothing. In a similar fiction of aesthetic disembodiment, Mauberley has "drifted . . . drifted precipitate, / Asking time to be rid of . . . / Of his bewilderment," where the ellipses score an open space into the fabric of the language and so, in the visual prosody of the page, provide a complement for the imagery of airborne insubstantiality (*P*, 197). The concomitant project in the poetics of decadence is the denaturalizing of the literary fiction of voice. So, in the next stanza, Pound repeats the gesture of the ellipsis and lowers the signal word in Maltby's book title into the affective silence of a parenthetical aside: "To be certain . . . certain . . . / (Amid aerial flowers) . . . time for arrangements – / Drifted on / To the final estrangement" (*P*, 197).

To "Mauberley," which provides the title of the second part of the sequence, Pound adds the subtitle date: "1920" (*P*, 196), so to complement the "1919" date on the last poem of the E.P. section. He may be nodding toward the successive-year plan in the story of the rise and fall of that joint personage Maltby-Braxton. Moreover, in a literary fiction that has featured the record of the 1910s so extensively, this framing designation of the next year also conveys an overpowering sense of *afterward*. This is the primary imaginative tense in the literary sensibility of decadence, and Pound implements it diversely through the second part of the sequence.

In echoes, to begin with, already in the second quatrain of the first poem of this second part, where the stirring phrase in the likeness Pound has drawn between himself as E.P. and the Odyssean hero – "His true Penelope was Flaubert" – recurs, but within a set of inverted commas – "His true Penelope / Was Flaubert" – which turns this repetition into a citation, a reference to an earlier version, all in all, a secondary reference (*P*, 185, 196). This sense of a diminished second is reinforced as the recurrence occurs across the turn of a verse, which breaks the momentum of the earlier, grander claim. The same rhythm of diminuendo shows where the enjambment brings the rhythm around in this next line to touch the upswing syllable "Was": the simple copula of the verb "to be" in the past tense fails to sustain the weight of any stress and lets the cadence fall accordingly. These techniques all contribute to our felt understanding that this Flaubert, being known above all for creating Madame Bovary, is not so grand after all as the Homer who gave us Penelope. The French novelist is in every sense a second-comer to the Hellenic poet of mythical firsts. The downturn of this parabolic tale extends in the larger design through the change of E.P. into Mauberley, who, in echoing the figures of his erstwhile original, is also and most of all a diminished reiterative.

"THE AGE DEMANDED." Quoted as well as capitalized, the title of the third poem in the second part shows Pound echoing this signal phrase from the second poem of the first part:

> The age demanded an image
> Of its accelerated grimace,
> Something for the modern stage,
> Not, at any rate, an Attic grace; . . .   (*P*, 186, 198)

Against the "age" that "demanded" an "image" of itself and its "accelerated" tempo of change, Pound expresses his self-conscious sense of his place in modern time. His modernism shows thus as a *modern*ity against itself. This is an imaginative apprehension of an instantaneousness – a *today*, a radical Now – that is constantly sought, always lost. In the longer story of his career as well as the sequence as a whole, this temperament has been established and reinforced by the sensibility of "decadence," which, in response to what the "age" has "demanded," excepts itself from the prevailing standards of a progressive present, whose presence is obviously impossible.

And so, already in this vignette from the first part of the sequence, in the next stanza but one, Pound submits those coerced and coercive words to the circling action and reversing effect of inverted commas. "The 'age demanded' chiefly a mould in plaster . . ." (*P*, 186). Heckling echo it may be, but echo it is. The decadent is taking exception to the claim of this "age," that is, by submitting the claim of this present day to a weakening repeat of itself.

The poetics of repetition in the sensibility of literary decadence is working to the purposes of demonstration, then, not only of expression. Consider those look-alike eye-rhymes in the terminal words of the preceding quatrain. Here is a lexical image of the reiterative visual consistency of contemporary mass culture. This, we remember from Henry James's signal figure of Beach Donner, demonstrates an age of mechanical reproduction in the weakening repeats of decadent temporality. So, here, in the poetic experience, the expectation of rhyme in these final syllables effects an acoustic confusion, a phonic wobble that smudges the distinctness of individual words, as of individual things in the commodity productions of public culture. The dissonance is demonstrative.

As with the fiction "demonstrating decadence" in the novels of the historical moment of the turn of the century, Pound is showing these conditions of contemporary history under the forms he is drawing from the resources of literary decadence especially. This demonstration is as extensive, in the second part of the sequence, as the dominance of a particular literary idiom in its rhetorical fiction. This is a Latinity that, as with the elaborated Latinisms of the *Homage*, presents no donnish obfuscations. Where the excess is a measure of his reinvention of this lexicon of literary decadence, it is also a gauge for the greater inventiveness of an anti-modern modernism, whose sense of special time comes with this feeling of being out of time.

Conspicuously so, in the third poem of this second part, where a Latinate register takes over the diction:

> Invitation, mere invitation to perceptivity
> Gradually led him to the isolation

> Which these presents place
> Under a more tolerant, perhaps, examination.
>
> By constant elimination
> The manifest universe
> Yielded an armour
> Against utter consternation . . .   (*P*, 199)

In the manifestly (and chokingly) dead language of these Latinisms, the poet offers the tense of afterward as the condition of literary English in his own time. As in the *Homage*, then, the Latinate vocabulary presents anything but a retreat from a sense of contemporary history. This poetic language provides a stronger characterization of "these presents," where the otherwise oddly plural number of this noun offers a stylization as arch as the idea of a timely Latinity.[43] Ponderously comic as it suitably is, the verbal wit of this passage is instinct with the conceit that has provided a dominant concept in the modernism of the later 1910s for Pound. The historical self-consciousness of the modernist finds the boldest and most inventive gestures of literary representation in this feeling of being out of time and, so, presents itself in the dead language Latinisms of literary decadence.

"Gladstone was *still* respected," the sixth poem in the first part of the sequence opens by gesturing, "Swinburne / And Rossetti *still* abused" (*P*, 189). The emphases added to the recurrence of this temporal adverb underscore an ambivalence about cultural time and duration. Here, in the beginning of the sixth poem in the first part of the sequence, as Pound turns to the circumstances of a first literary decadence in the narrative of literary history that he is telling within his own story, he begins this history in the first poem to follow those extraordinary war lyrics he provides in the fourth and fifth poems. So, "still" hinges the literary and cultural history of decadence into a suggestive continuum with wartime. This impression is intensified insofar as the narrative of literary history in the sequence is moving now in *backward time*, going in the reverse direction that the *anachronisms* so special to the temporal imaginary of decadence tend to feature. Obliquely, but revealingly, this reversal complements the effect of the war in those master narratives of Progress, against which the modernist and decadent define themselves.

More, and more particularly: the connection Pound intimates between a first and second decadence in English literary history, between the Nineties of his forerunners and the Teens of his companion talents, deepens through the experience of genius dying young. His generation will have realized this conceit at a scale unimaginable in the more fanciful circumstance of the century ending with that earlier decade. References to Swinburne and Rossetti thus crest in this account into episodic narratives that feature the representative instances of ruined youth in the Nineties legends. We hear stories of Dowson and Johnson, who were famed for their premature demises, but also, more interestingly because less famously, Victor Plarr (*P*, 189–90). Even more inconspicuous here under his synonym of M. Verog, Plarr will have followed the parabolic narrative of the Maltby and Braxton story perfectly. He has been the one-book wonder of *In the Dorian Mood*, published appropriately in the year of Maltby's demise, 1896. (A roman-à-clef reference to his author Beerbohm comes under the pseudonym of "Brennbaum," the title and figure of the next poem in the sequence.) Accordingly, in the biographical fiction of M. Verog's place of nonliterary employment in a science laboratory, the "pickled foetuses" lying around the remains of his poetic career blazon that fin-de-siècle legend of literary birth as death (*P*, 190).

Just two months after completing the sequence, Pound wrote a retrospective, roundup review of Arthur Symons, whom he appreciates as one of the hallmark poets of the English Nineties. In the process, he includes a considered assessment of this career in relation to himself and his own time. He appreciates Symons as the author of the "best of the Paterine prose books of the nineties," and he identifies him more discerningly as a representative of the best of "decadence." Those inverted commas return to circle the word Pound will have spent the last half-decade disclaiming and reclaiming for himself and his own generation. Accordingly, he distances and qualifies his estimation of Symons, who now "has reappeared as if still in the land of '95, writing still of Javanese dancers . . . Poem after poem strikes one as not quite the thing to convince a younger audience that Symons was, in the nineties, a permanent poet."[44] In this measured assessment, the period feeling of the Nineties – epitomized in the year that locates the moment of reversal, which provides in turn the defining event of the "fall" in that decade of de*cad*ence – both prescribes and limits the validity of Symons. And what, except years, has intervened? "I am deliberately beginning this essay from memory, and in the surety that there has been no book of Symons on my shelf since some vague period 'before the war.'"[45] Where Symons's "decadence" belongs for Pound's sense of cultural history to "some vague period 'before the war,'" this second set of inverted commas signals just that self-consciousness about historical time that is the defining sensibility of the modernist. In the much less "vague" sense of his own "period" during as well as after wartime, Pound obviously holds the war to account for his generation's outliving the appeal of the Nineties myth. In that ordeal, as recorded in the poetry and prose he has generated for these last five years, he and they have also lived out that legend in their own time, on their own grander scale. This is no obscure testament to the ongoing power of a tradition that Pound has made new, and newly representative as well as expressive. In that accomplishment, he has offered the basis for our understanding of it as a sensibility in which these two terms, now enriched historically, may combine meaningfully. "Modernism" and "decadence" are the signals of two inter-penetrating and reciprocating conditions. Pound has brought these together as the achievement of the first part of a career that, if it does not represent the whole of his generation, does at least (it is no small thing) bring the sense of his time to one of its acutest presentations.

Reforming Decadence: Late Romanticism, Modernism, and the Politics of Literary History

"Poets are the unacknowledged legislators of the World."[1] Shelley's dictum tends to be repeated most frequently to lay stress on the legislative force of literature. An equal emphasis should fall on the point that this law making is unacknowledged. This assertion does not constitute a plea for public recognition of poets. Rather, it is an indication that literature works its political effects indirectly, that is, through ways of happening that are characteristic of a literary imagination, say, through some enhanced fashioning of a common language. If this understanding sees the political power of poets, not as the result of their address to specific social issues, but instead as a function of their artistic making, another dictum from another age comes into view, but only as readily as it comes up as a problem in the politics of Shelley's poetics. "Art for art's sake": the more art works to its own apparent purposes, following the logic of Shelley's promise, the better it exerts its legislative effect. Yet the social contract drafted by poets in this formulation would seem to be written in invisible ink. How legible, let alone legislatorial, is it? What possible *use* could it be?

The question is accentuated when the "art for art's sake" adage is attached to that moment in literary and cultural history in which it originated – to the aestheticism of a late-nineteenth-century Anglo-French literary culture, which includes the attitudes stemming from the poet most identified with it: Baudelaire.[2] In his emphasis on the absolute value of art, which involves a strident defiance of the socially or morally improving uses of art, the French poet is seen as the defining type of the fallen – de*cad*ent – artist. At this extremity, the issue of the political utility of art is focused at a revealing extreme. Decadence appears on this site to be equally revolutionary and useless: it overturns the presumptive understandings of social as well as literary culture but to no evident purpose, not even nihilism or anarchism. This attitude becomes well known among some of the most contrarian artistic groupings in the subsequent century, which include avant-garde factions as various as vorticism and fauvism. As their major challenge and substantial dare, these programs promote a sort of intransitive revolution. Although the manifesto culture of the avant-garde reveals a history and memory of class warfare, including "The Communist Manifesto," this political tradition is elliptical and fragmentary, so that, by the early twentieth century, many of these documents tend to stimulate artistic events whose political consequences are invoked en large rather than claimed in particulars. They work in the mood of a future subjunctive, where the imperative present serves usually as a rhetorical fiction of consequence: the rebellion eventuates mainly in the making of the artistic event itself.[3]

This particular brand of aesthetical politics can be seen as a formation stemming from the literary and cultural time of post-revolutionary France. Here there is a long process of detaching from the millenarian possibilities of revolutionary romanticism – without wholly absconding from them. Admitting that the renewal of historical time through the poetic spot of time is already an intentional rather than an actual event, Shelley's statement represents a further attenuation. He is relocating the framework of political change from the external and historical realm to the internal and personal dimension, but, in the wording of that memorable phrase, he does not forego the political consequence entirely. And the move from revolution to legislation is not the most significant development here. It is, rather, an ongoing attenuation of the relevance of an art that remains connected to some original myth of political applicability. The sensibility of decadence, for which the useless beauty of art is its use and which anticipates the avant-garde conceit of an aesthetically intransitive revolution, registers a development and a complication of this precedent: the ongoing promises of early romanticism will have lived forward into the artistic practices and imaginative attitudes of decadence, where, as we saw in a number of representative instances in Chapter I, they constitute a sometimes productive impossibility, providing sources of significant and particularly eloquent distress. Where, in turn, the sensibility of decadence will have been regained as a powerfully present memory within the literary modernisms of Pound and (next) Eliot, its ongoing life in the political imaginary of this next century shows in the intensification, not in the resolution, of that problem of a revolutionarily useless art. This escalation presents a stage in the developmental history of modernism, one that provides a substantial dimension of understanding for some of the most controversial extremities in the politics of modernists.

I am not attempting to provide a comprehensive account of a politics of modernism (which is, of course, individual and various). Nor am I seeking to blame, let alone to forgive, any of the tendencies these artists may evidence individually. Rather, I want to reposition our understanding of the development of the political sensibilities of these two poets in the framework of a cultural history that is longer than the one usually provided. A literary history that has regained decadence as a sensibility within modernism will restore an essential context for our understanding of the presumptive place of poetry in political history and, in this way, provide a new perspective on the development of what is understood to be a reactionary politics in modernism.

This aspect of its political character has already generated a significant critical history. This critique reaches its deepest memory and furthest implication where it is extending a Marxist commentary. Its baseline understanding, informed by the principle of the economic determination of literature, is inflected sometimes in readings of considerable ideological subtlety, but it tends as a matter of course to situate a modernist sensibility in the middling position of a European middle class. From this location, an antipathy to socialist futures (to be won through revolutionary class struggle rather than evolutionary humanist progress) is, arguably, most motivated and intense. And the commitment to the possibility of this future among Marxist critics compels a searching interrogation of an antiprogressive sensibility within modernism.

The place of "decadence" in this antiprogressive temperament is at once highly charged and relatively unexamined in this critical tradition. This term is readily available and often availed of in a judgmental sense in Marxist historiography, where it designates a backsliding from the forward-oriented direction of progressive destiny. What is the relevance and significance of "decadence" to the political question in a specifically *literary* history, however? How do we think of the political involvements of modernist authors in terms of a literary history that is informed by the sensibility of decadence in general but constituted most particularly, as in Shelley's understanding of poetry's unacknowledged legislation, by the workings of its specifically formal, technical sensibility?

The most comprehensive Marxist response to these fundamental questions comes from Georg Lukács, in *The Meaning of Contemporary Realism* (1957). This book, which emphasized the origins of literary modernism in literary as well as cultural decadence, characterized "the ideology of modernism" (the title of his first chapter) as a reaction formation, which was working to reverse the ideals of emancipatory revolution in the literature of European socialism. On one side, as a Marxist, Lukács was still defending socialism as the best form in which to actualize human "potentiality" (his word for progress, to be won through revolution) and "realism" as its literary vehicle and expedient. On this other side, as a literary critic, he was character-izing modernism as a sensibility that, in its aversion to the progressiveness of social history, demonstrated a morbid self-absorption assignable to the attitudes and practices of artistic decadence.[4] Thus he critiques in most livid particulars Benjamin's analysis of allegory in German baroque drama, which, as we have seen, adumbrates that critic's interest in a poetics of decadence specifically. Most particularly: the emphasis on death and the deathly in baroque dramatic allegory, as in the poetics of decadence that Benjamin is prefiguring in it, provides Lukács the most vivid and indicative instance of the "annihilation of history" that is "the aesthetic consequence of modern-ism."[5] So Lukács finds a critical model for the modernism he loathes the most, which, in his understanding, works from a position of decadence to subvert those currents of historical futurity that he identifies with the aims and ends of progressive socialist revolution. Taking this critique several turns further, he would draw a forceful connection between a regressive direction in this ideology of modernism and a reactionary political orientation, which was manifest most dramatically in an attraction to fascism.

This is the critical tradition I wish to pick up in several of its most developed iterations, in the later work of three of its most prominent practi-tioners: following a further reading of Lukács into Theodor Adorno and Fredric Jameson. Writing across the last half of the twentieth century and into the first decade of the twenty-first, these writers continue to influence the attitudes of contemporary critical practice. The *idéoligiecritique* which they feature has informed a turn in the last several decades to a critical emphasis on a counter-modern quality in modernism, which ranges in its centers of attention from a reactionary character in fascist politics to a dystopian view of the future. It extends so widely now that a census is at once unnecessary and impossible. Routinely, however, this tradition fails to take coherent account of the influence of decadence as a specifically literary history, that is, as a composite of technical attitudes and formal practices, in the reckoning of modernist politics. In the earlier modernism we are looking at in this book, the relative dearth of explicit position papers or political screeds puts the work of interpretation more heavily in the texts of the literature itself, which Shelley would designate as the scene of most meaningful political action. However, as we shall see in this inter-chapter, this sector of evidence goes significantly missing in the formative Marxist critiques, and the reasons for its absence locate issues specific to this critical tradition.

A close consideration of the poetics of decadence in the formation of modernism and a politics of modernism was foreclosed, in adamant and sweeping fashion, by Lukács himself. This is a principled resistance, beginning in a Marxist understanding and characterization of the technical inventiveness in modernism. He sees this already celebrated quality as a tactical but symptomatic deflection of authorial responsibility. Not the broader sort of "perspective" (*weltanschauung*), which a socialist realist would rightly take as a vantage on the bigger-picture issues of political history, modernism demonstrates a myopic preoccupation with inconsequential procedures, an all-absorbing obsession with trivial manners in literary practices, which provide the sands, as it were, in which the elegant but vestigial form of the modernist ostrich hides its unknowing head. A similar image attends the critic getting lost in the verbal recesses of modernist literature, where the discredited efforts of literary technique and the devalued practice of close reading are joined as the earlier and later phases of bourgeois "decadence." This term, which implies as usual a backsliding from the progressive destinies of a socialist future, works mainly as a term of rhetorical and ideological judgment but also, as Lukács's commentary on Benjamin suggests, as a designation relevant to literary history.[6] Where "decadence" appears as the antimatter of historical advance in the ideology of Marxism, then, it disappears as the matter of analytical work in this critical account of the literature of major record.

In the continuance of this Marxist tradition after Lukács, however, and as an extension of his own practical disregard for the actual texts of modernism, there is a significant ambivalence in the values attributed to "technique." Avoidance of the written words of modernism leaves this category of literary activity and critical analysis largely vacant and, so, open for projection. And the political interests being imposed on this otherwise blank category are interestingly and revealingly conflicted. Here, even while the "backward" character of the technical preoccupation of a bourgeois modernism is sometimes asserted, a significant line in Marxist criticism demonstrates an extension of the scholarly understanding of modernism that Edmund Wilson so influentially modeled, where its methods and ethics are aligned with those of progressive revolution. This contradiction is worth identifying and following through to a conclusion, which is the opening it offers for a new (close) reading of some of the key texts of early modernism. Its cultural politics may be positioned anew in relation to some of its restored sources in literary decadence.

Political Prepositioning

Adorno is commonly acknowledged as the subtlest dialectician in Marxist literary and cultural criticism, and he represents the most flexible sensibility when it comes to the value of art as art. He routinely abjures the claims for consequential novelty among any number of assignably "modernist" authors, but his criteria for this exclusionary judgment tend to be not political but aesthetic. Among other things, he is important to modernism for the rapprochements he establishes between his political principles and the modernist artistry of his favored figures. Joyce and Beckett, Schoenberg and Kafka: these authors are second to none in the idiosyncrasy and inventiveness of their aesthetic craft. Just so, however, they are seen to be working in the spirit of the revolutionary and emancipatory ideal that Adorno posits as an ultimate value for art, which, in the end, achieves these effects only indirectly, as art, and never intentionally. "Insofar as a social function can be predicated for artworks, it is their functionlessness," he proposes in his last (posthumously published) book, *Aesthetic Theory* (1970), his summa, where he elaborates and clarifies this apparent paradox. "Through their difference from a bewitched reality, [artworks] embody negatively a position in which what is would find its rightful place, its own. Their enchantment is disenchantment."[7] Only in being removed from explicit political purpose, that is, can art achieve the power to transform its historical world. It provides the means of its own exceptionality to challenge the standards and conventions of a class-based ownership of the means of cultural production, which serves as the most insidious form of imprisonment for the sensibility of its unwitting consumers. In this evaluation, at its bleaker extreme, much of the acknowledged or attributed novelty in modernist technique is unpromising: any but the most extreme and austere technical inventions – Schoenberg's, say, or Beckett's – will be appropriated and normalized to the existing order by the market forces of commodity capitalism.[8]

Adorno sets out these formulas with the embittered eloquence of his critique of the "culture industry" in the later twentieth century. He looks back tellingly to the previous century, however, when he reserves a place for the political working of "art as art" in *Aesthetic Theory*. "It was plausible that socially progressive critics should have accused the program of *l'art pour l'art*, which has often been in league with political reaction, of promoting a fetish with the concept of a pure, exclusively self-sufficient artwork."[9] Acknowledging the potentially *reaction*ary character of an art that removes itself from political history in general and progressive destiny in particular, he proceeds to engage this standard Marxist rationale for judging the apparently backward-tracking politics of an "art for art's sake" attitude. Here he qualifies the expected objection that an aesthetics of this kind wrongly exempts itself from an awareness of the material circumstance and social conditions (the labor), which work of any kind entails. Indeed, he goes so far as to suggest that art of any type involves itself necessarily in a "nexus of guilt" about its fetishized character, not to reiterate that guilt but, it is the force of this subtle consideration to suggest, to forgive it.[10] This forgiveness of art for its own sake may be made in view of the ultimate efficacy of art's exceptionality to the standards and conventions of existing history. But this is a remission of the sin, in the judgmental lexicon of Marxist historiography, of nothing less – or more – than "decadence" itself.

The sensibility of decadence, it is essential to recognize, is being converted to a poetics and a politics of progressiveness: the work of art as art is forgiven insofar as its exception to the conventions of history opens up all the possibilities of a social novelty that it models. This is a point of ramifying import in *Aesthetic Theory*. The negotiation is in process throughout the book, and, in the historical framework of Adorno's attentions, it extends through the successive eras of "*l'art pour l'art*" and modernism, where this banner of progressivity is carried by "technique" and "form" as wholly abstract categories of value. We can follow its consequences through *Aesthetic Theory* and into Jameson's later work, where we may see the extremes it reveals in their shared understanding not only of a politics of early modernism but of later modernism, too.

Again and again Adorno revisits the possibility of the social and specifically progressive and indeed revolutionary efficacy of modernist formal and technical inventions. Now discrediting Lukács's campaign against the "importance of form" in modernist art as a "philistine call to arms,"[11] he frames an antithetical understanding of technique and its political content and consequence. It appears to be important both substantially and effectively, holding out the possibility of transitive force, indeed a transformational power, in the social and political history in which it is otherwise inevitably embedded. "There are historical moments in which forces of production emancipated in art represent a real emancipation," he avers, and these "moments" are concentrated predominantly in the consciousness of modernism. "[T]he modern," he proposes to further this possibility, "is not a chronological concept but the Rimbaudian postulate of an art of the most advanced consciousness, an art in which the most progressive and differentiated technical procedures are saturated with the most progressive and differentiated experiences," which, for him, are social and political experiences. This claim is remade and expanded as this last passage continues. Here, as he repeats the keyword "advanced," he invokes the social transitivity of modernist technique as a radiating efficaciousness and progressiveness: "the substantive element of artistic modernism draws its power from the fact that the most advanced procedures of material production and organization are not limited to the sphere in which they originate. In a manner scarcely analyzed yet by sociology, they radiate out into areas of life far removed from them ....."[12]

This estimate shows the power of an underlying mythology of progressive revolution and emancipation in the scholarly understanding of modernist art. Adorno localizes it in the historical era of early modernism most particularly. Ahead of the momentous history of the twentieth century, so this legend goes, a kind of mythical modernist beforetime witnesses the integration of advanced technical experiment and revolutionary political impact. This fabled moment is framed retrospectively and nostalgically from the late 1960s. "The relation of social praxis and art, always variable, may well have changed radically once again over the last forty or fifty years," he opens regretfully, but then counters to the positive with this turn to an earlier time: "During World War I and prior to Stalin, artistic and politically advanced thought went in tandem: whoever came of age in those years took art to be what it in no way historically had been: *a priori* politically on the left."[13] These socially "advanced" energies of early artistic modernism are co-opted as coercively in the new Soviet Union as in the old and new worlds of European capitalism and Hollywood America, but the fatalism of this critical account preserves the first years of the century as the time in which this progressive ideal was indeed realized.

This is an idealized conception that he makes every effort to protect in the defensive gestures and strenuous exceptions of his next sentences. Here he takes account of complications in the evolving politics of the historical avant-garde in that fabled moment of early modernism. "Avant-garde doctrines," he opens,

> if their opposition to *communis opinio* is grasped with sufficient abstraction and if they remain to some degree moderate, are sometimes susceptible to elitist reinterpretation, as has been the case with Pound and Eliot. Benjamin already noted the fascist penchant in futurism, which can be traced back to peripheral aspects of Baudelaire's modernism. All the same, when Benjamin in his later work distanced himself from the aesthetic avant-garde at those points where it failed to toe the Communist Party line, Brecht's hatred of Tui intellectuals may well have played a part. The elitist isolation of advanced art is less its doing than society's ...[14]

While the "case with Pound and Eliot" will be taken up through the next sections of this inter-chapter, it is the case of Adorno and Benjamin that is most relevant in this passage. What Adorno seems to be recalling is their disagreements on the mass-cultural capacity of avant-garde art, which worked in accord with a liberating technology of mechanical reproduction for Benjamin and the regrettable vulgarizations of the culture industry for Adorno. What is interesting and revealing in this representation, however, is the forcefulness with which Adorno overrides those differences and presents an imaginatively shared understanding about the potential for progressive revolutionary politics in the "aesthetic avant-garde" of this early moment of modernism. Note how he relegates any regressive or fascist tendency to "peripheral aspects" in the background to that period and the vicissitudes of "later" developments, which include those necessarily second-stage "abstractions" and "*re*interpretations." While these developments include Soviet as well as fascist elaborations of an earlier avant-garde, and while such a future has obviously already happened by 1970, it is the effort of this passage to disconnect those developments from the early modernism he has otherwise mythologized with a strongly contrary quality and promise.

Similar complexities move toward the same resolutions in Fredric Jameson's *A Singular Modernity* (2002). A firm intention to observe the antirevolutionary aspect of the modernist technical regimen is complicated by a residual faith in a fabled beforetime of modernism, when, in that legend of early days, a verve of artistic experimentation coincided with a power of active resistance to existing systems, exerting a pressure for emancipatory change. Even as Jameson can follow Adorno's understanding of capitalist market forces working equally to stimulate and suborn the inventions of modernist aesthetic, he also agrees that the "work of art thus seeks by ever greater objectivation to generate a substantiality that cannot be absorbed by commodity logic."[15] What cannot be "absorbed" in this way is also what cannot be explained by commodity logic, and this excess locates the substance of Jameson's most important critical claim. This fugitive material carries the trace of the energies he enshrines in this account of the "forms" of early modernist art, which work to the effect of a "liberation" in contemporary history that is consistent in every way with the miraculous powers Adorno has fabled in his account of modernism's antediluvian time:

> No matter that it is for the most part only in the forms left behind by modernism that we detect the traces of this momentous moment – one of whose tendencies, the technological one, was shattered by World War I, the other, that of social ferment, arrested and exhausted by the end of the 1930s by Stalinism and Nazism. Yet the forms still, as symbolic acts, testify to immense gestures of liberation and new construction which we can only glimpse retrospectively, by historical reconstruction.[16]

The historical content and literary references of "this momentous moment" are spelled out in an adjacent passage, in an approving paraphrase of a "path-breaking essay" by Perry Anderson on the long turn-of-the-century circumstance of early modernism. In Jameson's account, Anderson's essay decisively locates "modernism within the force field of several distinct emergent currents in late-nineteenth-century European society," which includes "political suffrage and the growth of the labour unions and the various socialist and anarchist movements." Here, concurrently, "the artists of the modern" participate through technical instruments and aesthetic measures in the promise of revolutionary political transformation. "[T]heir own vocation for aesthetic change and new and more radical artistic practices finds itself powerfully reinforced and intensified by the dawning conviction that radical change is simultaneously at large in the social world outside,"[17] where the movements he cites in the paraphrase of Anderson's essay are operating as the power of dominant political promise. This account provides not only a substantial enhancement of Anderson's story but a forceful simplification of it,[18] testifying all in all to the force of the mythology of the modernist beforetime, "this momentous moment," which he is reiterating and reinforcing.

What is especially notable in these constructions of early modernist form and technique is the virtually complete absence of quotation and readings, in brief, of any close critical analysis of these actual technical practices. This absence is remarkable in the cases of both Adorno and Jameson, whose analyses of literary language can in other contexts extend to the molecular level of inspection. If this omission looks back for its ideological model to Lukács's Marxist embargo on the poetics of bourgeois "decadence," the category of practice that it leaves empty of evidence opens as a place of possibility, of projection. And the contradictions that are witnessed in the political significances attributed to this open space are revealing.

These contradictions indicate a shifting back and forth between two moments of fall in the literary and political history of Europe: two locations of incipient decline and ultimate decadence provide alternate grounds and separate references for understanding a politics of modernism. To the earlier side, there is the long *durée* of revolutionary history and post-revolutionary sensibility, where the failing ideals of advancing emancipation decamp into the attitudes and practices of artistic *décadence*. The memory of this original loss and earlier fall seems to have fallen out of the effective record in the Marxist version of literary history that we have just read, however. Here the swerve occurs in the early-mid twentieth century, so that, in effect, an ongoing possibility of socialist progress is intercepted by events in the twentieth century rather than forestalled already and first of all in the activity and aftermath of a first revolution. The ideological motive attending this omission is not hard to infer; it preserves the promissory power of a primary revolution in much the same way that it holds onto the progressive potential of early modernism. Most important, it represents another stage in the forgetting of decadence as a force in the formation of literary modernism and a factor in the understanding of modernist politics. This omission allows the mythologies of progressive revolution and liberation – in play in the understanding of modernism from the time of Wilson – to be reclaimed, such is their endurance.

As a related consequence, in the scholarship on the politics of modernism in particular, a certain paradox of provocation takes its powerful and effective place. In this critical discourse, modernism is acknowledged as technically advanced and forward looking, experimental and so progressive, while a reactionary politics may be assigned either to personal compromises of this original energy or to enveloping historical forces. Where this contradiction needs to be explained, a certain form of intellectual mourning is endorsed, a mood of political dismay is sustained, so that the commentary may at once sympathize with "the modernist project" (understood as progressive by intention) and condemn a regrettable political retrograde, inevitable or not.[19]

A close attention to the texts of early modernism in the Pound and Eliot line tells a different story of origins and consequences. It reveals the development of technical methods that are embedded heavily in the precedent conventions of artistic decadence. These forms may be understood as the representation of an imaginative attitude more than impassively opposed to an ideology in which futurity is an establishing value. The political "turns" Pound and Eliot take through the 1920s and 1930s may be seen in this way not as a contradiction of original promises, not as the belying of some better-minded younger time, but as the continuance, perhaps the completion, of a more than century-long process. The coherence of this longer story is the point of my critical account, and it changes the premises and tenor of the discussion of modernist politics. Here the attitudes we characterize as reactionary are not accidental, not the result of or the response to the catastrophes in twentieth-century history alone, but are consistent with those traditions of decadence that are present as legacies in the memory of modernism.

This is a story whose origins in late romanticism might bring us to look first at a modernist whose affinities with that movement in general, and with Shelley in particular, seem to be the strongest. Whose connection with the culture of *décadence* in the French (and English) fin de siècle was also intense. And whose involvement with political history in its material sphere as well as in his poetic imagination is among the densest: Yeats. As a poet, however, Yeats plays a relatively small role in this present book. As we saw in the prose tales he wrote in the mid-1890s, he narrated his detachment as a poetic activist from the political powerlessness of literary decadence. His aversion was as strongly compelled and aggressively maintained, after all, as his commitment to the cultural nationalism of a young Ireland, in whose birth he could imagine himself to be assisting as a poet, as we also saw in Chapter I. The historical conditions in which Yeats evolved the politics of his poetry are significantly different to those of Pound and Eliot, however, and this difference tells most particularly in the development of the politics of their modernism.

These modernists develop the sensibility of decadent aestheticism through the last-days feeling of the Great War. In doing so, they bring the long-standing aftermath of Shelley's romanticism to its climax and climacteric. Here the political potency of poetry is the determining issue. "For poetry makes nothing happen," W. H. Auden notes as a matter of historical fact in the prosaic middle section of his 1939 elegy to Yeats – but not before a good deal has in fact happened to the aspirational value of a revolutionary early romanticism.[20] Their story forms accordingly as a record of mourning for the lost potential that is the legacy of romanticism within decadence. That promise of political application, though not accomplished, is not itself lost, but, rather, intensified in its impossibility. The promise is returned to with an insistence that indicates absorption or, indeed, obsession; the more the impossibility of a poetic politics is acknowledged, however, the more extreme the redress of political measures. This is a destiny that follows on decadence as a consequence of that original failure of romantic revolutionary art. Substantial as a legacy in the drafting of the poetics of Pound and, as we shall see, Eliot, it is formative also, as we may see, of crucial aspects in their developing politics, which, in our understanding, gain the coherence of an intellectual history as well as a literary tradition.

This is an understanding we may gain through a triangulation of our view on the two poets. It comes through the prose writer and painter who was not only their companion talent but also their severest critic and closest reader: Wyndham Lewis.

Lewis

In 1934, in *Men Without Art*, Lewis's close reading deploys the newly developed critical systems of I. A. Richards to frame a consideration of a number of writers, Eliot primarily. Of the formulas Richards has offered to analyze literary practice, the most relevant to Eliot, in Lewis's view, is pseudo-statement, where, according to Richards, the imaginative writer crafts sentences of apparent rationality only. To Lewis, Eliot's verbal reason is just a series of grammatical moves, logic not a consequential proposition but a verbal posture merely. Richards sees a number of motives underlying this modern practice, including the poet's need to simulate the appeal to empirical reason in physical science and a wish to retrieve a feeling of assurance compatible with that of traditional religion, where it takes the comparable form of pseudo-belief.[21] Lewis takes the practice instead as the most vivid instance of the constrictions imposed on the modern artist, who, in writing out pseudo-statement and signing onto pseudo-belief, is confined to make-believe assertions, to pretend value.[22] Here the logic of a proposition, which might otherwise provide the basis of an operative political recommendation, shows as the merest piece of verbal self-hypnosis. In other words, this artist works the material and means of the political world in other words – in the well-formed but intransitive order of verbal art.

And so Lewis continually moves Richards's pseudo-statement theorem into the characterizing company of the "art for art's sake" group, which, in this grouping, emphasizes the aestheticism of decadence. This association of pseudo-statement with decadence comes in its most striking instance for Lewis in that primer for a poetics of decadence: in Wilde's *The Decay of Lying*. This is a work that not only dissembles ingenuously but, in doing so, appears to make the sort of seriously true statement – about the compulsory falseness of art – that Wilde says art cannot make. Accordingly, Lewis reads this tract as both an example and a formulation of decadence in its most exemplary poetics. Wilde's is the charter document of an art that means nothing beyond its own *mise-en-abyme*.[23]

His fierce censure of these decadent proclivities in modernist – Eliotic – art seems to presume Lewis's exclusion from this condition. The special intensity of his rebuke can actually be taken as evidence of the reverse. His involvement in the condition he is otherwise critiquing is not just implied, it is, ultimately, admitted. His is an "opposition from within." And this contrarian involvement in the poetics of decadence and the condition of politics by other means may be taken, ultimately, as one source of his most particular political positions, which, in turn, may help us to position the political sensibilities of his modernist companions.

At the end of his introduction to the volume, Lewis uses the Richards-Eliot nexus he has sketched (in advance) to locate a condition that he admits is general for all artists in this time, including himself:

Is not however "the present writer," as are all other writers, suspect? Certainly he is! Time alone can show which of us, of all these figures engaged in this pell-mell confusion, has preserved the largest store (and at the best it must be modest) of what is rational and the least affected with rank bogusness.

Where the practice of pseudo- or bogus statement signals the decadent writer's acceptance of the conditions restricting the artist's efficacy, Lewis indicates not so cheekily that he is laboring in this same circumstance. With all evident sincerity, as he writes in the preceding paragraph, he is attempting "to discover how we can *use*, to the advantage of such light as is vouchsafed us, even the darkest and most fantastic solemnities – even the most *inconsequent* of pseudo-systems."[24] Although we do not know what specific "*use*" any of these "*in*consequent pseudo-systems" can be put to, and while this uncertainty is itself significant, Lewis represents his work in terms of this all too apparent paradox of useful inconsequence, not to discredit it, but rather to speak a deeper conceit.

Let us call it "reforming decadence" – a phrase that allows decadence to be at once the agent and the object of reform. This formulation bespeaks Lewis's honest wit. While he concedes the uselessness to which the artist is evidently relegated, and which offers itself accordingly as the target of reform, he makes the compensatory effort to turn this condition to use, indeed, to take it as the advantaging stance for some practicable recommendation. Perhaps the outsider status of the decadent writer endows this figure with some exceptional authority, and this vantage locates a possibility we will return to. Yet the paradox is resolved only hypothetically, verbally. It is a linguistic riddle. And this riddle emerges with some of the compulsive force he discloses in this otherwise untoward preamble. The riddle is compelling and inexorable, it is as residual in his sensibility as the legacy of the foregone promise of early revolutionary romanticism, which abides as an echo fading but not disappearing in the memory of a decadence that extends into the consciousness of modernism. This long story of loss informs a performance of mourning that is as expressive as the rueful eloquence of this last sentence. What comes of the intense problematic of this legacy is the subject of this inter-chapter, which takes Lewis in advance as an example of a pattern manifesting itself in Pound as well as in Eliot.

For Lewis, this riddle signals a conflict to which he responds in an extremely telling way. The difficulty intrinsic to this ideal of legislating aesthetes, of reforming decadents, of a political prepotency for poetry or any art, helps to compel a response of specific political type. The failure of the grand ambitions of Shelley's particular brand of revolutionary romanticism is undergone and, in a reaction that is contrary but understandable or even necessary, turned around. In this counterrevolutionary turn, many of the liabilities that have been assigned to the decayed romanticism of decadence are shifted into a *general* debility, to which a political solution, indeed an extreme solution, will be applied. This is the condition to which Lewis will address his advisory tracts of social behaviorism, such as *The Art of Being Ruled*. Specifically: where the pseudo-statements of literary decadence express meaning of a wholly subjective basis, where truth is the sheerest truth-feeling, where validity is relative, these conditions of permissiveness – under which the artist of late romanticism or early decadence might offer imaginative models of political possibility – are turned into the chartering attitudes of a compromised and chaotic state, which is fitted to images of a caricature, carnivalesque liberalism. To this condition, authority is the ultimate solution. And if my characterization of the politics of Lewis's reactionary modernism is familiar, what I am saying most specifically is that the target of the invective in this political complaint is also its major source of energy. It draws powerfully upon the ongoing experience of that lost promise of romanticism, which is the legacy of decadence within modernism, which, in turn, has taken the loss of the promissory mythologies of modernity as its own point of creative grievance. It is a next stage, one that turns back upon its origins with a retributive force which, understandable as it may be regrettable, also recalls those origins in ways that can be seen and, in being seen, reveal the coherence of this longer story within literary history.

Consider Lewis's depiction of Eliot in that same essay of 1934. This was written seven years after the poet has made his famous self-declaration as royalist in politics, classicist in literature, and Anglo-Catholic in religion. These positions find their signal principle in the reference Lewis makes here to *Criterion*, title of the journal Eliot founded a few years before his declaration. It provides the namesake value for the absolute standards to which a reactionary conservatism could be seen to be reverting. But with a difference, in Lewis's perception and representation, which he telegraphs with a truncated spelling, indeed a mutilated version, of Eliot's standard-bearing title:

> Mr. Eliot, sardonic but decorous, goes perfectly in his *pseudo* way! ... perfectly ready that his first mate should steer the good ship *Cri* for *any* port – the most *liberal* in the world, or the *reddest*, for that matter, in the universe ... perfectly agreeable that navigation should be conducted upon the best relativist principles, with the Einstein chronometer and the Marx sextant, or any other instruments whatever, however heterodox ...[25]

Visual satirist that he is, Lewis drafts this representation with an exaggerating, emphatic hand. No hyperbole, however, could fashion such unlikely references for the positions of reactionary conservatism that Eliot has taken up in his cultural politics. Marxism? Liberalism? Red communism? The relativity principle in Einstein's model of space-time, which provides a scientific basis for the subjectivism to which *Criterion* offers the riposte of its title? The riddle is thickened in its ongoing iterations in Lewis's essay. In cartoon frame after cartoon frame, Lewis brings a radical liberalism – dressed variously as Einsteinian relativism and Arcadian communism as well as decadent aesthetics – into the visual depiction of Eliot's conservatism. Reconstituted thus, Eliot's current position is brought correctly (if ironically) under the critical heading of the last word in the preceding quote: *heterodoxy*. This animus may seem surprising for a congenital skeptic like Lewis. It makes sense, however, within the bigger picture being traced here. The lack of a single coherent belief system is synonymous for Lewis both with *liberal*ism (which, in its radical ideal, *frees* itself from the constrictions of any orthodoxy) and with an inability to act out of any stable basis of practicable value. This condition, in the discursive rebuke of the rest of Lewis's essay, is chartered in the language of pseudo-statement and professed in terms of pseudo-belief, and it is synonymous in turn with a poetics of art for art's sake. This complex recalls the now long gone but not foregone promise of art for change's sake, which Shelley had framed as his already late version of the millenarian promise of early romanticism. This is the promise that the poets of decadence kept going, characteristically, as the glowing but dying ember of a fire already spent in their own characterizing time of afterward. Lewis brings it to a bonfire-of-the-vanities blaze in Eliot. In this depiction, and in Eliot's explicitly conflicting positions, Lewis is presenting a more than hundred-year-long political and literary history as the genetic memory of a complexly, densely compounded politics.

If the several stages of this legacy appear in this depiction as a serial cartoon, Lewis is providing a vindictive element that is also highly significant. The whole picture shows Eliot's authoritarian orthodoxy resting insecurely, restively, above the memory of its inverse identity, which is being rebuked by Lewis only as fiercely as it is unforgettably present – as the constituting force it actually exerted in Lewis's, as well as Eliot's, formation. Conversely put: those positions of authoritarian orthodoxy represent a reactive but also compensatory measure, one which is bound in its negative intensities to the liberal relativism in the residual dream that has disappointed them but, just so, cannot be negated. Its principles are iterated in the reverse-image rear-view mirror vision of a history that, in having failed them, becomes the source of a retributive political vision, of a reactionary antiliberalism above all.

And the special vindictiveness of this depiction is the indicator of the developmental turn in this longer story. The promise of romantic millenarianism, lost but then recovered in decadence as the source of expressive distress in being lost, is finally absconded from in modernism – and with a vengeance that expresses the sense of a *terminus ad quem*, a finalizing turn. Like Eliot and Pound, I am saying, Lewis can be seen to be reacting to this long disappointment of liberation poetics by bringing himself right into line – into line on the right – in a politics of authoritarianism, a radical secular orthodoxy. This position may be understood as a redressing of the extremity to which the principles of a now failed poetic ideology, which is an ideology of poetry's ultimate if indirect potency, has brought history: to the mess of liberalism. In this understanding, the decadence that is the now restored legacy and memory of modernism provides a powerful coadjutor to the formation of a modernist politics of authority: this comes as the final demise of the grand romantic plan of a politically applicable poetry. The story is told most closely in a view of Eliot's longer career, which can then be seen in a more intensive reflection and expansive application in Pound's.

Eliot and Pound

It is worth recalling the subtitle to Eliot's 1934 book, *After Strange Gods: A Primer of Modern **Heresy***. "Heresy" is the orthodox Eliot's stronger characterization of Lewis's "heterodoxy," but the condition is fitted in much the same intellectual and cultural position. In a rather astonishing trope in the preface to the book, Eliot depicts the relativist, subjectivist, "free-thinking" society, one in which the "strong convictions" of orthodoxy are impossible or unacceptable, as "*worm*-eaten with *Liberalism*."[26] The freedom that is the namesake value of "Liberalism" is identified with the condition of decay, which is the obsessive concern of this book. Eliot repeats the association when he remarks that, in his preferred society, "any large number of free-thinking Jews" would be "undesirable."[27] Here, in a way of thinking as grimly familiar as the phobic logic it follows, free thought is attributed to the ethnic group held presumptively, prejudicially, as the source of societal decay. Worm-eating, or the insidious work of Semitic free thought, is activity; indeed, it is rabid activity, but it is activity with no concerted or practicable purpose. So it comports loosely – and all the more powerfully – with the outlook of art for art's sake, that furious inconsequence of decadent poetics. And the peculiar virulence of

Eliot's cartooning of this attitude may be examined in view of his more specific address to the underlying aesthetic issues, which appear within the history of his own literary criticism.

In 1920, in his essay "Swinburne as Poet," Eliot appreciates a language practice in his subject that comports already with the critical formulas Richards would enunciate six years later. This is the signature method of the poetics of decadence for Lewis: pseudo-statement. Describing a poetic chorus from Swinburne's *Atalanta*, Eliot remarks on its sheer meaning-seemingness: "it is sententious, but it has not even the significance of commonplace." He expands: "This is not merely 'music'; it is effective because it appears to be a tremendous statement, like statements made in our dreams."[28] A sententious statement that translates back into the unreal and meaningless formulation of dream talk: here is pseudo-statement with a vengeance, but with little vengeance from Eliot himself, who clearly appreciates its "effect." But if it is "effective," as Eliot claims, what *does* it effect? That word wavers in its reach for a referent between intransitive and transitive senses: between the sensationalism we might expect of an art-for-art's-sake poetics and the ultimate utility, efficaciousness, which Shelley's poetic legislators might claim.

It is an effect of both kinds in Swinburne's verse that Pound invokes in a review of a recent Swinburne biography in 1918, where he appreciates that poet's "magnificent passion for liberty."[29] What Pound is celebrating is a freedom connatural to the aesthetic sensibility, where this decadent's fundamental distance and difference from social convention underlies and, with a perfectly understandable if paradoxical logic, underwrites and makes credible the artist's social recommendation. This is a capacity to model political values and ideal possibilities beyond the traditional, outside the historically approved, beyond the actual, certainly beyond the rational. There is a visionary dimension to this great calling for art, and this social vocation, this political potency for literature, breathes under Pound's phrase in a way that turns back to the millenarian inspiration of early romanticism (in Shelley's adjustment of it) and that will bring us back to it when we turn to his furtherance of this possibility.

What, in the meanwhile, does Eliot do with this capacity to expand the possibilities of politics along the imaginative lines of poetry? When he repeats the "art for art's sake" adage in the introduction to *The Use of Poetry and the Use of Criticism* (1933), he does so in the same paragraph in which he recalls Shelley's claim on the poet's legislative function, unacknowledged as it is. This now more than hundred-year-long literary history is told thus by Eliot:

My point here is that a great change in the attitude towards poetry, in the expectations and demands made upon it, did come, we may say for convenience towards the end of the eighteenth century. Wordsworth and Coleridge are not merely demolishing a debased tradition, but revolting against a whole social order; and they begin to make claims for poetry which reach their highest point of exaggeration in Shelley's famous phrase, "poets are the unacknowledged legislators of mankind." . . . The decay of religion, and the attrition of political institutions, left dubious frontiers upon which the poet encroached; and the annexations of the poet were legitimised by the critic . . . . the next stage is best exemplified by Matthew Arnold . . . [who] discovered a new formula: poetry is not religion, but it is a capital substitute for religion – not invalid port, which may lend itself to hypocrisy, but coffee without caffeine, tea without tannin. The doctrine of Arnold was extended, if also somewhat travestied, in the doctrine of "art for art's sake." . . . [which] was really a hopeless admission of irresponsibility . . . . In our time we have moved, under various impulses, to new positions . . . ."[30]

The misquotation of Shelley's "World" as "mankind" suggests the work of personal memory rather than retrieved reference; Eliot has lived with the import of this "famous phrase," and he is retelling its consequences with an intense imaginative apprehension. Thus, if Shelley's vision of the poet's capacity for transformational change looks back to the revolutionary romanticism of that poet's immediate forebears, it looks forward for Eliot to the poetics of decadence, as enunciated in the value of art for its own sake. Compounding the elements of religion with politics in his own developing appropriation as a poet, Eliot depicts a tradition that finds both a *terminus ad quem* and a *terminus a quo* in his own age, in himself. The rejoinder he enters as the mark of difference between himself and that nineteenth-century tradition leads to somewhat uncharacteristic flannelling about the interventions which some of the "new positions" of intellectual understanding, the study of "psychology" and "sociology" most notably, have brought to the expectation of what poetry is, or can be, or should do. What he is leaving unsaid or talking away is the fact that the tradition of imaginative thinking about a politically efficacious poetry, which he outlines so cleanly and perceptively, has not only failed; it has failed his age; it has failed him. Suspended as he is at the end of that tradition, drawing scant solace from the contributions the psychologist or sociologist might offer for the uses of poetry and dwelling accordingly in the loss of those primary possibilities, his rhetoric of skepticism about the problems of that tradition obviously leaves open the question of redress.

The development of this possibility takes strong account of the ideology that failed, and that failed him in particular. It gives an absolute value now to religious and political orthodoxy – the lectures on which this book is based were given the year before *After Strange Gods*. The relativist meanings that are the expression of a libertarian impulse; the *potentialist* truths that are recorded in practices such as Richards's pseudo-statement and that hold the promise of an art liberating and improving the world by being itself, acting much like Swinburne's version of a reforming decadence as it exhibits a similarly "magnificent passion for liberty": these are characterized now as "coffee without caffeine, tea without tannin." Play money. In that characterization, I suggest, we may read a record of the falling rhythm of a once powerful music. It is a script for the final failure of Shelley's attempt to extend (even as he attenuates) the dream of early revolutionary romanticism: it is a failure to remedy a world on its (art's) own terms. By now, in the late postwar world of the mid-1930s, even the memory of that lost possibility, which once provided the solace of an otherwise disconsolate decadent, is no use. This is the longer story that eventuates in the turn Eliot takes out of the tradition that fails him, which, at this endpoint, turns back upon the origins of the disappointment, turning its liberationist creed to its redress in the corrective strictures of authority in orthodoxy.

A similar exchange of aesthetic possibility for political certitudes might be found at a particular moment in Pound's career, in 1919–1920. It is in 1919 that he undertakes a study of political economics in his intensive, soon-to-be committed readings of Major Douglas's social credit theories. Now, Pound scholarship may be haunted by its own version of the Indiana Jones Quest for the Temple of Doom. Poundians (rather like the later Pound himself) search for the Root of all Evil, for the one moment or single reason that would afford some understanding of how this exceptionally innovative and "forward-looking" artist would be led to espouse social ideologies which, despite a rhetoric of address to egalitarian, implicitly socialist and arguably progressive values, ends up supporting regimes as "backward," reactionary, and authoritarian as Mussolini's. In a limited but anticipatory way, it is authority of this sort that speaks a powerful appeal to Pound in late 1919. And whatever subsequent political history might do to the motives that led him in this direction to begin with, we can see evidence, at least in terms internal to his poetic career, of some of the forces shifting him initially in this direction.

For the turn of the years 1919 and 1920 encloses the moment in which he is composing the poems in the sequence *Hugh Selwyn Mauberley*. In this fictional autobiography, as we have seen, he depicts the formative force of his poetic career in the condition of decadence. This story draws a greater complexity, now, in the political context of the literary history we are reviewing. For Pound is representing his earlier life as a poet as initially falling in line with the high visionary possibilities of Shelley's dream of legislating the world through poetry, as poetry, which, as history, ultimately falls through. In the difference between that poetic ideal and the reality of unchanged history, Pound's autobiographical story dwells in the decadence that is the imaginative circumstance left behind by that failure: it is the pervasive imaginative circumstance of the poem. Returning to that sequence and retelling its story in relation to poetry's unaccomplished political possibilities is appropriate now. This rereading provides an understanding not only of the disappointments that underlie the representations of decadence in the sequence but of the compensations and consequences in the more explicitly political career just now emerging, in the specially anti-decadent sense of the phrase, in earnest.

This rereading may be framed by a second look at the piece that provided the opening anecdote for this book, which is another signal moment in the early career: the 1 January 1914 editorial in *The Egoist*, where Pound was introducing his artistic generation to literary London. "We have attained to a weariness more highly energised than the weariness of the glorious nineties, or at least more obviously volcanic."[31] On the evidence of this sentence, the first number of the journal Pound will join Lewis in producing in June 1914 could be advertising itself not as *Blast*, but rather as *BALANCE*; not as volcanic, but rather as demure. Any advance tremor is assimilated to one of those balanced sentences that Pound has identified as the primary stylistic sign of writerly artifice in the Nineties. The elegance of the sentence affirms the identity he seeks, otherwise, but not disturbingly enough, to contest. Indeed, he has great faith in the artfulness he otherwise wants to disbelieve in. This complexity stays with him, we may see, when another signal statement from that 1914 screed – "And in the face of this are we in the heat of our declining youth expected to stretch the one word *merde* over eighteen elaborate paragraphs?"[32] – is juxtaposed to its echo and riposte, in 1917. Here, in correspondence with his British friend Edgar Jepson, he is setting out his editorial vision for his part of the *little review*. "My corner of the paper is *BLAST*," he claims, establishing a continuity he proceeds immediately to qualify,

> but *BLAST* covered with ice, with a literary and reserved camouflage. (I mean, that's what I want: a classic and impeccable exterior: [deleted expletive] enunciated with an exquisite politeness. *BLAST* in which the exuberance has given way to external decorum of phrase.[33]

The elaborate artifice Pound ostensibly rejected but more than discernibly exhibited in 1914 – in a sentence that rose impeccably to its rhetorical question, its own rhetorical period – is not just tolerated now. It is openly cultivated and indulged because it is seen as an instrument to provide or even expedite delivery of the energy which the vulgarity represents. This is the agreement he has brokered with the aesthetes of the Nineties: an artistry, which is so highly developed it would seem to have no evident aim beyond its own technique, is seen as the expedient for a force of convention- and standard-altering kind. This conceit lies as the generative concept within the earlier record of his negotiations with the Nineties. This exchange brings with it the longer memory of the difficulty of political applicability for poetry – all in all, the legacy of the late or decayed romanticism, particularly of an early revolutionary romanticism, in literary decadence. Of this complexity the poetic art and imaginative fiction of *Hugh Selwyn Mauberley* will prove remarkably representative.

The character of its first part, Ezra Pound's initialed counterpart E.P., has about him the obvious qualities of the heroic adversary: "For three years, out of key with his time" (*P*, 185). His *aesthetic* standards can be seen as those Pound espouses in his 1917 letter to Jepson: a finesse of artistic finish, the fineness of a "'sculpture' of rhyme" (*P*, 186), all in all, the decorous measures of "'the sublime' / In the old sense" (*P*, 185). Granted, this poet-character's program never speaks the word, with exquisite politeness or not, in French or not, of barbaric vulgarity, which, from the backwoods millenarianism of Pound's "half savage" American background (*P*, 185), may be taken as the instrument to change the world at it is. That silence is matched by the absence in the poetry we associate with E.P. of any evidently renovating connection to the world of affairs. For E.P.'s rhythms are indifferent to those of "the march of events," his gaze is deflected from the "mottoes on sun dials" (*P*, 185), whose timely words are obviously too motley, and his "image[s]" vigorously resist a depiction of the "accelerated grimace" that the "age demanded" (*P*, 186). Indeed, and in particular, that comic off-rhyme of "image" and "grimace" trivializes the demand of the contemporary record, while the set of inverted commas he places around the phrase "the march of events" certainly heckles any attempt to subject his message to an ideal of historical advance or even a standard of contemporary relevance. In view of the greater complexity of the literary history Ezra Pound is reliving in E.P., however, the social distance and political diffidence of the aesthete needs to be seen within a longer story of political engagement and, ultimately, disappointment.

While it is difficult to fix opinions in the narrative consciousness of the poem, which is also difficult to fix, the text is riddled with evidence of the witness to political realities that E.P. does *not* take up. As an idealized identity, that is, E.P. may be held to the expectations of his author's own compound myth of the Nineties in the Teens: he is a decadent aesthete who could blast the social world into some new order through art, as art – just as intensely as the world seems intent in belying that possibility. Its more positive possibility is recalled and affirmed as surely as it is put down by its opponents' ignoble spokesman, that would-be advisor and literary counselor to E.P., "Mr. Nixon," who, speaking from the "cream gilded cabin of his steam yacht," places himself pretty clearly in the received order of things. Who calls to the speaker's mind a relevant saying and anecdote: "Accept opinion. The 'Nineties' tried your game / And died, there's nothing in it" (*P*, 191–92). Pound might rewrite Mr. Nixon, as counsel to his contrarian side, thus: do *not* accept opinion, because the "*game*" of art plays out the high mission of art for art's sake, a reforming decadence in that signal decade of "The 'Nineties,'" where poetry, as poetry, can change things as they are. The failure of this possibility is as momentous in the sequence as the sumptuousness of Mr. Nixon's yacht is tawdry. In the pointing of such details in the sequence, the sorrows of a young poetry grown useless, which once drew powerfully on the mythological solace that is extended to those woes from the legends of decadence, have moved into retributive caricature.

This longer literary history provides both a reference and a model for the parabolic quality in the imaginative narrative of *Hugh Selwyn Mauberley*. In the chronology of the sequence, the still surviving piece of heroic romanticism in E.P. dissolves and turns down into the decadent aestheticism of Mauberley. This process also occurs within the architectural fiction Pound has drawn from that parable of Nineties decadence. Beerbohm's "Hilary Maltby and Stephen Braxton," we may now see, takes the longer literary history underpinning its fiction of ambition dying young – it recalls and absorbs the story of the failure of the rejuvenation and renewal of history in revolutionary romanticism – and recasts that memory in a narrative Pound can graft onto the autobiographical fiction of his experience.

What Pound left unsaid in 1920 is what Eliot revealed more clearly in 1933: the compensation (and consequence) of the failure of poetry's efficacious powers in those extreme forms of religious – and political – authoritarianism. If it is more prudent to attribute significance to what does *not* appear in the *Cantos*, given the omnivorous display of personages and ideas in that poetic encyclopedia, a striking and suggestive juxtaposition occurs in Canto XLVI, when Pound is revisiting in memory the offices of A. R. Orage's *New Age*. Here he was introduced to the economic doctrines of Major Douglas. Appearing with Douglas in this vignette is the otherwise unlikely figure of Max Beerbohm, who, in this context, specifically in its 1919 setting, recalls the story he offered Pound at this time as the narrative parable of the decadence onto which the sorrows of a failed revolutionary romanticism could be grafted. While any tendency toward critical simplification of this often tortuous history must be resisted, this is a failure that, now, at the next turn of this story, will be turned into the orthodox and soon-to-be authoritarian economics of social credit. Not as a formulaic truth, to be sure. These two personages are converging in Canto XLVI in a story that is filled out, in its remembrance of 1919, with the statistics of death in the recently concluded war.[34] This is the Great War that will have provided Eliot as well as Pound the confirmation of the historical imaginary of decadence and, in doing so, provided the truth and warrant for the poetic expression of the pessimism that has attended the evolution of modernism over the long turn of the century. But it also proved the untruth of the older hopes of romanticism within aesthetical decadence for the political prepotency of poetry. At this further turn of the story, the solaces of poetry in the older mythology of decadence are also withheld. The rest, as they say, is history – poor, bare, and not to be accommodated by a poetry of visionary political possibility, which has been turned in their view into the sort of libertine chaos their authoritarianism will next redress.

This position may not have been an inevitable result, even if the literary and political history provides a logic of continuity. It is in many respects all too evidently regrettable as an outcome. But it should not provide a vantage from which, reading literary history backward, we impose this end as a condemnatory consequence alone. It might be understood better, instead, as the most eventful measure of the complexities and tensions in the development through history of a poetics of decadence that, in Eliot's oeuvre, remains still to be read.

CHAPTER IV

T. S. Eliot: 1910–1922

When T. S. Eliot sailed to Europe in July 1914, he was resuming a journey he had begun in November 1910 – on several levels. As a student, he had spent that earlier academic year in Paris, where he attended lectures at the Sorbonne and officially, if somewhat diffidently, furthered his work toward a doctorate in philosophy at Harvard. As a poet, however, he drew deeply from the Parisian scene. One of the primary sites in the poetics of urban modernity, the city offered him the spirits of Baudelaire and Laforgue and the legacy of a heady French *décadence*. The atmosphere went straight to his head as the muse of youth and crested into a period of poetic productivity as intense in its energy as it was promising in quality. Now, in 1914, the doctoral student was using a fellowship to bring his dissertation to completion, beginning with summer study at the University of Marburg in Germany and continuing at Merton College, Oxford. The mood was professional, dutiful, resigned. And the maturing poet ... well, this poet was, in his own view, not maturing at all: the correspondence from that summer shows him already thinking of himself, in the conceit of a witticism for another stalled career, as a young poet "with a great future behind him."[1]

Outgrowing the suit of poetic clothes that Parisian *décadence* has tailored for him? One way of reading Eliot's early verse, offered lucidly by Ronald Schuchard, puts this work on a developmental trajectory of specifically religious convictions. This critical and interpretive narrative leads the youthful poet through the deviant manners and wayward attitudes of poetic decadence; it brings him toward the moral and spiritual understandings that culminate in his conversion to Anglo-Catholicism later in the 1920s.[2] In Schuchard's account, this is no simple or straightforward process, of course. If this biographical story becomes end-directed, however, it can lose the reality and dimensionality of what occurs along the way. Here the imaginative temperament of decadence develops its own content and depth. For the appeal of that sensibility represents no simple whim of late adolescent fashion for Eliot. It bespeaks an intensity of connection, which he will regain and strengthen in the next years. In this later period, which includes his taking up residence in London, an impulsive marriage, his shifting between jobs, and his rather swift affiliation with English life, he is also – and most notably – experiencing, and to some great degree undergoing, the national struggle of the Great War. This is a richly difficult history. It affords the young American an understanding of a sensibility particular to Europe and specific to "decadence": an imaginative apprehension of living in a late historical age, of time winding down, all in all, of *decay* as a condition of current circumstance and, more generally, of historical existence.

A presentiment of this kind was not unavailable to Americans, as I have suggested, especially to Americans of the cultural class of privileged white Protestantism to which Eliot, with Pound, belonged: a class equally elevated and precarious. The anxiety which their American experience has bequeathed them will be relocated in the European experience of the next several years, where, if it is newly grounded, it is also profoundly deepened. Here the experience of immense, unprecedented levels of death is recalibrated in the imaginative calculus familiar to the sensibility of decadence: the metric of empire falling, where the scale of imperial grandeur in collapse provides a frame of reference adequate to the magnitude of present distress. Simultaneously with Pound's *Homage to Sextus Propertius*, and not independently, Eliot takes the prospect of imperial decline from the historically informed vocabulary of literary decadence and, as we shall see, makes it one of the most expressive registers in his poetic lexicon. Following a trajectory similar to the one we observed in the work of Pound, Eliot moves from a youthful fluency in the poetic conventions of literary decadence to a usage matured as much by history as personal development. If one of the consensus understandings of earlier literary history has featured Pound and Eliot outgrowing the poetries of the decadence in which they dabbled as adolescents, I am reversing that current and suggesting as strongly as possible that they matured into this sensibility.[3] It is the difficult privilege of their shared experience to find in the shaking earth of that Great War the ground and warrant of the decadence they had taken on, in earlier days, as the muse of youth.

Like Pound, too, Eliot left the record of his early exchanges with the poetics of decadence mainly out of view – in notebooks not subsequently published in his lifetime. These cahiers include poems that are manifestly complete. Whether this ongoing oversight had to do with his perception of inexpert work or, subsequently, with vagaries in the management of literary estates, the fact remains that already by 1972, the year in which the messy legacy of *The Waste Land* manuscripts came into public view, there was every reason for making this earlier work available. And whether the suppression of decadence as an element in the core story of poetic modernism had already so firmly occurred by the three-quarter mark of the century (Kenner's *Pound Era* appeared in 1971), the import of this submerged work may be claimed now at its greatest range of implication and consequence – now that the parallel record of Pound's early immersion in literary decadence has been restored as a memory and identity in the canonical work. Not only does this poetic archive demonstrate the sensibility of literary decadence as its most consistent, coherent, and, indeed, constitutive influence, but, reclaimed, this material provides a vantage from which the best known poems of Eliot's next phase will reveal a new coherence. These poems will demonstrate the temper of decadence that is essential to them and, in the larger sense, essential to the production of one of the major strains in the canon of poetic modernism. In keeping with the idea that the long turn of the century defines a line of continuing and deepening crisis in the cultural imaginary of Europe, and in the most accurate sense of the term "modern*ism*," the acutest self-consciousness of this modern moment is coming again in Eliot through this renewed imaginative language of decadence.

Beginning this consideration in the poetry Eliot wrote between 1910 and mid-summer 1914, we may establish a basis for reading the subsequent verse of *Poems* (1919), *Ara Vos Prec* (1919), and *Poems* (1920), which provide the record of an extension of that original sensibility of literary decadence. A concluding consideration of *The Waste Land* (1922) will demonstrate the lengthened life cycle of the poetics of decadence, whose developmental curve describes the main lines of growth in the period which, by a fairly ready critical consensus, is the most important moment of his poetic career and of the literary history of modernist poetics.

1. The Singing Schools of Decadence

An inventory sampling the figures of literary decadence in the early poetry would show the extent to which Eliot is prepossessed by this sensibility. Its extensiveness will be suggested in the course of our readings, and, while the examples could be multiplied, the critical question takes shape not so much in the documented quantity of decadent motifs but in the intensity of Eliot's imaginative apprehension of what matters most for him as a poet. So, the great range of decadent images and themes can be narrowed for analysis to his preoccupation with the signal interest of time – thematically and figuratively, to begin with, and, ultimately, technically, rhythmically, poetically.

A phrase that dates the temporal imaginary of decadence in its now recognizably late day – "even in this later age" – comes as idiomatically and readily as this unadorned wording in "Convictions (Curtain Raiser)."[4] Whether this presentiment is connatural to the American version of the fin de siècle that Eliot underwent, it shows in his poetry in a figure indicative of the sense of an ending in the imaginative vocabulary of the English Nineties, that is, most expressively, where it touches the young. It appears in his poetry in the frequent figure of the adolescent aging under sunset colors – or, most strikingly, of an already posthumous young man: "I feel like the ghost of youth / At the undertakers' ball" (*IMH*, 17).

This figure of ruined youth in "Opera" appears as one expression of a generalized understanding of the absconded promise of the nineteenth-century mythology of Progress, whose promissory future has been removed. Eliot's critical apprehension appears in the semi-discursive work of the meditative lyric "Silence." "This is the hour for which we waited – // This is the ultimate hour," the poem gestures to frame its center of attention as the destined end of time, which, too, brings the sensibility of the poem to a surcharged present, some ultimate Now. Eliot uses that break between its two verse paragraphs to indicate that time is passing, even – or especially – during this

> ultimate hour
> When life is justified.
> The seas of experience
> That were so broad and deep,
> So immediate and steep,
> Are suddenly still.
> You may say what you will,
> At such peace I am terrified.
> There is nothing else beside.   (*IMH*, 18)

The imaginative challenge of this brink instant brings a young poet to the extremity of the final statement, but this hyperbole provides its own measure of the pressure and density of an ongoing crisis of time.

The compelling but impossible promise of this "*ultimate* hour" defines more particularly a predicament with inclusive time, all in all, the absconded promise of the synthetic temporality of the romantic spot of time. This crisis exists already among the most powerful provocations of the temporal imaginary of literary decadence. This is evidenced in the sensibility of a poet with whom Eliot would have a life-long intimacy: Baudelaire (his "spleen" and "Cythère" are invoked like naturalized companions elsewhere in Eliot's early verse).[5] For the French poet, in the conditions of the modern city, the quickening rhythms of perception and sensation generate the intense but elusive attractions of the quicksilver instant, flickering with the significance that disappears with its appearance. And so, more gravely and discursively but with no loss of intensity, in Eliot's lines, where, as Paul de Man observed of Baudelaire's experience of the time of decadence, the momentary is sensed as always already *falling away* from its ideal totality. Eliot presents the instantaneous whole of this "ultimate hour" as a vertiginous thrill. At once alluring and beautiful but also and especially terrifying, this version of an older poetic sublimity goes beyond the representations of a conventional sublime. In this special effect of dreadful emptiness (or empty dreadfulness), the poem presents the evidence – a sort of emotional precipitate – of what is left behind an unattainable possibility. With the personal turn of the young philosopher, this passage presents a processing of the original conceit of decadent temporality with an affective concept all his own.

What else has been left behind by the unfulfilled promise of the meaningful completion of time? A poetic tempo, surely, which presents one register of existence in the remains of time. A sort of remnant temporality appears in the rhythm and syntax of parataxis. Where phrase is laid against phrase in the absence of any larger syntactic pattern, poetic representation occurs in a series that, if it hinges one fragment to the next, also isolates each of these local instants, leaving it outside a temporal progression of meaningful syntactic sense. Phrases are left behind, in this prosody, not carried forward. Thus objects in catalogues, which provide the most frequent form of organization for this formal sense of poetic time, are most indicatively the images of temporal remnants – ruins, leftovers, vestiges. "With ashes and tins in piles, / Shattered bricks and tiles / And the débris of a city" (*IMH*, 15); "Bottles and broken glass, / Trampled mud and grass; / A heap of broken barrows" (*IMH*, 13). So, respectively, in "Second Caprice in North Cambridge" and "First Caprice in North Cambridge" goes the record of life in the midst of the temporal residuum, where, in detail after detail, the paratactic imaginary envisions the condition of existence as aftermath, as a series of relicts, just as, in its syntax, it encompasses sequence without consequence; just as, in the numerical titles of these two poems, a sense of numbered progression is projected to no summary understanding at all.

Or, as in the final poem of the sequence "Goldfish (Essence of Summer Magazines)," where the syntax expands to the hypotactic integration of this first verse paragraph:

Among the débris of the year
Of which the autumn takes its toll: –
Old letters, programmes, unpaid bills
Photographs, tennis shoes, and more,
Ties, postal cards, the mass that fills
The limbo of a bureau drawer –
Of which October takes its toll
Among the débris of the year
I find this headed "Barcarolle."   (*IMH*, 29)

The census of these objects of remnant temporality – the "débris" of "old letters," "photographs" (after-images), "unpaid bills" (the record of uncompleted time), "ties" (moments of fashion ever ready to be outdated already in the early century), and "limbo" (an afterlife without salvation or damnation or expiation, that is, an afterward without any experience of the meaningful completion of time) – occurs within dashes, which set this register of the remains of time outside any sense of temporal linguistic progression. This interval reads as the quintessential expression of the condition of the temporal remnant in the syntax of parataxis in the poetics of decadence in Eliot's early work.

An additional dimension of significance comes with the pattern of hypotactic syntax that encompasses this catalogue of the remains of time. Note how the completion of the periodic sentence involves a return to the first and second lines of this verse paragraph in the antepenultimate and penultimate lines. Thus Eliot inscribes the sense of directed development in the time of the poem into a form of circular return, which, referring at the opening and closing of this passage to "autumn" and "October," he also attaches to the temporal model of the annual seasonal round. If the syntactic form of the whole verse paragraph mimics the circular return of the year, however, there is no sense of the promissory renewal of time in the seasonal scheme: "Among the débris of the year / Of which autumn takes its toll"; "Of which October takes its toll / Among the débris of the year." An unpromising autumn presents the sense of an ending in a linear scheme which is outlined by a periodic syntax which, in effect, arrives at its own depletion: an autumn of history, all in all, the feeling of a late but also last historical day. This composite sense is both prompted and corroborated by that otherwise incongruous reference to "Barcarolle": this is the term for the song sung by gondoliers in Venice, which, as the isle of perennial decadence, provides the readiest reference in its ever-sinking condition to the entropic quality of cosmic time.

The fluency Eliot demonstrates with the temporal imaginary of decadence leaves him the more challenging task of composing poems that, as
moments of their own, present this sensibility as the lived condition of the
time they take. What is needed here is nothing short of a new way of telling
poetic time. The formal time of the romantic lyric, which involves a form of
emotional or affective closure within the poetic moment, and which provides the more distant original of Eliot's early work, needs to be replaced.
This is the challenge to which one of his early poems responds with a
revealingly partial degree of success.

"Fourth Caprice in Montparnasse" is probably the first poem (despite the
number in its title) Eliot wrote after arriving in Paris in autumn 1910. The
poem offers a primer in the figures of decadence, suitably recited as soon as
the young poet has arrived at its cultural capital. The moment of this
dramatic lyric is poised within the imaginative understanding of time that
he graphs in the movement from its first to second lines:

> We turn the corner of the street
> > And again
> Here is a landscape grey with rain
> On black umbrellas, waterproofs,
> And dashing from the slated roofs
> Into a mass of mud and sand.
> Behind a row of blackened trees
> The dripping plastered houses stand
> Like mendicants without regrets
> For unpaid debts
> Hand in pocket, undecided,
> Indifferent if derided.   (*IMH*, 14)

At the turn from the first verse into the second, the instigating vignette is
presented already as "again," already repetitive, unoriginal, secondary. This
is the special time of literary decadence. This secondary temporality shows
in a prospect being "grey with rain," which, in the shadow reality it
witnesses, also diminishes the sense of original distinction. A climatic
condition, a kind of emotional twilight, this atmospheric version of decadent temporality provides the tonic visual chord into which Eliot will
resolve many of the poetic prospects in *Prufrock and Other Observations*
(1917, though nearly all of these poems were written before 1914), a volume
whose substantial advance on mainstream traditions Marjorie Perloff has
aptly characterized in relation to avant-garde experiments continuing into
our present day.[6] In its own time, that volume preserves the echoing
memory of the sensibility of literary decadence that is at work most urgently

and directly in these earlier poems, where he engages the most manifest challenge in the temporal imaginary of literary decadence. How, if at all, does he shift this experience of secondary time from a static spatiality to a lived temporality, to tempo?

A variation to the mood music of its visual prospect occurs in the turn the verses take in the seventh line, where the poet moves on the trope of "mendicants" toward the underside of urban modernity, into the company of those beggars and misfits who are the habitués of Baudelaire's poetry. As soon as he strikes this note, the pace shifts unpredictably, even wildly, turning the cadences of lyric description into the hurdy-gurdy rhythm and rigmarole music of Gilbert and Sullivan multiple-syllable rhymes. This new music might seem to force those seamier aspects of the city into the trivializing rhythms of musical farce, but this alternative poetic tempo is prolonged as well as sudden – it goes on for four lines – and so presents a substantial variation on the prosodic pace of the piece so far. This rhythmic shift offers a signal instance of the changes that the poetic tempos of decadent temporality ring on the literary traditions they are challenging.

This mechanical-piano cadence provides a rhythmic figure for that category of value we understand in the aesthetics of decadence as the inorganic – marionettes not people, effigies not bodies. These are the features of an imaginative episteme for an historical phase that has outlived the cycle of regenerative nature; a last age, or, indeed, an aftermath. This move in the verse music runs true to that new chord in the poetics of decadence, and it is a rhythm that Eliot will develop to maximum potential in the quatrain poems of 1917–1919. If that later accomplishment stands in the longer view as the marker for his progression in the temperament of aesthetic decadence, it also shows this earlier work as unseasoned in the subtler but profounder understandings of that poetic sensibility. Whatever we may say about a new poetics introducing novel concepts of poetic experience and so new forms of order, even of disorder, it is simply not yet within Eliot's ken to make an effective, let alone a newly coherent, use of it. For the three-line finale that follows on the last words quoted changes cadence again, not in a new or related variation but in an effortful attempt at poetic closure of an older, conventional kind:

> Among such scattered thoughts as these
> We turn the corner of the street;
> But why are we so hard to please?   (*IMH*, 14)

Following the otherwise odd gesture of retrospect (on a poem barely twelve lines long) in this attempt at gathering its "scattered thoughts," the rhetorical question attempts a final synthesizing sweep, while the return to the speaking personage of the first verse in these last two also shows the circling form of an older kind of enclosure. This "we," however, has exerted no pressure along the way, and the absence of its presence in this interval is felt most when the poem places the greater weight of expectation on it at the end. This "we" appears as the lyric subject *ex machina*: an automatic memory, drawn not from those categories of the mechanical and inorganic that locate the new value in the poetics of decadence but from the residual, lasting legacy of a romantic poetry that has featured the lyric first person as its dominant consciousness. Where the sensibility of decadence represents a late or decayed romanticism, this new music of mechanical humanity cannot be assimilated so easily to the formal and affective structures of those poetic precedents. Unfit as it may be, Eliot's finale reveals the substantial challenge a poetics of decadence is setting to that tradition.

The importance of this new idea of mechanical humanity for Eliot's early oeuvre shows as it recurs in "Convictions (Curtain Raiser)." "Among my marionettes I find / The enthusiasm is intense!" (*IMH*, 11): thus, in the opening lines of this poem, Eliot's speaker positions himself among the figures of puppets that feel, indeed, in his own exclamatory fashion. The conceit of the human as artifact serves to locate this poem in a tradition of literary decadence that it echoes as well by its title, which recalls that of the overture piece in Symons's *London Nights*, "Prologue: Before the Curtain." There, too, in the first line, the figure of the marionette, the effigy, the secondary or shadowy human – "We are the puppets of a shadow-play" (*PAS*, I, 79) – provides an echo in advance of the notes Eliot will strike and amplify as his own puppet show goes on. Here he deploys these "marionettes" as characters in the developing dramatic vignette:

> Two, in a garden scene,
> Go picking tissue paper roses;
> Hero and heroine, alone,
> The monotone
> Of promises and compliments
> And guesses and supposes.
>
> And over there my Paladins
> Are talking of effect and cause,
> With "learn to live by nature's laws!"
> And "strive for social happiness
> And contact with your fellow-men
> In Reason: nothing to excess!"
> As one leaves off the next begins.   (*IMH*, 11)

Eliot's puppet humans serve as the orienting point on a prospect that inventories an equally conventional store of decadent motifs and figures. Those "tissue paper roses" present an image of the organic gone artificial. The normative attitudes of nineteenth-century liberal humanism – progressivism, which includes a gradualism both natural and rational, and, in the avoidance of any extremity, the favoring of evolution over revolution – are placed within those marks of quotation that express, most of all, this poet's supercilious distancing of them. Where, however, is the poetic measure and imagined music for this new value of the antinatural, antirational, antihuman? The prosody of the catalogue – "promises and compliments / And guesses and supposes" – touches a point where the paratactic and the mechanical overlap, but only momentarily, only as the exception that defines the standard he cannot expand into a comprehensive tempo. If, as his companion talent Pound will have said, "I believe in technique as the test of a man's sincerity,"[7] this paint-by-numbers approach to the canvases of cultural and literary decadence shows the hand of one whose "convictions" have not reached that sincerer level of technique. And while the verse he publishes from this period in *Prufrock* will certainly succeed as tone poems in the key of *décadence*, playing the mood music of the aftermath and long dying fall in their atmospheric prospects, the more daunting aspects of this sensibility appear as an undertone at the edge of consciousness. Its rhythms are intermittent and mainly hidden, its mechanical imagination a notional or momentary reverberation, all of which dissolves under the pressure of existing, longer-lived traditions.

Another challenging aspect of this sensibility shows in counterconventional sexuality, more specifically, the queerness theme. This subject has been much discussed in recent Eliot criticism, which has been preoccupied with homo*sexual* and homo*erotic* references.[8] One unnoticed aspect of this wide-ranging interest includes the representation of queer temporalities. Following the challenge to the values of reproductive futurity, these are clearly inscribed in the prosodies of remnant temporality and, more fitfully and momentarily, in the mechanical and non-"natural" character of the machine-age meters in Eliot's early poetry. These metrics, at one particular extreme, follow the model of the obsessive repetitions that Edelman has explained in relation to the death-drive compulsion in his Freudian source. This understanding serves at least to index the convention-dismaying character of this sensibility. In the partial success it witnesses in Eliot's early poetry, we find a measure of the magnitude of the challenge it represents. In the anticipation these poems provide of the extraordinary performance he will provide for this tempo in the quatrain poems later in the decade, most important, this early work offers a record of the deepening achievement in this particular aspect of the poetics of decadence. Granted, the "queerness" of this representation needs to be understood as a condition that is attenuated from an embodied original; it is a cultural commodity that can be accessed by any writer. Nonetheless, the character of the "homo-sexual" appears as a point of reference for this sensibility in the early poetry. It is forced to a revealing focus in "The Love Song of St. Sebastian," where it demonstrates the same kind of hesitations as those other aspects of the decadent imaginary in the early work.

This poem is first mentioned in a letter of 19 July 1914, to Conrad Aiken. It combines a description of Eliot's new German locale with an allusion to Swinburne. "Marburg is ... a wonderfully civilised little place ... The houses have beautiful unkempt gardens, with great waves 'where tides of grass break into foam of flowers'!"[9] The quotation is from Swinburne's "Laus Veneris," or "Praise of Venus," which, as the proximate muse for Eliot's "*Love Song* of St. Sebastian," invokes for this poem one of the most important representatives of the sexual adventuring identified with deca-dence – with Baudelaire, first of all, whom Swinburne had served as self-appointed advocate in Britain, but also with this English poet, whose record of transgressing sexual behavior had become as notorious as the French poet's.[10] Eliot's poem takes this wheel a turn further in his representation of erotic psychopathology in his St. Sebastian. In this tortured song of thwarted eros, the speaker ranges across a spectrum of sado-masochistic fantasies: a self-loathing wish to be annihilated in the sexual act dovetails into a compulsion to murder the beloved, a vision which Eliot spells out thus in manuscript: "You would love me because I have strangled you / And because of my infamy. / And I should love you the more because I have mangled you" (*IMH*, 78). In the margins of this transcription, Eliot alters "infammy" to "infamy" and adds "*Not* to rhyme with 'mammy'" (*IMH*, 79n.35). He can joke about a slip which, if it cannot be rid of psychological content for the Freudian reader in its original, does at least in this second version avoid the sort of awkward comedy he falls into in the pratfall consonance of "strangled you" and "mangled you." Does this mechanical cadence of triple-syllable rhyme complement the assignably "unnatural" aspect of homosexuality with an equally artificial music? Momentarily, but not lastingly: entering the labyrinth of sexual malady that Baudelaire had opened, briefly augmenting its daunting aspect in that rhythmical figure of a rudely mechanical time, Eliot withdraws from that extremity into the regular pace of the next two lines, "And because you were no longer beautiful / To anyone but me" (*IMH*, 79). Here the poem ends – on the sort of diminuendo we recognize in these early poems as the chord into which Eliot resolves the disturbances he seems so often just on the verge of stirring up. The composure is charged, nonetheless, with the disquiet of those discordant lines.

In a second letter to Aiken of 25 July, which includes the manuscript copy of the poem, Eliot presents an interestingly contradictory record of his attitude to the poetic material of the decadent. On one hand, he suggests that he has come to a poetic impasse: "I enclose some *stuff* . . . [I] wonder whether I had better knock it off for a while – you will tell me what you think. Do you think that the *Love Song of St. Sebastian* part is morbid, or forced?" (*LTSE*, 44). *Morbidity*, attributed by critics of *décadence* as its saliently objectionable characteristic, is the category of value from which Eliot is nervously asking to be detached. On the other hand, he is unable to jettison the sensibility of decadence as his primary form of literary ambition. For the rest of this letter projects a sequence that will use the "Love Song" as the weight-bearing element – weakened beam or not – for a poetic structure that arises, in this prospectus, as a virtual temple of literary *décadence*. There will be a "recurring piece quite in the French style," he proposes: this is the national marker for a manner represented in this early verse by the several hands of Baudelaire and Laforgue (and perhaps also Tristan Corbière), that is, the poets of a Parisian *décadence*. Here, more specifically, he quotes the poem he will write, showing a young woman, who "Wraps her soul in orange-coloured robes of Chopinese"; she will lead the reader to a masked ball, the state occasion for a celebration of life as artifice (*LTSE*, 44). And St. Sebastian, otherwise known as the martyr (witness) of the queer subculture of *décadence*?[11] "[T]here's nothing homosexual about this," Eliot protests to Aiken (*LTSE*, 44). Whether or not we accept the Freudian adage that yes is yes and no is a stronger yes, the point of sexual transgression that he is identifying in that contested trait holds an affiliation with which he is unwilling to accept affiliation – dismissing any question of queer identity for himself, also rejecting the fall from the norm that provides the defining identity of de*cad*ence.

Given the stress registered by these denials and self-questionings, it is not hard to understand why Eliot feels he might need to "knock it off for a while." In his developing relation to the poetics of decadence, he has in fact reached a choking point. The technical and thematic conventions of this temperament have overfed his mind, which has gone undersupplied by the establishing circumstances of decadence. After all, he has not really experienced the unreason of history or the impossibility of progress, he has not realized the lie that human nature gives en masse to the idealizing constructions of humanism. He could have hardly known that all of this was coming. "We rejoice that the war danger is over," he remarks at the end of this second letter to Aiken (*LTSE*, 44). The forward irony of his comment would be realized in less than a week, when, with the lack of expectation he shared with *les autres jeunes* in the summer of 1914, he would be carried toward the conflagration of his generation.

2. War and Empire

"[I]f I could only get back to Paris," Eliot writes to Aiken on 30 September 1914, from London; "But I know I never will, for long. I must learn to talk English" (*LTSE*, 58). In his five-finger exercises in decadence, Eliot *has* been writing a kind of French poetry in English. So this letter expresses dissatisfaction with almost everything he has composed since "Prufrock" (1910–1911). It indicates his awareness that a change needs to be made. In the next few years he will find the location of this change, where the attitudes and practices of French *décadence* will undergo not so much a breach as an expansion – in the awareness history visits on him.

This is the burden of the developmental biography he sketches nearly three years later in a letter to the Englishman Robert Nichols, a poet whose combat verse has moved him into a new national visibility. Citing the recent appearance of *Prufrock*, most of whose poems had been written before he came to England, Eliot indicates clearly his felt need to "be able to forget, in a way, what one has written already" (*LTSE*, 191). This new orientation, fitful at first, represents a reassessment from the present of the legacy extending into the atmospherics of many of the poems selected for *Prufrock*. From wartime, that is, the legacy of decadence in his earliest verse may be reclaimed and reconstituted. This is a resource he calls up explicitly with a reference to Symons, whose *Symbolist* [that is, "Decadent"] *Movement in Literature* is hailed in this letter as having provided the material essential to his poetic identity and survival (*LTSE*, 191). Suggestively, but unmistakably, Eliot indicates that this youthful enthusiasm provides the substance of this contemporary, necessary change. And its occasion is a war that will have made real the presentiments of a late age in the actuality of history. This is a development we need to situate in relation to the historical circumstance of this war, understanding the special imaginative vocabulary in which Eliot registers it.

The record the war leaves in Eliot's poetry of the late 1910s is not nearly so explicit a history as may be found in other civilian poets. What is visible and consistent in this verse is an end-of-empire-days feeling, which finds an intense literary witness in Eliot's own lengthened end-of-the-war moment. With a complexity, with a density that registers the historical thickness of his work of this period, he marks his sense of late imperial time. His connection to the ethics of empire may be sourced to a strong familial feeling, typified by his mother's role as president in the local chapter of the Colonial Dames of America; indeed, her formulation of the supportive role this society should provide Britain in the American involvement in the war received strong approval by her son.[12] Accordingly, the record of his imaginative relation to the historical and ideological institutions of empire is substantial and meaningful. The feeling of loss that is centered and enlarged in this framework of imaginative reference is the primary matter in Eliot's recovery of an historically enriched poetics of literary decadence. And so, to begin with particulars, we should ask: what did empire really mean to Eliot; and what did the Great War, in light of the political history of the century, impart to his imaginative understanding of the imperial project?

Two pieces of prose – an essay on Virgil, written in 1951, the other on George Wyndham, the "Romantic Aristocrat" of the British nineteenth century, in 1919 – may stake the wider frame of this historical terrain. By 1951, with a major phase in the process of decolonization underway, Eliot readily concedes the discrepancy between the ideals of empire and the historical actuality of its institutions. He admits that, in many respects, existence in the Roman Empire was "coarse and beastly"; his Virgil nonetheless "set an ideal for Rome, and for empire in general, which was never realized in history; but the ideal of empire as Virgil sees it is a noble one." This ideal features a quality in the sensibility of the Roman poet that Eliot especially appreciates: in a word, "unity." He dwells on the difference between the myriad miscellany (as well as geography) of an imperial program and what he calls "an attitude towards *all* these things," a capacity to see "a *unity* and an order among them," a capacity so fundamental to Eliot it receives no further explanation – for him this need of "unity and order" is simply "an attitude towards life."[13] Similarly, thirty years earlier, when he is citing Wyndham's work in service to the far-flung empire, which included "a campaign in Egypt . . . service in South Africa accompanied by a copy of Virgil . . . a career in the Commons, a conspicuous career as Irish Secretary . . . [and finally] a career as a landowner – 2400 acres," he makes an important point in that singular detail of the "copy of Virgil" that Wyndham brought with him to the farthest point of his imperial career. Although he concedes that this is an inventory of "apparently unrelated occupations," he frames it with an invocation of the same quality he will identify in his later appreciation of Virgil: these various activities make sense in view of the "*unity* of Wyndham's mind."[14] If this special capacity for "unity" identifies the ideal temper of the imperial sensibility for Eliot, its significance may be heightened by virtue of its unlikelihood here. After all, Wyndham appears in this piece as the sheerest amalgam of assigned roles and stylized impulses, which Eliot brings under the tenuously generic heading of "this peculiar English type": as "the aristocrat, the Imperialist, the Romantic riding to hounds across his prose, looking with wonder upon the world as upon a fairyland."[15] When this "fairyland" is seen as the previously unknown regions of the globe, however, the various personae Wyndham projects into that dimension may be formed in accord with a single trajectory – the imperial unifier, subjoining the various areas and exotic qualities of an unknown world under one rule. The buccaneering wonder that Eliot attributes to this outward-bound voyager – "Wyndham was enthusiastic, he was a Romantic, he was an Imperialist"[16] – is supported strongly then by the rights of empire, which not only authorize an attitude to the world but, for Eliot, precede and provide for Wyndham's single, unifying orientation toward it.

This ideal of unity locates a primary point of attraction in Eliot's imperial imaginary. The value suggests a regimen of authority coextensive with the regulated domains of empire. In Eliot's case, moreover, a quality of formal order speaks most clearly of the appeal the imperial scheme exerted for him in the circumstances of his own first exposure to it as an historical reality – not substantially in the (ex)colonial America of the turn of the century, but, beginning in August 1914, in Britain, chiefly in London. He begins to inhabit the capital of world empire at the moment it is being most strenuously contested as a center of reference, not only strategically but ideologically. There is the increasingly entrenched stalemate of the continental war, whose old imperial rationale of a "campaign for civilisation" was certainly belied in the day-by-day experience of hitherto untold atrocity. Beginning at Easter 1916, moreover, there is the worsening circumstance of Ireland, the signal instance of Britain's fading colonial domain. In this manifold circumstance, the ideals of empire are to equal degrees jeopardized and prized, so that, as the threat to their former hegemony escalates, so the intensity of his imaginative attraction to them may also rise. These are the conditions under which the apprentice work he has done in the poetics of decadence will find its enriching condition and expressive extension.

But from what position may this young penurious American participate imaginatively in the drama of Britain's late imperial age? A decisive location can be found in the same place where an improvement in Eliot's early poetic fortunes may also be discerned: in his taking up employment, on 19 March 1917, in the "Colonial and Foreign Department" of Lloyds Bank in London. After a dry period of nearly three years, which had begun roughly on his arrival in England, the move to Lloyds coincided with a revival of his ability to compose poetry. Already on 11 April 1917, he can write his mother: "Then too I have felt more creative lately ... I have been doing some writing – mostly in French, curiously enough it has taken me that way – and some poems in French will come out in the *little review* in Chicago ["Le Directeur," "Mélange Adultère de tout," and "Lune de Miel," as well as "The Hippopotamus"]" (*LTSE*, 175). A subsequent rush of productivity is chronicled for his mother only nineteen days later by Vivien, who attributes the extraordinary activity she records to the happy circumstance in the bank: "not one of his friends has failed to see, and to remark upon, the great change in Tom's health, appearance, spirits, and literary productiveness since he went in for Banking .... No one could be more surprised than I am ... Only when he began to be more bright and happy and boyish than I've known him to be for nearly two years, did *I* feel convinced – and only when he has written *five*, most *excellent* poems in the course of one week, did Ezra Pound and many others, believe it possible" (*LTSE*, 177–78). The surge of work that Vivien references so emphatically includes the verse Eliot composed in the prevalent form of his work in this period, the quatrain, whose brisk rhythms and witty rhymes evidence the energy she references in palpable prosodic qualities. This will be the dominant stanza in the major poems of this moment.

While Eliot's creative strength is reinforced by the features of this poetic form, the energy stems from a sense of excitement that is rising out of his work at Lloyds. His feeling of personal agency appears proportionate indeed to the ranging domain of his "*Colonial* and Foreign Department." He seems already eager to claim the whole scope of this department as his own in a letter written only two days after starting there. "Lloyd's is one of the banks with largest foreign connections, and I am busy tabulating balance-sheets of foreign banks to see how they are prospering. My ideal is *to know the assets and liabilities* (*of every bank abroad that Lloyd's deals with*) for ten years past!" (*LTSE*, 165–66). Two months later, in a 13 June letter to his father: "The man who taught me my job has gone on his holiday, and I have *full control* over it now. *All the money* coming in ... *passes through my hands*. ... The foreign work is I believe the most interesting part of banking, especially at the present time, when one can from time to time *see very big things happening*" (*LTSE*, 184). Eliot's report seems untroubled by the fact that his personal work, which involved translation and asset- and account-tabulation for those various colonial and foreign banks, occurred at a fairly low level of importance. If he was but a "cog in the machine of Britain's commercial empire," as Peter Ackroyd characterizes his position,[17] the machine swept him up and obviously enlarged his sense of himself, and in a way that the emphasis added to the letters of this moment is not needed to reveal. The occasional grandiosity of personal power in his report scales it all the more accurately (if fantastically) to the order and proportion that his "*Colonial* and Foreign Department" calls up through its title, which invokes not only a worldwide range of activity but an imperial orientation toward it.

The point of this observation goes to an understanding of Eliot's feeling of literary empowerment in these years. He connects his cresting recognition as a man of letters to his mounting power at Lloyds, implicitly but irresistibly, in a lengthy letter to his mother on 29 March 1919. "They are organising some new work," he begins, "a new department, in fact, of a very interesting and important kind," one whose global dimension measures the import of his own role in it: "There is a man from the Foreign Office coming in too," Eliot makes a point of noting, and his own work "will be on a *large scale*, with *numerous assistants*" (*LTSE*, 279–80). He proceeds then to a review of his situation as a writer, which includes an emphatic assertion of the place he claims in literary London, indeed, in Anglo-American literary history: "I really think that I have far more *influence* on English letters than any other American has ever had, unless it be Henry James" (*LTSE*, 280). Allowing for the exaggerations a letter to his mother might prompt, it seems necessary to note in response to this claim that, at this moment, Eliot's published writing adds up to one slim volume of verse, a few poems appearing subsequently in periodicals, a clutch of occasional essays, and a somewhat desultory series of reviews. While he has earned considerable repute, the acclaim is barely a year old, and if his influence is registered intensely where it is felt, it is confined mainly to a micro-climate of cognoscenti – hardly the sort of "bigger picture" of literary history to which the importance of Henry James is scaled. In the rhetorical economy of the letter, however, the authority Eliot enjoys at Lloyds is being carried over into his poetic account. In this transaction, as it were, he is cashing in the savings he has built up through his work at the bank – in the coin of a literary repute, it is important to note, that is still backed by the real gold of empire.

Consider the trans-Atlantic dimension of reference in this letter. The "*influence*" Eliot has earned in the "Colonial and Foreign Department" at Lloyds, at the financial capital and emblematic center of empire, tells its import as his personal story within the structure of literary history. As this (former) colonial poet comes (back) to London, that is, he is continuing and completing the work of that other returning American, Henry James. And here he gains the authority – the authenticity – which is the former imperial power's singular capacity to confer. "[F]or an American," he confides to his mother in July 1920, "getting recognised in English letters is like breaking open a safe" (*LTSE*, 392). The trove in which Eliot images the literary distinction England now yields to him clearly suggests the reference of Lloyds Bank and, for him, the cultural bullion in its vault. It hints at the status he attaches silently to that institution a year earlier, when, in effect, his position as imperial financier, fantasized or not, underwrites and legitimates the power with which this American poet in Britain now endows himself. The empire has served its returning servant well.

Eliot's investment in the enterprise of empire shows most of its imaginative value and literary interest, however, in the poetic uses he makes of its undoing. For the assurance he draws from this structure of authority is balanced, and expressively counterbalanced, by an awareness of its declining condition in contemporary history. Curiously, perhaps in a kind of retrospective self-explanation, his later essays on the role of empire in the literary imagination – in Kipling as well as Virgil – suggest that imperial feeling becomes available for literature mainly or only in the demise of its institutions and ideologies.[18] This is the same attitude that Pound expressed already in 1912 in "Patria mia," which registered the most important effect of the imperial episteme as an ideal unrealized. It exists mainly or only for poetry, that is, in the feelings to be experienced from its failure, its fall. This is a way of saying that empire provides a metric and a reference for the sense of loss and fall that is otherwise so widely working in the temporal imaginary of decadence, whose conditions may differ from Britain to America but whose literary representations stem from the same European literary and political history.

The deep literary memory for this moment in European time is recalled in the opening motions of the poem Eliot finished in July 1919, within days of the signing of the Versailles Treaty. The "little old man" who is the title character and speaker of "Gerontion" centers the references of failing empire in his own historical present:

> Here I am, an old man in a dry month,
> Being read to by a boy, waiting for rain.
> I was neither at the hot gates
> Nor fought in the warm rain
> Nor knee deep in the salt marsh, heaving a cutlass,

Bitten by flies, fought.
My house is a decayed house . . .[19]

The "hot gates" constitute an allusion to the Battle of Thermopylae (*thermo-pylae*, hot gates) in the Persian Wars, an event that marks a climacteric in the history of the Persian Empire and that the speaker appropriates, accordingly, as the scene of his own challenge and crisis in the most recent imperial war. He is a member of the generation too old by 1914 to have fought in that campaign, which was characterized critically, insistently, increasingly, as a war authored by the old but fought by the young. ("Young blood and high blood, / fair cheeks and fine bodies," Pound writes in the first of the two war lyrics in *Hugh Selwyn Mauberley*, where youth "walked eye deep in hell / believing in old men's lies" [*P*, 188].) Where this circumstance accounts for Eliot's speaker's self-presentation entirely in negatives, using the conjunctions "neither . . . Nor . . . Nor" to hinge his various disabilities, it also locates diminishment as a general or systemic condition. "My house is a decayed house." Given the representative identity of this speaker, the "house" that is "decayed" is more than an individual's dwelling. This is the "house of England" – a comprehensive, national habitation. Those several references in 1919 serve then to locate "Gerontion" in geopolitical space and historical time as a moment of late empire in which the sense of decay is at once extensive and concentrated.

Especially concentrated, in this account of the makeshift rituals in the ersatz religion the speaker records:

In depraved May, dogwood and chestnut, flowering judas,
To be eaten, to be divided, to be drunk
Among whispers; by Mr. Silvero
With caressing hands, at Limoges
Who walked all night in the next room;
By Hakagawa, bowing among the Titians;
By Madame de Tornquist, in the dark room
Shifting the candles; Fraulein von Kulp
Who turned in the hall, one hand on the door.   (*1920*, 14)

A "depraved May" calls up the conceit of contrary nature in decadence. The fall from the natural order is echoed suggestively in the moral domain in the name of Fraulein von Kulp, which provides an interlingual rhyme with the Latin *culpa*: wrong, fault, or fall. Another fall awaits the "caressing hands" of the man with the slippery name "Silvero." Along the same lines, there is a "flowering judas": through an allusion to the disciple who betrayed Jesus with a dishonest kiss, Eliot gestures suggestively – in a passage so dense with references to a culture of decadence – to the dishonesty that Oscar Wilde championed in *The Decay of Lying* as the poetic spirit of decadence, which is indeed flourishing in this milieu. Comprehensively, then: a nature gone wrong is echoed in a human fall that is focused in the transgressions of the queer and a poetics of dissembling; there is even the substitute religion of art in "Hakagawa, bowing among the Titians." With an extraordinary concentration, the attitudes and practices of artistic as well as attitudinal decadence are woven into this scene as a comprehensive interior prospect.

"After such knowledge, what forgiveness?" goes the antiphonal question in the poem (*1920*, 14). There is no substantial answer. The response is the poetry Eliot has been writing for the last several years, which provides the substance of the next section of this chapter, which follows his representation of this condition of late empire and its related declines in the verse of the late 1910s. Here the sense of contemporary history that we have established provides a basis for a renewed language of literary decadence.

3.   Four-Square Decadence: A Prosody for Modernism

Eliot's references to the decline of empire emerge through the poetic form that dominates the prosody at this moment: the rhymed, tetrameter quatrain. In this stanza an extreme regularity of cadence, formalized by often strong rhymes, effects an energy of palpably mechanical character. His critical writings of this moment, as Nigel Alderman has documented (in an article that reminds us how little scholarly attention has been paid to the poems of this moment), strongly emphasized aspects of the mechanical in the literary imagination; this is a characteristic valued particularly by Wyndham Lewis, on whose work Eliot also bestows a good deal of praise in the last years of the decade.[20] The machine-made feeling of these tetrameter quatrains bespeaks a motive interest perhaps in the personal circumstances of the versifier, who may have needed to gin up the tempo thus in order to break the nearly three-year writing block that had set in upon his arrival in Britain. But the cadence also echoes suggestively back through a literary philology, which includes an extensive use in the poetry of the ur-*décadent*, Théophile Gautier, whom Eliot has also acknowledged as a model.[21] Gautier's recognizably mechanical cadence provides a rhythmic figure for that category of value we may identify in the aesthetics of decadence as the inorganic, featuring puppets in lieu of living bodies, effigies or dead replicas instead of vital human life. These are the insignia of an imaginative understanding of an historical present that has, in effect, outlived the life cycle of renewable organic time; these are the features of a late or last age, an aftermath, where the machine has lost its discernibly human value or utility and stands as the sign of antihuman time. This sensibility is at once realized and intensified in the current historical circumstance, in the negative apocalypse of modern technology that the war constitutes. So, a prosody that takes the suitably complex measure of this historical time dominates a poetry that shows the poetics of decadence as the timeliest, the most definably modernist, of Eliot's early poetic temperaments.

Three of these quatrain poems present the personage who centers the framework of contemporary historical reference: "Sweeney." The title character of "Sweeney among the Nightingales" and "Sweeney Erect" appears also in the somewhat unlikely setting of "Mr. Eliot's Sunday Morning Service," where, in the closing lines, "Sweeney shifts from ham to ham / Stirring the water in his bath" (*1920*, 34). This recognizably Irish patronymic points in one direction to the situation in Ireland, which, following the Easter Rising in April 1916, continues through the remainder of the war and into the next decade as the most vivid and impending register of the end of imperial domain – and not just on that island. For, in the other direction, the failing campaign in the continental war reinforces the Irish message on a grander scale, taking the event of the rebellion to a totality of implication that Eliot claims, we shall see, in making Sweeney relevant as well to the European catastrophe.

"Sweeney among the Nightingales" opens in caricature, rhythmical as well as imagistic:

> Apeneck Sweeney spreads his knees
> Letting his arms hang down to laugh,
> The zebra stripes along his jaw
> Swelling to maculate giraffe.   (*1920*, 35)

While the figure of the simian Irishman is familiar as ethnic cartoon, it also presents an illustration of the late-nineteenth-century obsession with the process of reverse evolution, or degeneration. The promise of progress belied is imaged in this figure of the human reversed to the ape. So in tempo: the bestiary of human features coincides with the form of the tetrameter quatrain, stiffened considerably by the unexpected hard rhyme in the final line; there is an animal-mechanical character to this measure, which moves in striking and revealing contrast to the organically elastic rhythms of the "free verse" measures Eliot will have perfected in *Prufrock and Other Observations*. This new tempo taps into an imaginative apprehension of the decadent present, as it turns the pulse of human feeling down into this uncanny likeness, or canny unlikeness, of our human selves: a creaturely machine time lives out the failure of the ideal time of human improvement through progress, which, after all, history has now outlived. The poet is writing in an aftermath typified by the dead language factor so emphatically struck in the final line in the Latinate "maculate." Similarly, in "Sweeney Erect" –

> Morning stirs the feet and hands
>   (Nausicaa and Polypheme),
> Gesture of orang-outang
>   Rises from the sheets in steam . . . .
>
> Sweeney addressed full length to shave
>   Broadbottomed, pink from nape to base,
> Knows the female temperament
>   And wipes the suds around his face   (*1920*, 19–20)

– where the bestiary of primate likenesses expands within a rhythm reiterating a now familiar point. Automatic tempo is the late time of humankind, which, having disproved the truth of its improvement through progressive evolution, reverts now to the animal-mechanical feeling Eliot projects from this compound of imagery and rhythm.

This representation of the temporal imaginary of decadence shows its local time and historical instigation through several references in the same poem. Consider the bawdy double entendre in the title, which is irresistible once it is listened for: "Sweeney Erect" is the "Irish[man] Rising." This is not an accidental pun but a verbal figure consistent with a lexicon of canny representations. Where, in that third stanza, that "Gesture of orang-outang / *Rises* from the sheets in steam," the small heave of the trochaic stress on "Rises" serves to underscore the major historical event it emphatically names. And, more subtly but still more indicatively, in the second of the first two quatrains, which provides his mock-epic invocation of the Muses:

> Display me Aeolus above
>   Reviewing the insurgent gales
> Which tangle Ariadne's hair
>   And swell with haste the perjured sails.   (*1920*, 19)

The shifting of two letters in the last word of the second line turns "insurgent gales" to "insurgent Gaels." "Insurgent" was a word very much in play in the journalistic reportage of the Rising, as in the headline of the *New York Times* on 7 May, "Major M'Bride Shot as Irish *Insurgent*," where the ethnography is more idiomatic than the learned version of Eliot's poem, that mock-erudite catalogue of mythological muses.[22] Or, with less pretense, but no less guile, in that Sunday Morning Service of Mr. Eliot, where,

as "Sweeney shifts from ham to ham / Stirring the water in his bath," the
Irish caricature is broad and blunt: Paddy's pig provides the basis for the
wordplay in representing the character's "hams," whose "stirring" invokes
by a subtler synecdoche the motions of those other Paddies, the Easter
Rising of Sweeney's countrymen barely a year earlier. Unsubtle the other
aspects of this characterization, which, once the several notes are decoded,
present a livid picture of current circumstance.

Beyond caricature? An additional dimension of feeling comes with this
perceptible shift in rhythm and imagery in the final quatrains of "Sweeney
among the Nightingales":

> The host with someone indistinct
> Converses at the door apart,
> The nightingales are singing near
> The Convent of the Sacred Heart,
>
> And sang within the bloody wood
> When Agamemnon cried aloud
> And let their liquid droppings fall
> To stain the stiff dishonoured shroud.   (*1920*, 36)

These tetrameters are not metronomic but stately; by the end, they have
created and sustained a sense of processional solemnity. The cadence goes
strong but also strange and fateful as the first word of the final stanza marks a
turn toward formal closure with its coordinating conjunction, when the
rhythm builds into the sublimity of the final prospect. This is a quality
enhanced in the penultimate line with the replacement of "droppings" by
"siftings," a change offered initially by Pound on the manuscript and
preserved in the first appearance of the poem in the *little review* in 1918
and subsequently in *Poems* (1919) and *Ara Vos Prec* (1920) (*IMH*, 382). The
imagistic lightening turns a picture of dropping bird turds into a fairy
filigree of birdsong. Here the beauty of the wood, lit up with the incandescence of nightingale music, mingles with the terror of the memory of the
violent demise of Agamemnon, whose dying words in the play by Aeschylus
also provide the epigraph for Eliot's poem. The hero returning from the
Trojan War to the murderous plot of his wife Clytemnestra is doubled by
Sweeney, surrounded in the seedy bistro of contemporary London by a
mélange of women as menacing as that "Rachel *née* Rabinovitch," who
"Tears at the grapes with murderous paws" (*1920*, 36). In view of this
modern counterpart's simian character, however, the likeness should hardly
entail the exhilaration of the sublime. So, where does the majestic sentiment
of this finale come from?

It comes in good part from a poet's *pre*sentiment about the events that background the Sweeney character and that texture the identification of this figure with his mythic double. For, like Agamemnon, Sweeney is a returning soldier. Those "zebra stripes along his jaw" depict the creases of fat cut into the neck by the tight, stiff collar of the military dress uniforms that were worn at this time. (In 1974, Marshall McLuhan told me that Eliot had said to him that the model for Sweeney was an Irish-Canadian airman, billeted in London during the war.) And when Sweeney reappears in *The Waste Land*, it is in the company of Mrs. Porter and her daughter, the (not so lofty) subjects of a song sung by Irish and Australian troops in the Gallipoli campaign in 1915.[23] Sweeney's connection to the soldiery of this contemporary war is of primary importance; it is the Great War as much as the Trojan War that provides the back story in the framework of imaginative association. Indeed, the Agamemnon references come late and last in the process of composition: it is only in the final draft of the poem that the Greek epigraph is added (perhaps in response to a suggestion by Pound, who has recently reviewed the Browning translation of *Agamemnon*).[24] The classical hero functions in a rhetoric of final irony, where, in imaginative comparison, he recalls a standard that Sweeney fails but that also makes available a range of exalted feeling in the poem, here of exalted loss. And no small sense of loss attends the perception that Britain's "Great War for Civilisation" is being fought – and lost – by this "Apeneck" Irishman, the simian representative of that unevolved province and now insurgent colony. Imperial decline, degenerative time, and a tempo turning from a memory of mechanical brutality to emotional diminuendo: the historical conditions and expressive measures of the poetics of decadence locate Eliot's most intense register of the import of the current day, which, in the exceptional degree of self-consciousness he exhibits about this time, registers as a particularly modernist day.

As a measure of its pressure in the historical imaginary of decadence in Eliot's present, the Irish situation provides a point of major reference in an otherwise unlikely site, Venice. This is the location for "Burbank with a Baedeker: Bleistein with a Cigar." The connection surfaces through Eliot's correspondence around the time of the poem's composition. In a letter to the British novelist and travel writer Douglas Goldring, Eliot refers to the controversy Goldring has touched off with his 1917 critique of the Irish literary revival, *Dublin: Explorations and Reflections of an Englishman*. This book singled out for criticism one of the more conspicuous spokespersons of the Celtic movement, Ernest Boyd, who retaliated with "Broadbent's Baedeker" – a review of Goldring's volume in the Dublin weekly, *New*

Ireland, which accused Goldring of cultural imperialism. Goldring's ironically patronizing riposte, "The Importance of Being Ernest," stirred a further rejoinder from Boyd, "A Boy of the Bulldog Breed."[25] Writing to Goldring on 7 November 1918, Eliot refers to "the cuttings from *New Ireland*" and claims: "my opinions nearly coincide with yours" (*LTSE*, 253). Whatever difference "nearly" intimates, the "Baedeker" reference and the conspicuous alliteration of "b"s in Eliot's title obviously recall the headlines in the *New Ireland* controversy. Not that this reference is necessary to establish a theme of imperial decline in the Venetian scene: the city situated on its coastal plain is perceived to be ever surrendering its cultural treasure, which is the booty of marine empire, into the sea; it is a capital city in the Baedeker of decadence. But those reminders in Eliot's title of the decline of imperial rule in Ireland establish the condition of decadence at a closer focus, which may account for the particular imaginative intensities and linguistic interests of this poem.

The English center of the Venetian scene emerges in the final quatrain in references as oblique but certain as the Irish signals in the poem's title:

> Who clipped the lion's wings
> And flea'd his rump and pared his claws?
> Thought Burbank, meditating on
> Time's ruins, and the seven laws.   (*1920*, 18)

Beyond the insignia of the degraded lion of St. Mark's, this prospect of the decline of imperial-mercantile power for the Venetian state looks farther away and closer to Eliot's current home for its sources of concern. The "seven laws" make reference to *The Seven Lamps of Architecture*, where Ruskin enumerates the "laws" of moral order in public construction in general, not only in Venice in particular. Here, as in *The Stones of Venice*, the image of "ruins," "Time's" and tides' but also of "laws," that is, of social as well as material and natural degeneration, comprises but exceeds its specific topic and provocation in the Venetian state. For Ruskin's motives in *The Stones of Venice* included a wish to turn the story of its fall into a cautionary tale for England as a marine imperial power. That is a warning which Eliot's last stanza answers with his representation of imperial power in diminuendo, focusing that point through the English name of his first title character.[26] It is the assimilated point of the history he has experienced in the preceding years, no less closely than in the Irish trouble that lies in the background sound of his title.

Here the place the Irishman Sweeney has taken in the poems featuring his name is taken by the nominal Jew. Eliot's representation of "Bleistein" may open the ethical problematic as well as the imaginative dimensionality of his relation to contemporary decadence. In this representation, "Bleistein" provides the most extreme illustration of the backward-turning process of reverse evolution: "A lustreless protrusive eye / Stares from the protozoic slime" (*1920*, 18). More: in the company of other Jewish characters-in-name, in the familiar fiction of Jewish conspiracy, in an explanatory paradigm equally long-standing and newly current after the war, Bleistein stands as the primary cause (not just an illustrative or even instrumental figure) of time's "decline":

> The smoky candle end of time
>
> Declines. On the Rialto once.
>> The rats are underneath the piles.
> The jew is underneath the lot.
>> Money in furs. The boatman smiles,
>
> Princess Volupine extends
>> A meagre, blue-nailed, phthisic hand
> To climb the waterstair. Lights, lights,
>> She entertains Sir Ferdinand
>
> Klein.   (*1920*, 18)

If the irregular syntax in this passage gives the tetrameter prosody a more variable cadence and so a less mechanical character than is usual now in Eliot's quatrains, the sense of late time comes through auxiliary resources in the poetic temperament of decadence: the repetition that fades. "Declines" and "Klein," rhyming in the otherwise unobtrusive position of the initial word in their respective lines, but focused in that placement by the indentation of alternate lines, are linked additionally as second halves in the pattern of enjambment they share; the rhyming syllables come together as an echo distended across the span of two quatrains, to be heard not in the usual and conspicuous position of end-stopped rhymes but by an inner ear relying on a reader's eye. The feeling of diminishment in reiteration is reinforced by the additional sense of smallness that the meaning of the German word brings into the sense of the Jewish name, which, turning diminishment into belittlement, takes a presentiment of declining time even lower.

While the question of Eliot's anti-Semitism has centered a good deal of scholarly commentary in the last two decades,[27] it is worth noting those simultaneous and equally intensely negative representations of the Irish.

Not that these two groups need to compete as subjects of prejudice and enmity; nor that Eliot be judged, or spared judgment. An understanding of these figures, especially as the Irish and Jews are linked as subjects of denigration, comes with that larger framework of conception we recognize as the temporal imaginary of decadence. In this scheme, the figures of the downturn of time are seen predictably in the instances of the two religions – Judaism for "Bleistein" and Roman Catholicism, presumably but irresistibly, for "Sweeney" – which, from the otherwise enlightened Protestantism of Eliot's background, are deemed to be superstitious, irrational, fetishistic, reversionary. Whether these images depict his personal attitudes or some exaggerated version of a standard language of prejudice, they emerge in representations whose controversy is not just a provocation to be reacted to but a critical and interpretative issue to engage.

A point of comparison to highlight and offset Eliot's methods in these poems on the Irish and the Jews comes in the otherwise infamous "King Bolo" verses. These are the poetic outrages he was pulling off at roughly the same time and secreting in private correspondence to selected friends.[28] Crude not only in their sexual and racist humor, the barrack-room balladry in which these verses were composed offers a point of telling contrast to the poems we are considering here.

Notice how an especially artful concoction of enjambments and distant echoic rhyme provides the setting for his representation of the "jew."[29] In a similar complication, "Apeneck Sweeney" blends into the figure of poetic sublimity in the elegiac finale of that poem. The composite product is no less offensive and morally objectionable than it is poetically refined, a quality that is heightened in relation to the ransom-gamble mechanical-piano cadences that dominate the quatrains otherwise. These unsettling figures emerge from within the most exquisite of poetic measures. This complication of ethics by aesthetics represents a special extension of the anti- or pseudo-morality of the poetics of decadence, as formulated by Wilde in *The Decay of Lying*. In the extraordinary artfulness of its moralistic subversion of truth as a category of artistic value, this tract participates in that profounder complication of good aesthetics and bad morals, which identifies one of the strongest provocations of the English fin de siècle. So, too, in Eliot's poems of this moment, which take this attitude to an extremity registered equally in the odiousness of those figures and the suavity of their representation in the poems: the shift from the machine-made cadences of the standard quatrain measures to the rhythms of a more finely pointed poetic time moves in perfect synch with the transgression of finer feelings. Whether Eliot be judged or spared judgment for this demonstration, he is clearly participating in the conundrum of aesthetical ethics, which provides one of the primary registers of the ongoing crisis of the meaning and value of art over the long turn of the century.

The feeling of loss that attends this eventuality shows in the elegiac feelings that dominate the moments in which this problem of aesthetical ethics is demonstrated. This apprehension finds a most specific application in the language imaginary of "Burbank." Here, in the perceptibly waning days of empire, in the late historical age of decadence, we are reading a poetic lexicon rifted with signals of antiquity and mortality. Thus "Princess Volupine extends / A meagre, blue-nailed, phthisic hand." The rare and recherché and virtually unpronounceable adjective – "phthisic" means *decay* – provides the last Word in the poetics of English decadence in particular, as, in general, in the poetics of decadence, language is a material always already lapsing into an unliving condition. This is the unvoiced condition of printed existence; its word is a verbal substance going . . . going . . . gone from vital exchange, into a quasi-paleographic craft. Eliot's "phthisic" is a word sent like a message in a bottle from that floating island of perennial decadence, which we are reading, it seems, millennia after its original sound died on the air.

Not only in that poem: there is "Mr. Eliot's Sunday Morning Service." Here the automatic tempo of the late-time imaginary in Eliot's standard wartime-issue quatrain coincides with an idiolect familiar from the lexicons of decadence. It is rifted with the memory of an antiquity no longer living in Eliot's contemporary English language:

> Polyphiloprogenitive
> The sapient sutlers of the Lord
> Drift across the window-panes.
> In the beginning was the Word.
>
> In the beginning was the Word.
> Superfetation of τὸ ἒυ,
> And at the mensual turn of time
> Produced enervate Origen. *(1920, 33)*

"In the beginning was the Word" recalls a pristine original moment of language, some Adamic unity of verbal sign and referential meaning, which capitalizes "Word" as a noun proper to its referent in that myth of verbal origins. This quality has fallen into the polyglot composite of words that are obviously not in referential life and use, of words learned or obsolete or rare or unusually formed, of words that look back to ancient roots that do not stir with current life. If there is a piece of Eden in each root, the root is dead, and the composite language of the passage, preposterous as it seems, is just this dead matter of fossilized radicals. (Recall that Pound used the same ultra-Latinate form of "superfetation" in referring to the mechanical characters in the Russian ballet he was using as an example of postwar "decadence.") This is the linguistic condition of a decadent script, of the Scripture of Decadence. If it looks wanly or even nostalgically back through the verbal comedy to the topos of a foregone origin, it looks across to John Bull's Other Island for its local provocation, its timely content and historical depth. Here, in the final quatrain, "Sweeney shifts from ham to ham / Stirring the water in his bath" (*1920*, 34): the stirring of Sweeney's countrymen in the Irish Rising is recalled in the particular imagistic details and verbal configurations we noted earlier. These combine with the appearance of Sweeney in other poems of this moment to join the undoing of imperial rule in Ireland with the declining fortunes of empire in an apparently unending but ever worsening war on the continent.

This sense of downturn in the current war also locates a moment of feeling in "A Cooking Egg" as powerful as it is subtle. Initially, this poem might be dismissed as the brittle and trivial wit of Eliot's quatrain art, his music box prosody. The dominant voice is the know-nothing know-it-all, a sort of rhetorical zero:

> I shall not want Capital in Heaven
>   For I shall meet Sir Alfred Mond:
> We two shall lie together, lapt
>   In a five per cent Exchequer bond.   (*1920*, 22)

This caricature in voice is interrupted and significantly altered, however, as the poem turns toward conclusion:

> But where is the penny world I bought
>   To eat with Pipit behind the screen?
> The red-eyed scavengers are creeping
>   From Kentish Town and Golder's Green;
>
> Where are the eagles and the trumpets?
>
>   Buried beneath some snow-deep Alps.
> Over buttered scones and crumpets
>   Weeping, weeping multitudes
> Droop in a hundred A. B. C.'s.   (*1920*, 23)

Syntactically and rhythmically, "The red-eyed scavengers are creeping / From Kentish Town and Golder's Green" recalls the pattern and pacing in "The nightingales are singing near / The Convent of the Sacred Heart." And where those two lines in "Sweeney among the Nightingales" lead to the "turn" of the final stanza, which pivots on the initial coordinating conjunction "And," a similar modulation occurs in "A Cooking Egg." For the cadence changes with the surplus verse: as the quatrain stanza-pattern breaks into the additional line, the variation marks a difference in emotion that matches the shift in the finish to "Sweeney." The intensification in "A Cooking Egg" includes, too, an allusion to present conditions in the Great War. The human cost of this first mass war is scaled to the proportion of "[w]eeping, weeping multitudes" and imaged in the pathos of its conscripted masses' typical lives, in the figures of the "buttered scones and crumpets" that are served in a hundred public canteens, the Aerated Baking Companies. Eliot is sustaining a frame of war reference from the mention of "Sir Alfred Mond" and the "five per cent Exchequer bond," where the minister in the war cabinet is linked, from his former career as prominent financier, with the instruments used to fund the war.

As in "Sweeney among the Nightingales," Eliot is taking the war as a source of poetic feeling that is amplified through a framework of imperial reference. The softly sardonic comedy in the rhyming of "crumpets" and "trumpets" includes a muted, ironically protected perception of the relation between the common food of the cannon fodder and the insignia of an imperial pageant, "the eagles and the trumpets" of a Roman *triumphus*. A gloss on the imperial content of these images comes in Eliot's later (1932) poem, "Coriolan: Triumphal March," where that rite of the Roman Empire, a procession of treasure and captives through the capital city, is featured in these images for the regalia of a modern military parade: "You can see some eagles. / And hear the trumpets."[30] Fancied in 1932, already foregone in 1917: that rhetorical question asks, *ubi sunt*, where are these numinous things of yesteryear? It is as a lost source of order and authority that this memory of the Roman triumphal march exerts its particular poetic power, which is measured, indeed, in its distance, its *ir*relevance – in the poor, bare, *un*accommodated lives of these somber conscripts in the mass army of the failing empire.

If Eliot can experience the imperial episteme chiefly as a fallen or compromised ideal, he comes back again (and again) to the war as the event that establishes his relation to empire as *materia poetica*. This is the material reference for the diversely working poetics of decadence. This sensibility provides a key for interpretive work and a frame of critical analysis that reveal the coherence of a major interval in his development. If these quatrain poems are constantly acknowledged as important and indeed canonical, they are also routinely overlooked in those literary histories that focus instead on the major work on either side of them, respectively, *Prufrock and Other Observations* and *The Waste Land*. One reason for this omission has been the absence of a developed understanding of the poetics of decadence in Eliot's early work. It is a decadence that is particularly and emphatically modernist insofar as the feeling of aftermath, which shows in the mechanical cadences as well as imaginative temporality of decadence, appears as the critical perception of the present, as the crisis of time, in this poet's acutely and self-consciously modern day.

4. *The Waste Land*: Dracula's Shadow, and the Shadow Language of Decadence

A single passage in the manuscript history of *The Waste Land* recapitulates Eliot's development of an historically enriched poetics of decadence. This first draft is dated 1914 by Valerie Eliot:

> A woman drew her long black hair out tight
> And fiddled whisper-music on those strings
> The Shrill bats quivered through the violet air
> [**Sobbing**] Whining, and beating wings.
> > distorted
> A man, [**one withered**] by some mental blight
> > contorted
> Yet of abnormal powers
> > Such a one crept
> I saw him creep head downward down a wall
> And upside down in air were towers
> Tolling reminiscent bells –
> > And [**there were**] chanting voices out of cisterns and of wells.[31]

The figure of the man crawling "head downward down a wall" contains a memory of the vampire Dracula in the first sighting by Bram Stoker's narrator Jonathan Harker: "But my very feelings changed to repulsion and terror when I saw the whole man slowly emerge from the window and begin to crawl down the castle wall over that dreadful abyss, *face down*, with his cloak spreading out around him like great wings."[32] In the double "down" of "head downward down," Eliot replicates the force of the shock that Harker's (Stoker's) own emphasis strikes into the "*face down*" of his representation. And the likeness that Harker draws between the cloak and "great wings" accounts for the presence of the figure of the bats, from which the human figure in this scene emerges and into which he disappears ultimately in the published, 1922 version:

> And bats with baby faces in the violet light
> Whistled, and beat their wings
> And crawled head downward down a blackened wall
> And upside down in air were towers
> Tolling reminiscent bells, that kept the hours
> And voices singing out of empty cisterns and exhausted wells.
>
> (*TWL*, ll. 145, 379–84)

An intermediate version of late 1921 presents the otherwise missing link of this re-inscription of the man-vampire into the bats:

> A woman drew her long black hair out tight
> And fiddled whisper music on those strings
> And bats with baby faces, in the violet [**air**] light,
> Whistled, and beat their wings
> A [**man**] / form crawled downward down a blackened wall
> And upside down in air were towers
> Tolling reminiscent bells, that kept the hours.
> And voices singing out of cisterns and exhausted wells.   (*TWL*, 75)

Though deleted, "man" preserves the human figure into this last draft and so locates the Dracula character as the main point of continuity and development over these years.

In the first casting of this passage in 1914, the Dracula figure prompts a rhetoric of censure that emerges from a vantage shared with the standards of progressive civilization. That is the value which this figure of reversion so explicitly contests, as we saw in our earlier consideration of the novel. It is weirdly overheated but revealing nonetheless as a measure of the strongly conditioned quality of some aspects of Eliot's earlier sensibility. He is holding onto the values that decadence defies but that history has not yet given the lie to, at least not yet on the grand scale of the Great War. The exercises in literary decadence that he has inscribed heretofore have been woven largely out of his head; they represent an appropriation, often a masterful appropriation, of the postures and gestures that are available to him mainly from literary tradition.

The recasting of this passage in 1921–1922 demonstrates Eliot's assimilation of the history that has intervened. He relocates the scene from the twilight atmospheric of the "evening" scene in 1914 and inserts it into a geographical and historical prospect that he labels quite specifically, in his note to this section of the published poem, as the "present decay of eastern Europe" (*TWL*, 148). This eastern European location takes the atavistic challenge that the Dracula figure represents in his homeland into the instigating site of the Great War. And this challenge is writ large in the epic perspective of those "hooded hordes swarming / Over endless plains" (*TWL*, ll. 145, 368–69) – the vision of a European continent overrun by barbarian hordes recalls the end of the Roman Empire and, just so, invokes the present day as a moment in a history whose chaos is also framed as imperial decline. Unsurprisingly, then, Eliot provides an epigraph to the 1921 manuscript of the poem that reads as the last words of the imperial dream – "The horror! The horror!" (*TWL*, 3) – from Conrad's *Heart of Darkness*.[33] Kurtz's last words are uttered at the outer verge of commercial empire; they locate the *terminus ad quem* of the imperial project, the limit where Western progressivism and rationalism fail.

This figure is reiterated as the end of another imaginative voyage, which appears in the penultimate draft of Part 4 of the sequence:

> One night
> On watch, I thought I saw in the fore cross trees
> Three women [**with white hair**] leaning forward, with white hair
> Streaming behind, who sang above the wind
> A song that charmed my senses, while I was
> Frightened beyond fear, horrified past horror, calm.
> (Nothing was real) for, I thought, now, when
> I like, I can wake up and end the dream.   (*TWL*, 67)

"The horror! The horror!" that Conrad's character groans is repeated in the doubling emphases of this speaker's being "horrified past horror." As at the limit of commercial empire, from which Kurtz sees the irredeemable savagery of the human condition and so knows the folly of the imperial project as a civilizing mission, Eliot's speaker inhabits a zone of foreclosed possibilities as well. The "horror" of his "dream" retains the memory of the historical circumstance that spurred it, that spurred Kurtz's words first of all, but he is shifting the conditions of late imperial days into a figure of romantic fantasy. Suppressing this passage as well as the epigraph at Pound's direction, probably because "The horror!" did not enclose a major affective chord of the sequence, Eliot nonetheless leaves this evidence of an end-of-empire-days feeling, which is an establishing circumstance of the decadent imaginary, as one of the instigating stimuli of the poem.

The restored memory of this omission puts in summary perspective the extent of references in the poem to empire, which work together to inscribe a *memento mori* to imperial ambition. The marine empire of Phoenicia is seen in the body of the drowned Phoenician sailor, which circulates famously through the text. A major moment of reversal in imperial fortunes is recalled in the naval battle at Mylae near the end of "The Burial of the

Dead" (*TWL*, l. 70, 136). The early and late days in Britain's maritime empire are bracketed in "The Fire Sermon," where the Thames, which "sweats / Oil and tar" (ll. 142, 266–67) nowadays, runs back through the allusion to Elizabeth and her ceremonial vessel on the "brisk swell" (l. 142, 284) of a seaborne tide to the sap years of marine imperial reign, now foregone. In a more immediate *mise-en-scène*, in the interior view of "A Game of Chess," references to the life cycle of empire dominate the prospect. Allusions to Dido (l. 92, 137) and Cleopatra (l. 77, 137) recall their male counterparts Aeneas and Antony and so locate their respective moments at the early and late turns of the mythology – and history – of the Roman state and the Roman Empire. In this chambered space, the atmospheric feeling belongs decisively, overwhelmingly, to a late imperial age: a room loaded with stuff, artistic or not, is choked with the sheer material surfeit that those references identify as the spoils of empire, here as empire spoiled. This is the most quantitative and so indicative metric of distress in the historical circumstance, which is also the temporal imaginary, of decadence.[34]

The decadent imaginary in *The Waste Land* is manifest at a profounder depth with the evidence indicating the extent of its presence in the developing manuscript of the sequence. These materials represent far more than a poetic documentary of regrettable circumstance in current history; they present a kind of submerged imaginative intelligence in the poem, all in all, a literary sensibility that is constitutive of the poem as a literary record of its day. What lies behind or beneath the lines of the completed poem may serve, as the early unpublished verse has done for the work of major poetic record in *Poems* (1920), as an inner history of textual memory which, once recovered, may reveal the coherence and power of the decadent sensibility in this landmark poem of literary modernism.

Consider "Elegy," which, with a sequence of other pieces, Eliot considered as an extension of the sequence (ending as we now know it on "Shantih") but, on Pound's advice, ultimately withdrew.

> The sweat transpirèd from my pores!
> I saw [the] sepulchral gates, [thrown]/flung wide,
> Reveal (as in a tale by Poe)
> The features of the injured bride!
>
> That hand, prophetical and slow
> (Once warm, once lovely, often kissed)
> Tore the disordered cerements,
> Around that head the scorpions hissed!

> Remorse unbounded, grief intense
> Had striven to expiate the fault –
> But [interfere] poison not [with] my [nightly] present bliss!
> And keep within thy charnel vault!
>
> (*TWL*, 117)

Written in 1919, these quatrains recall the powers of four in the major verse in *Poems* (1920). Here the form of the tetrameter quatrain frames the references to Poe and extends his sensibility in a fashion equally extravagant and exact. The erotic pathology is centered in the necrophilia for which Poe is well known, but the death-in-life of corpse love finds its indicative metric in a machine-made cadence that also impersonates vitality. This is the aftermath imaginary of the sensibility of decadence, which lives in and as the morbid modernity of the mechanical, post-organic condition which Eliot typifies as such. If it had been left in place, it would provide its own sense of an ending as one of the final notes from the decadent imaginary in the sequence.

This note would be amplified with the inclusion of the otherwise fragmentary "Dirge," which, written in 1921, represents the advance echo of his later adaptation of these lines from *The Tempest* in the published poem:

> Full fathom five your Bleistein lies
> Under the flatfish and the squids.
>   man's
> Graves' Disease in a dead jew's eyes!
> Where the crabs have [nibb] eat the lids.
> Lower than the wharf-rats dive
>   Though he suffer[s] a sea-change
>   Still expensive rich and strange.   (*TWL*, 119)

Focused earlier in the title figure in "Burbank with a Baedeker: Bleistein with a Cigar," Bleistein returns in the fate of his "expensive" life as Jewish profiteer, and so agent of decay, in the typical anti-Semitic fiction. Its justice is very rough: this passage samples the sort of moralistic postures Eliot can assume to explain and punish the transgression of his fascination with decadence. It is a record of that fascination and another indicative measure of its pressure as the poetic sensibility of this poem.

Eliot's fascination with the imaginative conditions of decadence begins in his life as a writer. This is an inward history that remains in the manuscript of *The Waste Land* and that shows remarkably in another poem included in that series of additional pieces: "The Death of St. Narcissus." Dated 1915 by Valerie Eliot and Christopher Ricks, this poem was submitted by Pound to *Poetry* in August of that year, when it was set up in type but not printed; it was published only in 1950, when, included in a privately printed collection titled *Poems Written in Early Youth*, it seems to be framed and distanced as a piece of juvenilia.[35] Its diminishment begins in the completed text of *The Waste Land*, where, in a substantially curtailed form, it is taken into Part I in the "Come under the shadow of this red rock" passage. The full text provides a record of Eliot's early and ongoing absorption with issues intrinsic to the sensibility of literary decadence.

This poem engages the psychodrama of self-representation in poetry, all in all, the process of self-abstraction in language, which appears in the figure of the mirror-gazing Narcissus in the title. In manuscript and fair copy version, the experience of self-representation in the simulacrum of language is dramatized as a confrontation between the speaker and some imagined "you," who, in being confronted with various "shadows" of himself, may be seen as a displaced "he," that is, as the poet "I." The shadow cast in language, in the otherwise insubstantial word, is the advancing "shadow" figure of this passage, which crests toward its end into its most striking instance:

> Come under the shadow of this grey rock
> Come [(**and sit**)] under the shadow of this grey rock
> And I will show you a shadow different from either
> Your shadow sprawling over the sand at daybreak, or
> Your shadow huddled by the fire against the redrock.
>   cloth   [**bloodless**]
> I will show you his bloody [**cloth**] coat and [**green**] limbs
>   grey
> And the [**blue**] shadow between his lips.   (*TWL*, 91)

The poetic drama casts the adversarial relationship between the written and living versions of himself. A "you," who is the self that has been distanced in being written, is drawn back into and confronted in the poet's cave, where the difference between person and persona is emphatically drawn. The difference is most vivid in the person's asserting the bodily reality of himself, the "bloody coat" and "limbs." Alternately "green" and "bloodless," these limbs configure the favored shade of Wilde's queer chromatics and a more than suggestive connection to the non-vital condition, which extends the theme of non-reproductive queerness to this extreme. These insignia of the decadent imaginary may be focused in relation to writing most vividly in that enigmatically "blue shadow" on his lips, which are blued by more than the chill of death. For this is the color of the specifically blue ink that Eliot used as a younger poet,[36] whose vital life as a speaker is chilled to that "blue shadow between his lips" in the act of writing. The subsequent change from "blue" to "grey" carries a shift from a primary color to shadow chromatics as one measure of this process of loss, of disembodiment in verbal representation. It occurs first in the mouth but also and especially on the page, where ink is spilled, and so, associatively at least, where he sees the grey into which the black of print and the white of the page coalesce as the one dim shade of secondary intensities.

All in all, this passage takes the emphases of the poetics of decadence into an imaginative involvement with disincarnating, thus extending the anti-reproductive theme in the direction witnessed in Pound's emphasis on disembodiment: "shadow" recurs no less than six times. And so, to the most important point of the development that modernist poets are giving to the poetics of decadence, this passage asks the question of Eliot's furtherance of the legacy, first in this St. Narcissus fragment, then in the published version of *The Waste Land*.

In the fair copy of the 1915 manuscript, this last passage extends into several images of narcissistic self-involvement, variously visual and authorial:

> His eyes were aware of the pointed corners of his eyes
> And his hands aware of the tips of his fingers . . .
> Then he knew that he had been a fish
> With slippery white belly held tight in *his* own fingers,
> Writhing in his own clutch, his ancient beauty
> Caught fast in the pink tips of his new beauty.   (*TWL*, 95–97)

If "writhing" is the word plus the letter "h" for "writing," the fish is the pen but also, and most obviously, it is the penis. The action catches a masturbation fantasy: the autoerotic quality draws the intensive of possession of "*his* own" twice, which Eliot himself underscores in the first instance. In this spilling of seed without the possibility of begetting life, the written word on the page appears clearly indeed as the dead letter of the litterateur. The establishing circumstance in the literary imaginary of decadence, this condition is enhanced in the extraordinary bizarreness of the next vignette:

> Then he had been a young girl
> Caught in the woods by a drunken old man
> Knowing at the end the taste of her own whiteness
> The horror of her own smoothness,
> And he felt drunken and old.   (*TWL*, 97)

In the succession of projections and personages that are rolled off in the poem, the speaker has imagined himself as the young girl who, Narcissus-like, experiences herself and her own attractiveness in the "drunken old man" pursuing her. She experiences her features not as concrete particularities, however, but as generic abstractions: "whiteness" and "smoothness" are formations that match the class concepts which words provide for the specificities of their referents. If this is what language, especially written language, does to the material of physical experience, so, in Dowling's formulation on literary decadence, the special condition of that late day of history, of the history of language, is featured in the image and condition of printed language. This is the ossuary for the fossils and shells, the dead carapaces, of the once living quick of the spoken word. That circumstance of the late day of history may be projected intuitively in the figure of the "drunken old man," who, in coveting the subject of verbal representation, feels old already and first of all in a (still) young poet's experience of the ever-aftermath of language. In the oblique script of these extreme perceptions, and under the pressure of its exceptional imaginative intensity, the passage clearly suggests that the record of an older decadence is going to be pushed into new iterations.

This expectation may be realized in the otherwise enigmatic tableau in the finale, where the "he" of the poem shifts into the figure of St. Sebastian. This personage carries the considerable weight of his legacy in the literary and artistic culture of decadence, where his suffering configures the forbidden eros of homosexuality. Appearing recently in this wise in Eliot's "The Love Song of St. Sebastian," this figure reappears now as martyr and witness, but in a different configuration, which includes the difficulties specific to linguistic representation that Eliot has been elaborating in this series.

"So he became a dancer to God," this verse paragraph opens,

> Because his flesh was in love with the burning arrows
> He danced on the hot sand
> Until the arrows came.
> As he embraced them his white skin surrendered
>   itself to the redness of blood, which satisfied him.
> Now he is green, dry and stained
> With the shadow in his mouth. (*TWL*, 97)

"As he embraced them his white skin surrendered / itself to the *redness* of blood, which satisfied him." The intense physicality we are given to infer from the bodily experience of the pain of the arrows shifts at its climacteric into a representation that captures, not the intense physicality of that experience, but, rather, the abstraction of the verbal counter, the class concept of the word. As in the earlier *mise-en-scène* of an old man and a young girl appreciating her own "*whiteness*," this tableau repeats and in its repetition emphasizes as essential the crucial point of attention: the "ness" of the verbal generality for the specific is what establishes, engages, and indeed "satisfies" this figure of the verbal artist of decadence. This figure also reiterates the image and point of the "shadow in his mouth," which recycles the motif of the bodiless quality of the verbal counter for the thing. And where "green" repeats the color assigned to his "limbs" in the first verse paragraph, Wilde's signal color comes back into view to suggest the connection again between the unliving condition of literature (print) and the non-reproductive quality in Edelman's notion of queer temporality, which has provided one of the main imaginative tenses of decadence for Eliot.

Where Eliot has lived the legacy of decadence forward into the manuscript history of *The Waste Land*, this sensibility extends into the published version of the sequence in ways that may now be seen. These might be typified initially in the passage from which we turned into the archive history of the poem. In that scene from the beginning of "A Game of Chess," where the remnants of empire establish the external (historical) circumstances of decadence, its poetics are working internally in the disposition of its language, most strikingly in its syntax, which, at the exceptional length of its first sentence, witnesses an extraordinary elaboration of periodic structure:

> The Chair she sat in, like a burnished throne,
> Glowed on the marble, where the glass
> Held up by standards wrought with fruited vines
> From which a golden Cupidon peeped out
> (Another hid his eyes behind his wing)
> Doubled the flames of sevenbranched candelabra
> Reflecting light upon the table as
> The glitter of her jewels rose to meet it,
> From satin cases poured in rich profusion;
> In vials of ivory and coloured glass
> Unstoppered, lurked her strange synthetic perfumes
> Unguent, powdered, or liquid – troubled, confused
> And drowned the sense in odours; stirred by the air
> That freshened from the window, these ascended
> In fattening the prolonged candle-flames,
> Flung their smoke into the laquearia,
> Stirring the pattern on the coffered ceiling.
> Huge sea-wood fed with copper
> Burned green and orange, framed by the coloured stone,
> In which sad light a carvèd dolphin swam.   (*TWL*, ll. 77–96, 137)

What is the subject of the verb "doubled"? Is it the "Chair" or "the glass" or the "standards wrought"? This confusion enters the sequence of the subsequent phrases, where "unstoppered," whether or not it is a word (it is not), wobbles oddly between the status of a participial adjective and an active verb (working in consort with "lurked"). Similarly confusing is the unhinging of that already ponderous conglomerate of three adjectives – "Unguent, powdered, or liquid" – from the noun "perfumes," whose placement ahead of them inverts the standard word order of English. This confusion leads to a part-of-speech double take in "troubled, confused," words that look like participial adjectives, but, with the entry of "And drowned the sense," appear to be active verbs in series. The rationalist of a Latinate English, who might be commanding the ratios of greater and smaller units in the relation of main and subordinate clauses of this periodic sentence, inscribes a failure of the syntax of logical proportion which, by irresistible suggestion in this imagined prospect, reads also as a record of the collapse of the portioning authority of empire, whose rise and fall are recalled through the allusions to Dido and Cleopatra, so to Aeneas and Antony, so to the inaugural moment of Rome and its immanent political decline in the extensions of empire. The seemlier outlines of empire have been run down already by the evidence in the scene of the choking overload of imperial spoil. In the external circumstance of the historical and temporal imaginary of decadence, Eliot inscribes its fall in a syntax of collapsing mastery that makes the linguistic sensibility of literary decadence so expressive.

   This appreciation helps to make evident the pressure of a most particular text of decadence in Eliot's representation of this interior chamber. It is an extended reference to a scene of Venice in *The Wings of the Dove*. "[T]he sun on the stirred sea-water, flickering up through open windows," James overtures in a now familiarly decadent emphasis on reflected and secondary light,

> played over the painted "subjects" in the splendid ceilings – medallions of purple and brown, of brave old melancholy colour, medals as of old reddened gold, embossed and beribboned, all toned with time and all flourished and scalloped and gilded about, set in their great moulded and figured concavity (a nest of white cherubs, friendly creatures of the air) and appreciated by the aid of that second tier of smaller lights . . .[37]

The general resemblance in the atmospheric lighting of the two scenes may be seen in the recurrence of the verb "stirred." More particularly, the parenthetical aside in Eliot's reference to the second of the "Cupidons" recalls the same typographical gesture James makes in presenting his "cher-ubs." And where the "melancholy colouring" of James's scene appears as a representation of "all" this splendor being "toned with time," the feeling of the transient and insubstantial in an otherwise overwhelming sumptuary of stuff is reflected in the correspondingly "sad light" in Eliot's. The Venetian original for Eliot's lines connects this sensibility to the sinking city and failing mastery of marine empire, that island of decadence perennial. This association is borne out in his own text in a compositing of cultural times that recalls the English and Irish overlay on the Venetian scene of "Burbank with a Baedeker: Bleistein with a Cigar." In the allusions graphing the rise and fall of the Roman Empire (through Dido and Cleopatra to Aeneas and Antony) in the adjacent lines, the Venetian and Roman histories coalesce as the determining story for the second (or third) decadence of Eliot's British present.

Commenting on this scene in "A Game of Chess" in one of the first reviews of *The Waste Land*, Edmund Wilson acknowledges the epic des-olation it reflects. Anticipating his consideration of this poem and the modernist sensibility it represents in *Axel's Castle*, however, he already identifies a "freedom and illumination of the soul" as the functions of the "spring of memory" that Eliot is tapping as one source of personal redemp-tion in the sequence.[38] This image of the "spring of memory" and the redemptive measure it suggests has served as a touchstone for a particular line of critical appreciation. Here, despite the status *The Waste Land* owns as the hallmark representation of the "Lost Generation," emphasis falls on the primary importance of the restoration quest in the medieval Grail romances of the Waste Land, which, in its completed form, Eliot's authorial notes claim as template for his organizational plan for the sequence (*TWL*, 147). In the broadest terms, this dimension of attributed significance decisively overrides and leaves behind the pressure of decadence as an ordaining sensibility in the poem, relegating it to the status of a condition from which the better maker of this poem would be delivered.

This emphasis on redemption and transcendence needs indeed to be understood in relation to the heavy intervention exerted on the manuscript by Pound. Where the poetic drafts arrived in his hands in late 1921 or early 1922 in the textual image of its first working title, "He Do the Police in Different Voices" (*TWL*, 4), the medley of divergent characters in voice centered Pound's attention most aggressively. Acting already on the chal-lenges he would encounter in his renewed work on the *Cantos*, for which he was already seeking the (ever-elusive) organizational "plan," Pound set out to unify this composite of "Different Voices." Sometimes disembodied and magically detached from the present circumstance of the narrative fiction, these "voices" are "spoken" most of all in and as print – in and as the diverse styles of various literary manners and eras, which, especially in the third part, Eliot is exercising and demonstrating at exceptional length. To the purpose of putting this variety to work to one concerted end, Pound's heaviest pressure comes in encouraging Eliot to maintain and develop Tiresias as a centering personage and a unifying sensibility, so that, in accentuating the sexual distress which this dramatic character embodies and witnesses, he also frames the motive force for redressing the condition that Tiresias represents. This decision establishes a narrative mandate and momentum for the otherwise undirected sequence of the manuscript pieces. In the now dominant character of the prophet suffering his own ambivalent sexuality, Eliot merges this figure into the rhythms of purgation and transcendence that he initiates in the closure of the third part. He develops this as the main direction in the remainder of the poem. The fourth part reduces under Pound's slashing blue pencil from about ninety-five lines to the ten-line image of purgative cleansing in the figure of the disintegrating sailor, when the fifth part takes its imaginative transit to sites of ritual purgation and spiritual fulfillment in the ancient East. While the circumstances that attended the writing of Part V in particular are still somewhat uncertain, it is striking that the manuscript of this narrative of spiritual progress, which brings the ritualized cadences of a now single and sustained speaking character to spiritual destination, is virtually untouched by Pound. He doubles his approval on this section with the heading "OK OK from here on *I think*" (*TWL*, 71). Whether Eliot wrote this fifth part in response to the orientation his editor had initiated (after receiving back the "corrected" manuscripts of the first four parts), or left it already written as it now is in his first offering to Pound,[39] it is clear that the completed poem establishes a telos to which the whole sequence appears to proceed. It is equally clear that Pound is decisively influential in moving it toward this end in the final version, which he protected against Eliot's attempts to keep it going in appending those additional poems. So that, in reading forward toward this end, we also read backward from it and, accordingly, diminish the significance of what intervenes. And what intervenes between the reader's experience of the whole sequence and the high, sustained voice of the single lyric speaker in the ceremonial finale?

It is all that residual matter: the textual medley of divergent *performances* ("He *Do* the Police . . .") in the first three parts. Whether or not every poetic enunciation is a "performance" of some sort, the succession of Eliot's highly mannered dramatic and literary characters in Parts 1–3 may serve to raise performance to the status of a poetic principle. It is the principle which Wilde enshrined in *The Decay of Lying*, that primer on the poetics of decadence, where it opposes "sincerity" as the enemy of true (false) art. And where this principle is witnessed across the span of Parts 1–3, it comes in a variety of literary styles and particularity of poetic personae that resist any fusion into a speaking personage of sincere individual interest or earnest personal intention. It is manifest most conspicuously in the central dramatic representation of the third part.

   This is the sexual encounter between the "young man carbuncular" and "the typist home at teatime." Developing this scene in the manuscript draft, Eliot returns to the form of the quatrain stanza, which has served to further a poetics of decadence in all those manifest ways in the major work of *Poems* (1920). Hold those famous quatrain poems as background sound and you can hear how Eliot realizes the potential for performativity in this verse measure. His hard rhymes accentuate a sense of mechanical comedy, while the metric is regular enough to register its discrepancies not as an expressive variation but as another note *in* that mechanical comedy. This all develops into a feeling of verse burlesque. In a roughhouse verbiage of cartoon and lampoon, these gestures of invective and caricature move in and out of the forced cadences of music hall farce, in a poetically but not wholly attenuated form of a variety act:

> I Tiresias, old man with wrinkled dugs,
> Perceived the scene, and foretold the rest,
> Knowing the manner of these crawling bugs,
> I too awaited the expected guest.
>
> A youth of twentyone, spotted about the face,
> One of those simple loiterers whom we say
> We may have seen in any public place
> At almost any hour of night or day.
>
> Pride has not fired him with ambitious rage,
> His hair is thick with grease, and thick with scurf,
> Perhaps his inclinations touch the stage –
> Not sharp enough to associate with the turf.
>
> He, the young man carbuncular, will stare
> Boldly about, in "London's one café",
> And he will tell her, with a causal air,
> Grandly, "I have been with Nevinson today."
>
> Perhaps a cheap house agent's clerk, who flits
> Daily, from flat to flat, with one bold stare;

> One of the low on whom assurance sits
> As a silk hat on a Bradford millionaire.
>
> He munches with the same persistent stare,
> He knows his way with women and that's that!
> Impertinently tilting back his chair
> And dropping cigarette ash on the mat.
>
> The time is now propitious . . .　　　　　　　　　　(*TWL*, 45)

The massive contraction of this passage is well known:

> I Tiresias, old man with wrinkled dugs
> Perceived the scene, and foretold the rest –
> I too awaited the expected guest.
> He, the young man carbuncular, arrives,
> A small house agent's clerk, with one bold stare,
> One of the low on whom assurance sits
> As a silk hat on a Bradford millionaire.
> The time is now propitious . . .　　　　(*TWL*, ll. 141, 228–35)

Whatever standard of poetic value we may apply to the product of Pound's heavy intervention, it is certain that, once the original form of this passage is reclaimed, the memory of that underlying and ramifying pattern of performed styles is impossible to expunge. It retains the now vivid shadow of the principle of poetic decadence that has been evidenced in the textual memories and imaginative recesses of the poem as we know it. And where a poetics of decadence is displayed through the working drafts of the sequence, surfacing undeniably in that exceptional flourish of poetic performances that Eliot is posturing in his quatrain art in the third part, the value of spiritual sincerity, which the finale imposes in the poetic fiction of a single and sustained lyric speaker, finds no stage for the importance of being so earnest. Which is to say: there is a sensibility of decadence at work in this poem; its record has been buried through the circumstances we have followed, but it deserves to regain its place as a formative force in the writing of this iconic piece of modernist poetry.

Its suppression represents an early gesture on Pound's part of the subduing of decadence in his own poetic record, which will eventuate in the selection of poems for the definitive collection of the 1926 *Personae*. This turn involves any myriad number of factors, including his dedication to issues of political economics. In the secondary elaboration of the religious significance in *The Waste Land* as completed, Eliot's complicity with Pound's poetic counsels no doubt signals and witnesses his inwardness with a spiritual orientation that his subsequent personal and poetic biography will of course bear out. And while the sensibility of decadence is no stranger to religious feeling, it is inseparable for poets such as Baudelaire from the otherwise "fallen" conditions that are intrinsic to the temperament of a decadent poetics and that deserve accordingly to be brought back into place as a primary determinant in the work of *The Waste Land*.

It was given this place in one of the most engaged of the initial reviews of the poem, which, unlike Wilson's, refused to waver between the positive and negative feelings of the sequence. As the main point of its summary judgment, it provides a census of the elements of literary decadence that is remarkably adequate to the density of this sensibility in the poem – even as initially published. In the intensity of its rebuke, moreover, it offers an assertion of those standards and categories of value that still define the exceptionality of this literary convention. "Among the maggots that breed in the corruption of poetry," F. L. Lucas gestures comprehensively to begin his piece in the *New Statesman*,

> one of the commonest is the bookworm. When Athens had decayed and Alexandria sprawled . . .; when the Greek world was filling with libraries and emptying of poets, growing in erudition as its genius expired, then first appeared . . . that *Professorenpoesie* which finds in literature the inspiration that life gives no more, which replaces depth by muddiness, beauty by echoes, passion by necrophily. The fashionable verse of Alexandria grew out of the polite leisure of its librarians, its Homeric scholars, its literary critics . . .. The malady reappears in Rome . . .. in the gloomy pedantry that mars so much of Propertius; it has recurred at intervals ever since.[40]

Writerliness; the loss of the living original of voice in the secondary dimension of books, where an early Homeric epos is heard going over to the silence of late Roman satire; a reference in the "malady" (the word occurs several times in the review) to *Les Fleurs du Mal*, one of the texts that allegedly started this process; and this fall of poetry showing its most consequential measure as the "decay" of an early capital of classical civilization, Athens, is repeated and epitomized in the imperial "sprawl" of another, Alexandria, and another, Rome. The literary history Lucas is telegraphing in this account culminates in the livid figure of "necrophily," which, whether or not it is a word (it is not), summarizes in its lumpy and ugly way the juridical view of those conditions of decadent verbalism and of an existence that, in this perversion, has outlived the norms of a natural life. This is the age of the secondary and the circumstance of the posthumous, which takes the deathliness of print as its representative image and the sensibility of decadence as its prevailing temper. This is the imaginative circumstance within which Eliot has been developing the sensibility of decadence over the last dozen years. He has moved from intimation to realization of its historical reality as the establishing condition of his poetry. In the hallmark status that *The Waste Land* owns in any literary history of modernism, we may reclaim the sensibility of decadence as a substantial, substantiating content.

Barnes and Beckett, Petropi of the Twilight

"Sometimes in a phrase the characters spring to life so suddenly that one is taken aback," T. S. Eliot writes in his introduction to Djuna Barnes's *Nightwood* (1936), "as if one had touched a wax-work figure and discovered that it was a live policeman."[1] Eliot's point is reiterated in this description of one of Barnes's many characters, Count Onatario Altamonte: "'The living statues,' she said, 'He simply adores them'" (*N*, 13). If the puppet imperso-nating the human provides an image of the poetics of decadence, so the artificial, post-natural, aftermath imaginary of its historical understanding is demonstrated extensively in this novel and centrally in the biographical fiction of her protagonist. In a family lineage of dubious (the German patronymic originates in "a Jew of Italian descent") but ever declining title, Baron Felix Volkbein is a figure "born to holy decay" (*N*, 1, 107). He lives in the backward-oriented fantasy of his aristocratic background, cen-tering a representation of the remnant temporality that provides for the poetic tempos as well as imaginative narratives in literary decadence. The repetition that fades in the poems of Swinburne and Rossetti, of Pound and of Eliot too, shows in the dissipating strength of the family name, whose doubtful origin also recalls the degraded state of originality itself in the attitudes and practices of decadent writing.

Revolving its fiction around the Parisian capital that Barnes moved through in the years after the Great War, *Nightwood* revisits the scenes and recasts the themes of that "breviary of the Decadence," Huysmans' *À Rebours*. Not a ritual repetition, and no diminishing reiterative, Barnes's recasting furthers the concerns she features in the circumstances of that doubtful baron – in the equally dubiously titled "Dr. Matthew O'Connor, an Irishman from the Barbary Coast (Pacific Street, San Francisco)" (*N*, 14):

> A pile of medical books, and volumes of a miscellaneous order, reached almost to the ceiling, water-stained and covered with dust. Just above them was a very small barred window, the only ventilation . . . .

> In the narrow iron bed, with its heavy and dirty linen sheets, lay the doctor in a woman's flannel nightgown.
>
> The doctor's head, with its over-large black eyes, its full gun-metal cheeks and chin, was framed in the golden semi-circle of a wig with long pendant curls that touched his shoulders, and falling back against the pillow, turned up the shadowy interior of their cylinders. He was heavily rouged and his lashes painted. (*N*, 78–79)

Lying abed during the day, this "Dr." lives the same counterclockwise life as the antinatural calendar of Huysmans' Des Esseintes. There is the complementary contrary of the effeminized male. And where the room unopened to the world images the circumstance of unnatural artifice, so the geological deposit of books has supplanted nature in general and typified in particular the condition of print within which the language imaginary of decadence operates.

More consequentially, this scene provides the dramatic tableau and staging area for the casting of Dr. O'Connor's character in voice, which, in every available sense of the word, *performs* in the novel as its dominant consciousness. The immense stretches of the uninterrupted text of his "talk" (his prompts come from the nominal presence of auxiliary characters) proceed with the autonomous quality of continuous print. A book talking as though it were human, the personage of O'Connor provides one version of the living statues that Altamonte likes, of the live waxworks that Eliot admired – of a marionette language. O'Connor presents and represents the mechanical humanity of a post-natural age, which is the circumstance of current history in the decadent imaginary.

This is the condition Barnes fills out for its representative through allusions sometimes predictable and sometimes striking. Reference to *The Decline and Fall of the Roman Empire* (*N*, 128) makes the usual move and situates O'Connor's sensibility in the late and failing day of a great age. This identification also places his page-bound talk in the archive of the silence that the now dead language of Latin exemplifies. Thus O'Connor characterizes the unliving speech of his bookish talk: "I am a doctor and a collector and a talker of Latin ..." (*N*, 92). And, as a signal of the inventiveness Barnes exerts in the condition which Latinity typifies, he moves beyond the quasi-professional idiolect of the would-be medical man into the improvisatory mock-Latin that provides the basis for the title of this Afterword: "... and a sort of petropus of the twilight" (*N*, 92).

A word neither in Latin nor in English, "petropus" is a piece of language facticity that captures not only the utter dubiety of O'Connor's utterances but, as a function of the irresistible suggestiveness of its syllables, something of the petrified and extinct creature of the speech it typifies. A corpse performing human talk, a literature devolved to a corpus that abides in an archive and that impersonates life only in personages as doubtful as O'Connor: this character signifies the sense of an ending in cultural history – his "petropus" is "of the twilight" – that the sensibility of decadence may be taken to reflect and, in its various ways, to make coherent. Indicative of literary decadence in particular, the character of O'Connor's radical and unflagging loquacity takes its place as a figure of its own in a style of dramatic exchange in literary fiction that is also particularly and signally modernist. This is a genre of fictional "dialogue" which Fredric Jameson has set out to define in the primary example of Wyndham Lewis. This account may be turned in conclusion toward a new understanding of the difference that a recognition of the constitutive role of decadence within modernism makes in our critical understanding of this signal feature.

"Dialogue is too weak a term for such exchanges," Jameson observes of these interactions, "which, in their violent *stichomythia*, define a veritable *agon* between the polar adversaries. This is the very element of Lewis' novelistic world." Jameson's critical description of this *agon* features a "combative, exasperated, yet jaunty stance of monads in collision, a kind of buoyant truculence in which matched and abrasive consciousnesses slowly rub each other into smarting vitality."[2] For Jameson, this is the extreme representation in literary fiction of those circumstances of cultural history in which modernist literature takes its exemplary stand. In his understanding, these autonomous characters in voice provide emblems and instances of

> the newly autonomous realm of aesthetic language. The modernist gesture is thus ideological and Utopian all at once: perpetuating the increasing subjectivization of individual experience and the atomization and disintegration of the older social communities, expressing the anxiety and revulsion of intellectuals before the reification of social life and the ever intensifying class conflicts of industrial society, it also embodies a will to overcome the commodification of late nineteenth-century capitalism, and to substitute for the mouldering and overstuffed bazaar of late Victorian life the mystique and promise of some intense and heightened, more authentic existence.[3]

Isolating and radicalizing the character of the individual in this circumstance of late modernity, Jameson's author makes the "gesture" which he denominates properly as "modernist" insofar as it represents, in the impasse into which Lewis moves the figure of this isolated individual, a heightened self-consciousness of the fundamental struggle of his age.

This is a struggle whose resolution is configured for Jameson in the values he invokes at the close of this passage: a "promise of some intense and heightened, more authentic existence." Developing this promise as a concept, he frames it in a term he adapts from Nathalie Sarraute: "the 'sub-conversation.'" Here, "beneath the routine and insignificant, contingent exchange of spoken words," which are "brittle with cliché" and "corroded by publicity and received ideas," the possibility of "some more fundamental human contact, some deeper wordless groping struggle or interaction" is conjured by the novelist as the accomplishment of supreme value. "The task of the novelist then becomes the recuperation of that more authentic reality and the invention of a new and fresh, nonalienated, *originary* language in which the latter's preverbal or nonverbal events and incidents can somehow, beyond all fallen speech, be adequately rendered."[4]

Whether or not those "preverbal or nonverbal" events can be "adequately rendered" in literary fiction, there is a dimension of invocatory possibility that retains the emphasis Jameson strikes into his signal word: "*originary*." This original speech provides at once the means and ideal of that "fundamental human contact" that he retains as supreme aim and value; as one measure of its merit, this original speech would be generated with a degree of "invention" sufficient to overthrow the great weight of dead matter that Jameson uses to characterize the oppositional lot of the common, public Word. What happens under these adversary circumstances, in Jameson's formulation, is a fragmentation of the individual subject and a displacement of the expressive center into a dialogical form of narration, where the fiercely contested exchanges of the speaking characters make a story in effect of their residual tension and a "subconversation," as it were, of the articulate parts of the whole they formerly comprised. Thus, even if "Lewis' relational universe has no place for a thesis about human nature" in Jameson's admission,[5] the formal ideal of the autonomous but interactive and articulate human subject remains in formative play in the fundamental work of the pseudo-couples in Lewis's fiction.

It is the status of this "*originary*" speech in a critical understanding of the modernism that Jameson uses Lewis to typify that must come under review. In his characterization of the pseudo-dialogues of Lewis's fiction, Jameson appropriates the hyper-signifying term of the expressive individual from Lewis's own armoury of values. This is the basis for Lewis's redoubtable claim about the existence of that "autonomous realm of aesthetic language," where the emphatic and collaborating value of the "*originary*" is also strongly in play. And where Jameson's emphasis on the "*originary*" in this "aesthetic language" of Lewis seems correct, it also provides an explanation for why Lewis takes no greater place in my study, which has revealed the overwrought but fraught and ultimately unavailable notion of the "original" in the traditions of decadence subsisting within modernism. Giving this difference its due, it also serves to anticipate the ways in which the literary decadence that I am following from the English fin de siècle into the modernism of early Pound and Eliot is maintained and developed well into the middle of the century.

In summary understanding, then, Barnes's O'Connor is no figure of an individually "autonomous realm of aesthetic language" in which an "*originary*" speaker takes ownership and authority. He is a quotation, marked off as such by the punctuation on the page in a formal irony and, in the affective fashion of the book's dramatic fiction, assigned to the silence which the absence of authentic response frames for him. He is in the end an automaton of language, inhabiting that status in the manifest absence of meaningful communication with reciprocating human individuals. In these several ways, O'Connor's personage brings into summary form the essential tenets of the decadence that Barnes has demonstrated so extensively otherwise in this novel. In the intense demonstration this novel provides of the agony of the pseudo-couple, she dramatizes as well a struggle so fundamental to cultural modernity that its self-consciousness in this regard makes it a quintessentially modernist testament.

This sensibility lives forward as well as backward from Barnes, and our recognition of its importance in the formation of modernism may qualify existing understandings. This course may be followed from the source of the wording Jameson uses to title the chapter in which he analyzes those figures of dramatic exchange: "Agons of the Pseudo-Couple." The "pseudo-couple" is Samuel Beckett's term.[6] In the elaborate pathos of interaction between dramatic characters that it signals in Jameson's elaborated title, it finds no shortage of examples in the dramatis personae of Beckett's own plays: Vladimir and Estragon, Hamm and Clov, Nell and Nagg, etc. etc. These dramatic pairings match up in a rough and ready way with the analytical conceptions in Jameson's chapter: speaking to and beyond each other, they locate the essential dramatic tension on stage. Whether or not their exchanges may be subtended by the "subconversation" of a once articulate individual, their more immediate origins in the two-man teams of Irish as well as English and American vaudeville recall a form of mechanical comedy (machines speaking beyond each other) that is a primary point of reference. These dialogic teams belong equally to farce and Barnes's own farcically billed "Dr. Matthew Mighty O'Connor" (*N*, 84), that is, to the mechanical, post-natural, aftermath imaginary of literary decadence. And it is in the fiction from which Jameson's title phrase is taken that the decadent premise for this new understanding of literary modernism may be staked at a revealing extreme: Beckett's great postwar trilogy *The Unnamable* (*Molloy*, 1951; *Malone Dies*, 1951; *The Unnamable*, 1953).

The circumstances of literary decadence that Barnes establishes for O'Connor are matched strikingly for the first personage of the trilogy, already in its first words, which feature the presumptive author of the book:

> I am in my mother's room. It's I who live there now. I don't know how I got there. Perhaps in an ambulance, certainly a vehicle of some kind. I was helped. I'd never have got there alone. There's this man who comes every week. Perhaps I got there thanks to him. He says not. He gives me money and takes away the pages. So many pages, so much money ... The truth is I haven't much will left. When he comes for the fresh pages he brings back the previous week's. They are marked with signs I don't understand.[7]

The invalid physicality of the writer; the self-enclosed chamber of writing; a language that exists in the condition of continuous print and which, as one index of its detachment from the otherwise natural language of voice, has been denaturalized into a mysterious and arbitrary set of written insignia: Beckett begins with a configuration it will have taken a long legacy of literary decadence to fashion as its most typical *mise-en-scène*. This is also a legacy of literary Latinity. Where the dead matter of language is typified by Barnes's O'Connor and his cultivation of Latin, it works for him also and most of all as an idiom of fantastical mendacity, which also serves the principles of Wilde's primer for poetic decadence in *The Decay of Lying*. So Beckett's trilogy finishes with the main personage of its third novel turning an admitted pig-Latinity into a language of comic prevarication: "But it is not to speak of her that I have started lying again. *De nobis ipsis silemus*, decidedly that should have been my motto. Yes, they gave me some lessons in pigsty Latin too, it looks well, sprinkled through the perjury."[8]

What gets "sprinkled" through the "perjury" of decadent poetics is more than a literary Latinity, of course. This "sprinkle" may be taken as a critical metaphor for one of the most important imaginative actions in Beckett's fiction. It provides one of the final points in the massive transformations he will have worked on this legacy of literary decadence as it turns toward the second half of the century.

Consider the little bits of phrasal interjection, comic appositives really, which, in the first of the three novels, are sprinkled through this representative passage:

> But I am human, *I fancy*, and my progress suffered, from this state of affairs, and from the slow and painful progress it had always been, whatever may have been said to the contrary, was changed, *saving your presence*, to a veritable calvary, with no limit to its stations and no hope of crucifixion, *though I say it myself*, and no Simon, and reduced me to frequent halts. Yes, my progress reduced me to stopping more and more often, it was the only way to progress, to stop. And though it is no part of my tottering intentions to treat here in full, *as they deserve*, these brief moments of the immemorial expiation, I shall nevertheless deal with them briefly, out of the goodness of my heart, so that my story, so clear till now, may not end in darkness, the darkness of these towering forests, these giant fronds, where I hobble, listen, fall, rise, listen and hobble on, wondering sometimes, *need I say*, if I shall ever see again the hated light, at least unloved, stretched palely between the last boles, and my mother, to settle with her, and if I would not do better, at least just as well, to hang myself from a bough, with a liane.[9]

These interjections interrupt a momentum of words that is apparently autonomous. Its compelled progress may be followed along the line of the extended series of coordinating conjunctions, which swing the clauses ahead relentlessly if, ultimately it seems, to a point which, by the end, has lost any sense of the period it is completing beyond the death into which its forward sense eventuates. Here is a vivid instance of language on the page as the mechanical tour-de-forceless energy that literary decadence has now whirred down to. And it is within this rhythm that Beckett's typical figure of the comic automaton, at once more and less than human, both the glory and the jest of creation, comes into prominence. His is the voice of those comic appositives, of which "need I say" might be most demonstrative. This interjection is of course exactly what is not needed, it seems, to compel the mechanism that is generating clause upon clause. Unnecessary, gratuitous, a gift in its own right (or wrong), each of these interruptions offers one of those "brief moments of immemorial expiation" which, with the self-protective irony of its hyperbolic phrasing, Beckett's character-in-language invokes as the ultimate possibility of this cross-braid design. Beckett is working to his most concerted purposes within this rhythm and counter-rhythm of apparently mechanical language and the putatively human uses of interruption. "The only way to progress," goes the wording of a motto in the same passage for this counter-rhythm, is "to stop," because it is in the brief pause of the stop that the moment of difference to the *perpetuum mobile* of language is felt in its contrary quality.

This is in its own small but exact way a moment of *modernism*, which, in the precise sense of this word, registers and intensifies the self-conscious difference of the time it occupies, the instant it inhabits so indicatively here.

It is a moment recurring again and again in Beckett's fiction. Between the mechanical action of language and the declining fortunes of the corporeal machine, which are the complementary recognitions of literary decadence, "need I say" enters gratuitously, a grace note, a moment of exception. It signals the difference of its instant in the self-consciousness of its comedy and so hollows out its place as the most minimal but typical moment of modernism. This is the form of a temporality which, recalling the point I have used critics as various as Raymond Williams and Paul de Man to make, is the moment constantly dissolving from the possibilities of presence that it invokes. So, need I say, Beckett's exquisitely provisional and momentary gesture pronounces something of the lasting significance of the sensibility whose literary history has been told here.

Notes

INTRODUCTION   THE CODES OF DECADENCE: MODERNISM AND ITS DISCONTENTS

1. Ezra Pound writes the editorial as "Ferrex on Petulance," *The Egoist*, 1 January 1914, 9.
2. Pound, "Ferrex on Petulance," 9–10.
3. Pound, "Ferrex on Petulance," 9.
4. Arthur Symons, "The Decadent Movement in Literature," *Harper's New Monthly Magazine*, November 1893, 858–67, 858, 859, 866.
5. Arthur Symons, *The Symbolist Movement in Literature* (1899; rpt. London: Archibald Constable & Co., Ltd., 1908), 6, 4.
6. "May I dedicate to you this book on the Symbolist movement in literature, both as an expression of a deep personal friendship and because you, more than any one else, will sympathise with what I say in it, being yourself the chief representative of that movement in our country? .... How often have you and I discussed all these questions, rarely arguing about them, for we rarely had an essential difference of opinion, but bringing them more and more clearly into light .... It is almost worth writing a book to have one perfectly sympathetic reader, who will understand everything that one has said, and more than one has said, who will think one's own thought whenever one has said exactly the right thing, who will complete what is imperfect in reading it, and be too generous to think that it is imperfect. I feel that I shall have that reader in you; so here is my book in token of that assurance" (v–vii).
7. Thus, summarily, in the claim Yeats makes in *Autobiographies* (London: Macmillan, 1961), 193: "Whatever I came to know of Continental literature I learned of him."
8. Since *The Symbolist Movement in Literature* is the prevailing document, the "Symbolist" attribution comes along with the name Symons, whose formative importance is attested by the poets themselves. Eliot, for example, in a review of Peter Quennell's *Baudelaire and the Symbolists* in the *Criterion* (January 1930), writes: "I myself owe Mr. Symons a great debt: but for having read his book, I should not, in the year 1908, have heard of LaForgue or Rimbaud; I should probably not have begun to read Verlaine; and but for reading Verlaine, I should not have heard of Corbière" (357). Although Ezra Pound did not provide such a public testament to the indispensability of Symons's critical

book, his indebtedness to that collection was easily inferred from a publication that occurred in a scholarly journal of established importance at a moment in which the canons of modernist criticism were being formed: in 1962, when G. Thomas Tanselle recovered and published some of Pound's early (1911) letters to Floyd Dell, the associate editor of the *Friday Literary Review of the Chicago Evening Post*. It is here that Pound nominates Symons as one of his "gods": "Two Early Letters of Ezra Pound," *American Literature*, 34.1 (1962), 114–19, 118.

9. Remy de Gourmont, "Souvenirs du Symbolisme: Jean Moréas," *Le Temps*, 27 December 1910, n.p. (microfilm), "Malgré un petit journal éphémère, *Le Symbolisme*, lancé à cette époque par Moréas lui-même, avec Paul Adam et Gustave Kahn, l'épithète de décadent prévalut longtemps et eut même son heure de gloire avec la décadence et avec le décadent surtout, qui sembla un instant avoir centralisé le nouveau mouvement littéraire .... Symboliste, ce même mouvement va prendre une tout autre apparence. Il exhibe du coup de hautes prétentions esthétiques et même philosophiques."

10. Remy de Gourmont, "Souvenirs du Symbolisme: De Baju à René Ghil," *Le Temps*, 24 January 1911, n.p. (microfilm), on Anatole Baju, as founding editor of *Le Décadent*: "La vie publique d'Anatole Baju fut sans éclat; il en est de même de sa vie privée, dont la modestie fait tout le charme. Je n'en connais pas l'histoire, mais seulement la légend .... La plume sans doute oscillait dans ses mains bleuies par les étincelles d'acier, habituées au lourd marteau à deux pointes."

11. Patrick McGuinness, "Introduction," *Symbolism, Decadence, and the Fin de Siècle: French and European Perspectives*, ed. Patrick McGuinness (Exeter: University of Exeter Press, 2000), 1–3.

12. This translation is in *One Hundred and One Poems by Paul Verlaine: A Bilingual Edition*, trans. Norman R. Shapiro (Chicago: University of Chicago Press, 1999), 126–27.

13. Symons, *The Symbolist Movement* (1899; 1908), 3.

14. Symons emphasizes this aspect in Baudelaire in *The Symbolist Movement in Literature*, rev. ed. (London: Dutton, 1919), 140–42. The Swedenborgian schemes are elaborated at greatest length in 1908 (1899) in the chapter on Gérard de Nerval (30 ff.).

15. Walter Benjamin, *The Writer of Modern Life: Essays on Charles Baudelaire*, ed. Michael W. Jennings (Cambridge, MA: Harvard University Press, 2006), e.g., 198.

16. Symons, *The Symbolist Movement* (1899; 1908), 139. *Against Nature*, trans. Margaret Mauldon, ed. Nicholas White (Oxford: Oxford University Press, 1998); the title may also be translated as "Against the Grain."

17. Oscar Wilde, *The Picture of Dorian Gray* (1890, 1891), Norton Critical Edition, 2d ed., ed. Michael Patrick Gillespie (New York: Norton, 2007), 104, 121, 254, 268. Hereafter reference will be made parenthetically to this edition as *PDG*, which, besides including both the 1890 and 1891 versions, reprints some of the reviews of the first edition: see esp. "A Study in Puppydom," from *St. James Gazette*, 352 ff.

18. Glenn Hughes, *Imagism and the Imagists* (London: Oxford University Press, 1931), 6.

19. Frank Kermode, *Romantic Image* (1957: rpt. New York: Routledge, 2002), 130.

20. Hugh Kenner, *The Pound Era* (Berkeley: University of California Press, 1971), 179.

21. Kenner, *The Pound Era*, xi.

22. Kenner, *The Pound Era*, 183.

23. Kenner, *The Pound Era*, 186.

24. Ezra Pound, *Hugh Selwyn Mauberley*, in *Personae: The Shorter Poems*, ed. Lea Baechler and A. Walton Litz (New York: New Directions, 1990), 188.

25. T. S. Eliot, "Gerontion," in *Collected Poems 1909–1962* (1963; rpt. New York: Harcourt Brace, 1991), 29.

26. Michael North, *Novelty: A History of the New* (Chicago: University of Chicago Press, 2013), 162–71.

27. Lewis M. Dabney, *Edmund Wilson: A Life in Literature* (New York: Farrar, Straus and Giroux, 2005), 123.

28. Wilson, "Symbolism," *Axel's Castle: A Study in the Imaginative Literature of 1870–1930* (1931; rpt. New York: Scribner's, 1971), 1–25.

29. See the letter to Auguste Villiers de L'Isle-Adam, 24 September 1866 (or 1867), in *Selected Letters of Mallarmé*, ed. and trans. Rosemary Lloyd (Chicago: University of Chicago Press, 1988), 50.

30. Wilson, *Axel's Castle*, 23.

31. Wilson, *Axel's Castle*, 1–2.

32. Wilson, *Axel's Castle*, 12.

33. Wilson, *Axel's Castle*, 22.

34. A good discussion of Wilson's attitudes to the intersection of literature and politics is provided by Dabney, *Edmund Wilson*, 202.

35. Robert Spiller, "The Influence of Edmund Wilson: The Dual Tradition," *The Nation*, 22 February 1958, 164.

36. Allen Tate, "Three Types of Poetry," *The New Republic*, 28 March 1934, 181, 182.

37. F. O. Matthiessen, "A Critic of Importance," *Yale Review*, June 1931, 856.

38. F. R. Leavis, "Criticism of the Year," *The Bookman*, December 1931, 180. Leavis presents William Empson's *Seven Types of Ambiguity* as 1931's best book of criticism.

39. Robert M. Adams, "Masks and Delays: Edmund Wilson as Critic," *Sewanee Review*, Spring 1948, 273.

40. This is an adaptive capacity managed well by Pericles Lewis, who, in his developing work on religion and modernism, attempts specifically to extend "Edmund Wilson's claim, in 1931, that 'the literary history of our time is to a great extent that of the development of Symbolism and of its fusion or contact with Naturalism.'" Thus Lewis proposes that the mystical significance which symbolism includes – not so much from Wilson, but from Symons, whom Wilson is extending in this tradition of developing adaptation – may be fused with the otherwise barren patterns of naturalistic detail in modern fiction in

order to provide a loose and attenuated but nonetheless effective "sense of the sacredness of the everyday in modernist novels." Valid as an indicator for the particular set of effects that Lewis is observing, this sense of symbolism reflects one development out of a multiplex potential in the legacy it represents, one that acquires a life of its own in these secondary elaborations, where the sense of the potential of the symbol has become detached from the *décadence* with which it was originally intertwined. Pericles Lewis, "Churchgoing in the Modern Novel," *Modernism/modernity*, 11.4 (2004), 669–94, 671, 672, and later, *Religious Experience and the Modernist Novel* (Cambridge: Cambridge University Press, 2010), esp. 36 ff.

41. Robert Scholes, "The Epoch of the Small Reviews," *Modernism/modernity*, 17.2 (2010), 421–29, 423; Morag Shiach, "'To Purify the Dialect of the Tribe': Modernism and Language Reform," *Modernism/modernity*, 14.1 (2007), 21–34, 25; Andrew John Miller, "'Compassing Material Ends': T. S. Eliot, Christian Pluralism, and the Nation State," *ELH*, 67.1 (2000), 229–55; Raphael Ingelbien, "Symbolism at the Periphery: Yeats, Maeterlinck, and Cultural Nationalism," *Comparative Literature Studies*, 42.3 (2005), 183–204, 183. Scott Hamilton's *Ezra Pound and the Symbolist Inheritance* (Princeton: Princeton University Press, 1994) does not engage with modernism as a critical category or historical reference, but extends the attitudes of Kermode and Kenner, taking "symbolism" as the name of the major tradition Pound is living forward and including "decadence" as a mainly undesirable subordinate within that dominant counter. The composite of critical documents that Cyrena Pondrom assembles in *The Road from Paris: French Influence on English Poetry 1900–1920* (Cambridge: Cambridge University Press, 1974) is extremely important recovery work, but it gives no place to "decadence." This list of critical works could be extended to far greater length. Another word that does the work of substitution but occurs less frequently is "aestheticism," which projects the "art for art's sake" emphasis in the poetics of decadence of Baudelaire and Gautier. In a special issue of *Modernism/modernity*, 15.3 (2008), which is dedicated to bridging the difference between "modernism" and "decadence," "aestheticism" is attached to "decadence" in the framing piece by Cassandra Laity, "Beyond Baudelaire: Decadent Aestheticism and Modernity" (427–30); it is then echoed in word or in substance in most of the essays that follow. In large part, "aestheticism" identifies an aspect of the legacy separate from what I am attempting to recover for our understanding of modernism: a sense of imaginative temporality that is a constitutive part of the modernist sensibility – all in all, an overriding prepossession of last days or an aftermath circumstance. Some of the essays in the *Modernism/modernity* special issue do engage other significant aspects of decadence in relation to modernism. See especially Laity's "The Dissipating Nature of Decadent Paganism from Pater to Yeats," 431–46; Carolyn A. Kelley's "Aubrey Beardsley and H.D.'s 'Astrid': The Ghost and Mrs. Pugh of Decadent Aestheticism and Modernity," 447–75; and Robin Blyn's "*Nightwood*'s Freak Dandies: Decadence in the 1930s," 503–26.

42. Paul de Man, "The Rhetoric of Temporality," in *Blindness and Insight: Essays in the Rhetoric of Contemporary Criticism*, 2d ed. (Minneapolis: University of Minnesota Press, 1983), 187–228, esp. 208, where he writes in conclusion to section I. "Allegory and Symbol": "On the level of language the asserted superiority of the symbol over allegory, so frequent during the nineteenth century, is one of the forms taken by this tenacious self-mystification. Wide areas of European literature of the nineteenth and twentieth centuries appear as regressive with regards to the truths that come to light in the last quarter of the eighteenth century. For the lucidity of the pre-romantic writers does not persist. It does not take long for a symbolic conception of the metaphorical language to establish itself everywhere, despite the ambiguities that persist in aesthetic theory and poetic practice. But this symbolical style will never be allowed to exist in serenity; since it is a veil thrown over a light one no longer wishes to perceive, it will never be able to gain an entirely good poetic conscience."

43. Walter Benjamin, *Origin of German Tragic Drama*, intro. George Steiner, trans. John Osborne (London: Verso, 1998), 159–60.

44. See Benjamin, *The Writer of Modern Life*, "Introduction," 7–8.

45. See Benjamin, *The Writer of Modern Life*, passim, esp. "Baudelaire, or the Streets of Paris," where the days of decadence in Roman antiquity are linked with the conditions of allegory: "That Baudelaire was attracted to late Latin culture may have been linked to the strength of his allegorical intention" (163).

46. Benjamin notes a congruency between Early Modern and Baudelairean allegory in *The Writer of Modern Life*, 154: "'L'appareil sanglant de la Destruction': the household effects scattered, in the innermost chamber of Baudelaire's poetry, at the feet of the whore who has inherited all the powers of Baroque allegory."

47. Paul de Man, "The Rhetoric of Temporality," 207: "The relationship between the allegorical sign and its meaning (*signifié*) is not decreed by dogma . . . We have, instead, a relationship between the signs in which the reference to their respective meanings has become of secondary importance. But this relationship between signs necessarily contains a constitutive temporal element; it remains necessary, if there is to be allegory, that the allegorical sign refer to another sign that precedes it. The meaning constituted by the allegorical sign can then consist only in the *repetition* (in the Kierkegaardian sense of the term) of a previous sign with which it can never coincide, since it is of the essence of this previous sign to be pure anteriority."

48. Benjamin, *Origin*. This sense of the mock human or effigy extends in Benjamin's heavily metaphorical formulation (226), where the bodies of dead gods are the concepts of the allegory, whose meanings are the transmuted substance of the now murdered deities of ancient religion. This is the critical story of the origins of allegory, and it explains the deadness factor in the landscape as well as language imaginary of it (166): "Whereas in the symbol destruction is idealized and the transfigured face of nature is fleetingly revealed in the light of redemption, in allegory the observer is confronted with the *facies*

hippocratica of history as a petrified, primordial landscape. Everything about history that, from the very beginning, has been untimely, sorrowful, unsuccessful, is expressed in a face – or rather in a death's head. And although such a thing lacks all 'symbolic' freedom of expression, all classical proportion, all humanity – nevertheless, this is the form in which man's subjection to nature is most obvious and it significantly gives rise not only to the enigmatic question of the nature of human existence as such, but also the biographical historicity of the individual. This is the heart of the allegorical way of seeing." Benjamin turns this idea decisively in the direction of the poetics of decadence, which he is already engaging in his work on Baudelaire, in this summary formulation in "Central Park" (*The Writer of Modern Life*, 168), where the "corpse," which is the "key figure in early allegory," is seen in the attenuated but no less deathly figure of "the 'souvenir' [*Andenken*]."

49. See Eve Kosofsky Sedgwick, *Epistemology of the Closet* (1990), 2d ed. (Berkeley: University of California Press, 2008), 165–66, where, however, she also notes how the queer element is also being displaced by an increasingly conventionalized understanding of modernism: "Reading *Dorian Gray* from our twentieth-century vantage point where the name of Oscar Wilde virtually *means* 'homosexual,' it is worth reemphasizing how thoroughly the elements of even this novel can be read doubly or equivocally, can be read either as having a thematically empty 'modernist' meaning or as having a thematically full 'homosexual' meaning." Rita Felski, *The Gender of Modernity* (Cambridge, MA: Harvard University Press, 1995), 103: "From a present-day perspective, the affinities and parallels between the self-conscious aesthetic sensibility of early modernism and the social articulation of modern homosexuality appear striking."

50. This is a way of reading that is outlined revealingly in its paradigmatic example by Herbert Butterfield in *The Whig Interpretation of History* (1931; rpt. New York: Norton, 1965), esp. "The Underlying Assumption," 9–33.

51. Ann Ardis, *Modernism and Cultural Conflict, 1880–1922* (Cambridge: Cambridge University Press, 2002); see especially "Introduction: Rethinking Modernism, Remapping the Turn of the Century," 1–14; "Inventing Literary Tradition, Ghosting Oscar Wilde and the Victorian Fin de Siècle," 45–77; and "Conclusion: Modernism and English Studies in History," 173–76.

52. This story expands the dimensionality of modernism, and critics such as Kirsten MacLeod and Cassandra Laity have told it variously and well: Kirsten MacLeod, *Fictions of British Decadence: High Art, Popular Writing, and Fin de Siècle* (Basingstoke: Palgrave, 2006); Cassandra Laity, *H.D. and the Victorian Fin de Siècle: Gender, Modernism, Decadence* (Cambridge: Cambridge University Press, 1996). Another valuable contribution to an understanding of progressive decadence comes from Matthew Potolsky, *The Decadent Republic of Letters: Taste, Politics, and Cosmopolitan Community from Baudelaire to Beardsley* (Philadelphia: University of Pennsylvania Press, 2013).

53. Lee Edelman, *No Future: Queer Theory and the Death Drive* (Durham: Duke University Press, 2004), 1–66, 27.

54. Edelman, *No Future*, 41–50, 54–58, 10–11.

55. Representative examples include José Esteban Muñoz, *Cruising Utopia: The Then and There of Queer Futurity* (New York: New York University Press, 2009); *Queer Universes: Sexualities in Science Fiction*, ed. Wendy Gay Pearson, Veronica Hollinger, Joan Gordon, (Liverpool: Liverpool University Press, 2008); and *Trans/Forming Utopia: The Small Thin Story*, vol. 2, ed. Elizabeth Russell (Bern, Switzerland: Peter Lang, 2009).

56. Heather Love, *Feeling Backward: Loss and the Politics of Queer History* (Cambridge, MA: Harvard University Press, 2007), 4.

57. Love, *Feeling Backward*, 6 ff.

58. Walter Benjamin, "Theses on the Philosophy of History," in *Illuminations*, ed. Hannah Arendt, trans. Harry Zohn (New York: Schocken, 1969), 253–64, 257–58.

59. Love, *Backward*, 147. Theodor Adorno, *Minima Moralia: Reflections from Damaged Life*, trans. E. F. N. Jephcott (1951; rpt. London: Verso, 1974), 235.

60. Richard Gilman, *Decadence: The Strange Life of an Epithet* (New York: Farrar, Straus and Giroux, 1979), 5.

61. Gilman, *Decadence*, 6–7.

62. Daniel Pick, *Faces of Degeneration: A European Disorder, c.1848–c.1918* (1989; rpt. Cambridge: Cambridge University Press, 1996).

63. Gilman, *Decadence*, 56.

64. Walter Jackson Bate, *The Burden of the Past and the English Poet* (Cambridge, MA: Harvard University Press, 1970), passim.

65. Gilman, *Decadence*, 138.

66. Karl Heinz Bohrer, *Suddenness: On the Moment of Aesthetic Appearance*, trans. Ruth Crowley (New York: Columbia University Press, 1994), passim, esp. "The Prehistory of the Sudden: The Generation of the 'Dangerous Moment,'" 39–69; Fredric Jameson, *A Singular Modernity* (2002; rpt. London: Verso, 2012), 189–93.

67. Raymond Williams, *The Politics of Modernism: Against the New Conformists* (London: Verso, 1989), 32. Williams is dealing for the most part with "modernism" as a term in scholarly accounts – that is, as a retrospective designation that came into academic vocabulary only in mid-century. "'Modernism' as a title for a whole cultural movement and moment has then been retrospective as a general term since the 1950s, thereby stranding the dominant version of 'modern' or even 'absolute modern' between, say, 1890 and 1940" (32).

68. Paul de Man, "Literary History and Literary Modernity," in *Blindness and Insight*, 142–65, 156–57.

69. The work that moved first in this direction is David Weir's *Decadence and the Making of Modernism* (Amherst: University of Massachusetts Press, 1995), where the title indicates the preponderance of interest in the earlier phase of its literary history. The understanding Weir proposes in this account involves ideas of historical successiveness. The features he catalogues in a phenomenology of "decadence" constitute not so much a poetics of modernism as the material of a "transitional phase" to this later sensibility, which occupies only about a seventh of the book's contents and so, appropriately, focuses a good

deal less of its conceptual and analytical work. Weir's book is a valuable overview of those aesthetic concepts and qualities that are shared and varied across the schools of naturalism and aestheticism as well as modernism and decadence.

CHAPTER I   THE TIME OF DECADENCE

1. William Wordsworth, *Poetical Works*, ed. Thomas Hutchinson, rev. ed. Ernest de Selincourt (1936; rpt. Oxford: Oxford University Press, 1967), 577. "There are in our existence spots of time," Wordsworth overtures to begin his explanation in Book XII of *The Prelude*:

> That with distinct pre-eminence retain
> A renovating virtue, whence . . .
>
>   our minds
> Are nourished and invisibly repaired;
> A virtue, by which pleasure is enhanced,
> That penetrates, enables us to mount,
> When high, more high, and lifts us up when fallen.
> This efficacious spirit chiefly lurks
> Among those passages of life that give
> Profoundest knowledge to what point, and how,
> The mind is lord and master – outward sense
> The obedient servant of her will. Such moments
> Are scattered everywhere, taking their date
> From our first childhood. I remember well . . .   (ll. 208–25)

   The renovating strength that stems from these special moments of imaginative memory is linked with a power that can be "efficacious" insofar as it "penetrates" a range of physical aspects and intellectual activities. These various elements are integrated into a feeling of well-being that is general and systemic and, hierarchical as it may be, subjoined under its all-inclusive force.

2. Wordsworth, *The Prelude*, Book XII, in *Poetical Works*, 578, ll. 277–87.
3. Wordsworth, Book XII, 578, ll. 272–75.
4. Edelman, *No Future*, 10–11.
5. James K. Chandler, *Wordsworth's Second Nature: A Study of the Poetry and Politics* (Chicago: University of Chicago Press, 1984), 184–215, esp. 212: "the distinction between the past and the present dissolves into a relationship of thoroughgoing reciprocity, an epistemological circle."
6. Thomas De Quincey, *Confessions of an English Opium-Eater and Other Writings*, ed. Grevel Lindop (Oxford: Oxford University Press, 1998), 23.
7. De Quincey, *Confessions*, 37.
8. In Wordsworth, *Poetical Works*, 164, l. 81.
9. Thus, in framing his first exposure to opium, his memory seeks to discover for "the most minute circumstances" of "the place and the time" of his memory a feeling of "mystic importance" (De Quincey, *Confessions*, 37–38) – the same

intimation that Wordsworth experienced (in similar wording) in sensing that connection between times present and past. It recreates the dynamics of the spot-of-time consciousness, but in a shadow language and parody circumstance.

10. De Quincey, *Confessions*, 49.
11. Margaret Russett, *De Quincey's Romanticism: Canonical Minority and the Forms of Transmission* (Cambridge: Cambridge University Press, 1997), 14–91, 87.
12. Percy Bysshe Shelley, *The Major Works*, ed. Zachary Leader and Michael O'Neill (Oxford: Oxford University Press, 2003), 617, ll. 429–31; 618, ll. 434–36.
13. Shelley, *Major Works*, 609, ll. 165–69.
14. Shelley, *Major Works*, 620, ll. 518–26.
15. See, for example, the popularity of Jean-Baptiste Cousin de Grainville's *The Last Man, or Omegarus and Syderia, A Romance in Futurity*. (Trans., London, 1806. 2 vols. Facs., New York: Arno Press, 1978); and the parody of *The Last Man*, "A Dialogue for the Year 2130: From the Album of a Modern Sibyl," in *The Keepsake for MDCCCXXX*, ed. Frederic Mansel Reynolds (London: Hurst, Chance, & Co., 1829), 249–64. The piece is attributed to "The Author of Grandy." This volume features poems by S. T. Coleridge and "The False Rhyme, A Tale," by "The Author of Frankenstein."
16. Mary Shelley, *The Last Man* (1826), ed. Morton Paley (Oxford: Oxford University Press, 1998), 220, 423, 318.
17. Shelley, *The Last Man*, 317.
18. Shelley, *The Last Man*, 373 ff.
19. Shelley, *The Last Man*, 437 ff.
20. Shelley, *The Last Man*, 462, 467
21. Byron's representation of Rome in Canto IV extends through stanzas LXXVIII–CLXXV. Subsequent references in this paragraph are by stanza numbers in Canto IV, in Byron, *Poetical Works*, ed. Frederick Page, rev. ed. John Jump (1904; 2d ed. London: Oxford University Press, 1970), 237–42.
22. So Byron demonstrates an imaginative attraction to some of the readily available characters and easily accessible themes of a conventional decadence, most conspicuously in his closet drama *Sardanapalus: A Tragedy* (in *Poetical Works*, 453–92), where the title figure consumes his kingly privilege in a life of *luxuria* that also wastes the domains of a far-flung empire. Byron's difference from the sensibility of decadence shows in this work in the force of the heroic as a category of imaginative action and value, which Sardanapalus manifestly and expressively fails as a character. This lost possibility shows in Byron's political imaginary as a personalization of history, so that, even in view of the failure of recent as well as future revolution, personal heroism remains in place as a code of expected behavior and a standard of performative value; this understanding is conveyed clearly by Jerome McGann, in "Rome and Its Romantic Significance," in *The Beauty of Inflections: Literary Investigations in Historical Method and Theory* (Oxford: Clarendon, 1988), 313–33, 324–25.

23. Anna Laetitia Barbauld, *Eighteen Hundred and Eleven, A Poem* (Boston: Bradford and Read, 1812), 26, 29. This edition is not lineated.

24. Barbauld, *Eighteen Hundred and Eleven*, 32.

25. De Quincey, *Suspiria de Profundis*, in *Confessions*, 87–88.

26. De Quincey, *Suspiria*, 88. Max Nordau, *Degeneration*, n. trans. (1895; rpt. New York: Appleton, 1905); see esp. chapter IV, "Etiology," 36–39.

27. Benjamin, *The Writer of Modern Life*, "The Paris of the Second Empire of Baudelaire," 46–133, esp. 59.

28. Georg Lukács, *The Historical Novel*, trans. Hannah and Stanley Mitchell (London: Merlin Press, 1962), esp. chapter 3, "The Historical Novel and the Crisis of Bourgeois Realism," section 1, "Changes in the Conception of History after the Revolution of 1848," 172–83, and section 5, "The General Tendencies of Decadence and the Establishment of the Historical Novel as a Special Genre," 230–50.

29. Karl Marx, *The Eighteenth Brumaire of Louis Bonaparte*, in *Karl Marx: Later Political Writings*, ed. and trans. Terrell Carver (Cambridge: Cambridge University Press, 1996), 32.

30. Marx, *The Eighteenth Brumaire of Louis Bonaparte*, 33.

31. Marx, *The Eighteenth Brumaire of Louis Bonaparte*, 32–33.

32. Marx, *The Eighteenth Brumaire of Louis Bonaparte*, 33.

33. Ibid.

34. Ibid.

35. Nordau, *Degeneration*, 36–39.

36. Charles Baudelaire, "The Poem of Hashish," in *Artificial Paradises*, trans. Stacy Diamond (New York: Citadel, 1996), 33.

37. Baudelaire, "The Poem of Hashish," 51–52.

38. Baudelaire, "An Opium-Eater," in *Artificial Paradises*, 129.

39. Baudelaire, "An Opium-Eater," 129.

40. Charles Baudelaire, "The Artist, Man of the World, Man of the Crowd, and Child," in *The Painter of Modern Life and Other Essays*, trans. Jonathan Mayne (1964; rpt. London: Phaidon Press, 1995), 9.

41. Edgar Allan Poe, "The Man of the Crowd," in *The Complete Poems and Stories of Edgar Allan Poe, with Selections from His Critical Writings*, 2 vols., ed. Arthur Hobson Quinn and Edward H. O'Neill (New York: Knopf, 1946). vol. 1, 308–314, 308.

42. Samuel Taylor Coleridge, "Kubla Khan," in *The Complete Poetical Works*, ed. Ernest Hartley Coleridge (Oxford: Clarendon Press, 1912), 297–98, ll. 17–28.

43. Poe, "The Man of the Crowd," 314.

44. Poe, "The Man of the Crowd," 309. Emphasis added.

45. Poe, "The Man of the Crowd, 308, 311, 313–14.

46. Walter Pater, "Conclusion," in *Studies in the History of the Renaissance* (1873), ed. Matthew Beaumont (Oxford: Oxford University Press, 2010), 119.

47. Harold Bloom, "Walter Pater: The Intoxication of Belatedness," *Yale French Studies*, 50.1 (1974), 163–89, esp. 166, 180, 185, 188.

48. Siegfried Kracauer, "Photography," trans. Thomas Y. Levin. *Critical Inquiry,* 19.3 (1993), 421–36; originally published as "Die Photographie" in the *Frankfurter Zeitung,* 28 October 1927.

49. Thus, in an April 1892 account of "Colour-Blindness, Its Pathology and Its Possible Practical Remedy," an otherwise bland contributor to the magazine *The Nineteenth Century* is visited by an energetic compulsion to explain away the afterwardness of the image. This writer makes the adamant point that even the substitute color appears *instantaneously* with the original glimpse: "It is . . . necessary for us to realise that the after-image does not, as one might at first suppose, spring suddenly into being in the instant in which the eyes are removed from the paper. Rather, as Hering has shown, it begins to come into being in the instant in which the eyes are directed to the object, and it then gradually works its way up to our consciousness, through a retina which is becoming more receptive to its influence" (654). In these final clauses, the author expands the instantaneous moment of visual perception into a whole cognitive process, one that integrates and normalizes these several stages into a single organic span.

   That the after-image exerts the appeal of some counter-cultural value is suggested in an 1895 piece, "The Anthropometric Laboratory," which Francis Galton wrote for *The Contemporary Review.* "The persistence of impressions, especially if visual ones, is exceedingly various. Some persons are strongly affected by after-images and others are not." To those who witness the strongest proclivity in this direction, he gives a further group category and a telling indicator: "There can be little doubt that *the liability to after-images* is an important part of *the artistic temperament*" (XXXI, n.s., 337; emphasis added). In context, "liability" certainly does not suggest "responsibility" or "accountability," while the readier sense of "risk" or even "danger" fits "the artistic temperament" especially.

   Where the danger being attached to the after-image is concentrated and intensified in the sensibility of the artists to whom it is affixed, another article, "Colour Shadows," in *The Nineteenth Century* (May 1895), draws decadent painting into the force field of the after-image controversy. To the painter-laureate of decadence, James McNeill Whistler, this author attributes the signature strength of the after-image, acknowledging him as the "master" of the visual echoing this double vision effects. "And the skilful painter is the painter who knows how to manipulate his after-image phenomena . . . it is evidently the after-image of these purples that has reverberated back upon the yellow-greens in his high-lights. And, again, the really great colourist is the man who has acquired an absolute mastery over the after-image phenomena . . . Mr. Whistler, for instance, is a master of this art" (828–29). The shimmering of the after-image that this writer admires also shows most characteristically in the twilit atmospheric that Whistler's canvases feature as their distinctive prospect.

50. Bate, *Burden of the Past,* 31–107, esp. 103–107.

51. Poe, "Letter to B_____," *Complete Poems,* vol. 2, 858.

52. Poe, "Ligeia," *Complete Poems,* vol. 1, 222.

53. Poe, "Berenice," *Complete Poems*, vol. 1, 146.
54. Poe, "The Coliseum," *Complete Poems*, vol. 1, 49.
55. Algernon Charles Swinburne, "The Triumph of Time," in *Major Poems and Selected Prose*, ed. Jerome McGann and Charles L. Sligh (New Haven: Yale University Press, 2004), 82, ll. 3–6.
56. Swinburne, "The Triumph of Time," 82, ll. 9–16.
57. Yopie Prins, "Swinburne's Sapphic Sublime" and "P.S. Sappho," in *Victorian Sappho* (Princeton: Princeton University Press, 1998), 112–245, esp. 119, 139–41, 174–77, 195–97.
58. Dante Gabriel Rossetti, "Jenny," in *Collected Poetry and Prose*, ed. Jerome McGann (New Haven: Yale University Press, 2003), 67, ll. 278–79, 282–89.
59. Rossetti, "Sonnet XXXVIII. The Morrow's Message," in *Collected Poetry*, 144, ll. 1–8.
60. Some recent criticism has productively challenged the relevance of originality to the work of second-generation romanticism in particular. See the discussion of the literary and legal issues of plagiarism by Tilar J. Mazzeo, *Plagiarism and Literary Property in the Romantic Period* (Philadelphia: University of Pennsylvania Press, 2007), esp. chapter 4, "'The Slip-Shod Muse': Byron, Originality, and Aesthetic Plagiarism," 86–121.
61. *The Poetical Works of Lionel Johnson*, ed. Ezra Pound (London: Elkin Matthews, 1915), xvii.
62. Dowson, "Villanelle of Sunset," in *Poems of Ernest Dowson*, ed. Mark Longaker (Philadelphia: University of Pennsylvania Press, 1962), 44.
63. Dowson, "Villanelle of the Poet's Road," in *Poems of Ernest Dowson*, 110.
64. Dowson, "Villanelle of Acheron," in *Poems of Ernest Dowson*, 111.
65. *The Poems of Arthur Symons*, vol. I (New York: John Lane, 1909), 28. This two-volume edition, which represents Symons's own selection of poems in volumes published between 1889 and 1909, will hereafter be cited parenthetically as *PAS* by volume and page numbers.
66. Symons, "The Decadent Movement," *Harper's*, November 1893, 862; Symons, *The Symbolist Movement* (1899; 1908), 3.
67. W. B. Yeats, "Into the Twilight," from *The Wind Among the Reeds* (1899), in *Collected Poems of W. B. Yeats*, 2d ed. (1950; rpt. London: Macmillan, 1971), 65–66.
68. Yeats, "The Valley of the Black Pig," from *The Wind Among the Reeds*, in *Collected Poems*, 73.
69. Ibid.
70. Yeats, "The Man and the Echo," from *Last Poems 1936–39*, in *Collected Poems*, 393. "The Irish Dramatic Movement" in *The Collected Works of W.B. Yeats*, vol. III, ed. William H. O'Donnell and Douglas N. Archibald (New York: Scribner's, 1999), 410.
71. A good account of Yeats's Parisian experience is provided by R. F. Foster, *W. B. Yeats: A Life*, vol. I: *The Apprentice Mage 1865–1914* (New York: Oxford University Press, 1998), 138–39.

72. Yeats, "The Tables of the Law," in *The Secret Rose, Stories by W. B. Yeats: A Variorum Edition*, ed. Phillip L. Marcus, Warwick Gould, and Michael J. Sidnell (Ithaca: Cornell University Press, 1981), 151.
73. Yeats, "The Tables of the Law," 151.
74. Yeats, "The Tables of the Law," 155, 156, 157.
75. Yeats, "The Tables of the Law," 162.
76. Linda Dowling, *Language and Decadence in the Victorian Fin de Siècle* (1986; rpt. Princeton: Princeton University Press, 1989), 46–103.
77. Yeats, "The Adoration of the Magi," in *The Secret Rose, Stories by W. B. Yeats: A Variorum Edition*, ed. Marcus, Gould, and Sidnell, 164–72, 165. Oscar Wilde, *The Decay of Lying: An Observation* (1889), in *The Artist as Critic: Critical Writings of Oscar Wilde*, ed. Richard Ellmann (Chicago: University of Chicago Press, 1982), 290–320.
78. "Glamour," originally Scottish, was introduced into literary language by Walter Scott; it is recognized as a corrupt form of "grammar," for the sense of which cf. "gramarye": *OED*: obs. Exc. Archaic: 1) grammar, learning in general; 2) occult learning, magic, necromancy. This second sense provides the link with "glamour," which means 1) magic enchantment, spell; 2) magical or fictitious beauty. Yeats plays with "glamour" most extensively in the prose tale "Kidnappers," in *The Celtic Twilight* (1893; rpt. Gerrards Cross, Bucks: Colin Smythe, 1987), 91–96.
79. W. B. Yeats, "The Symbolism of Poetry," in Yeats, *Essays and Introductions* (New York: Macmillan, 1961), 162, 164.
80. See the several poems Lionel Johnson projects into this context, for example, "Ireland" and "Ireland's Dead" and "To Weep Irish," in *The Poetical Works of Lionel Johnson*, 137, 58, 47. Ireland provides the site for a projection of highly rhetorical emotion in these poems.

INTER-CHAPTER   THE CULTIVATION OF DECAY AND
THE PREROGATIVES OF MODERNISM

1. Felski, *The Gender of Modernity*, 91.
2. Sedgwick, *Epistemology of the Closet*, 167–81.
3. Sedgwick, *Epistemology of the Closet*, 170.
4. Friedrich Nietzsche, *Ecce Homo*, in *On the Genealogy of Morals and Ecce Homo*, trans. Walter Kaufmann (New York, Vintage, 1967), 223.
5. Nietzsche's position in relation to the condition he labels "decadence" is two-sided. He sees himself at once as its full-time critic and its wholly representative product. As he admits and emphasizes in *Twilight of the Idols* (1889), in *Twilight of the Idols and The Anti-Christ*, trans. R. J. Hollingdale (1968; rpt. London: Penguin, 1990), 44: "It is self-deception on the part of philosophers and moralists to imagine that by making war on *décadence* they therewith elude *décadence* themselves. This is beyond their powers: what they select as an expedient, as a deliverance, is itself only another expression of *décadence* – they *alter* its expression, they do not abolish the thing itself."

6. Nietzsche, *Ecce Homo*, 223.

7. Friedrich Nietzsche, *The Birth of Tragedy*, in *The Birth of Tragedy and The Case of Wagner*, trans. Walter Kaufmann (New York: Vintage, 1967), 84.

8. Nietzsche, *The Twilight of the Idols*, 39–40.

9. Friedrich Nietzsche, *The Case of Wagner*, in *The Birth of Tragedy and The Case of Wagner*, trans. Walter Kaufmann (New York: Vintage, 1967), 186.

10. Sigmund Freud, *Beyond the Pleasure Principle*, trans. James Strachey, The International Psychoanalytic Library (New York: Liveright, 1950), 49–50. Emphasis in the quoted text.

11. Freud, *Beyond the Pleasure Principle*, 51. Emphasis added.

12. Jacques Derrida, *The Post Card: From Socrates to Freud and Beyond*, trans. Alan Bass (Chicago: University of Chicago Press, 1987), 360n.7; 355.

13. Robert Pippin, *Modernism as a Philosophical Problem* (1991), 2d ed. (Oxford: Blackwell, 1999); see esp. xiv, xv, 29, 31, 44.

14. Edgar Allan Poe, "The Imp of the Perverse," in *The Complete Poems and Stories of Edgar Allan Poe, with Selections from His Critical Writings*, ed. Arthur Hobson Quinn and Edward H. O'Neill, vol. 2, 639–40.

15. Poe, "The Imp of the Perverse," 638.

16. Ibid.

17. Stephen Arata, *Fictions of Loss in the Victorian Fin de Siècle* (Cambridge: Cambridge University Press, 1996). In his "Conclusion: Modernist Empires and the Rise of English," 178–84, Arata touches suggestively on connections between certain themes of these "fictions of loss" and later modernist preoccupations, (e.g., 179, where the invasion fears of late-nineteenth-century literary and public culture reappear in the "hooded hordes" of Eliot's phantasmagoria in *The Waste Land*).

18. Thomas Hardy, *Tess of the D'Urbervilles* (1891), ed. Simon Gatrell and Juliet Grindle (Oxford: Oxford University Press, 2005), 140.

19. This outcome is imaged forebodingly in Hardy's representations of Jude's first Latin primers. These "*old* Dolphin editions" center the scene of his young exertions within the grip of old age, auguring the inevitability of death already for his incipient energies: "While he was busied with these *ancient pages*, which had already been thumbed by *hands possibly in the grave*, digging out the thoughts of these minds so remote yet so near, the *bony old horse* pursued his rounds, and Jude would be aroused from the woes of Dido by the stoppage of his cart and the voice of *some old woman* crying, 'Two to-day, baker, and I return this *stale one.*'" (Emphasis added). Thomas Hardy, *Jude the Obscure* (1895), ed. Patricia Inham (Oxford: Oxford University Press, 2002), 27.

20. Hardy, *Jude the Obscure*, 325.

21. Hardy, *Jude the Obscure*, 326.

22. Gillian Beer, "Hardy and Decadence," in *Celebrating Thomas Hardy*, ed. Charles P. C. Pettit (London: Macmillan, 1996), 90.

23. Beer, "Hardy and Decadence," 90.

24. H. G. Wells, *The Time Machine*, Norton Critical Edition, ed. Stephen Arata (New York: Norton, 2009), 18.

25. Wells, *The Time Machine*, 20.
26. Wells, *The Time Machine*, 26.
27. Wells, *The Time Machine*, 26, 28.
28. Wells, *The Time Machine*, 34.
29. Bram Stoker, *Dracula*, Norton Critical Edition, ed. Nina Auerbach and David J. Skal (New York: Norton, 1997), 164–65. Emphasis added.
30. Stoker, *Dracula*, 199.
31. Stoker, *Dracula*, 208.
32. John Picker, *Victorian Soundscapes* (New York: Oxford University Press, 2003), 134–37.
33. Stoker, *Dracula*, 195.
34. Stoker, *Dracula*, 198.
35. Stoker, *Dracula*, 196.

CHAPTER II   THE DEMONSTRABLE DECADENCE OF MODERNIST NOVELS

1. Henry James, *The Awkward Age* (1899, 1909; rpt. New York: Knopf, 1993), 148.
2. James, *Awkward Age*, 16.
3. Thomas Hardy, *The Pursuit of the Well-Beloved and The Well-Beloved* (1892; 1897; London: Penguin, 1997).
4. James, *Awkward Age*, 54.
5. James, *Awkward Age*, 68.
6. Walter Benjamin, "The Work of Art in the Age of Mechanical Reproduction," in *Illuminations*, ed. Hannah Arendt, trans. Harry Zohn (New York: Schocken, 1969), 217–51.
7. Its density of reference certainly exceeds the five entries that George Schoolfield indexes in his helpful *Baedeker of Decadence: Charting a Literary Fashion 1884–1927* (New Haven: Yale University Press, 2003).
8. Henry James, *The Wings of the Dove* (1902; 1909; rpt. New York: Knopf, 1997), 305–306.
9. James, *Wings of the Dove*, 336.
10. James, *Wings of the Dove*, 337.
11. James, *Wings of the Dove*, 348.
12. Ali Nematollahy, "Anarchist Dandies, Dilettantes, and Aesthetes of the *Fin de Siècle*," *Nottingham French Studies*, 48.1 (2009), 14–30.
13. Christopher E. Forth, "Nietzsche, Decadence, and Regeneration in France, 1891–95," *Journal of the History of Ideas*, 54.1 (1993), 97–117.
14. Adam Parkes, *A Sense of Shock: The Impact of Impressionism on Modern British and Irish Writing* (New York: Oxford University Press, 2011), 45, 219–20n.4, 224–25n.54.
15. Joseph Conrad, *The Secret Agent: A Simple Tale* (1907), ed. Bruce Harkness, S. W. Reid, and Nancy Birk (Cambridge: Cambridge University Press, 1990), 11–12. Hereafter cited parenthetically as *TSA*.
16. Symons, *The Symbolist Movement*, 139.

17. "Typical of this form of degeneracy – these drawings, I mean."

    "You would call that lad a degenerate, would you?" mumbled Mr Verloc.

    Comrade Alexander Ossipon – nicknamed the Doctor, ex-medical student without a degree . . .

    "That's what he may be called scientifically. Very good type too, altogether, of that sort of degenerate. It's enough to glance at the lobes of his ears. If you read Lombroso –" (*TSA*, 40–41)

18. Anthony Ashley Cooper Shaftesbury, "An Essay on the Freedom of Wit and Humour," *Characteristics of Men, Manners, Opinions, Times* (London: John Darby, 1732), 72.

19. A comprehensive account of the history and consequences of the establishment of Greenwich Mean Time comes from Adam Barrows, *The Cosmic Time of Empire: Modern Britain and World Literature* (Berkeley: University of California Press, 2011). Barrows' account of *The Secret Agent* (102–12) emphasizes the conflict between the artifice of the rationalized standard and the organic rhythms of Conrad's experience in the merchant marine, which, if desirable, are represented now as inaccessible.

20. A long-standing critical attitude, described thus by James F. English, "Anarchy of the Flesh: Conrad's 'Counterrevolutionary' Modernism and the Witz of the Political Unconscious," *Modern Fiction Studies*, 38.3 (1992), 615–30, 616.

21. English, "Conrad's 'Counterrevolutionary' Modernism," 619.

22. G. K. Chesterton, *The Man Who Was Thursday: A Nightmare* (1908; rpt. New York: Random House, 2001), 3–5. Hereafter cited parenthetically as *MWT*.

23. Fredric Jameson, "Modernism and Imperialism" (1990), in Jameson, *The Modernist Papers* (London: Verso, 2007), 152–69.

24. Arthur Balfour, *Decadence* (Cambridge: Cambridge University Press, 1908), 6–7. Hereafter cited parenthetically as *D*.

25. This is the censure that comes from the effort of definition of this elusive signifier in St. John Lucas's essay, "The True Decadence," *Macmillan's Magazine* (June 1902), 133. The "true decadence" ends up being a repository of everything menacing to "true" Englishness (133–42). Most notably, in relation to the connections made in the novels of Conrad and Chesterton, decadent authors are seen to "behave like abandoned literary anarchists" (133).

26. C. F. G. Masterman, *The Condition of England* (London: Methuen, 1909), 79. Hereafter cited parenthetically as *TCE*.

27. *The Letters of D. H. Lawrence*, vol. II (June 1913–October 1916), ed. George J. Zytaruk and James T. Boulton (Cambridge: Cambridge University Press, 1981), 441.

28. An account of the textual history of the novel is provided helpfully by David Bradshaw, ed., *Women in Love* (Oxford: Oxford University Press, 1998), xxxix–xli. Hereafter cited parenthetically as *WIL*.

29. Sandra M. Gilbert and Susan Gubar, "Soldier's Heart: Literary Men, Literary Women, and the Great War," in *No Man's Land: The Place of the Woman Writer in the Twentieth Century*, vol. 2, *Sexchanges* (New Haven: Yale University Press, 1989), 258–323.

30. David Trotter, *The English Novel in History 1895–1920* (London: Routledge, 1993), 126.
31. The two versions of this line (5.1.196) are flanked in the introductory "textual note" to *Hamlet*, in *The Norton Shakespeare*, vol. 2, *The Later Plays*, ed. Stephen Greenblatt, et al. (New York: Norton, 2008), 113.
32. I have examined these issues in broad historical context in "The Novel and the First World War," in *The Oxford History of the English Novel*, vol. 4, *The Reinvention of the British and Irish Novel 1880–1940*, ed. Patrick Parrinder and Andrzej Gasiorek (Oxford: Oxford University Press, 2011), 402–16.
33. *Hamlet*, 2.2.227–31: "Hamlet: Then you live about her waist, or in the middle of her favour! Guildensterne: Faith, her privates we. Hamlet: In the secret parts of Fortune? O, most true –, she is a strumpet."
34. The novel was first published pseudonymously as *The Middle Parts of Fortune* by "Private 19022" in 1929 and then in an expurgated version in 1930 as *Her Privates We*. The unexpurgated version is the basis of the current edition: Frederic Manning, *Her Privates We*, ed. William Boyd (London: Serpent's Tail, 1999), 205.
35. Manning's friendships with Pound and Eliot and his writing for Eliot's *Criterion* are recalled by Boyd in his "Introduction," xii–xv.
36. See W. H. R. Rivers, *Instinct and the Unconscious: A Contribution to a Biological Theory of the Psycho-Neuroses* (1924) (Cambridge: Cambridge University Press Archives, 2001). The "fugue" state is described and analyzed at greatest length under "Dissociation," 71–84.
37. Rebecca West, *The Return of the Soldier*, intro. Samuel Hynes (1918; rpt. London: Penguin, 1998), 4. This edition follows the first British edition (London: Nisbet, 1918). Hereafter cited parenthetically as *RS*.
38. The allusive intention of names is confirmed by the figure of "Bert Wells, nephew of Mr Wells who keeps the inn at Surly Hall" (*RS*, 51), who recalls of course H. G. Wells, the father of the infant son whom West was already caring for. See the account of their relationship by Carl Rollyson, *Rebecca West: A Life* (New York: Scribner's, 1996), 50–71.
39. See esp. "Space-Craft," in *The Pound Era*, 23–40.
40. Ezra Pound, *Hugh Selwyn Mauberley*, in *Personae: The Shorter Poems of Ezra Pound*, ed. Lea Baechler and A. Walton Litz (New York: New Directions, 1990), 186.

INTER-CHAPTER IMAGISM

1. Claire Healey recreates this occasion from various sources in "Amy Lowell Visits London," *The New England Quarterly*, 46.3 (1973), 442–46.
2. The identifications of secondary critical headings such as "decadence" are not the interest in the definitive literary history, that is, Helen Carr's *The Verse Revolutionaries: Ezra Pound, H.D., and the Imagists* (London: Jonathan Cape, 2009), which provides an extraordinarily well-detailed circumstantial history (nearly 1,000 pages). One of the major outcomes of this history is a

diminishment of Pound's significance in Imagism, and an accordingly greater importance for the previously subsidiary talents of Flint and Aldington. Along the same lines, it is the poetic temperament that these various talents join to represent that centers the interest in my reading here.

3. "Imagisme," *Poetry*, March 1913, 199. The essay was Flint's, but Pound inserted these three points. See Christopher Middleton, "Documents on Imagism from the Papers of F. S. Flint," *The Review*, 15 (April 1965), 36–37.

4. *Poetry*, March 1913, 200–207.

5. Wilson, *Axel's Castle*, esp. 12–20.

6. See also Stanley K. Coffman, Jr., "Imagism and Symbolism," in his *Imagism: A Chapter for the History of Modern Poetry* (Norman: University of Oklahoma Press, 1951), 74–103.

7. F. S. Flint, "Contemporary French Poetry," *Poetry Review*, August 1912, 355–414; 365–66.

8. Flint, "Contemporary French Poetry," 357.

9. Flint, "Contemporary French Poetry," 411.

10. Margaret Storm Jameson, "England's Nest of Singing Birds," *The Egoist*, 1 November 1915, 175–76. Emphasis added.

11. Jameson, "England's Nest of Singing Birds," 176.

12. The "Lecture" is dated thus by Hynes; T. E. Hulme, "A Lecture on Modern Poetry," in *Further Speculations: T. E. Hulme*, ed. Samuel Hynes (1955; rpt. Lincoln: University of Nebraska Press, 1961), xvii. Hynes understands this "Lecture" to be an essential precedent to the later Imagism of Pound and Flint.

13. Hulme, "A Lecture on Modern Poetry," 68–69.

14. Hulme, "A Lecture on Modern Poetry," 70 ff., esp. 73–75.

15. Hulme negotiates the visual content promised by the term "Imagism" in a contemporary companion piece, his "Notes on Language and Style." Here he depicts the image largely as a matter of "poetic analogy," where visible images appear as the figurative terms of similes and metaphors. On this secondary level of elaboration, the visual image emerges as a decorative rather than essential element – a status he emphasizes in according it the value of lightness, even capriciousness. "Analogies in poetry, like the likenesses of babies, to be taken half seriously, with a smile." The visual similitude, he indicates, is really just a happy accident of perception, whose "inspiration is a matter of an *accidentally* seen analogy or unlooked-for resemblance . . . . Fertility of invention means: remembrance of *accidental* occurrences *noted* and arranged (cf. detective stories)" (all but final emphasis added); Hulme, "Notes on Language and Style," in *Further Speculations*, 84, 85. In the poems, then, Hulme's "visual images" appear characteristically as the surprisingly, often humorously, always casually apprehended term of comparison. "Like a red-faced farmer" goes his deflating trope for that old poetic favorite, "the ruddy moon." More wistfully, even less imposingly, the moon in "Above the Dock" is seen as "but a child's balloon, forgotten after play." Or with the comic surprise of seeing himself in passage "to the final river," floating "Ignominiously, in a sack, without sound / As any peeping Turk to the

Bosphorus": as published in an appendix to Pound's 1912 volume *Ripostes*; rpt. *Personae: The Shorter Poems of Ezra Pound*, ed. Lea Baechler and A. Walton Litz (New York: New Directions, 1990), 267–68.

16. In the appendix to *Ripostes*; rpt. *Personae*, 268.
17. In the appendix to *Ripostes*; rpt. *Personae*, 266.
18. Max Beerbohm, *The Works of Max Beerbohm* (London: John Lane, The Bodley Head, 1896).
19. *Selected Letters of Ezra Pound, 1907–1941*, ed. D. D. Paige (New York: New Directions, 1950), 11.
20. *Poetry*, March 1913, 198.
21. *Des Imagistes: An Anthology* (London: The Poetry Bookshop, 1914; New York: Albert and Charles Boni, 1914), 2. Poems in this collection will be cited parenthetically as *DI*.
22. Dowling, *Language and Decadence in the Victorian Fin de Siècle*, 46–103.
23. Beerbohm, "Diminuendo," in *Works*, 150.
24. Hulme, "A Lecture on Modern Poetry," 73.
25. *Cadences* (London: The Poetry Bookshop, 1915); *Some Imagist Poets, 1916: An Annual Anthology* (Boston: Houghton Mifflin, 1916), viii–ix.
26. See *Imagist Poetry*, ed. Peter Jones (Harmondsworth: Penguin, 1972), 148.
27. Of the five poems Flint contributed to *Des Imagistes*, one other ("The Swan," *DI*, 35) finds a rhythm similar to the London piece.
28. *Some Imagist Poets: An Anthology* (Boston: Houghton Mifflin, 1915), 16.
29. *Some Imagist Poets, 1916*, 7.
30. *Some Imagist Poets, 1916*, 8–9.
31. Cassandra Laity, *H.D. and the Victorian Fin de Siècle: Gender, Modernism, Decadence* (Cambridge: Cambridge University Press, 1996), esp. "Introduction: Dramatis Personae: The Aesthete Androgyne and the Femme Fatale," ix–xix, "The Rhetoric of Anti-Romanticism: Gendered Genealogies of Male Modernism," 1–28, and "H.D.'s Early Decadent Masks and Images: *HER, Sea Garden*," 29–60.
32. For the growing importance of the racial or ethnic factor in American national identity and the relevance of these developments for the continental American modernism of the 1920s and after, see Walter Benn Michaels, *Our America: Nativism, Modernism, and Pluralism*, (Durham: Duke University Press, 1995), esp. 6–13.
33. T. J. Jackson Lears, *No Place of Grace: Antimodernism and the Transformation of American Culture, 1880–1920* (1983), 2d ed. (Chicago: University of Chicago Press, 1994), esp. 4–7, 26.

CHAPTER III   EZRA POUND: 1906–1920

1. R. A. Scott-James, "Modern Poetry," in *The Daily News*, 9 July 1909, 3; R. A. Scott-James, *Modernism and Romance* (London: John Lane, The Bodley Head, 1908), passim, esp. chapter XIV, "The New Romance," 214–35.
2. Edward Thomas, "Two Poets," *English Review* (1909), 627.

3. This resistance includes a bloody- and single-minded denunciation of "The Decadents" (*Modernism and Romance*, chapter VI, 69–85) and a willful inscription of "The New Romance" on the otherwise unlikely site of Conrad's novels of the late imperial age, the import of which he summarizes thus: "The idea forces itself upon us that our civilisation so far from being very old is really in its infancy" (*Modernism and Romance*, 234–35). The strenuousness of this assertion, especially in reference to the historical pessimism of Conrad's fiction, measures the strained nature of Scott-James's case, which, in turn, says a good deal about the force of the presentiments he is resisting, as revealed in other locations. "It is a wearisome tale to tell ... he is happy indeed who does not understand what I have sought to suggest rather than to explain ... if he has not felt these and all the other parts of our *over-developed community shaking and shivering in self-conscious postures*, groaning in the agonies either of actual physical pain or the self-imposed torture of affectation, then he belongs to the happy few who have not been compelled to witness the 'ache of modernism'" (*Modernism and Romance*, 33; emphasis added). Attempting to counter the understanding of Hardy's Tess, which undermines an idea of progressive futurity in the modernism she experiences chiefly as "ache," Scott-James is in fact equating modernism with decadence. Its signs appear not just as the contemporary disease but as the disease *of* the contemporary – of a modernity that stands at the forward edge of developmental history, of "our *over-developed* community." Here the sense of the ultimate present that provides the "ism" of the "modern" with its principal meaning involves a recognition not of some triumph of progressive time, but of its inversion; Progress is consummated in the contorted products he depicts here, all too clearly, as the febrile exhaustion of fin-de-siècle types. In this sense "decadence" is an initial and constitutive modernism, and the resistance Scott-James puts up to admitting this equivalence says a good deal about its significance.
4. Thomas, "Two Poets," 627.
5. Ezra Pound, "M. Antonius Flamininus and John Keats, a Kinship in Genius," *Book News Monthly*, February 1908, 446.
6. Ibid.
7. *The Collected Early Poems of Ezra Pound*, ed. Michael King (New York: New Directions, 1976), 205. This collection brings together poems published in book-length collections, poems published in periodicals but uncollected subsequently, and poems composed but not published, and provides useful bibliographical information. Hereafter cited parenthetically as *CEPEP*.
8. A first point of documented connection comes in 1911, near the time at which Nietzsche's collected works was published in English translation. In "Redondillas, or something of that sort," a poem withdrawn from the manuscript of *Canzoni* (1911) and not published subsequently until late in his lifetime, Pound turns Nietzsche's infamous anti-Christianity into an unlikely point of praise:

> I believe in some parts of Nietzsche,
> I prefer to read him in sections;

In my heart of hearts I suspect him
 of being the one modern christian;
Take notice I never have read him
 except in English selections.   (*CEPEP*, 217)

The tonal complexity of this passage includes the archly assumed celebrity of a not-quite-emergent twenty-five-year-old poet, who pretends that his reading practices are worthy of "notice" even in their precise calibrations. Seriocomic or not, Pound's disclaimer about the limited conditions of his knowledge of Nietzsche is belied by the "heart of hearts" register of his response.

9. Kathryn V. Lindberg, *Reading Pound Reading: Modernism after Nietzsche* (New York: Oxford University Press, 1987). Whereas, in one instance (31), Lindberg notes Nietzsche's complicity in the decadence he so fiercely critiques, she does not develop this aspect of his sensibility in any substantial way in connection with Pound or Poundian modernism.
10. Kenner, *The Pound Era*, xi, 179.
11. Propertius's Latin provides the title for Dowson's piece, in *Poems of Ernest Dowson*, 90.
12. Ezra Pound, *Personae: The Shorter Poems of Ezra Pound*, ed. Lea Baechler and A. Walton Litz (New York: New Directions, 1990), 41. Poems in this edition hereafter cited parenthetically as *P*.
13. Christine Froula, "War, Empire, and Modernist Poetry, 1914–1922," *Cambridge Companion to the Poetry of the First World War*, ed. Santanu Das (Cambridge: Cambridge University Press, 2013), 210–26, 216, 226n.46.
14. *The Poetical Works of Lionel Johnson*, 35.
15. Ezra Pound, "Through Alien Eyes III," *New Age*, 30 January 1913, 300.
16. J. K. Huysmans, *Against Nature [À Rebours]* (1884), ed. Nicholas White, trans. Margaret Mauldon (Oxford: Oxford University Press, 1998), 29–31.
17. See, for example, Benn Michaels, *Our America*, esp. 6–13.
18. Pound, "Patria mia VI," *New Age*, 10 October 1912, 564.
19. Pound, "Affirmations VI. Analysis of This Decade," *New Age*, 11 February 1915, 409.
20. Pound, "Affirmations II. Vorticism," *New Age*, 14 January 1915, 277.
21. Pound, "The Renaissance III," *Poetry*, May 1915, 90.
22. Also, Jacob Epstein "has had 'form-understanding'; he has not fallen into the abyss, into the decadence of all sculpture that is 'the admiration of self'"; in Pound, "Affirmations III. Jacob Epstein," *New Age*, 21 January 1915, 312. Again in Pound, "This Super-Neutrality," *New Age*, 21 October 1915, 595, where President Woodrow Wilson is seen as "a 'safer' type, in ordinary circumstances, than the decadence of its opposite, i.e., the frothy type which receives too many ideas."
23. Pound, "Affirmations V. Gaudier-Brzeska," *New Age*, 4 February 1915, 381.
24. Pound, "What America Has to Live Down V," *New Age*, 12 September 1918, 314; "List of Books: Comment by Ezra Pound [on *Certain Noble Plays of Japan*, inter alia.]," *little review*, August 1917, 6; "Hellenist Series VI," *Egoist*,

March/April 1919, 24; "Art Notes: Parallelograms," *New Age*, 17 October 1918, 400; "Mr. James Joyce and the Modern Stage: A Play and Some Considerations," *Drama*, February 1916, 131.

25. Pound, "James Joyce: at Last the Novel Appears," *Egoist*, February 1917, 22.
26. Pound, "The Revolt of Intelligence IX," *New Age*, 11 March 1920, 301.
27. Letter of 3 May 1916, from London, in *Pound/Lewis: The Letters of Ezra Pound and Wyndham Lewis*, ed. Timothy Materer (New York: New Directions, 1985), 35.
28. *Blast: War Number*, ed. Wyndham Lewis (1915; rpt. Santa Rosa: Black Sparrow Press, 1993), 34.
29. Letter of 29 February 1916, from Stone Cottage, in *The Selected Letters of Ezra Pound to John Quinn, 1915–1924*, ed. Timothy Materer (Durham: Duke University Press, 1991), 64.
30. A good contextualization of this poem in relation to other early attempts by Pound to write about the war comes from James Longenbach, "War Poets by the Waste Moor," *Stone Cottage: Pound, Yeats, and Modernism* (New York: Oxford University Press, 1990), 105–34.
31. Footnote, signed: "E.P.," to Frederic Manning's "M. de Gourmont and the Problem of Beauty," *little review*, February/March 1919, 26–27.
32. Pound, "Art Notes, by B. H. Dias, On the Russian Ballet," *New Age*, 23 October 1919, 427.
33. Ibid.
34. Ibid.
35. Pound, "On the Russian Ballet," 428. Cf. Virginia Woolf, *Jacob's Room* (1922; rpt. New York: Harcourt, 1991), 155–56: "Like blocks of tin soldiers the army covers the cornfield, moves up the hillside, stops, reels slightly this way and that, and falls flat, save that, through field-glasses, it can be seen that one or two pieces still agitate up and down like fragments of broken match-stick."
36. Pound, "On the Russian Ballet," 428.
37. Ibid.
38. In a letter to the *English Journal* dated 24 January 1931; in *The Selected Letters of Ezra Pound, 1907–1941*, 231.
39. Max Beerbohm, "Hilary Maltby and Stephen Braxton," *Seven Men and Two Others* (New York: Vintage, 1959), 38. This edition, hereafter cited parenthetically as "HMSB," reprints the 1919 (Heinemann) text of the story.
40. See Holbrook Jackson, *The Eighteen Nineties: A Review of Art and Ideas at the Close of the Nineteenth Century* (1913; rpt. Atlantic Highlands, NJ: Humanities Press, 1976), passim, e.g., 89: "Dandy of intellect, dandy of manners, Oscar Wilde strutted through the first half of the Nineties and staggered through the last."
41. Under the pseudonymously initialed "T. J. V." in "The Culinary Vein," a review of the play "Come Out of the Kitchen," *Athenaeum*, 26 March 1920, 424. In the sequence, Beerbohm appears in the cameo of the soundalike "Brennbaum" (*P*, 191), where, in addition to the similarity between the "circular infant's face" and the images Beerbohm presented of himself in visual caricature, the final epithet – "Brennbaum 'The Impeccable'" – quotes and

knowingly varies Shaw's well-known phrase "The Incomparable Max." "Impeccable" may also echo the sense of the epigraph to *The Works of Max Beerbohm*, "I am utterly purposed that I will not *offend*" (n.p.).

42. Undated letter (1936; probably November) from Pound to Montgomery Butchart (Beinecke Library, Yale University), and letter of January 1937 from Pound to Butchart (Beinecke Library). The negotiation became a three-way correspondence, including Laurence Pollinger with Butchart. The exchange lasted into March because Pound would not dismiss the possibility, at least not strongly enough to force Butchart to drop his recommendation. The assignment's appeal to Pound is recorded in another letter of November, as he writes "The Life and TIMES, that could rise marrveleus and effulgent."

43. So, too, where the mischievously Latinate title of his contemporary collection – *Umbra [Shadows]* – combines with the descriptive indicator of its subtitle: *The Early Poems of Ezra Pound* (London: Elkin Matthews, 1920).

44. Ezra Pound, "Arthur Symons," *Athenaeum*, 21 May 1920, 663.

45. Ibid.

INTER-CHAPTER REFORMING DECADENCE: LATE
ROMANTICISM, MODERNISM, AND THE POLITICS
OF LITERARY HISTORY

1. Shelley, "A Defence of Poetry," in *The Major Works*, ed. Leader and O'Neill, 701.

2. So associated by Gautier, in his introduction to an early collection of Baudelaire's poetry; in *The Complete Works of Théophile Gautier*. XII, trans. F. C. DeSumichrast (New York: Bigelow, Smith & Co., 1910), 39–40.

3. For a good analysis of the political complications in the history of the avant-garde manifesto, see Martin Puchner, *Poetry of the Revolution: Marx, Manifestos, and the Avant-Gardes* (Princeton: Princeton University Press, 2006), passim, esp. 3, where Puchner anticipates his account of a "crucial moment in the emancipation of the art manifesto from the socialist manifesto [in] Filippo Tommaso Marinetti's fascist critique of Marxism. This critique, drawing on the French syndicalist Georges Sorel, allowed him to break with the communist reverence for the original *Manifesto* and to forge a new manifesto, one that continued to function as a political document but whose primary purpose was now artistic."

4. Georg Lukács, "The Ideology of Modernism," *The Meaning of Contemporary Realism*, trans. John and Necke Mander (London: Merlin Press, 1963), 17–46, esp. 24, 29–33.

5. Lukács, *The Meaning of Contemporary Realism*, 40–44, 41. The complexity of Benjamin's place in Marxist cultural and literary criticism, particularly his relation to Adorno, is analyzed well by Eugene Lunn, "Part III: Benjamin and Adorno," *Marxism and Modernism: An Historical Study of Lukács, Brecht, Benjamin, and Adorno* (Berkeley: University of California Press, 1982), 149–279.

6. Lukács, *The Meaning of Contemporary Realism*, passim, e.g., 33–35, 68, 76, 80.
7. Theodor W. Adorno, *Aesthetic Theory*, trans. Robert Hullot-Kentor (Minneapolis: University of Minnesota Press, 1979), 227.
8. Adorno, for example, in *Aesthetic Theory*, 29: "The shadow of art's autarchic radicalism is its harmlessness: Absolute color compositions verge on wallpaper patterns. Now that American hotels are decorated with abstract paintings *à la manière de* . . . and aesthetic radicalism has shown itself to be socially affordable, radicalism itself must pay the price that it is no longer radical." Adorno's ellipsis.
9. Adorno, *Aesthetic Theory*, 227.
10. Ibid.
11. Adorno, *Aesthetic Theory*, 141.
12. Adorno, *Aesthetic Theory*, 33–34.
13. Adorno, *Aesthetic Theory*, 254.
14. Ibid.
15. Jameson, *A Singular Modernity*, 152.
16. Jameson, *A Singular Modernity*, 136.
17. Jameson, *A Singular Modernity*, 134–35.
18. Cf. Perry Anderson, "Marshall Berman: Modernity and Revolution," *A Zone of Engagement* (London: Verso, 1992), 25–55.
19. A useful roundup review of the critical work dedicated to the deliberation of this apparent paradox of an aesthetically progressive poetics and a socially reactionary politics – William Chace, Raymond Williams, Alastair Hamilton, and Fredric Jameson – is provided by Marjorie Perloff in "The Politics of Modern Poetry," a review of Cairns Craig's *Yeats, Eliot, Pound, and the Politics of Poetry*, in *Contemporary Literature*, 25.1 (1984), 88. The provocation in the paradox, which Craig rehearses in the opening pages of his book (Pittsburgh: University of Pittsburgh Press, 1982), 2–3, pushes him to propose somewhat plaintively that the field of literary language provides all three poets a great democratic leveler, that is, a medium of positive purification of these regrettable political inclinations (2–3). The otherwise unresolvable quality in this problem can push critics to extreme solutions: in *The Sense of an Ending: Studies in the Theory of Fiction* (1967; rpt. New York: Oxford University Press, 2000), 110–11, for instance, Frank Kermode dissolves the evident discrepancy of aesthetic experimentation and reactionary politics by asserting "that the radical thinking of the early modernists about the arts implied, in other spheres, opinions of a sort not normally associated with the word radical. It appears, in fact, that modernist radicalism in art – the breaking down of pseudo-traditions, the making new on a true understanding of the nature of the elements of art – this radicalism involves the creation of fictions which may be dangerous in the dispositions they breed towards the world"; those ultimate political solutions, in other words, were instinct already and first of all in the early radicalization of art. The difficulties inherent in the critical task of reconciling experimental aesthetics and reactionary politics push commentators to assert opposite but absolute partisan values for the same literary figures

and institutions in early modernism. So, in "Seafarer Socialism: Pound, *The New Age*, and Anglo-Medieval Radicalism," *Journal of Modern Literature*, 29.4 (2006), 1–21, Lee Garver maintains that the poetic experimentation undertaken in the radical project of Pound's Anglo-Saxon translation accords wholly with the concurrent (1911) work of labor unrest and social emancipation in England, for which *The New Age* was the appropriate partisan venue, whereas, in "*The New Age* and the Emergence of Reactionary Modernism Before the Great War," *Modern Fiction Studies*, 38.3 (1992), 653–65, Charles Ferrall maintains, as his title suggests, a totally opposite political character and value in this journal. A good overview of the critical problem comes in "The Politics of Modernist Form," *New Literary History*, 23.3 (1992), 675–90, where Marianne DeKoven rehearses the various claims that are made for the politically revolutionary and socially progressive dimensions of modernist technical and formal experimentation (677). DeKoven notices that the work of female modernists seems far more readily identifiable with the convention-dismaying efforts of a liberating political ideology than, say, Pound, Eliot, or Joyce (680–81).

20. W. H. Auden, "In Memory of W. B. Yeats" (1939), in *Collected Shorter Poems 1927–1957* (London: Faber, 1961), 142.

21. I. A. Richards, *Science and Poetry* (New York: Norton, 1926), esp. 21–22, 67–70.

22. "There is one main subject to be studied in connection with anything that can be described as Mr. Eliot's critical system," Lewis proposes in the framing statement of "T. S. Eliot, The Pseudo-Believer," and then specifies, emphatically: "namely the whole question of *sincerity*, in all its ramifications. That notion, with all the values attaching to an actual doctrine of *Make-Believe*, has gradually become for Mr. Eliot, as for Mr. Richards, the central affair." Wyndham Lewis, "T. S. Eliot, The Pseudo-Believer," in *Men Without Art* (1934), ed. Seamus Cooney (Santa Rosa: Black Sparrow Press, 1987), 55–82, 58.

23. Lewis, "T. S. Eliot, the Pseudo-Believer," *Men Without Art*, 66–67.

24. Lewis, "Introduction," *Men Without Art*, 16. Emphasis added.

25. Lewis, "T. S. Eliot, the Pseudo-Believer," *Men Without Art*, 77–78.

26. T. S. Eliot, *After Strange Gods: A Primer of Modern Heresy* (New York: Harcourt, Brace, and Co., 1934), 12. Emphasis added.

27. Eliot, *Strange Gods*, 20.

28. T. S. Eliot, "Swinburne as Poet," in *The Sacred Wood* (1920); in *The Sacred Wood and Major Early Essays* (Mineola, NY: Dover Publications, 1998), 86–87.

29. Ezra Pound, "Swinburne versus Biographers," *Poetry*, March 1918, 329.

30. T. S. Eliot, "Introduction," in *The Use of Poetry and the Use of Criticism: Studies in the Relation of Criticism to Poetry in England* (1933; rpt. Cambridge, MA: Harvard University Press, 1964), 16–17.

31. Pound, as "Ferrex on Petulance," in *The Egoist*, 1 January 1914, 9.

32. Pound, "Ferrex on Petulance," 9–10.

33. In *Selected Letters of Ezra Pound*, ed. Paige, 112.

34. Ezra Pound, "Canto XLVI," *The Cantos of Ezra Pound* (1973; rpt. New York: New Directions, 1986), 231–35.

CHAPTER IV T. S. ELIOT: 1910–1922

1. James Joyce, *Ulysses* (1922), in *The Corrected Text*, ed. Hans Walter Gabler et al. (New York: Vintage, 1986), 118, 7.875–76.

2. Ronald Schuchard, *Eliot's Dark Angel: Intersections of Life and Art* (New York: Oxford University Press, 1999), esp. 8–24, 76–86.

3. Eliot's connection to the 1890s comes mainly through Wilde in Ronald Bush's well-documented account, "In Pursuit of Wilde Possum: Reflections on Eliot, Modernism, and the Nineties," *Modernism/modernity*, 11.3 (2004), 469–85.

4. T. S. Eliot, *Inventions of the March Hare: Poems 1909–1917*, ed. Christopher Ricks (New York: Harcourt, Brace, 1996), 11. This collection brings together the poems in the manuscript-notebook, for which Eliot provided this title; Ricks provides helpful editorial commentary. Quotations from poems in this collection hereafter cited parenthetically as *IMH*.

5. See, for example, "Embarquement pour Cythère," the second poem in the sequence "Goldfish (Essence of Summer Magazines)" (*IMH*, 27).

6. Marjorie Perloff, "Avant-Garde Eliot," *21st-Century Modernism: The "New" Poetics* (Oxford: Blackwell, 2002), 7–43.

7. Under "Credo," in "A Retrospect" (1918), in *The Literary Essays of Ezra Pound*, ed. T. S. Eliot (London: Faber, 1954), 9.

8. This subject has been explored in a widening inquiry, which includes Colleen Lamos's *Deviant Modernism: Sexual and Textual Errancy in T. S. Eliot, James Joyce, and Marcel Proust* (New York: Cambridge University Press, 1998); Suzanne W. Churchill's "Outing T. S. Eliot," *Criticism*, 47.1 (2005), 7–30; Gabrielle McIntire's "An Unexpected Beginning: Sex, Race, and History in T. S. Eliot's Columbo and Bolo Poems," *Modernism/modernity*, 9.2 (2002), 283–301; and John Paul Riquelme's "T. S. Eliot's Ambiviolences: Oscar Wilde as Masked Precursor," *The Hopkins Review*, 5.3 (2012), 353–79. See also the four essays in part I, "Homoeroticisms," in *Gender, Desire, and Sexuality in T. S. Eliot*, ed. Cassandra Laity and Nancy Gish (New York: Cambridge University Press, 2004): Colleen Lamos, "The Love Song of T. S. Eliot: Elegiac Homoeroticism in the Early Poetry," 23–42; Tim Dean, "T. S. Eliot, Famous Clairvoyante," 43–65; Michele Tepper, "'Cells in One Body': Nation and Eros in the Early Work of T. S. Eliot," 66–83; and Peter Middleton, "The Masculinity Behind the Ghost of Modernism in Eliot's *Four Quartets*," 83–104.

9. *The Letters of T. S. Eliot*, vol. I (1898–1922), ed. Valerie Eliot (London: Faber, 1988), 40–41. References to letters in this collection hereafter cited parenthetically as *LTSE*.

10. Swinburne, "Laus Veneris," in *Major Poems and Selected Prose*, ed. McGann and Sligh, l. 55, 72. For a good account of Swinburne's relation to Eliot in regard particularly to sexual themes, see Cassandra Laity, "T. S. Eliot and A. C. Swinburne: Decadent Bodies, Modern Visualities and Changing Modes of Perception," *Modernism/modernity*, 11.3 (2004), 425–48.

11. A good account of the broader historical context and its relevance to the homoerotic interest of the poem is provided by Richard Kaye, "'A Splendid

Readiness for Death': T. S. Eliot, the Homosexual Cult of St. Sebastian, and World War I," *Modernism/modernity*, 6.2 (1999), 107–34.

12. In a letter of 1 July 1917, to his mother (*LTSE*, 187): "I was particularly interested in your Colonial Dames circular which I thought very well written and a model of its kind."

13. Eliot, "Virgil and the Christian World" (1951), rpt. Eliot, *On Poetry and Poets* (London: Faber, 1957), 124, 126, 127. Emphasis added.

14. "A Romantic Aristocrat" was included as a section in "Imperfect Critics" (1919), which was gathered in *The Sacred Wood* (1920); in *The Sacred Wood and Major Early Essays*, 15. Emphasis added.

15. Eliot, "A Romantic Aristocrat," 16.

16. Ibid.

17. Peter Ackroyd, *T. S. Eliot: A Life* (New York: Simon and Schuster, 1984), 79.

18. Eliot, "Rudyard Kipling" (1941), rpt. Eliot, *On Poetry and Poets*, 245.

19. "Gerontion," in *Poems* (New York: Alfred A. Knopf, 1920), 13–16, 13. References to poems in this collection will be given parenthetically as *1920*.

20. Nigel Alderman, "'Where are the Eagles and the Trumpets': The Strange Case of Eliot's Missing Quatrains," *Twentieth Century Literature*, 39.2 (1993), 129–51, esp. 136, 138 ff. For a cogent analysis of the importance of the mechanical in Lewis's work, in relation particularly to the experience of technological war, see Jessica Burstein, "Waspish Segments," *Cold Modernism: Literature, Fashion, Art* (University Park, PA: The Pennsylvania State University Press, 2012), 65–86; Burstein extends this understanding to a wider modernism, 86–94.

21. Eliot recalls his conversations with Pound about their respective turns to the quatrain in the late 1910s, and the particular example of Gautier, in a 1959 *Paris Review* interview with Donald Hall, "T. S. Eliot, The Art of Poetry No. 1," which is collected in Hall's *Their Ancient Glittering Eyes: Remembering Poets and More Poets* (New York: Ticknor and Fields, 1992), 265.

22. "Major M'Bride Shot as Irish Insurgent": headline in *New York Times*, 7 May 1916. Emphasis added.

23. "O the moon shone bright on Mrs. Porter / And on her daughter / They wash their feet in soda water": *The Waste Land*, ll. 199–201, *The Waste Land: A Facsimile and Transcript of the Original Drafts Including the Annotations of Ezra Pound*, ed. Valerie Eliot (New York: Harcourt Brace Jovanovich, 1971), 140. In his note to line 199, Eliot writes: "I do not know the origin of the ballad from which these lines are taken; it was reported to me from Sydney, Australia" (*The Waste Land*, 147). For the singing of the song (Eliot has corrected the bawdier parts) by the Australian troops in the Gallipoli assault, see B. C. Southam, *A Guide to the Selected Poems of T. S. Eliot*, 6th ed. (Orlando, FL: Harcourt Brace Mifflin, 1996), 168–69.

24. Ricks (*IMH*, 381) notes that the "Greek epigraph (misquoted) is added to both [carbon typescripts] in pencil (no space left for such, so it is not just that there was no Greek on his typewriter)." Both carbon typescripts contain suggestions by Pound. His review of Browning's translation of *Agamemnon* appears in "Hellenist Series V. Aeschuylus," *The Egoist*, January-February 1919, 6–9.

25. Ernest A. Boyd, "Broadbent's Baedeker," *New Ireland*, 19 May 1917, 24–25; Douglas Goldring (signed "Broadbent"), "On the Importance of Being Ernest," *New Ireland*, 26 May 1917, 49–50; Boyd, "A Boy of the Bulldog Breed," *New Ireland*, 2 June 1917, 62–63.

26. For the concern with cycles of cultural vitality and decline, see the opening paragraph of *The Stones of Venice* (1851; rpt., 3 vols., Boston: Estes, 1899), I, 15. The moral dimension of this account is revealed most clearly in *Seven Lamps of Architecture* (1849; rpt. Boston: Estes, 1900), especially in the first and last essays gathered into this collection: "The Lamp of Sacrifice" and "The Lamp of Obedience."

27. See, for example, Anthony Julius, *T. S. Eliot, Anti-Semitism and Literary Form* (1995; rpt. Cambridge: Cambridge University Press, 1997). A special issue of *Modernism/modernity*, 10.1 (2003) was devoted to the question of Eliot's anti-Semitism; a framing essay by Ronald Schuchard, "Burbank with a Baedeker, Eliot with a Cigar: American Intellectuals, Anti-Semitism, and the Idea of Culture," 1–26, was responded to by David Bromwich, 27–31; Ronald Bush, 33–36; Denis Donoghue, 37–39; Anthony Julius, 41–44; James Longenbach, 49–55; and Marjorie Perloff, 51–56. Schuchard concludes with "My Reply: Eliot and the Foregone Conclusions," 57–70. A subsequent issue of *Modernism/modernity* (10.3) in the same year opens with Cassandra Laity's "Editor's Note on Eliot and Anti-Semitism: The Ongoing Debate II," 417, and follows with Jonathan Freedman's "Lessons Out of School: T. S. Eliot's Jewish Problem and the Making of Modernism," 419–29; Bryan Cheyette's "Neither Excuse nor Accuse: T. S. Eliot's Semitic Discourse," 431–37; Ranen Omer-Sherman's "Rethinking Eliot, Jewish Identity, and Cultural Pluralism," 439–445; and Jeffrey M. Perl's "The Idea of a Jewish Society," 447–54.

28. These poems are collected as appendix A in *IMH*, 305–21.

29. David Bromwich discusses the lower case spelling of "jew" in his response to Schuchard's article in *Modernism/modernity*, 10.1 (2003), 29.

30. Eliot, *Collected Poems 1909–1962*, 125.

31. T. S. Eliot, *The Waste Land: A Facsimile*, 113. This volume includes the text of the first published edition of the poem (New York: Boni and Liveright, 1922). References to the facsimile drafts (page numbers) and the published poem (page and line numbers) hereafter cited parenthetically as *TWL*.

32. Stoker, *Dracula*, ed. Auerbach and Skal, 39.

33. Joseph Conrad, *Heart of Darkness* (1899), ed. Ross C. Murfin (New York: St. Martin's Press, 1989), 85.

34. Other sites in the manuscript in which the presence of decadence can be vividly seen include the long, largely discarded overture to the central encounter of the typist and the young man carbuncular in Part III, "The Fire Sermon." Here the focus falls on "Fresca," an embodiment of the fashionable vamp, which Eliot presents as an accumulation of references to literary decadence: "Fresca was [**baptised in**] born upon a soapy sea / Of Symonds – Walter Pater – Vernon Lee" (*TWL*, 27). Earlier he has put her in line with Rossetti's "Jenny," giving her this name and echoing a refrain line of that poem:

Fresca! in other time or place had been
A meek and [**lowly**] weeping Magdalene;
More sinned against than sinning, bruised and marred,
The lazy laughing Jenny of the bard.   (*TWL*, 27)

35. T. S. Eliot, *Poems Written in Early Youth* (New York: Farrar, Straus and Giroux, 1967), 28–30. Printed privately in Stockholm in 1950.
36. See Lyndall Gordon, *T. S. Eliot, An Imperfect Life* (New York: Norton, 2000), 33.
37. Henry James, *The Wings of the Dove*, 300.
38. Edmund Wilson, Jr., "The Poetry of Drouth," *The Dial*, December 1922, 613, 614.
39. In the account of this process by Peter Ackroyd, *T. S. Eliot: A Life*, 115–17, Eliot brought a substantial amount of the manuscript in December to Pound in Paris and remained long enough to receive back the edited pages before departing to the sanatorium in Lausanne; here, Ackroyd proposes, Eliot composed Part V and completed the poem, which he brought with him to Paris in January on his way back to London. An alternative account is provided by Lawrence Rainey, ed. *The Annotated Waste Land, with Eliot's Contemporary Prose*, 2d ed. (New Haven: Yale University Press, 2006), 23–24, who proposes that Eliot brought the material of all five parts (and more) to Pound in early January.
40. F. L. Lucas, "The Waste Land," *New Statesman*, 3 November 1923, 116.

AFTERWORD   BARNES AND BECKETT, PETROPI
OF THE TWILIGHT

1. Djuna Barnes, *Nightwood*, intro. T. S. Eliot (1937; rpt. New York: New Directions, 1961), xiv. References are to this edition and are hereafter cited parenthetically as *N*.
2. Fredric Jameson, *Fables of Identity: Wyndham Lewis, The Modernist as Fascist* (Berkeley: University of California Press, 1979), 37.
3. Jameson, *Fables of Identity*, 39.
4. Jameson, *Fables of Identity*, 40–41.
5. Jameson, *Fables of Identity*, 47.
6. Samuel Beckett, *The Unnamable*, in *Molloy, Malone Dies, The Unnamable* (New York: Grove Press, 1959), 409.
7. Beckett, *Molloy*, in *Molloy, Malone Dies, The Unnamable*, 3.
8. Beckett, *The Unnamable*, in *Molloy, Malone Dies, The Unnamable*, 456.
9. Beckett, *Molloy*, in *Molloy, Malone Dies, The Unnamable*, 103.

Index